Teaching the Bible in the Liberal Arts Classroom

Works by Jane S. Webster:

Ingesting Jesus: Eating and Drinking in the Gospel of John, Atlanta, GA: Society of Biblical Literature; Leiden, NL: Brill Academic Publishers, 2003.

Works by Glenn S. Holland:

Gods in the Desert: Religions of the Ancient Near East, Lanham, MD: Rowman & Littlefield, 2009.
Co-editor (with John T. Fitzgerald and Dirk Obbink), *Philodemus and the New Testament World,* Leiden, NL: Brill Academic Publishers, 2004.
Divine Irony, Selinsgrove, PA: Susquehanna University Press, 2000.
The Tradition that You Received from Us: 2 Thessalonians in the Pauline Tradition, Hermaneutische Untersuchungen zur Theologie 24, Tubingen: J.C.B. Mohr (Paul Siebeck), 1988.

Copyright © 2012 Sheffield Phoenix Press

Published by Sheffield Phoenix Press
Department of Biblical Studies, University of Sheffield
45 Victoria Street, Sheffield S3 7QB

www.sheffieldphoenix.com

All rights reserved.
No part of this publication may be reproduced or transmitted in any form or by any means, electronic or mechanical, including photocopying, recording or any information storage or retrieval system, without the publisher's permission in writing.

A CIP catalogue record for this book
is available from the British Library

Typeset by the HK Scriptorium
Printed by Lightning Source

ISBN 978-1-907534-63-8 (hbk)
ISBN 978-1-907534-81-2 (pbk)

TEACHING THE BIBLE
IN THE
LIBERAL ARTS CLASSROOM

Edited by
Jane S. Webster and Glenn S. Holland

SHEFFIELD PHOENIX PRESS
2012

*To those teachers
who have inspired us and challenged us to grow*

Contents

DAVID J.A. CLINES
Foreword — xi

PREFACE — xiii

CONTRIBUTORS — xv

JANE S. WEBSTER AND GLENN S. HOLLAND
Introduction — 1

PART I: BIBLICAL STUDIES IN THE LIBERAL ARTS — 11

MATTHEW C. BALDWIN
'The Touchstone Text': A Forensic Rationale for Biblical Studies in American Liberal Education — 12

SUSANNE SCHOLZ
Occupy Academic Bible Teaching: The Architecture of Educational Power and the Biblical Studies Curriculum — 28

STAN HARSTINE AND PHILLIP WISELEY
Challenges in Teaching Biblical Literature as a General Education Requirement — 44

GLENN S. HOLLAND
'Not as the Scribes': Teaching Biblical Studies in the Liberal Arts Context — 56

MURRAY JOSEPH HAAR AND ANNA MADSEN
What Do Athens and Jerusalem Have to Do with Sioux Falls? — 65

CHRISTIAN M. BRADY
'God Is Not in This Classroom' or Teaching the Bible in a Secular Context — 73

MARGARET PARKS COWAN
Engaging Diverse Students in a Required Biblical Studies Course — 80

SHARON BETSWORTH
Arts Integration and Service-Learning in Introduction
to Biblical Literature 91

BENJAMIN WHITE
Pedagogical Iconoclasm: The Role of the Upper-Level
Biblical Studies Seminar in the Context of Undergraduate
Religious Studies Programs 99

**PART II: PEDAGOGICAL THEORY AND
BIBLICAL STUDIES COURSES** 115

SHANE KIRKPATRICK
Teaching the Material and Teaching the Students:
Reflections on Introductory Courses for Non-Majors 116

JANET S. EVERHART
Service-Learning in the Undergraduate Biblical Studies Classroom 130

J. BRADLEY CHANCE
The Bible and World Construction: The Reality
of Multiple Voices in Biblical Religion 140

ALISON SCHOFIELD
Collaborative Learning and the Pedagogy of the Bible
in the Liberal Arts Context 151

BRYAN D. BIBB
From Biblical Literature to Ultimate Questions:
Shifting Contexts and Goals for Introducing the Bible 165

PART III: CASE STUDIES 177

JONATHAN D. LAWRENCE
Bible-Trek, Next Generation: Adapting a Bible Survey Course
for a New Audience 178

JANET S. EVERHART
Dildos and Dismemberment: Reading Difficult Biblical Texts
in the Undergraduate Classroom 184

AMY C. COTTRILL
Reading Textual Violence as 'Real' Violence
in the Liberal Arts Context 192

Contents

CARL N. TONEY
*Engaging Students Online: Using Wiki Technology
to Improve your Class Notes* — 199

MARGARET E. RAMEY
*What's the Harm in Harmonization? Using Jesus Films
in the Classroom to Examine the Crucifixion Narratives* — 209

JANE S. WEBSTER
Teaching with Meta-Questions — 217

RUSSELL C.D. ARNOLD
*Course Design and the Use of Meta-Questions
in an Interdisciplinary First-Year Seminar on the Ethics
of Biblical Interpretation* — 223

RODNEY K. DUKE
Biblical Studies and Metacognitive Reading Skills — 233

SUSAN E. HYLEN
Teaching Revelation to the Left Behind *Generation* — 245

BIBLIOGRAPHY — 254

INDEX OF SUBJECTS — 271

INDEX OF AUTHORS — 276

Foreword

The flourishing of courses in biblical studies in institutions other than seminaries and theological faculties in universities is a relatively recent development, but one that is now deeply embedded in many colleges and universities especially in the English-speaking world. It is a development that is good for students, who can study the Bible as part of a degree program in literature or cultural studies, and it is good for the health of the discipline, since it offers opportunities to approach our familiar texts in new intellectual contexts, with resultant gains for diversity and for freshness in interpretation.

The contributors to this volume have had to strike out on new paths for the shape of their curricula and for the teaching of students who in many cases have no particular religious commitment to the Bible. The program unit of the Society of Biblical Literature devoted to teaching the Bible in the liberal arts college has supported their practice and sustained them in a sense of collective adventure. The present volume is a remarkably rich and deeply thoughtful outcome of those sessions.

Teaching the Bible in the Liberal Arts Classroom has a very definite focus on the USA, and all its contributors are from the USA, but there is not a teacher of Bible in the world who is not addressed here and will not profit from reflecting on each of the essays here. I wish I were back in the classroom again myself so as to begin implementing as many as possible of the brilliant ideas in this book.

David J.A. Clines
University of Sheffield
President, Society of Biblical Literature, 2009

Preface

This book was born out of need. When Jane moved from Canada to the United States to take up a faculty position at Barton College in North Carolina, she was introduced for the first time to the concept of a liberal arts education with its emphasis on diversity of studies in support of a particular major or professional program. She was also confronted with the task of teaching students who were not particularly interested in biblical studies, but who either claimed to know what the Bible said and 'believed every word', or who considered the Bible to be a relic of an archaic age. Because she was educated in Canada in a seminary and graduate school context, she had no models for instruction. At that point, she turned to her professional organization—the Society of Biblical Literature—for some help. Although there were several program units on teaching, most of the papers she heard discussed ways that ethics or theology might be taught through the use of the Bible. Few presentations addressed the principles of pedagogy, best practices in learning, and the particular needs of the undergraduate liberal arts context. Together with Susanne Scholz, she proposed a new program unit in order to create some space at the annual meetings where these conversations might take place. The program unit 'Teaching Biblical Studies in the Undergraduate Liberal Arts Context' (affectionately known as TBSULAC) was born.

Glenn was one of the presenters during the first year of the group's operation. He was drawn to the group both by a long-standing interest in effective pedagogy and by a dearth of colleagues with whom he could discuss the particular challenges involved in teaching biblical studies at a secular liberal arts college. Since none of his courses was required, the viability of his biblical studies courses, like the other offerings of the department of philosophy and religious studies, was based solely on the instructors' ability to attract students consistently year after year. But teaching courses in Hebrew Bible, New Testament, and other biblical topics entailed difficulties his departmental colleagues' courses did not. The annual sessions of TBSULAC provided the sort of forum that Glenn had been hoping for, a continuing conversation among academic instructors facing the same sorts of problems in trying to teach the subject they love to undergraduates in as effective and enlightening a way as possible.

The program unit quickly attracted a group of dedicated teachers struggling with many of the same issues with which Jane and Glenn have contended, and has grown into a community of self-reflective educators who encourage, support, and laugh with each other over the challenges we face in doing our job well. We have experimented together and discussed our results. We have raised questions and pondered the answers together. We have shared our favorite 'tricks of the trade' with willing spirits; we have shared our course plans, learning objectives, assessment strategies, and best practices. This volume is a sampling of the continuing conversation and an invitation to others to join us.

Our program unit has completed its first six years and is now looking ahead to new challenges. Since the recession of 2008, unemployment has been on the rise and parents and students alike are defining the purpose of a college education differently: where once a college education was meant to produce an 'educated effective citizen', now it is meant to provide a well-paying job. As college tuitions rise, students are more than ever committed to finding employment quickly in order to attend to their student loans. Many colleges across the country see this urgency to enter the workforce reflected in fewer students taking Humanities courses and more taking professional degrees. As the numbers of religion majors and class sizes drop, institutions begin to cut courses, faculty, and curriculum requirements. Governments give priority to funding mathematics and science programs and let the humanities and arts slide. At the same time, religious issues continue to remain on the forefront of public discourse, often ill-informed or misrepresented, yet teachers in biblical studies have had to work harder to justify their contribution to education. In many institutions, these teachers have had to extend their expertise, shifting from discipline-specific instruction to general education requirements such as writing, speaking, service-learning, or critical thinking. While this volume addresses some of these issues, the conversation has just begun.

We hope that this collection of essays—and the love and dedication to the task of teaching and to the students that they represent—will offer hope to the discouraged, vision for the weary, and strategies to the flummoxed. We welcome you into the conversation.

JANE S. WEBSTER and GLENN S. HOLLAND

Contributors

Russell C.D. Arnold, DePauw University, Greencastle, Indiana, USA
Matthew C. Baldwin, Mars Hill College, Mars Hill, North Carolina, USA
Sharon Betsworth, Oklahoma City University, Oklahoma City, Oklahoma, USA
Bryan D. Bibb, Furman University, Greenville, South Carolina, USA
Christian M. Brady, Pennsylvania State University, University Park, Pennsylvania, USA
J. Bradley Chance, William Jewell College, Liberty, Missouri, USA
Amy C. Cottrill, Birmingham-Southern College, Birmingham, Alabama, USA
Margaret P. Cowan, Maryville College, Maryville, Tennessee, USA
Rodney K. Duke, Appalachian State University, Boone, North Carolina, USA
Janet S. Everhart, Simpson College, Indianola, Iowa, USA
Murray Joseph Haar, Augustana College, Sioux Falls, South Dakota, USA
Stan Harstine, Friends University, Wichita, Kansas, USA
Glenn S. Holland, Allegheny College, Meadville, Pennsylvania, USA
Susan E. Hylen, Vanderbilt University, Nashville, Tennessee, USA
Shane Kirkpatrick, Anderson University, Anderson, Indiana, USA
Anna Madsen, OMG: Center for Theological Conversation, Sioux Falls, South Dakota, USA
Jonathan D. Lawrence, Canisius College, Buffalo, New York, USA
Margaret E. Ramey, Messiah College, Grantham, Pennsylvania, USA
Alison Schofield, University of Denver, Denver, Colorado, USA
Susanne Scholz, Perkins School of Theology, Southern Methodist University, Dallas, Texas, USA
Carl N. Toney, Hope International University, Fullerton, California, USA
Jane S. Webster, Barton College, Wilson, North Carolina, USA
Benjamin White, Clemson University, Greenville, South Carolina, USA
Phillip Wiseley, Edison State College, Fort Myers, Florida, USA

Introduction

The traditional home of biblical studies among institutions of higher learning is the seminary, the divinity school, and the church-related college or university. These settings reflect the place of biblical studies as a subsection of the field of theology, as a means for better understanding divine revelation and so also better understanding God's will for faithful people. The origins of major private universities as church-related institutions for many years ensured the teaching of biblical studies within their ivy-covered walls as well, but with increasing secularization came a growing discomfort with a field of study apparently justified only by a confessional bias. In state universities in particular, the field of biblical studies poses a definite problem, and survives most often on the basis of the Bible's place as the touchstone, with Shakespeare, of Western European literature and, with the inheritance of the classical world, of Western European art.

Similarly, many people might ask whether the academic study of the Bible has a proper place in the curriculum of a liberal arts college or university, a curriculum whose ostensible purpose is to produce well-educated citizens. Both the United States and Canada are constituted as secular nations whose citizens are free to subscribe to any religion or none, and as places where religious convictions are largely relegated to the private sphere; we may well ask whether in-depth knowledge of one set of texts authoritative for only one or two religious communities is really necessary for good citizenship in those nations. If good citizenship is the goal of the liberal arts, does biblical studies have a proper place in the liberal arts classroom?

In fact, the same question might be asked for the academic study of religion in general. Does the discipline of religious studies have a real and unique contribution to make to the liberal arts curriculum, a contribution other fields of study not only cannot provide, but in fact need to provide if they are to do their own work well? In the October 2008 edition of *Religious Studies News*, the AAR-Teagle group, led by Timothy Renick of Georgia State University, presented the findings of a joint 18-month study of this question, 'The Religion Major and Liberal Education'.[1] Participating in this study were '300 faculty

---

1. Timothy Renick *et al.*, 'The Religious Studies Major in a Post-9/11 World: New Challenges, New Opportunities', *Religious Studies News* (October 2008), pp. 21-24.

members and stakeholders on more than a dozen campuses'.² The report highlights the essential place of the study of religion in the liberal arts curriculum.

Part of the importance of religious studies, according to the report, lies in the importance of religion to vast proportions of the world's population. The report notes, for example, that membership in the four major world religions—Judaism, Christianity, Islam, and Hinduism—increased from 67% in 1900 to 73% in 2005 and is projected to rise to 80% in 2050.³ These figures have political consequences; the authors agree with the *Economist* that 'these days religion is an inescapable part of politics'.⁴ Especially after the 9/11 attacks on the World Trade Center in New York, it has become painfully clear that religious ignorance among a nation's citizens is a serious hindrance to understanding what motivates many other nations and peoples. The official name of the report, in fact, is 'The Religious Studies Major in a Post-9/11 World: New Challenges, New Opportunities', testifying to the centrality of the terrorist attacks of late 2001 to the American public's renewed concern with religion and religious issues.

The growing public interest in religion is reflected in the growing number of religious studies majors in institutions of higher learning. The numbers increased by 22% over the decade 1997 to 2007, with some 47,000 students majoring in religious studies in the final year; in public institutions alone the increase was an astonishing 40%. Moreover, according to the report, 'the number of religion degree programs that are housed in freestanding religion departments also appears to be on the rise, with the total now topping 50 percent'.⁵ Clearly the attention (and academic support) devoted to the study of religion in institutions of higher learning is on the rise.

The increase in enrollment has also driven a shift from courses concentrating on close readings of key texts, an approach typical of seminaries or private universities, to more culturally relevant survey courses of different religious communities to serve a larger, more skeptical, and perhaps less knowledgeable, cohort of students.⁶ According to the AAR-Teagle group, 'departments and curricula in religious studies at public, private, and church-related institutions are gradually, persistently, and unevenly shifting from a "seminary model" for the study of religion (in which courses in Bible, Christian history, and Christian doctrine are seen as primary and courses on other religions and aspects of religion are deemed secondary or even unnecessary) to a comparative model (in which the focus is on promoting student understanding of the beliefs, practices, and histories of multiple religious traditions in a comparative context)'.⁷ The

---

2. Renick *et al.*, 'Religious Studies Major', p. 21.
3. Renick *et al.*, 'Religious Studies Major', p. 21, citing World Christian Database, 2007; cf. *The Economist*, November 1, 2007.
4. Renick *et al.*, 'Religious Studies Major', p. 21, citing *The Economist*, November 1, 2007.
5. Renick *et al.*, 'Religious Studies Major', p. 22.
6. Renick *et al.*, 'Religious Studies Major', p. 22.
7. Renick *et al.*, 'Religious Studies Major', p. 22.

seminary model of the religion major emphasizes the primacy of Christianity both as a focus of study and as the definitive example of religious thought and action. The comparative model, on the other hand, grants all religious traditions a more or less equal footing. Courses taught might include not only surveys of different religious traditions but a focus on religious phenomena as they are manifested in a number of different religious communities or traditions. The comparative model is well suited to the needs of those seeking a more comprehensive understanding of religious beliefs and practices compatible with the lines of inquiry in other academic disciplines in the liberal arts curriculum. But at the same time, it would seem that this shift to a comparative model of inquiry would lessen the relevance of biblical studies, or even the need for biblical studies courses at all.

The AAR-Teagle report affirms the need to establish a dialogue for 'the nature and value of a religious studies major, the substance and shape that it should have, and the multiple ways in which it contributes to broader institutional and educational objectives'.[8] With this assertion, the report provides a useful framework for a discussion of the place of biblical studies among the liberal arts. The report identifies five 'obvious and strong affinities' or characteristics of religious studies that reflect a consensus among religious studies major programs in the liberal arts context. This consensus is reflected by the section heading that introduces each of the five, 'The religious studies major is, by its very nature . . .'.[9] In other words, the majority of religious studies departments contributing to the survey identify these 'obvious and strong affinities' as inherent in the very nature of the academic study of religion.

The first inherent characteristic is that religious studies is 'intercultural and comparative:' 'The major explores more than one religious tradition and engages the phenomena of religion comparatively across and within cultures'.[10] In order for students to undertake comparative work, they must be able to understand and articulate the assumptions and ideas that undergird their own cultural traditions. For many students, that means they must have some knowledge of the themes and stories found among the books of the Bible. At the same time, however, biblical literature is itself 'intercultural and comparative'. It represents the thinking of many different people in different places, at different times, in different socioeconomic locations, responding to different historical events in different cultural contexts. This means that biblical texts may be considered in terms of difference as well as in terms of similarity. Rather than presenting the Bible as a history of God, one might just as easily focus on the Bible as a history of people trying in different ways to make sense of their world, in the light of their belief that their God was intimately involved in their lives and their world.

The second characteristic identified by the AAR-Teagle Report is multidisciplinarity: 'The major promotes the understanding and application of a

---

8. Renick *et al.*, 'Religious Studies Major', p. 23.
9. Renick *et al.*, 'Religious Studies Major', p. 23.
10. Renick *et al.*, 'Religious Studies Major', p. 23.

range of methodological and theoretical approaches to religious phenomena'.[11] Biblical studies is also inherently multi-disciplinary. Instructors may take a variety of approaches to the biblical texts, incorporating various methodological approaches or hermeneutical perspectives. Instructors may choose to introduce different methodologies in different areas, or use a specific hermeneutical trajectory, such as feminist, African American, or post-colonial, or focus on a literary category such as rhetoric, which draws on both literary and historical critical methods, buttressed by examples taken from literature, art, music, and media.

The third inherent characteristic is the critical approach: 'The major teaches students to examine and engage religious phenomena, including issues of ethical and social responsibility, from a perspective of critical inquiry and analysis of both the other and the self'.[12] Since most of those students who come to class with some biblical knowledge gained that knowledge through experiences in church, the critical approach to the Bible may present them with a considerable challenge they are often reluctant to engage. This is especially so when actions taken by Yahweh or his servants in the biblical stories run counter to prevailing modern standards of right and wrong. Students seem to become aware of both their own cultural bias and the very different biases that shape the biblical texts. Their awareness of the biases informing the conquest narratives in Joshua, for example, can lead to classroom conversations about the ethics of the European conquest of North America or the more recent American conquest of Iraq. Biblical studies thus can provide ample opportunities for 'critical inquiry and analysis of both the other and the self'.[13]

The fourth characteristic is that the religious studies major is integrative: 'The major applies theoretical knowledge of religious phenomena to lived, practical contexts, both historical and current'.[14] Whereas a seminary model might focus on 'what the Bible might teach us about our lives and our relationship with God', the comparative model will situate the biblical texts within the general religious phenomena of sacred texts or use the Bible as a source text for the description of religious histories, rituals and traditions, among other things. As such, the Bible becomes only one source among many for ideas about religious experience, instead of the only source, or the normative / authoritative source, or worse, the lens through which every other religious tradition is con-

---

11. Renick *et al.*, 'Religious Studies Major', p. 23.
12. Renick *et al.*, 'Religious Studies Major', p. 23.
13. In *Teaching and Learning in College Introductory Religion Courses* (Malden, MA: Wiley-Blackwell, 2008), Barbara E. Walvoord concludes that most instructors teach courses in religion in order to promote critical thinking among their students and so tend to avoid the personal. But ironically, she finds, students most often take courses in religion because they are searching for personal meaning. Instructors may choose to resolve this conflict in expectations in various ways, but a critical approach to the biblical texts can serve to encourage students to assess and critique their beliefs in light of a clearer idea of the content of the biblical texts, texts many of them consider authoritative.
14. Renick *et al.*, 'Religious Studies Major', p. 23.

sidered. This might be the essential difference between biblical studies in an overtly confessional context, and biblical studies in a liberal arts context. In the latter, for example, an instructor might ask students, 'What does it mean to call these stories sacred? On their authority should we condone child sacrifice on the model of Abraham or Jephthah, or the abuse of women, such as that suffered by Hagar or the Levite's concubine, or racism on the order reflected in Chronicles?' Or one might link the rituals and festivals described in the Bible with contemporary rituals and festivals explicitly based on them, such as Passover, Hanukkah, and the Lord's Supper, to consider both similarities and differences between the ancient models and their modern manifestations.

Finally, the fifth characteristic is that a religious studies major is inherently creative and constructive: 'The major employs knowledge of religious phenomena and the skills of religious studies in the solving of complex problems, including those raised in the personal and social engagement of issues of life, death, love, violence, suffering and meaning'.[15] It seems apparent that the Bible has had a significant role in defining the issues of life, death, love, violence, suffering, and meaning in the American context. The challenge is perhaps that the Bible has been used uncritically to speak to these issues. Within a comparative context, it becomes possible to distinguish the *range* of contemporary American values at least ostensibly based on biblical texts. So for example, in a political context, one might compare the prophetic preference for the poor with modern political attitudes, or compare the diverse biblical responses to war and peacekeeping. Presenting the *range* of possibilities presented in the Bible in response to a given subject can provide fertile ground for discussion and can help students come to informed and ethically responsible conclusions.

The AAR-Teagle White Paper provides a useful model for understanding and exploring the challenges and opportunities of teaching biblical studies in the liberal arts classroom. How have individual instructors responded to these challenges and opportunities by the way they structure their courses? Timothy Peoples, in a survey of syllabi from introductory courses in biblical studies taught at liberal arts institutions, finds such courses fall into three general analytical categories according to the dominant paradigm, whether historical-critical, post-modern, or religious.[16] The historical-critical paradigm attempts to overcome the cultural chasm between the ancient writer and the modern reader: 'Professors from this perspective aim to train students to understand the time period so they may understand the meaning of the text'.[17] The post-modern paradigm asserts that the cultural chasm cannot in fact be overcome, and instead focuses on the modern reader's reaction to and assimilation of the ancient text.

---

15. Renick *et al.*, 'Religious Studies Major', p. 23.
16. Timothy Peoples, 'Pedagogy of the Bible in the Liberal Arts Context: Paradigms and Perspectives', unpublished paper presented to the Teaching Biblical Studies in the Undergraduate Liberal Arts Context group of the Society of Biblical Literature, Annual Meeting, November 19–22, 2011, p. 2.
17. Peoples, 'Pedagogy of the Bible', p. 3.

Peoples quotes A.K.M. Adam: 'Postmodern biblical criticism engages the reader and the Bible not on the terms that any privileged institution (the academy, the synagogue, the church, or the state) sets, but on the terms that interest particular readers and their audiences'.[18] The religious paradigm insists on the centrality of the religious affirmations made or implied by the biblical text, with a particular focus on its moral and ethical implications. Peoples writes, 'This method is less a discovery of something new [than] a critical appropriation of ways that faithful readers have interpreted Scripture and sought to direct their hearts, souls, minds and strength toward God'.[19]

Peoples collected eighty-eight syllabi for introductory biblical studies courses from liberal arts institutions and classified them into these three categories through analysis of how each syllabus described the associated course, through 'direct statements, indirect statements, and other implicit indicators'.[20] On this basis, he identified forty syllabi as most consistent with the historical-critical paradigm, thirty with the post-modern paradigm, and eighteen with the religious paradigm. As Peoples notes, 'Clearly, students throughout the United States are learning to analyze and interpret the Bible in a variety of ways and no one particular approach appears dominant'.[21] The upshot, he argues, is that how a course is taught is less important than why, and that biblical studies courses should reflect the interests and goals of the liberal arts.[22]

The question now is, what practical steps can instructors in biblical studies courses take in the classroom to be true to the study of religion in the liberal arts college as it is outlined in the AAR-Teagle Report, and at the same time reach students who come from a wide variety of religious and cultural backgrounds with a greater or lesser store of knowledge and experiences to prepare them for the academic study of religion? That question is the concern of the essays that make up this volume.

Part 1 of this volume, 'Biblical Studies in the Liberal Arts', include essays that address the question: How should we teach biblical studies in the setting of a liberal arts college? What conditions in the liberal arts college and outside it determine how we understand and carry out our work of teaching? How should our approach differ (or should it?) from the approaches taken in the seminary or the strongly denominationally-defined church-related college or university? To what extent do we who teach Bible in liberal arts colleges face a unique pedagogical situation, distinct from the pedagogical situation faced by our professional peers in other sorts of institutions and even from that faced by other faculty at our own institutions? In 'The Touchstone Text:' A Foren-

---

18. A.K.M. Adam, *What Is Postmodern Biblical Criticism?* (Minneapolis: Fortress, 1981), p. 74, cited by Peoples, 'Pedagogy of the Bible', p. 4.

19. Peoples, 'Pedagogy of the Bible', p. 6. In this connection, Peoples cites A.K.M. Adam, *Faithful Interpretation* (Minneapolis: Fortress, 2006), p. 18.

20. Peoples, 'Pedagogy of the Bible', p. 9.

21. Peoples, 'Pedagogy of the Bible', p. 10.

22. Peoples, 'Pedagogy of the Bible', pp. 10-11.

sic Rationale for Biblical Studies in American Liberal Education', Matthew C. Baldwin reviews questions surrounding the place of biblical studies in the liberal arts both from a historical perspective based on seminal documents and a contemporary perspective provided by an assessment of such indicators as biblical studies textbooks, outcome statements, and analyses offered by critics of biblical studies as a discipline. Susanne Scholz, in 'Occupy Academic Biblical Teaching: The Architecture of Educational Power and the Biblical Studies Curriculum', considers the various institutional, political, and economic forces that have shaped biblical studies as an academic discipline in the past and work to prevent a necessary re-imagining of the biblical studies curriculum in the present. Stan Harstine and Phillip Wiseley's 'Challenges to Teaching Biblical Literature as a General Education Requirement' uses the results of a survey conducted at Friends University in 2006 to assess student attitudes and expectations regarding the biblical literature courses taught within the general education curriculum at a Christian-identified college. '"Not as the Scribes:" Teaching Biblical Studies in the Liberal Arts Curriculum' by Glenn S. Holland considers pedagogical strategies for courses in biblical studies that are also intended to help students cultivate traditional liberal arts skills such as intelligent reading, effective speaking and writing, and incisive critical analysis. The ideals of liberal education are also in view in 'What Do Athens and Jerusalem Have to Do with Sioux Falls?', in which Murray Joseph Haar and Anna Madsen consider the tension between the expectation that biblical studies courses in a religiously-affiliated institution will encourage students' faith commitment and the liberal arts mandate, which places a premium on the freedom to challenge all assertions regardless of the outcome. Similarly, Christian Brady in '"God is Not in This Classroom" or Reading the Bible in a Secular Context' argues that teaching in a secular liberal arts environment requires allowing texts to speak for themselves, so students might hear what the texts have to say—which may not necessarily be what they want to hear.

Several essays consider the place of biblical studies courses in the context of the larger liberal arts college community and its various concerns. In 'Engaging Diverse Students in a Required Biblical Studies Course', Margaret P. Cowan considers the difficulties of conveying both the content of a course and promoting the goals of liberal education while engaging students who enter college with wide-ranging levels of academic preparedness, and offers some practical suggestions for doing so. Sharon Betsworth's 'Arts Integration and Service-Learning in Introduction to Biblical Literature' examines how both arts integration and service learning are key components to improve student learning and pique interest in Introduction to Biblical Literature as a general education course at a church-affiliated institution. By way of contrast, Benjamin White in 'Pedagogical Iconoclasm: The Role of the Upper-Level Biblical Studies Seminar in the Context of Undergraduate Religious Studies Programs' considers the ways a course with a narrower focus, one that depends on some biblical knowledge and sophistication among its students, might help equip them with the necessary tools for becoming successful, life-long students of biblical texts.

The essays in Part 2, 'Pedagogical Theory and Biblical Studies Courses' describe a range of pedagogical models and techniques that have proven useful to their authors when teaching liberal arts undergraduates. Shane Kirkpatrick, in 'Teaching the Material and Teaching the Students: Reflections on Introductory Courses for Non-Majors', addresses the pedagogical challenges of teaching a required introductory Bible course to non-majors at a church-related college. Organizing the course around 'authority' understood as a developmental, educational, and religious issue, he suggests ways to use course materials to promote development of students' capacity for critical thinking, creative problem-solving, and a sense of responsibility as global citizens. 'Service-Learning in Undergraduate Biblical Studies Courses', by Janet S. Everhart explores the advantages and challenges of integrating academic service-learning into undergraduate biblical studies courses in the liberal arts setting. J. Bradley Chance's 'The Bible and World Construction: The Reality of Multiple Voices in Biblical Religion' explores an interdisciplinary approach to biblical studies that employs the sociology of knowledge as presented in Peter Berger's *The Sacred Canopy* to provide students a model for how society works as a human construction. Alison Schofield in 'Collaborative Learning and the Pedagogy of the Bible in the Liberal Arts Context' offers useful ways of teaching both new content and new methods relevant to biblical studies through cooperative learning groups, an approach with the potential to help students achieve learning outcomes that are otherwise often difficult for them to reach in an academic quarter. Bryan Bibb also addresses specific goals in 'From Biblical Literature to Ultimate Questions: Shifting Contexts and Goals for Introducing the Bible', which explores the opportunities and challenges of transitioning from an introductory course in 'biblical literature' in a broadly religious context to a course on 'the Bible and Ultimate Questions' that addresses an institutional 'Ultimate Questions' requirement in a mostly secular context.

In Part 3, 'Case Studies', essays reflect on the more specific issues of the undergraduate liberal arts context, such as how to design appropriate unit assessments, integrate technology, or engage diverse or resistant students. Jonathan D. Lawrence in 'Bible-Trek Next Generation: Adapting a Bible Survey Course for a New Audience' describes an introduction to Old Testament course that was narrowed to focus on only five stories in order to emphasize close readings, interpretations, and analysis to fit the needs and expectations of the current generation of undergraduate students. 'Dildos and Dismemberment: Reading Difficult Biblical Texts in the Undergraduate Classroom', by Janet S. Everhart, inspired by the liberal arts tradition of 'questioning old truths and looking for new perspectives', explains why it is important to acknowledge and incorporate problematic stories in undergraduate biblical studies courses and offers a few strategies for presenting them in the classroom. In a similar vein, Amy C. Cottrill's 'Reading Textual Violence as "Real" Violence in the Liberal Arts Context' argues that it is necessary to recognize and address the often horrific violence found in many biblical texts, and offers examples of how an instructor might help students to confront a range of their own assumptions about reading, language, the concept of the self, as well as violence itself.

Innovative teaching based in emerging technologies is the topic of Carl Toney's 'Engaging Students Online: Using Wiki Technology to Improve Your Class Notes'. Toney argues that The Web 2.0 wiki technology presents an opportunity for creating a dynamic and collaborative set of class notes on the internet that will allow students to prioritize their learning by highlighting class material they deem important.

One challenge facing biblical studies professors is to help students disentangle their images of a harmonized gospel narrative so they can begin to appreciate and evaluate each of the four gospels on their own terms. In 'What's the Harm in Harmonization? Using Jesus Films in the Classroom to examine the Crucifixion Narratives', Margaret E. Ramey explains how analyzing Jesus films is an excellent way to introduce this topic and to empower students to recognize how harmonizations may actually hinder their full appreciation of the portraits constructed by each evangelist. A similar concern with students' initial responses is the focus of Jane S. Webster's 'Teaching with Meta-questions'. She argues that developing a course around a 'meta-question' that will be meaningful for students regardless of background—Why do people suffer? What can we know to be true? How do we make choices?—can engage students from the start and lead them through the discipline into self-discovery. In 'Course Design and the Use of Meta-Questions in an Interdisciplinary First-Year Seminar on the Ethics of Biblical Interpretation', Russell C.D. Arnold describes how he designed a course based on the meta-question, 'how do we make moral decisions about interpretations?' and found this question useful in integrating student learning. Rodney K. Duke, in 'Biblical Studies and Metacognitive Reading Skills', argues that using the Bible to teach metacognitive learning, and specifically metacognition and reading strategies, can improve students' reading skills and comprehension of the biblical literature, as well as other sorts of reading across the disciplines. Finally, in 'Teaching Revelation to the *Left Behind* Generation', Susan E. Hylen deals with specific problems that arise from presenting Revelation to students who already have very definite ideas about how the book should be understood. She suggests several approaches that serve not to replace the student's former understanding of the text, but to enable them to see multiple possibilities within a single text.

It is our hope that these essays, addressing the place of biblical studies in the liberal arts college, suggesting methods of presenting biblical studies effectively, and providing case studies of particular course strategies and approaches, will contribute to a continuing conversation about philosophy, methodology, pedagogy, and associated issues in our academic discipline and institutional setting. In many ways, the liberal arts college offers an ideal setting for teaching and learning about biblical literature in a way that brings that literature into direct contact with the many disciplines that contribute to contemporary study of the Bible—literary studies, history, classical studies, languages, philosophy, and various aspects of the social sciences, among others—and allows both students and instructors to understand the biblical texts as one part of a more complex and more beautiful human tapestry.

Jane S. Webster
Glenn S. Holland
March, 2012

Part I

BIBLICAL STUDIES IN THE LIBERAL ARTS

The Touchstone Text: A Forensic Rationale for Biblical Studies in American Liberal Education

Matthew C. Baldwin
Mars Hill College[1]

Biblical Studies as a Privileged Occupation

In 2000, 2002, and again in 2004–2005, the American Academy of Religion conducted three important surveys of departments and programs in the study of religion in American colleges and universities.[2] As for the field as a whole, so also for those who teach biblical studies in the undergraduate liberal arts context, these surveys provide an unprecedented opportunity for self-reflection.

In reacting to the data, scholars of religion noted how the results of the 2000 and 2002 surveys failed to support the widespread notion that undergraduate religious studies in America had already moved steadily away from the 'seminary' and towards the 'comparative' model of education.[3] When measured by

---

1. Earlier versions of the main elements of this paper were presented at two separate Annual Meetings of the Society of Biblical Literature, in 2006 and 2009, in the Teaching Biblical Literature in the Undergraduate Liberal Arts Context New Program Unit.

2. The 2000 survey of undergraduate programs was conducted by NORC and sponsored by the Lilly Foundation. For information on this study see 'New Information on the Undergraduate Study of Religion', AAR Website, www.aarweb.org/programs/Department_Services/Survey_Data/Undergraduate/default.asp. The Lilly/NORC-sponsored survey of graduate programs was conducted in 2002; see 'Survey of Graduate Programs in Religion and Theology', AAR Website, www.aarweb.org/programs/Department_Services/Survey_Data/Graduate/default.asp. Results from these studies continued to be published from 2001 to 2004 in *Religious Studies News*. For the much smaller, internally conducted 2004–2005 survey of undergraduate programs see 'AAR Undergraduate Departments Survey Methodology', Focus on the Undergraduate Study of Religion, *Religious Studies News* (May 2008) p. 13; and 'AAR Undergraduate Departments Survey Shows Increases in Religious Studies', Focus on the Undergraduate Study of Religion, *Religious Studies News* (May 2008) pp. 11-12. Also see especially David V. Brewington, 'AAR Undergraduate Departments Survey Comparative Analysis of Wave I and II', Focus on the Undergraduate Study of Religion, *Religious Studies News* (May 2008) pp. 14-15. *RSN* May 2008 is available online at www.aarweb.org/programs/Department_Services/Survey_Data/RSN_UndergradSurvey_May2008.pdf.

3. See Edward R. Gray, 'What We Have Learned from the Census of Religion and Theology Programs', *Religious Studies News* 16.2 (Fall 2001) Special Pullout Section, pp. i-iii; Linell Cady, 'What Does the Census Data Say about the Study of Religion? A Public Sector Perspective',

the sheer volume of courses offered, and by the relative popularity of the various of concentration chosen by graduate students, 'religious studies' in the American context appears to be strongly focused on Christian history, theology and scripture. Across all undergraduate programs, the largest plurality of courses offered belonged to the field of biblical studies; such courses comprised nearly 30% of all sections, with the traditional introductory Bible survey course leading the pack.[4] This data correlated well with the 2002 graduate survey, which showed that twelve of the fifteen most popular areas of doctoral study are all related to Christian history, theology, and scripture, with the study of New Testament and Christian origins in the lead.[5] Reacting to these numbers, Richard A. Rosengarten, then dean of the Divinity School at the University of Chicago, called 'Christianity ... the de facto center of gravity', and astutely observed that 'the Bible remains the touchstone text for the study of religion in the United States'.[6]

As Edward R. Gray has pointed out, religion departments 'benefit strongly from institutional policies requiring students to take religion courses', a situation that describes fifty-five percent of all undergraduate institutions with religion programs.[7] Such institutional requirements very frequently can be met by introductory Bible courses. Frequently, even schools lacking such a 'religion' requirement still grant a general education credit for courses introducing the Bible. As Jonathan Z. Smith points out, 'this privileged category of requirement-fulfilling courses guarantees substantial enrollments, the coin of the realm with administrations'.[8] Thus, biblical scholars occupy an especially privileged

---

Religious Studies News 17.2 (March 2002), pp. 7, 21; Jonathan Z. Smith, 'What Does the Census Data Say about the Study of Religion? A Private Sector Perspective', *Religious Studies News* 17.2 (March 2002), pp. 7, 23; Carey J. Gifford, 'AAR Surveys of Religion and Theology Programs in the U.S.: Numbers Count', *Religious Studies News* 18.4 (October 2003), p. 14; Hans J. Hillerbrand, 'Going Our Way: The 2000 Survey of Departments of Religion', *Religious Studies News, AAR Edition* (March 2004), pp. 6, 19; and Richard A. Rosengarten, 'The AAR Graduate Survey at First Blush: Some Initial Thoughts on Institutional Definition and Doctoral Areas of Concentration' *Religious Studies News* 19.2 (March, 2004), pp. 7, 18.

4. Of all course sections offered, 11% were various 'Introduction to Bible'; 10.5% were on 'New Testament' topics; 8.4% were on 'Old Testament' topics. 45.1% of all courses were on Christian topics. See the raw survey results reported in Gray, 'What We Have Learned'.

5. The 2002 survey showed a total of 397 graduate students concentrating in New Testament (ranked 1st), and 241 in Hebrew Bible (ranked 4th); taken together these 638 students vastly outnumbered students in all other subjects. Among the top fifteen concentrations, only three stand outside explicitly Christian studies: Judaism (ranked 8th, with 127 students), Philosophy of Religion (ranked 11th, with 86 students), and Culture and Theory in Religion (ranked 14th, with 56 students). For analysis, see Rosengarten, 'Graduate Survey at First Blush'.

6. Rosengarten, 'Graduate Survey at First Blush', p. 18. But, as Linell Cady points out, 'the centrality of Christianity in the curriculum is, of course, not all that surprising given the roots of the field in the seminary model, the dominance of Christianity among the North American student body as a whole, and the Christian affiliation of over half of the responding institutions'; see Cady, 'A public sector perspective', p. 21.

7. Gray, 'What We Have Learned', p. i.

8. Smith, 'A Private Sector Perspective', p. 23.

position within the religion departments that house them, and within the undergraduate liberal arts curriculum in general.

The 2000 and 2002 surveys may have reassured professors of Bible, since the data suggested a steady demand for Biblicists in American colleges. Administrations and faculties seem to value the contribution of biblical scholarship to the liberal arts education of undergraduates. What the survey could not tell us, other than suggesting that religious studies in America still depends too much on a putatively outmoded 'seminary model' of study, was *how* biblical scholars fit into liberal education, *why* the institutions assign such value to our work, and *whether* they in fact *ought* to.

Questioning the Status Quo

Close on the heels of these first surveys, there emerged several challenges to the observed centrality of Christian and biblical studies in the study of religion. In 2004, the AAR announced its intention to separate its annual meetings from those of the Society of Biblical Literature.[9] At the time, the decision (since rescinded) sent tangible shock waves through the discipline. Although the separation was explained in entirely practical terms, many biblical scholars understood it as a repudiation of their field, as if the Academy was declaring, 'biblical studies is not a part of the study of religion'.

The uneasy alliance of biblical studies and religious studies has been the subject of debate for years. Consider, for example, the 1999 Society of Biblical Literature Plenary Address of J.Z. Smith, 'Bible and Religion'. In this thought-provoking address, Smith charged biblical scholars, and especially New Testament scholars, with neglecting 'religion' as a theoretical category, with substitution of interpretive 'method' for critical theory, and with failing to attend to the 'foundational' problem of the dialectic between 'insider' and 'outsider' perspectives in religious studies. In a memorable passage, Smith argues that

> scholarly study of the Bible remains, to a remarkably large degree, an affair of native exegesis. That is to say, [it produces] the sort of accounts that ... [could] constitute data for the student of religion.[10]

In other words, Smith suggests that biblical scholars interpreting biblical texts, however 'academic' their research may be, can be viewed as religious believers engaged in an implicitly religious practice. Arguing about the meaning of sacred scripture, in hopes of influencing the understanding of 'insiders' within a faith tradition, effectively makes one a 'native exegete', even if one's own

---

9. The reasoning behind the split was announced in the 'Report of the Task Force on the Independent Meeting' (American Academy of Religion, 2004); formerly published online, this document is no longer freely available on the internet.

10. Jonathan Z. Smith, 'Bible and Religion', *Bulletin of the Council of Societies for the Study of Religion* 29.4 (2000), pp. 87-93; see p. 88. This essay was reprinted in Smith, *Relating Religion: Essays in the Study of Religion* (Chicago: University of Chicago Press, 2004), pp. 197-214.

faith commitments have been tabled or temporarily set aside for the purpose of conducting objective research. Such 'native exegesis' is precisely the sort of activity that scholars of religion normally make the object of their study. If this perspective has validity, then arguably biblical scholarship is not really at home in the academic discipline of religion, let alone in the secular academy. The study of religion will only privilege particular data sets (e.g. biblical literature) in pursuit of developing a theoretical account of the larger subject matter.[11] If biblical scholarship is seen mainly as concerned with explicating the significance of biblical texts in an effort to challenge or support the ongoing self-construction of a particular religious tradition, then it cannot actually be doing the work of religious studies.

In the immediate aftermath of the AAR's decision, it was also argued by some that, in any case, biblical studies is becoming less and less central in the American study of religion. The second, 2004–2005 AAR survey has been interpreted as showing a decline in the preeminence of Christian studies in general and biblical studies in particular: so argues the widely distributed and discussed Teagle Foundation-funded White Paper of the American Academy of Religion on the Study of Religion in Liberal Education.[12] The White Paper's authors interpret the 2005 survey as showing that

> by most indications, courses in Christian Theology, Old Testament, and New Testament were all flat or down. Sections of Introduction to World Religions grew in number; sections of Introduction to the Bible declined.[13]

Using this analysis, the authors argued that, at last, the previous decade had brought 'a pronounced if uneven shift away from a seminary and toward a comparative model for the [religion] major'.[14]

This conclusion was premature, perhaps reflecting an aspirational rather than actual view of the field. Although the dominant theoretical and methodological paradigms used by scholars working in religious studies are in fact changing, the actual data on course offerings do not support the report's conclusion. In comparing the results of the 2000 and 2005 surveys, David V. Brewington showed that, while there may have been a slight decline in the total number of

---

11. See Smith, 'Bible and Religion', p. 87, quoting *Drudgery Divine* (Chicago: University of Chicago Press, 1990), p. 143.

12. See Timothy Renick *et al.*, 'The Religious Studies Major in a Post-9/11 World: New Challenges, New Opportunities', *Religious Studies News* (October 2008), pp. 21-24; available as 'The Religion Major and Liberal Education—A White Paper' on the AAR Website, www.aarweb.org/Programs/Religion_Major_and_Liberal_Education; and in an abbreviated form, 'The Religious Studies Major and Liberal Education', *Liberal Education* 95.2 (2009), pp. 48–55. See also Jane S. Webster, James J. Buckley, Tim Jensen, and Stacey M. Floyd-Thomas, 'Responses to the AAR-Teagle White paper: "The Religious Studies Major in a Post-9/11 World"', *Teaching Theology and Religion* 14.1 (2011), pp. 34–71, where the White Paper appears on pp. 34-47. Page numbers in this essay refer to the version published in *Teaching Theology and Religion*.

13. Webster *et al.*, 'Responses', p. 38.

14. See Webster *et al.*, 'Responses', p. 41.

institutions teaching biblically-related courses, there was, overall, a significant increase in the total number of *sections* offered in all introductory-level Bible and biblical courses (Intro Bible +25.3%, Intro NT +10%, Intro OT +7.1%).[15] There may be ample reason to believe that field is undergoing changes, but there is also reason to think that biblical studies not only remains a lively part of the mix, but retains its status as the leading, or *touchstone* sub-discipline.

The status quo has survived these challenges. As of 2011, the AAR and SBL had reconciled and resumed simultaneous meetings. It may seem like good news for biblical scholars, but the underlying tensions and criticisms remain. Critics may still raise tough philosophical questions about whether biblical studies deserve such a privileged status within the study of religion and liberal education.

It cannot be a coincidence that, since 2004, there has been a veritable explosion of self-reflective work done by biblical scholars intent on being much more explicit about the theoretical commitments of their research and the pedagogical aims of their teaching. Much of this work has been published on the internet, in a new venue, the *SBL Forum*. Some internal critics, such as Hector Avalos and Jacques Berlinerblau, have come close to arguing for the total abolition of biblical studies as an area of study in the secular academy.[16] Others have addressed the paradoxical and problematic realities of the interface of insider/outsider discourse in the biblical studies classroom, and others have defended the teaching of the Bible in terms drawn from critical pedagogies common to more clearly secular areas of study.[17]

---

15. Brewington compared the results of the 2000 and the 2005 survey by restricting his analysis to the 267 institutions who responded to both surveys; see 'AAR Undergraduate Departments Survey Comparative Analysis of Wave I and II', Focus on the Undergraduate Study of Religion, *Religious Studies News* (May 2008), pp. 14-15. www.aarweb.org/programs/Department_Services/Survey_Data/RSN_UndergradSurvey_May2008.pdf. Figures from the table on p. 15.

16. Jacques Berlinerblau, 'The Unspeakable in Biblical Scholarship', *SBL Forum* www.sbl-site.org/Article.aspx?ArticleId=503; also, Berlinerblau, 'What's Wrong With the Society of Biblical Literature', *Chronicle of Higher Education*, The Chronicle Review Section, 53.12 (2006), p. B13. Hector Avalos, 'The Ideology of the Society of Biblical Literature and the Demise of an Academic Profession', *SBL Forum* www.sbl-site.org/Article.aspx?ArticleId=520; see also Avalos, *The End of Biblical Studies* (Amherst, NY: Prometheus Books, 2007).

17. See, e.g. Elna K. Solvang, 'Teaching Difference: College Students and the Bible', *SBL Forum* www.sbl-site.org/Article.aspx?ArticleId=224C; Drew Smith, '"Between Athens and Jerusalem": Reading Liberal Books at Church-Based Universities', *SBL Forum* www.sbl-site.org/Article.aspx?ArticleId=389; Arthur Walker-Jones, 'New Life in the Biblical Studies Classroom', *SBL Forum* www.sbl-site.org/Article.aspx?ArticleId=423; Daniel J. Gaztambide, 'If You Can't Take the Heat, Stay Out of the Classroom: Re-evaluating the Student-Teacher Relationship, Classroom Ambiance, and Religion', *SBL Forum*; Mary Bader, 'Strategies for Moving Students from Faith-based to Academic Biblical Studies', *SBL Forum* www.sbl-site.org/Article.aspx?ArticleId=467; Daniel J. Gaztambide, Matthew W.I. Dunn, Shawn C. Madden, and Ron Clark, 'Responses to Bader Article', *SBL Forum* www.sbl-site.org/Article.aspx?ArticleId=473; Michael V. Fox, 'Bible Scholarship and Faith-Based Study: My View', *SBL Forum* www.sbl-site.org/Article.aspx?ArticleId=490; Michael Avioz, Ronald M. Hinson, Paul D. Brassey, K.L. Noll, James E. Bowley, 'In Response to the Fox Article', *SBL Forum* www.sbl-site.org/Article.aspx?ArticleId=502.

The most persuasive branch of the discussion has emphasized the ways that biblical studies, when taught in the right way, will positively contribute to the general educational outcomes that are desirable in a modern liberal arts setting.[18] But although it may be relatively easy for biblical scholars to convince administrations (or themselves) *that* biblical studies *can* fit into liberal education, there has yet to emerge a persuasive account of *why* biblical studies *ought* to remain in its demonstrably privileged position.

What is needed is a persuasive rationale for including biblical studies in the contemporary liberal arts curriculum. Such a rationale must go beyond the position that 'we meet your general education outcomes by teaching the Bible'. (Such arguments tend to sidestep the issue, because any subject at all can be taught so as to meet general learning outcomes.) *Ars longa, vita breva:* the real question is, why expend limited educational resources on this subject, rather than another?

The Origins of 'Religious Studies' in America

In attempting to answer this difficult question, it helps to consider our current situation from the perspective of history. Collegiate-level study of the bible in America has a distinctive and relatively short history which continues to shape our disciplinary practices today. It can be argued that the current institutional standing and privilege of biblical studies in the American college is actually a legacy of the strange history of the study of religion in the American college system.

In this endeavor, once again, it is J.Z. Smith's 1999 address that inspires the work and blazes the trail. Against forgetfulness of our professedly historical disciplines, Smith's address was a *pharmakon* for restoring repressed memories. Older scholars may have preferred to forget, and younger scholars to remain ignorant of, the disciplinary past invoked by Smith. But the gadfly provoked both groups towards greater self-examination.

In his address, Smith pointed out that the organization that eventually became the American Academy of Religion was first organized in 1909 as the Association of Biblical Instructors in American Colleges and Secondary Schools, with a mission to advance pedagogy in undergraduate biblical studies, then a relatively new field of study. In 1922 the Association changed its unwieldy name to the National Association of Biblical Instructors, henceforth being known by

---

18. On this latter point in particular see the remarks of Jane S. Webster, in Webster, *et al.*, 'Responses', pp. 48-51. See also R. Timothy McLay, 'The Goal of Teaching Biblical and Religious Studies in the Context of an Undergraduate Education', *SBL Forum* 4.8: www.sbl-site.org/Article.aspx?ArticleId=581; and Joseph A. Marchal, 'To What End(s)? Biblical Studies and Critical Rhetorical Engagement(s) for a "Safer" World', *SBL Forum* www.sbl-site.org/Article.aspx?ArticleId=550.

the 'portentous acronym' of NABI.[19] At the time of its founding, 'religious studies' did not exist as a discipline in American colleges. Instead, most members of NABI were housed in Departments of Bible. Only gradually, through the middle of the 20th century, did these Departments of Bible begin to transform into Departments of Religion. Finally responding to this trend, in 1963 NABI changed its name to the American Academy of Religion. In other words, until only about 50 years ago, the AAR shared with the SBL, at least in name, an organizational focus on biblical subjects, and emphasized undergraduate pedagogy over research.[20] Through more than half of the 20th century, NABI served as the pedagogical arm of biblical studies in American higher education, and its *Journal* was initially dedicated to problems of teaching Bible in the context of American undergraduate liberal arts education.[21]

Smith demonstrates that, during this early period American scholars had understood the term 'religion' in a way that made the membership of NABI, as he put it, 'in fact, an implacable foe of the academic study of religion as we have come to understand it'.[22] Which is not to say that 'biblical instructors' at the beginning of the 20th century did not intend their work to be 'religious studies', but only to claim that 'religious studies', at that time, was construed as something quite different than it is today. The members of NABI tended to view the teaching of religion and the teaching of Bible as coextensive tasks. For most of the members and their colleagues, the goal was to teach Bible (qua 'religion') in order to help students cultivate a mature, morally sophisticated, scientifically informed, spiritually rich and personal faith.[23]

The End of Biblical Instruction, According to NABI

We ought to dig further into this forgotten disciplinary history. Whereas Smith was concerned mainly with the way the membership of NABI positioned themselves with respect to the malleable taxon 'religion', it may also be useful to

---

19. Smith, 'Bible and Religion', p. 87. On the history of NABI, see Elmer W.K. Mould, 'The National Association of Bible Instructors: An Historical Account', *Journal of Bible and Religion* 18.1 (1950), pp. 11–28.

20. NABI was a sister to the older Society of Biblical Literature and Exegesis, founded in 1880, which supported advanced philological and historical-critical research. On the relations between the SBLE and NABI, see Ismer J. Peritz, 'Editorial: The National Association of Bible Instructors and the Society of Biblical Literature and Exegesis', *Journal of the National Association of Biblical Instructors* 1.2 (1933), p. 29. On the early history of the Society of Biblical Literature, see Ernest W. Saunders, *Searching the Scriptures: A History of the Society of Biblical Literature 1880–1980* (Biblical Scholarship in North America 8; Chico, CA: Scholars, 1983).

21. The *Journal of the American Academy of Religion*, now in its 74th volume, actually issued its 1st volume in 1933, under the title *Journal of the National Association of Biblical Instructors*. This title was changed to the *Journal of Bible and Religion* in 1937, and finally became the *JAAR* only in 1966. Smith, 'Bible and Religion', pp. 87–88.

22. Smith, 'Bible and Religion', p. 89.

23. See Smith, 'Bible and Religion', p. 88 and see p. 88 n. 10 (on pp. 91-92).

examine how they understood the relationship of their work to the task of liberal education in America.

In late December 1932, the *National Association of Biblical Instructors* held its 23rd annual meeting in New York City.[24] If the meeting's proceedings are any indication, in 1932 a distinctly pessimistic, or even eschatological mood pervaded the membership of NABI. The presidential address of Chester Warren Quimby, professor at Dickinson College, set the tone. According to Quimby, college teachers of Bible were working in a particularly difficult cultural context: 'ignored by students, passed up by the clergy, tolerated by the faculty, ours is often a lonely and discouraging task'.[25] At that time, membership of NABI consisted of professors working in 82 liberal arts colleges and universities, most of which are still in existence today.[26] Yet, according to Quimby, in the more than two decades of its existence, NABI had 'failed' in its mission to promote biblical instruction in America. He told the gathered teachers: 'any survey will show that college Bible is pretty much flat on its back'.[27] Apparently supporting this contention with quantitative data, Hugh Hartshorne from Yale reported that between 1927 and 1932 there had been a steep decline, both relatively and absolutely, in enrollments in courses on biblical subjects.[28]

To understand the mood of despair, one must attempt to understand the history of the discipline as it would have been seen by members of NABI. Prior to the Civil War, American undergraduate education had only rarely included formal study of the Bible in English translation.[29] During the 17th and 18th centuries, at America's small number of elite schools, a seminary model of education prevailed and students studied the Bible philologically, in preparation for ministerial careers; yet biblical studies itself was not a specialized collegiate discipline.[30] Curriculums changed in the early 19th century, with the introduc-

---

24. For a schedule of the conference, see 'Report of the Twenty-Third Annual Meeting of the National Association of Biblical Instructors, 1932', *Journal of the National Association of Biblical Instructors* 1.1 (1933), pp. 23–28. According to this report, the decision to publish the *JNABI* was made during the business session of this meeting (see item no. 6 on p. 24; Ismar J. Peritz was elected as its editor). The first issue, published in 1933, contained the conference proceedings.

25. Chester Warren Quimby, 'The Word of God', *Journal of the National Association of Biblical Instructors* 1.1 (1933), pp. 1–6 (p. 3).

26. Henry T. Fowler, 'The Place of the Bible in the College Curriculum', *Journal of the National Association of Biblical Instructors* 1.2 (1933) pp. 25–28, (p. 26). See 'Report', p. 28 for a list of members and their institutional affiliations.

27. Quimby, 'Word of God', 1.

28. Hugh Hartshorne, 'The Future of the Bible in the American College', *Journal of the National Association of Biblical Instructors* 1.1 (1933), p. 9-10.

29. See Fowler, 'Place of the Bible', p. 25.

30. W. Clark Gilpin, 'The Creation of a New Order: Colonial Education and the Bible', in *The Bible in American Education: From Source Book to Textbook* (ed. David L. Barr and Nicholas Piediscalzi; Philadelphia: Fortress, 1982), pp. 5-24. Compare also Mark A. Noll, 'The Revolution, the Enlightenment, and Christian Higher Education in the Early Republic', in *Making Higher Education Christian: The History and Mission of Evangelical Colleges in America* (ed. Joel A. Carpenter and Kenneth W. Shipps; Grand Rapids: Eerdmans, 1987), pp. 56–76.

tion of the 'Old Time College', but at these almost universally Christian early liberal arts institutions there was little curricular instruction focused on biblical subjects. Instead, unofficial but often compulsory Bible studies were a part of the schools' highly structured co-curricular activities.[31]

The end of the 19th century brought dramatic changes. By 1932, America stood at the end of six decades of growth in higher education: enrollments had exploded in size; the number of institutions had greatly multiplied, and the so-called 'Academic Revolution' was underway.[32] Also, after the Civil War, a new model of undergraduate education had emerged. The unified curriculum of the 'Old Time College' had given way to a curriculum featuring electives and a chosen area of concentration. The college major appeared for the first time in 1878.[33] By 1932, the practice of focusing education on a major course of study could be described somewhat skeptically by NABI member Henry T. Fowler, professor at Brown University, as 'almost universal'.[34]

During the post-Civil-War period, the critical results of modern biblical scholarship were beginning to emerge, and the discipline was taking shape as a distinct field.[35] In response, many colleges began to establish official departments of Bible—although these took various names—and English language instruction in the Bible was added to the undergraduate curriculum for the first time.[36] In 1894, according to Fowler, American schools included only three 'departments of Bible': at Yale, Bryn Mawr, and Smith.[37] By 1919, more than 250 undergraduate Bible departments existed nationwide.[38]

---

31. See William C. Ringenberg, 'The Old-Time College, 1800–1865', *Making Higher Education Christian*, pp. 77-97.

32. See Mark A. Noll, 'The University Arrives in America, 1870–1930: Christian Traditionalism during the Academic Revolution', *Making Higher Education Christian*, pp. 98–109.

33. Association of American Colleges and Universities (Jonathan Z. Smith, *et al.*), *The Challenge of Connecting Learning: Project on Liberal Learning, Study-in-Depth, and the Arts and Sciences Major* (Liberal Learning and the Arts and Sciences Major 1; Washington, DC: Association of American Colleges and Universities, 1990), p. 1.

34. Henry T. Fowler, 'The Place of the Bible', p. 25.

35. See George Dahl, 'The Scientific Approach to the Bible', *Journal of the National Association of Biblical Instructors* 1.2 (1933), pp. 1–4, for a NABI perspective on the revolution in 'scientific' biblical studies. For a later perspective on these same developments, see Thomas H. Olbricht, 'Intellectual Ferment and Instruction in the Scriptures: The Bible in Higher Education', *The Bible in American Education*, pp. 97-120.

36. So Fowler, 'Place of the Bible', p. 25. According to Fowler, 'the real era of the English bible in the American College curriculum began with the establishment of the Woolsey Chair at Yale in 1888' (p. 26). For a more recent perspective, see Charles R. Kniker, 'New Attitudes and New Curricula: the Changing Role of the Bible in Protestant Education, 1880–1920', *The Bible in American Education*, pp. 121-42.

37. Henry T. Fowler, untitled remarks from the 25th anniversary dinner of NABI, held in December, 1934, *Journal of the National Association of Biblical Instructors* 3.1 (1935), pp. 41–42.

38. The figure 250 was cited by Charles Foster Kent, in a 1919 address to the Midwest Branch of the Association of Biblical Instructors in American Colleges and Secondary Schools, who were then meeting in Chicago. The talk is discussed in Mould, 'An Historical Account', p. 14. Contra-

In its early years, the National Association of Biblical Instructors worked together with other professional organizations, such as the Religious Education Association, to establish relatively rigorous academic standards for the emerging college programs in Bible. They pressured schools to adopt higher standards by publishing graded evaluations of existing programs, considering both the qualifications of instructors and the implementation of the curriculum. They also worked with the College Entrance Board to establish standards for secondary school curricula and for advanced placement credit in college-level Bible courses, and worked to create a clearinghouse system for the placement of well-trained faculty in colleges and preparatory schools.[39] As a result of all these efforts, by 1933, as Fowler put it, there had been a 'very great advance in the recognition by college authorities that the Bible is entitled to *some* place in the curriculum'.[40]

Yet Quimby, Fowler and other members of NABI were acutely aware of mounting disciplinary changes. Starting in the 1920s many undergraduate departments of Bible had been transformed into 'Departments of Religion'; shockingly, some instructors in these departments were offering courses in subjects not directly related to biblical studies![41] Quite a few observers thought that this change spelled doom for the discipline. Reflecting on this trend of Bible departments turning into what he termed 'vague societies of religion', Quimby melodramatically echoed the lament of fugitive Elijah: 'although we only are left, they are seeking our life to take it away'.[42]

Of course, collegiate biblical studies survived its rough transition into the middle of the 20th century, and somewhat ironically, it actually emerged as a professional discipline *during* the transitional period that historian George Marsden has called 'the collapse of American evangelical academia'.[43] In the 19th century, most colleges directly reflected the culture of evangelical Protestantism which had dominated American public life from the beginning. The schools had been founded, were staffed, and were attended almost exclusively by Protestants of Western European descent. But this period of 'evangelical consensus' gave way, after the Civil War, to unstoppable demographic and

---

dicting this figure, slightly, we find that later in the same paper, Mould reports that there were 299 departments nationwide in 1918 ('Historical Account', p. 20).

39. On all these activities of the association, see Mould, 'An Historical Account', pp. 20–22; compare Fowler, untitled remarks, pp. 41–42. See also Eliza H. Kendrick, 'Twenty Five Years of the National Society of Biblical Instructors', *Journal of the National Association of Biblical Instructors* 3.1 (1935), pp. 37–40; esp. pp. 39–40.

40. Fowler, 'Place of the Bible', p. 28. Compare Quimby, 'The Word of God', p. 1, who lists the disdain of college administrators for biblical subjects as one of six challenges facing modern instructors of Bible.

41. Quimby, 'The Word', p. 1; Fowler, 'Place of the Bible', p. 25.

42. Quimby, 'Word of God', p. 1. The allusion is to 1 Kgs 19.10 (cf. Rom. 11.3). This passage from Quimby is also cited in Smith, 'Bible and Religion', p. 88.

43. George M. Marsden, 'The Collapse of American Evangelical Academia', pages 219–264 in *Faith and Rationality: Reason and Belief in God* (ed. Alvin Plantinga and Nicholas Wolterstorff; Notre Dame: University of Notre Dame Press, 1983).

intellectual developments. In contrast to today's academic environment, in which our 'millennial generation' (or 'post-modern') students are very likely to express skepticism towards scientific modes of understanding, and even preference for 'spiritual' or 'faith-based' perspectives, in the early 1930s the members of NABI were confronted by increasingly 'modernist', 'lost generation' students, while the faculty of the colleges were being shaped by a new academic spirit that emphasized liberty, criticism, reason, and science.

Almost to a person, the scholars working in NABI seem to have embraced this new spirit of academia, albeit cautiously, while they remained openly committed to Christianity and to the religious, or spiritual education of students via scientific study of the Bible. (In this same period, self-proclaimed fundamentalist Christians had begun a process of setting up a parallel system of schools designed, at least in part, to protect students from 'modernism' and the 'higher criticism' of the Bible that was taking root in the colleges.[44]) George Dahl of Yale University, referring to his subject area as the teaching of 'the classical documents of our religion' (note the insider's self-identification), suggested that the era of higher criticism had yielded 'a new atmosphere of invigorating and creative freedom' which had led to 'a truer appreciation of the supreme and abiding worth of the Bible'.[45] Others warned against a modernist drift away from spirituality and into materialism.[46] Even Dahl, who styled himself a staunch advocate of a scientific approach to biblical instruction, worried about the possibility that the 'cold intellectualism' of science might be behind part of what he termed 'the decline in popular enthusiasm for biblical studies today'.[47]

In 1933, many NABI members believed there was a need to re-shape biblical instruction in a way which could overcome this danger of 'cold intellectualism'. Several expressed reservations about the appropriateness of making critical scholarship the focus in the classroom. On these matters, Clara Willoughby Davidson of Randolph-Macon Women's College, rightly claimed to express what she called the 'group mind'.[48] Davidson, blaming the 'World War' for radically transforming American culture, asked NABI members to 'rethink the aims' of their work. She began by suggesting that 'the aim of college biblical instruction is at one with that of education in general', and then, having defined the goals of liberal education as 'the freeing of the individual for creative social living in his own day',[49] suggested that this meant that 'the educational process

---

44. See Virginia Lieson Brereton, 'The Bible Schools and Conservative Evangelical Higher Education, 1880–1940', *Making Higher Education Christian*, pp. 110–136.
45. Dahl, 'The Scientific Approach', p. 1.
46. See Florence Mary Fitch, 'The Historical Approach to the Study of the Bible', *Journal of the National Association of Biblical Instructors* 1.2 (1933), pp. 11–14. Apparently, in her classes Fitch represented 'fundamentalism' and 'modernism' as extremes to be avoided.
47. Dahl, 'The Scientific Approach', p. 1.
48. Clara Willoughby Davidson, 'Re-thinking Our Aims as Biblical Instructors', *Journal of the National Association of Biblical Instructors* 2.2 (1934), pp. 49–55, p. 49.
49. There is plenty of evidence that other members of NABI shared Davidson's understanding of the aims of education. For example, see Joseph Haroutunian, 'The Bible and Modern Education',

at its best is a religious process, that is to say, all true education is religious education'.[50] College faculty should recognize this 'essentially religious nature' of education, but especially so teachers of Bible, for the 'Jewish Christian' message of the Bible is the highest form of religion.[51] Accordingly, as she puts it, in 'the universities and colleges of countries avowedly Christian' we must teach the Bible. Historical-criticism was valuable, but could obstruct the real aim of education, which is, the development of religion.[52] She spoke of the 'desperate need' for such education, warning that 'the race' is threatened by 'disaster consequent upon materialism and self-interest'.[53]

Most contemporary teachers of the Bible will recognize that, over the past 80 years, both the context and the implicit purposes of our work have been dramatically transformed. Colleges once dominated by a culturally and religiously homogenous student body have become increasingly pluralistic, and, with the exception of faculty working in the most traditional and conservative collegiate programs, contemporary teachers of Bible no longer view their task as one of helping students cultivate a 'vital [Protestant, Christian] personal religion'. Instead teachers of Bible mostly embrace secular and/or non-sectarian accounts of their work and purposes. To be sure, there are parallels between the concerns of the Bible faculty of the 1930s, and concerns we find today. As we have seen, biblical studies once again faces the question of its relation to religious studies programs, and to the academy. There has also been a revival of debate on the role of 'scientific' methods in the classroom. For example, consider Dale Martin's recent, widely-reviewed book *The Pedagogy of the Bible*, which challenged the dominance of historical criticism in the education of theological students. The book has sparked both supportive and critical responses from colleagues across the spectrum of institutional contexts, including undergraduate programs.[54] To be sure even Martin himself insists on a 'radical difference' between the contexts of graduate theological studies and collegiate 'Arts and Sciences', saying that for undergraduates there is 'something liberative' in

---

Journal of the National Association of Biblical Instructors 1.1 (1933), pp. 10–15. Haroutunian names two principle aims for 'modern education', namely, 'making ... useful and effective members of society' and fostering 'the fullest development of personality, the realization of a rich selfhood', both of which aims can be condensed under one rubric, 'the building of character' (p. 10).

50. Davidson, 'Re-thinking Our Aims', p. 50. Fitch also argued that the outcomes towards which liberal education aspired could be attained through the passionate and faithful teaching of Bible for the purpose of cultivating 'vital, personal religion'. See Fitch, 'Historical Approach', p. 11.

51. Davidson, 'Re-thinking Our Aims', pp. 51–52.

52. Davidson, 'Re-thinking Our Aims', pp. 53–54. Compare the similar views of David E. Adams of Mount Holyoke College in 'The Teaching of Religion in the Liberal Arts College', *Journal of the National Association of Biblical Instructors* 2.2 (1934), pp. 56–60.

53. Davidson, 'Re-thinking Our Aims', pp. 53–54. It is not entirely clear what Davidson means by 'the race' in this passage.

54. Dale B. Martin, *Pedagogy of the Bible* (Louisville, KY: Westminster John Knox, 2008). For the recent debate see A.K.M. Adam, D.B. Martin, *et al.*, 'Should We Be Teaching the Historical-Critical Method?' *Teaching Theology & Religion* 12.2 (2009), pp. 162–187.

the traditional historical critical method.[55] There is little doubt that this view is widely shared in the field. These areas of debate will remain unresolved so long as we remain unclear about the proper rationale for including our subject in the curriculum.

Biblical Studies, Work and Faith in 21st Century America

One possible rationale for collegiate biblical instruction that might be raised is the claim that we need it to prepare the next generation of professional biblical scholars or members of the clergy. But this is nonsensical. As of January 2012, the United States has an adult population estimated at 242 million persons (out of a population of 313 million), of whom about 154 million are considered as a part of the labor force, with close to 142 million employed.[56] Thus, the roughly 9,000 member Society of Biblical Literature represents only around 0.006% (six one thousandths of one percent) of the US labor force. As for the professional clergy, at roughly 43,000 employed persons (not all of whom are Christian or Jewish), clergy represent only 0.03% (three one hundredths of one percent) of the US labor force.[57] In comparison with these numbers, the 2000 AAR survey estimated that, just in the year covered by the study, at least 700,000 students (0.4% of the US workforce) had enrolled in collegiate-level religion courses.[58] Recall that 30% of those courses were biblical. Each *year* we are sending hundreds of thousands of college graduates out into the public sphere armed with an introductory-level knowledge of biblical studies. Even if we set aside the fact that virtually all professional Biblicists and clergy have advanced graduate training, for which prior undergraduate level study of the Bible is not so very important, these demographic considerations underline the fact that we cannot justify collegiate biblical education as a kind of pre-professional course of study.

What then are our undergraduates doing with their studies of Bible? Again, a demographic approach to answering that question might suggest a more pragmatic rationale for our work.

The Pew Forum on Religion and Public Life reports that approximately 78% of American adults self-identify as 'Christian'.[59] That represents approximately

---

55. See Adam and Martin, *et al.* 'Should We Be Teaching', pp. 171-73.
56. Bureau of Labor Statistics, 'Economic News Release, Table 1-A, Employment Status of the Civilian Population by Sex and Age', US Dept. of Labor Website, www.bls.gov/news.release/empsit.t01.htm. Population statistics from US Census Bureau, 'Population Estimates', www.census.gov/popest/data/national/totals/2011/index.html.
57. Bureau of Labor Statistics, 'Occupational Employment and Wages, May 2010: Clergy', US Dept. of Labor Website, www.bls.gov/oes/current/oes212011.htm.
58. Hillerbrand, 'Going Our Way', p. 6.
59. Pew Forum on Religion and Public Life, 'U.S. Religious Landscape Survey', religions.pewforum.org/reports.

185 million adults.⁶⁰ Comparing the 154 million member workforce to the mass of 185 million adult 'Christians', I am tempted to quip that, in America, Christianity is even more popular than work.

We may safely assume that the majority of our students are now or one day will be counted as self-identified Christians. Moreover, the dominance of Christian self-identification in American life assures us that even our students who belong to other traditions or who reject any religious affiliation whatsoever are still likely have regular contact with self-professed Christians. Hector Avalos may be correct that in modern pluralistic America we have witnessed a 'dethronement of the Bible', such that it has lost its once unquestioned position of cultural authority.⁶¹ Yet the fact remains that a great many Americans embrace a religious identity in which the Bible has acknowledged authority as sacred scripture. The object of inquiry in a biblical studies classroom is considered sacred, or even sacrosanct, by, on average, about one third of the students, while most of the rest regard it as somehow highly important.⁶² In this society there are millions of people who are likely to recognize and in some cases explicitly assert the religious, political, cultural, historical, and even the scientific 'authority' of some aspect of biblical literature. At some point in their lives, for good or for ill, students will be confronted by public or social discourse rooted in biblical interpretation or biblical doctrine, proffered by peers or authorities who may or may not be trustworthy. I would maintain that this demographic reality creates a perennial pressure on the academy—and also on the public secondary schools⁶³—to include discourse about the Bible in the curriculum.

Forensic Training for 'Native Exegetes'

It may seem too historically contingent, if not a bit dangerous, to offer a rationale for collegiate biblical studies based on the continuing religious authority of the Bible in our society. After all, the religious studies departments that house us increasingly wish to be understood as promoting a non-sectarian, academic enterprise. How can training college students to read their own sacred scriptures (or the sacred scriptures of their neighbors) be squared with the mission of religious studies to promote the scientific study of religion?

---

60. Assuming an adult (over 18) population of approximately 238 million; 2010 estimates put the number of citizens under 18 years of age at approximately 74 million. See US Census Bureau, 'Population Estimates: National Intercensal Estimates (2000–2010)', www.census.gov/popest/data/intercensal/national/nat2010.html.

61. Hector Avalos, 'Wither Biblical Studies?' *Bulletin of the Council of Societies for the Study of Religion* 38.1 (2009), pp. 13–15 (p. 14).

62. I am here extrapolating from Pew Forum data on affiliations, which puts 26.3% of Americans in the 'Evangelical Protestant' category, and 6.9% in 'Historically Black Churches' category, both of which traditions have tended to promote a high view of biblical authority.

63. Since 2007, echoing the efforts of NABI in the 1920s and early 1930s, the SBL has been actively engaged in attempting to shape public secondary school curricula with respect to the Bible. See 'SBL Educational Resources', www.sbl-site.org/educational/thebibleinpublicschools.aspx.

Ultimately, the aims of collegiate biblical studies may be different than the aims of the collegiate study of religion. Even if we all equally disavow the 'seminary model' of education in religion, J.Z. Smith still seems right to suggest that most biblical studies remain 'an affair of native exegesis'. We certainly have no demographic basis for disputing his claim. It is easy enough to prove that much of what passes for biblical studies is Christians (and in some cases Jews) arguing about the meaning of their own (or someone else's) sacred scriptures, albeit in a formal, public manner. However zealously we stress an academically rigorous, religiously neutral approach to the Bible as a subject of historical-literary study, most of us, and most of our students, will continue to embrace some form of an 'insider' identity, even if we are, theologically and socially, 'outsiders' to variously particular expressions of the traditions we embrace.

In the 19th and early 20th century, Biblicists fought for the inclusion of the Bible in collegiate curricula, winning their case by embracing standards of 'scientific' and 'historical' methodology that remade the Bible into a proper object of academic study. As a subject viewed from the college classroom, 'Bible' is not understood as a closed canon of *sectarian scripture*, but rather as an open family of *ancient literature*. The various Bibles used in different traditions continue to be held sacred and used religiously by millions of insiders and 'natives', and yet, no sectarian institution controls 'biblical studies' as a field. Even its critics acknowledge that biblical studies have been successful at creating a space of disciplined ecumenical, interfaith, and critical theological dialogue.[64] It has also nurtured more independent viewpoints. As Berlinerblau puts it, we 'have legitimated and routinized the right of an individual to criticize the sacred'.[65] Biblical studies may depend on the work of 'native exegetes', but it does so in public, bringing outsiders in, and turning insiders outward. The discipline thus allows for a dialectical interaction between 'outsiders' and 'insiders', if they are willing to adhere to public and academic standards of discourse.

Such considerations make it easier to offer a rationale for why instruction in the Bible, in our time and place, should belong to a liberal arts education. The training offered by biblical studies is ultimately *forensic,* in the rhetorical sense of the term. To adopt any critical stance towards an object of study is to enter into the 'conflict of interpretations'. How much more so when the topic is biblical literature! To interpret the Bible, to make a claim about its significance (or lack thereof), is to enter into an ongoing public debate that has impact because of the 'authority' religious people assign to the text. Collegiate biblical studies provide academic training for critical engagement in many different public settings over the significance of a culturally important text, using the broadly accepted tools of a public discipline (such as history, geography, archaeology,

---

64. See Berlinerblau (n.p.), 'What's Wrong with the Society of Biblical Literature?' where he damns the membership of SBL with faint praise for its success in ecumenical and interfaith dialogue, an achievement of what he calls 'pseudosecularism' or 'soft secularism'.

65. Berlinerblau, 'The Unspeakable in Biblical Scholarship', n.p.

philology, textual study, etc.). Martin is surely right that there is 'something liberative' in such instruction. Because biblical rhetoric is a part of the public tradition in America, biblical studies empowers our students to assume a greater share of agency and responsibility as citizens, enhancing their abilities, both to persuade others, and to question and criticize the speech of other actors in the public sphere. Martin jokes that he has to warn his undergraduates, 'Don't think that just because I've given you these skills that you can go back to your dorm room and tell your Southern Baptist friends that they're necessarily wrong'.[66] Yet we have every reason to think that this is *precisely* what they might try to do with the skills that we teach them. May all concerned parties be well armed with the right skills for the ensuing argument.

Whether or not faculty teaching Bible are trained in or well disposed towards the scientific study of religion, or are even housed in religion departments, it seems clear that collegiate-level courses in biblical studies exist because they serve the needs of the *res publica* more so than they do the needs of 'religious studies'. It has become an American tradition to offer academic, 'scientific' (historically and literarily grounded) biblical studies as a way of fostering a more literate and responsible discourse among people—our students—who might have a pragmatic need to enter into critical debate over the meaning of biblical texts. In this sense biblical studies can readily be seen as a vital part of an American 'liberal education... that empowers individuals, liberates the mind from ignorance, and cultivates social responsibility'.[67] For the time being, this pragmatic rationale may be all that we need to make sense of our work.

---

66. Adam and Martin, *et al.*, 'Should We Be Teaching', p. 173.

67. See Carol Geary Schneider, 'Practicing Liberal Education: Formative themes in the reinvention of liberal learning', *Liberal Education* 90.2 (2004), pp. 6–11. Schneider's address is a summary of the 2002 report of the Association of American Colleges and Universities, *Greater Expectations: A New Vision for Learning as a Nation Goes to College* (Washington, DC: Association of American Colleges and Universities, 2002).

Occupy Academic Bible Teaching: The Architecture of Educational Power and the Biblical Studies Curriculum

Susanne Scholz
Perkins School of Theology, Southern Methodist University

If the Occupy Movement[1] included a critical analysis of the structures in which the academic teaching of the Bible takes place today, it would find that the power dynamics shaping the academic curriculum of the Bible in North American and European colleges and universities are extremely slanted, so much so that a comprehensive transformation of the biblical studies curriculum may even be futile. Internal and external forces have contributed to this curricular situation. In an article published in 2010 as part of an anthology on the transformation of the biblical studies curriculum, I analyzed some of the inner-disciplinary dynamics in need of change for an alternative curriculum to emerge.[2] I made the claim that the teaching of biblical studies in liberal arts settings faces similar curricular challenges to graduate school settings because 'the curricular structure of biblical studies, as taught at all levels of academic learning, is firmly stuck in a nineteenth-century Christian-Protestant vision, as initially articulated by Friedrich Schleiermacher'.[3] I substantiated this claim by highlighting three areas in the curricular design of biblical studies courses: I showed that the nineteenth-century curricular model still controls the basic assumptions of many undergraduate and graduate curricula; I examined teaching instruments, such as introduction books, to illustrate the ongoing popularity of teaching the Bible within the Schleiermacher model; and I outlined an alternative curricular vision for the teaching of biblical studies.

By examining the inner-disciplinary dynamics of the biblical studies curriculum, I maintained that a curricular transformation seemed not only nec-

---

1. For a brief description of the Occupy Movement, see http://en.wikipedia.org/wiki/Occupy_movement.
2. Susanne Scholz, 'Redesigning the Biblical Studies Curriculum: Toward a "Radical Democratic" Teaching Model', in *Transforming Biblical Education: Ethos and Discipline* (ed. Elisabeth Schüssler Fiorenza and Kent Harold Richards; Atlanta: Society of Biblical Literature, 2010), pp. 269-92.
3. Scholz, 'Redesigning the Biblical Studies Curriculum', p. 270.

essary but doable, possible, and even mandatory if we want biblical studies courses to meet the expectations of a liberal arts education, sometimes defined as 'provid[ing] students with knowledge, values and skills that will prepare them for active and effective participation in society'.[4] I suggested that a transformed biblical studies curriculum ought to be based on a 'radical democratic' educational vision developing in students 'intellectual-religious maturity', 'historical-cultural understanding', and 'literary-ethical engagement' with the world. A few examples illustrated this vision which champions a comprehensive redesign of the undergraduate and graduate curriculum fostering, developing, and encouraging in students a thorough understanding of culture, politics, and religion. In a sense, then, I analyzed the inner-disciplinary status quo to argue for a social-justice oriented vision of the biblical studies curriculum.[5]

Although no extensive curricular debate currently takes place in the field, my proposal does not stand alone. Some renowned Bible scholars envision curricular redesigns. For instance, R.S. Sugirtharajah explained:

> Those who teach biblical studies need to come up with fresh plans to increase students' knowledge of the Bible, but the success of these renewed plans to deepen biblical literacy depends largely on how biblical courses prepare students for responsible citizenship in an increasingly globalized world as well as in Western countries whose populations now have their roots in an array of cultures and histories.[6]

In the forefront of Sugirtharajah's vision for the biblical studies curriculum stands the development of 'responsible citizenship' in a 'globalized world'. In other words, he wants biblical studies courses to contribute constructively and critically to democratic society. Other scholars report of already transformed curricula. Archie Lee describes a curriculum for 'multiscriptural contexts'. More specifically, the graduate program of the Department of Cultural and Religious Studies at The Chinese University of Hong Kong promotes a 'cross-textual hermeneutic' that acknowledges the existence of Asian sacred texts and takes seriously students and their cultural contexts.[7] In other words, prominent scholars have urged to move the biblical studies curriculum from a historically defined curriculum toward a design advancing interdisciplinary, cross-cultural, and cross-textual hermeneutical explorations.[8] In accordance with these schol-

---

4. Carol M. Baker, *Liberal Arts Education for a Global Society* (2000), carnegie.org/fileadmin/Media/Publications/PDF/libarts.pdf.
5. I have been committed to this curricular vision and published accordingly; see, e.g. Susanne Scholz (ed.), *Biblical Studies Alternatively: An Introductory Reader* (Upper Saddle River, NJ: Prentice Hall, 2003).
6. R.S. Sugirtharajah, 'The End of Biblical Studies', in *Toward a New Heaven and a New Earth* (ed.; Fernando F. Segovia; Maryknoll, NY: Orbis Books, 2003), p. 136.
7. Archie C.C. Lee, 'Cross-Textual Biblical Studies in Multiscriptural Contexts', *Transforming Biblical Education*, p. 44.
8. See also, e.g. Elisabeth Schüssler Fiorenza, *Democratizing Biblical Studies: Toward an Emancipatory Educational Space* (Louisville, KY: Westminster John Knox, 2009).

arly observations, my 2010 article maintained that 'a move toward the radical-democratic teaching model is possible wherever we teach, and a sustained conversation on the biblical studies curriculum at all levels ensures that we develop a viable future for the field'.[9] It was an optimistic assessment for transforming the Bible curriculum despite the few inner-disciplinary efforts to systematically redesign the academic teaching of biblical studies.

Yet my article also hinted at the fact that the relative lack of developing alternative curricula is not only related to a general disinterest in the field. Powerful external forces impede such attempts, as they have put considerable pressure on most institutions of higher education during the past few decades. As William M. Plater, an English professor and former Executive Vice Chancellor and Dean of the Faculties at Indiana University, explained, faculty members have increasingly become arbitrary to the curricular design because many of them only hold contingent appointments and perform disaggregated work. They lack job security and comprehensive institutional integration that earlier generations of the professoriate took for granted. Plater observed:

> [M]ost American colleges and universities can no longer sustain an academic workforce based on an ideal of the 'complete scholar' engaged in coherent, integrated, and self-directed work across the full range of teaching, research, service, and governance. The predictable career path leading from graduate student to tenured full professor is no longer the norm.[10]

Plater's dire observation is part of a growing body of literature arguing that professors have increasingly joined America's low-wage workers. English professor, John Champagne finds that this situation 'proletarianizes the professoriate, subjecting it to increasing surveillance and regulating in greater detail how its work time is spent'.[11] In addition, accreditation agencies evaluate the health and viability of academic programs, departments, and, in fact, the teaching and research agendas of entire universities and colleges based on 'models of corporate business management'.[12] The future of higher education looks grim indeed.[13] The call by biblical scholar Abraham Smith that we 'use our analytical skills—as public intellectuals—to help to expose the full panoply of power arrangements in biblical discourse, whether our attention is devoted to texts,

---

9. Scholz, 'Redesigning the Curriculum', p. 292.

10. William M. Plater, 'The Twenty-First-Century Professoriate: We Need a New Vision if We Want to Create a Positive Future for the Faculty', *Academe Online* (July-August 2008), www.aaup.org/AAUP/pubsres/academe/2008/JA/Feat/plat.htm.

11. John Champagne, 'Teaching in the Corporate University: Assessment as a Labor Issue', *AAUP Journal of Academic Freedom* 2 (2011), p. 4, www.academicfreedomjournal.org/VolumeTwo/Champagne.pdf.

12. John W. Powell, 'Outcomes Assessment: Conceptual and Other Problems', *AAUP Journal of Academic Freedom* 2 (2011), p. 9, www.academicfreedomjournal.org/Previous/VolumeTwo/Powell.pdf.

13. See, e.g., Marc Bousquet, *How the University Works: Higher Education and the Low-Wage Nation* (New York: New York University Press, 2008).

interpreters, or the larger productive processes that seek to control thought, desire, and behavior'[14] demands to be heeded.

I was aware of these developments in my 2010 article, and so I advised that Bible scholars need to look beyond the inner-disciplinary debates when we think about the viability of transforming the biblical studies curriculum. This article follows my advice and turns to the external forces that limit curricular transformation. The pervasive architecture of educational power has come to shape institutions of higher education and prevents creative, innovative, and comprehensive redesign of the biblical studies curriculum at the undergraduate and graduate levels. In my view, these 'geometries of power'[15] do not give reason for much optimism. They also do not solely apply to biblical studies but also to religious studies, to the humanities, and in fact, to institutions of higher education as a whole. My concerns, however, remain focused on biblical studies. I examine in three steps how primarily three components form a pervasive architecture of educational power discouraging curricular transformation in the field. First, I highlight the neoliberal agenda prevalent in society during the early decades of the twenty-first century and correlate this agenda to the status of the biblical studies curriculum. Second, I turn to the notion of the university as a corporation and its effects on the biblical studies curriculum. Third, I elaborate on the pressures of degree marketability and what its absence means for the biblical studies curriculum. In short, the following sheds light on external political and economic forces that inhibit the transformation of the academic curriculum in biblical studies today.

One final thought in this introduction: Since the Occupy Movement has called for an opposition to the political and economic forces of Wall Street that also threaten institutions of higher education,[16] biblical scholars ought to be ready to ask why relative little curricular change has been realized despite the hermeneutical and methodological innovations in the field since the 1970s. Is it not the case that powerful external forces have sidelined academic disciplines that do not directly advance neoliberal and money-driven goals, and so curricular practices in biblical studies—and in the humanities in general—attempt to preserve at least the status quo? At worst, are these external forces not steadily nibbling away at any curricular ambition for a thriving humanities curriculum, including biblical studies, that develops in students 'critical think-

---

14. Abraham Smith, 'Taking *Spaces* Seriously: The Politics of Space and the Future of Western Biblical Studies', *Transforming Biblical Education*, p. 68.
15. A.E. Mazwi and R.G. Sultana, 'Editorial Introduction', in *Education and the Arab 'World': Political Projects, Struggles, and Geometries of Power* (ed. André E. Mazawi and Ronald G. Sultana; World Yearbook of Education 2010; New York/London: Routledge, 2009), p. 12. See also, e.g. Debbie Epstein *et al.* (eds.), *Geographies of Knowledge, Geometries of Power: Framing the Future of Higher Education* (World Yearbook of Education 2008; New York/London: Routledge, 2007). See also Smith, 'Taking Space Seriously', p. 64.
16. See, e.g. Henry A. Giroux, 'Why Faculty Should Join Occupy Movement Protesters on College Campuses', *truthout* (December 19, 2011): www.truth-out.org/why-faculty-should-join-occupy-movement-protesters-college-campuses/1324328832.

ing, dialogue, and those values that engage matters of social responsibility and civic engagement'[17]? The following analysis aims to contribute to a discussion about the institutional conditions in which we teach and to encourage bold proposals toward a transformed biblical studies curriculum on the undergraduate and graduate levels.

Neoliberalism, Historical Criticism, and the Biblical Studies Curriculum

When biblical studies became established as an academic discipline in Western countries during the early to mid-nineteenth century, the socio-economic and political conditions were also in the making.[18] European societies had moved into the industrial age under the newly emerging economic and political conditions. The renowned 1904 study by the sociologist Max Weber, entitled *The Protestant Ethic and the Spirit of Capitalism*, describes the 'elective affinities' between the Calvinist work ethic and the capitalist system.[19] Weber observed that Protestant theologies endowed moral and spiritual significance to hard work and economic success. They provided religious justification for an economic system that required the suppression of immediate gratification and stressed potential economic gains in the future.

The evolving historical method in biblical scholarship did not challenge this ethos. On the contrary, it supported it. The focus on the past, presumably divorced from issues prevalent at the time of those reconstructing biblical history, taught every reader to disregard contemporary concerns because they were classified as unscientific for understanding the Bible. In other words, historical criticism divorced the text from the social locations of readers and established biblical meaning exclusively in a distant past. Interestingly, historical criticism was initially contested by the theologically and methodologically conservative generation of Bible scholars in nineteenth-century Europe, as the career of Ernst Hengstenberg illustrates. Hengstenberg was a professor in Berlin from 1826 until 1869, and during these decades he prevented the appointment of any historical critic to the theological faculty. Only his retirement changed this situation, and the next group of scholars advanced the new method with full force. They also convinced colleagues in other fields that biblical studies fit into the scientific framework of the modern university,[20] and they established biblical studies as a legitimate academic discipline. Michael C. Lagaspi described the institutionalization of biblical scholarship in the eighteenth and early nineteenth

---

17. Giroux, 'Why Faculty Should Join'.
18. R.S. Sugirtharajah, 'The End of Biblical Studies?' p. 135.
19. Max Weber, *The Protestant Ethic and the Spirit of Capitalism* (Talcott Parsons, trans.; Mineola, NY: Dover, 2003).
20. For an analysis of the early stages of this development in the eighteenth century, see Michael C. Lagaspi, *The Death of Scripture and the Rise of Biblical Studies* (Oxford: Oxford University Press, 2010).

century and affirmed that 'the discipline is best understood as a cultural-political project shaped by the realities of the university'.[21]

Today the social, political, economic, cultural, and educational status quo is in great upheaval again and what was taken for granted forty years ago is now in flux. Intellectuals talk about 'the end' of everything: history, journalism, newspapers, the nation state, America, Europe, and even biblical studies.[22] Since 2008, most everybody in the Western world realizes that capitalist economies are in crisis mode, and some even speak of the end of capitalism, the economic system that in 1989 moved globally into the neoliberal mode, a development that began in the West in the 1970s.[23] Neoliberalism is defined as 'a market-driven approach to economic and social policy based on neoclassical theories of economics that stresses the efficiency of private enterprise, liberalized trade and relatively open markets, and therefore seeks to maximize the role of the private sector in determining the political and economic priorities of the state'.[24] A fundamental principle of neoliberalism concerns the privatization of public functions in society because of the conviction that private companies 'produce a more efficient government and improve the economic health of the nation'.[25] Privatization, deregulation, and 'financialization'[26] are key processes that have increasingly come to dominate Western societies.

Neoliberal interests endorse investments in business, engineering, and science departments while the humanities receive neoliberal glances of suspicion. This is a time of retrenchment in which curricular innovation in the humanities or biblical studies is marginalized, especially since neither area of learning holds much gain to neoliberal interests. Hence, academic disciplines

---

21. Lagaspi, *The Death of Scripture*, p. 7.
22. Hector Avalos, *The End of Biblical Studies* (Amherst, NY: Prometheus Books, 2007). See also Francis Fukuyama, *End of History and the Last Man* (New York: Free Press, 1992); Jean-Marie Guéhenno, *The End of the Nation-State* (Minneapolis: University of Minnesota Press, 1995); Naomi Wolf, *The End of America: Letter of Warning to a Young Patriot* (White River Junction, VT: Chelsea Green Publishing, 2007); Marie Bénilde, 'The End of Newspapers?', *New York Times* (March 16, 2010): www.nytimes.com/2010/03/17/opinion/17iht-edbenilde.html?pagewanted=all; David Marquand, *The End of the West: The Once and Future Europe* (Princeton: Princeton University Press, 2011).
23. See, e.g. Joel Kovel, *The Enemy of Nature: The End of Capitalism or the End of the World?* (New York: Zed Books, 2002); Anthony Faiola, 'The End of American Capitalism?', *The Washington Post* (October 10, 2008), www.washingtonpost.com/wp-dyn/content/article/2008/10/09/AR2008100903425.html; Eugene McCarraher, 'The End of Capitalism and the Wellsprings of Radical Hope', *The Nation* (June 27, 2011), www.thenation.com/article/161237/end-capitalism-and-wellsprings-radical-hope.
24. See en.wikipedia.org/wiki/Neoliberalism.
25. See en.wikipedia.org/wiki/Neoliberalism.
26. For a definition of 'financialization', see the one in Wikipedia (en.wikipedia.org/wiki/Financialisation): 'an economic system or process that attempts to reduce all value that is exchanged (whether tangible, intangible, future or present promises, etc.) either into a financial instrument or a derivative of a financial instrument. The original intent of financialization is to be able to reduce any work-product or service to an exchangeable financial instrument, like currency, and thus make it easier for people to trade these financial instruments'.

in the humanities, including biblical studies, seek to preserve the status quo; they are in survival mode. Money is tight, socio-cultural and political support often minimal, and intellectual space for curricular exploration rare. Neoliberal authorities demand justifications of the curricular status quo and if they are not forthcoming, degrees, departments, and even entire schools disappear.[27] When scarce job opportunities are added on top of these conditions, curricular transformation is seldom a goal.

Also in European countries, changes in the educational infrastructure are under way due to neoliberal advances. European universities developed 'solely as national institutions, in an era when economies were national', but nowadays 'the economic fulcrum is increasingly moving to a supranational level'.[28] This is important because some scholars posit that the economic and political pressures placed upon institutions of higher education reflect 'the changing nature of the relationship between capitalism and modernity'.[29] The societal developments in Europe affect departments of theology and religion in which biblical studies are housed. The departments operate in secularized societies which recognize religious traditions merely as historic relics. I am stating the following based on anecdotal evidence only, but it seems to me that theological departments at European universities exist on the margins holding on to past accomplishment, status, and method.[30]

The situation is worse in developing nations in which institutions of higher education are often in crisis mode. They face 'increasing demand, a lack of basic physical resources such as classrooms, a small number of skilled and committed academic and administrative staff and the absence of academic resources such as journals and basic scientific equipment'.[31] Educational imperialism and a growing dependence on neoliberal benefactors aggravate a situation that also applies to Christian educational institutions. Financial support comes often from organizations subscribing to neoliberal ideologies and located in developed countries, especially the United States.[32] Firoze Manji and Carol O'Coill elaborate on the effects of the neoliberal austerity measures that the Interna-

---

27. Champagne, 'Teaching in the Corporate University', pp. 7-8. See also, e.g. Richard Lake, 'Proposal would eliminate Nevada State College, other schools', *Las Vegas Review Journal* (March 10, 2011): www.lvrj.com; Laurel Rosenthal, 'Some California university degrees disappear amid budget cuts', *The Sacramento Bee* (July 9, 2011): www.sacbee.com.

28. Roger Dale, 'Repairing the deficits of modernity: The emergency of parallel discourse in higher education in Europe', in *Geographies of Knowledge*, p. 15.

29. Dale, 'Repairing the deficits of modernity', p. 16.

30. See, e.g. Erhard Gerstenberger, 'Liberation Hermeneutics in Old Europe, Especially Germany', in *The Bible and the Hermeneutics of Liberation* (ed. Alejandro F. Botta and Pablo Andinach; Atlanta, GA: Society of Biblical Literature, 2009), pp. 61-84.

31. Rajani Naidoo, 'Higher education: a powerhouse for development?' in *Geographies of Knowledge*, p. 252.

32. For an analysis, see, e.g. Kingsly Banya, 'Globalization, Social Justice, and Education in Africa: Neoliberalism, Knowledge Capitalism in Sub-Saharan Africa', in *Globalization, Education, and Social Justice* (ed. Joseph I. Zajda; Series Globalization, Comparative Education and Policy Research, vol. 10; Dordrecht, Netherlands/New York, NY: Springer, 2010), pp. 15-31. For a gen-

tional Monetary Fund (IMF) implemented in Africa during the 1980s: 'The outcome of these deliberations [by the IMF and African governments] was the "good governance" agenda of the 1990s and the decision to co-opt NGOs and other civil society organizations to a repackaged programme of welfare provision, a social initiative that could be more accurately described as a programme of social control'.[33]

Since then, international and some local NGOs, including churches, have been involved in charitable development and many of them have become co-opted by neoliberal interests. As a result, social institutions in health, education, and social welfare suffer under the externally imposed constraints in most African countries. More specifically related to the academic teaching of the Bible, this situation has fostered theological conservatism and the adherence to the literal-historicist hermeneutical paradigm with little concern for curricular innovation in biblical studies. However, it has to be stressed that progressive Christian organizations, churches, and select biblical studies scholars have organized to oppose these neo-colonial forces and developed alternative and indigenized readings of the Bible.[34]

It thus should not surprise that some politically progressive economists state that neoliberals have created 'a big structural crisis' in capitalist Western societies. To them, this crisis is grounded in a 'civilizational crisis'.[35] For instance, the members of the International Observatory of the Crisis—a group located at the Departmento Ecuménico de Investígaciones (DEI) in San José in Costa Rica and closely affiliated with liberationist theological movements in Latin and Central America—have looked at the financial crash of 2008 in conjunction with the ecological crisis, the increasing diminishment of natural resources, and the ongoing food and water crises. They conclude that the capitalist system is nearing its collapse. They see an urgent need for an alternative economic system based on values that 'reaffirm the lives of the majorities'[36] and built on

---

eral discussion beyond the educational realm, see James Ferguson, *Global Shadows: Africa in the Neoliberal World Order* (Durham, NC: Duke University Press, 2006).

33. Firoze Manji and Carl O'Coill, 'The Missionary Position: NGOs and the Development of Africa', *International Affairs* 78.3 (2002), pp. 567-83 (p. 578).

34. See, e.g. James Howard Smith and Rosalind I.J. Hackett, *Displacing the State: Religion and Conflict in Neoliberal Africa* (Notre Dame, IN: Notre Dame Press, 2011); World Council of Churches, 'African Women's Statement on Poverty, Wealth and Ecology' (November 5-6, 2007, Dar Es Salaam, Tanzania) available at: www.oikoumene.org/en/resources/documents/wcc-programmes/public-witness-addressing-power-affirming-peace/poverty-wealth-and-ecology/neoliberal-paradigm/african-womens-statement-on-poverty-wealth-and-ecology.html); World Alliance of Reformed Churches, 'Neoliberalism contradicts Christian faith, Argentine forum says' (May 2003): www.warc.ch/pc/confess/00.html. See also Gerald O. West and Musa W. Dube (eds.), *The Bible in Africa: Transactions, Trajectories and Trends* (Leiden/Boston/Köln: Brill, 2000).

35. Wim Dierckxsens *et al.* (eds.), *XXI Century: Crisis of Civilization: The End of History or the Birth of a New Society?* (DEI: San José, 2010), www.observatoriodelacrisis.org/what-encourages-us/?lang=en.

36. Dierckxsens, *XXI Century*, p. 110.

'the desire of the majority of the world population to live at peace with liberty, justice, mutual respect and integral democracy'.[37]

The question is how the Bible curriculum has contributed to these dire developments. It would also be interesting to explore how a biblical studies curriculum would look if it sought to focus on economic injustice as part of an alternative economic vision that is not based on greed and the exploitation of the 99 percent. For sure, teaching students how to do a word study on 'money in the Bible' would not satisfy the learning goals of such a newly transformed curriculum. Dramatic and radical curricular changes would be necessary, but it seems unlikely that universities and colleges, driven and shaped by neoliberal political and economic forces, would support faculty to teach in opposition to neoliberal forces prevalent today. And although academic freedom continues to be officially affirmed,[38] self-censorship among the faculty and intricate hiring processes ensure widespread silence on issues overtly critical of the political and economic status quo. Hence, like many other academics, scholars of the Bible often practice a preferential option for the curricular status quo in liberal arts colleges and elsewhere.

The University as a Corporation and Its Effects on the Humanities

One of the first articles that classified universities as corporations appeared in 1931. The author, M.M. Chambers, delivered a generally positive assessment of US-American universities as corporations because this status made universities no longer 'merely a creature of the legislature'.[39] Chambers outlined how various state universities moved from legislative control to 'the status of a constitutional corporation',[40] a welcome advancement because it enabled schools to grow and flourish undeterred from legislative interference.

This assessment has changed, probably because the perception about the nature and function of corporations has dramatically changed. Nowadays, the word 'corporation' has significant negative connotations, as articulated in many critical analyses. For instance, David C. Korten described the global spread of corporate power as 'enriching the few at the expense of the many, replacing democracy with rule by corporations and financial elites, destroying the real wealth of the planet and society to make money for the already wealthy, and eroding the relationships of trust and caring that are the essential foundation of

---

37. Dierckxsens, *XXI Century*, p. 111.

38. For a critical perspective on this statement, see, e.g. John M. Elmore, 'Institutionalized Attacks on Academic Freedom: The Impact of Mandates by State Departments of Education and National Accreditation Agencies on Academic Freedom', *AAUP Journal of Academic Freedom* (2011), www.academicfreedomjournal.org/VolumeOne/Elmore.pdf.

39. M.M. Chambers, 'The University as a Corporation', *The Journal of Higher Education* 2.1 (January 1931), p. 24.

40. Chambers, 'The University as a Corporation', p. 24.

a civilized society'.⁴¹ Or as a review of the *Publisher Weekly* stated it: Corporations are 'a malignant cancer exercising a market tyranny that is gradually destroying lives, democratic institutions, and the ecosystem for the benefit of greedy companies and investors'.⁴² These and other studies have contributed to an understanding of corporations as anti-democratic, profit-driven, unethical, and hierarchical entities that aim for the concentration of economic and political power.⁴³ When institutions of higher education turn to corporate principles, even though they are mostly non-profit organizations, some scholars express concern. They challenge the idea that universities or colleges should operate like corporations and be guided by profit-driven and efficient management principles. They argue that universities and colleges do not deliver measurable products but enable the cumbersome and long-winding processes of learning, teaching, and doing research.

Yet the scholarly criticism is not loud and influential enough. Increasingly, educational institutions rely on corporate management principles. Is there a professor left who has not heard the ubiquitous call for learning outcomes? Some critics thus classify institutions of higher education as 'ruined institutions'. Bill Readings is one of them stating in 1996 'that the market structure of the posthistorical University makes the figure of the student as consumer more and more a reality, and that the disciplinary structure is cracking under the pressure of market imperatives'.⁴⁴ Readings also observed that 'the professoriate is being proletarianized as a body and the number of short-term or part-time contracts at major institutions increases' while the production of knowledge becomes 'equally uncertain'.⁴⁵ In his view, the legitimating struggles within the humanities as well as the disputes over methods and theories within individual disciplines indicate the 'contemporary shifts in the University's function as an institution… [which] is now up for grabs'.⁴⁶ Readings' dire observation is alarming: 'It is no longer clear what the place of the University is within society nor what the exact nature of that society is, and the changing institutional form of the University is something that intellectuals cannot afford to ignore'.⁴⁷

---

41. David C. Korten, *When Corporations Rule the World* (West Hartford, CT: Kumarian, 2nd edn, 2001), p. 5.
42. See the quote on the back of Korten's book, *When Corporations Rule the World*.
43. See also, e.g. Russell Mokhiber and Robert Weissman, *On the Rampage: Corporate Power and the Destruction of Democracy* (Monroe, ME: Common Courage, 2005); Susanne Soederberg, *Corporate Power and Ownership in Contemporary Capitalism: The Politics of Resistance and Domination* (London/New York: Routledge, 2010); Luis Suzrez-Villa, *Globalization and Technocapitalism: The Political Economy of Corporate Power and Technological Domination* (Burlington, VT: Ashgate, 2011). See also the work of the International Forum on Globalization, available at ifg.org/index.htm.
44. Bill Readings, *The University in Ruins* (Cambridge, MA: Harvard University Press, 1996), p. 177.
45. Readings, *University in Ruins*, p. 1.
46. Readings, *University in Ruins*, p. 2.
47. Readings, *University in Ruins*, p. 2.

Things have certainly heated up since Readings. Nowadays, even mainstream newspapers and magazines publish analyses and commentaries on these issues. As Jane Kenway and Johannah Fahey note, contemporary universities are most 'interested in scientific and technological knowledge that can be applied and commercialized'[48] as institutions aim for international recognition and fame. Articles on 'The End of Tenure'[49] and 'The Crisis in Higher Education'[50] try to inform the general public that untenured and time-limited positions constitute the majority of academic appointments while tenured and tenure-track professors represent 'no more than 35% of the American faculty'.[51] William Deresiewicz summarizes the reason for these developments in one word: efficiency. He commented: 'Contingent academic labor, as non-tenure-track faculty, part-time and full-time, are formally known, is cheaper to hire and easier to fire.... Good, secure, well-paid positions—tenured appointments in the academy, union jobs on the factory floor—are being replaced by temporary, low-wage employment'.[52] He elaborated:

> What we have in academia…is a microcosm of the American economy as a whole: a self-enriching aristocracy, a swelling and increasingly immiserated proletariat, and a shrinking middle-class. The same devil's bargain stabilizes the system: the middle, or at least the upper middle, the tenured professoriate, is allowed to retain its prerogatives—its comfortable compensation packages, its workplace autonomy and its job security—in return for acquiescing to the exploitation of the bottom by the top, and indirectly, the betrayal of the entire enterprise.[53]

In an academic environment in which the 'middle class', i.e. tenured and tenure-track faculty, is squeezed, curricular innovation and change are not a priority.

Institutional disparities are further aggravated when the discrepancies between public and private institutions are taken into account. State schools enroll three-quarters of America's college students and yet their budgets are constantly attacked and reduced. Simultaneously, political and parental pressures push students into vocational programs, further sidelining the liberal arts curriculum in favor of so-called practical job skills. Attitudes about college education advance utilitarian principles because it has become too expensive to acquire an undergraduate education that does not translate into immediate employment skills after graduation.[54] As a result, the humanities, as well as

---

48. Jane Kenway and Johannah Fahey, 'Policy incitements to mobility', in *Geographies of Knowledge*, p. 171.

49. Christopher Shea, 'The End of Tenure?' *New York Times* (September 3, 2010): www.nytimes.com.

50. William Deresiewicz, 'Faulty Towers: The Crisis in Higher Education', *The Nation* (May 4, 2011), www.thenation.com.

51. Deresiewicz, 'Faulty Towers'.

52. Deresiewicz, 'Faulty Towers'.

53. Deresiewicz, 'Faulty Towers'.

54. See also Patricia Cohen, 'In Tough Times, the Humanities Must Justify Their Worth', *New York Times* (February 25, 2009), p. C1.

the social and some natural sciences (e.g. anthropology, physics) experience draconian faculty reduction and entire departments are closed when they do not advance instant educational payoff.[55] In short, money is at the center of the educational enterprise which C. John Sommerville bemoaned when he wrote:

> The secular research university has gotten caught up in the values of a secularized economy... now money has become the measure of them all. Students all too often want the majors that promise the highest starting salaries. Faculty are eager to leave one college if they hear of a 'better' job elsewhere. Administrators make their decisions with an eye to the financial advantage or security of their institutions. Taxpayers want the cheapest faculty available. Parents want the cheapest education on offer—unless they think a higher investment will guarantee an even higher return—and then too often wring their hands when they find out their children have chosen 'impractical' majors.
>
> The corporate model is essentially the view that the university has a product. The product is a degree, or more properly, the 'human capital' holding that degree.... [I]ts corporate character draws our attention to the one pseudo-value of money.[56]

The architects of corporate universities and colleges define education as a skill set that adapts students to the mainstream of the global economy. In this educational model, 'impractical' majors have no future; hence the declining prestige of a humanities education. This scenario also applies to the workers at degree-granting institutions, as English professor Marc Bousquet observed succinctly: 'Campus administrations have steadily diverged from the ideals of faculty governance, collegiality, and professorial self-determination. Instead they have embraced the values and practices of corporate management'.[57] In the same vein, education scholar Terri Kim stated: 'Universities are now managed as if they are corporations, competing in a global knowledge economy, in which hierarchies of power and wealth are generated by transactions in a new mode of knowledge

---

55. See, e.g. Reeve Hamilton, 'Budget Woes, Calls for Efficiency Imperil Physics', *The Texas Tribune* (September 16, 2011): www.texastribune.org/texas-education/higher-education/underenrolled-physics-program-fight-survival; Kayla Johnson and Gianna Cruet, 'Cost of cutting: Philosophy tied to campus', *The Nevada Sagebrush* (April 25, 2011), nevadasagebrush.com/blog/2011/04/25/cost-of-cutting-philosophy-tied-to-campus; Lisa W. Foderaro, 'Budget-Cutting Colleges Bid Some Languages Adieu', *New York Times* (December 5, 2010), p. MB1; Scott Jaschik, 'Turning Off the Lights', *Inside Higher Ed* (March 4, 2010), www.insidehighered.com/news/2010/03/04/clark; Stanley Fish, 'The Crisis of the Humanities Officially Arrives', *New York Times* (October 11, 2010), opinionator.blogs.nytimes.com/2010/10/11/the-crisis-of-the-humanities-officially-arrives; 'Reading confirms physics closure', *BBC* (November 21, 2006), news.bbc.co.uk/2/hi/uk_news/education/6159106.stm.

56. C. John Sommerville, *Religious Ideas for Secular Universities* (Grand Rapids: Eerdmans, 2009), pp. 27-28.

57. Marc Bousquet, *How the University Works: Higher Education and the Low-Wage Nation* (New York: New York University Press, 2008), p. 1. For an argument that universities cannot be labeled as corporations, see Lars Engwall, 'The university: a multinational corporation?' (Portland Press, 2008), www.portlandpress.com/pp/books/online/univmark/084/0009/0840009.pdf.

production'.[58] In this corporate environment curricular transformation of biblical studies courses seems like a quaint idea in which the study of religion and the Bible has little employment purpose for degree-seeking students.

In a nutshell, then, and to state the obvious, these developments have not benefited the academic study of the Bible. There are very few teaching positions whether part or full time, tenure-track or tenured. The pressure to conform to curricular expectations is intense. An overloaded teaching and service schedule produces work days filled with little time left for curricular explorations. Scholars choose narrow, safe, and conventional research topics in the hope to eventually be offered one of the few coveted tenure-track positions. Furthermore, teaching positions in biblical studies and other disciplines in theological and religious studies are often limited to religiously affiliated institutions that are theologically, hermeneutically, and ideologically conservative. Finally, salaries start low and remain relatively low, and few students major in biblical studies. Certainly, these conditions apply not only to the biblical field but to the humanities in general. As John Champagne put it bluntly, it is a situation in which 'the corporate university has colonized the humanities'.[59] Under such circumstances, the transformation of the biblical studies curriculum remains elusive.

On the Marketability of Biblical Studies Courses

Then there is the issue of the marketability of the academic study of the Bible. In secular-defined departments of religious studies a heavy emphasis on the Bible is too specialized, appears to lack comparative perspective, and seems to endorse a religious-cultural heritage linked to Western imperialism. In short, it seems biased, value-driven, and normative. The field is virtually unknown outside of theological and religious studies departments and not a safe bet for a post-graduation job. Biblical scholar Jacques Berlinerblau described the situation in the following way:

> Consider that 'biblical studies' as a college major is not exactly a booming industry. In secular universities, a department devoted solely to biblical studies is virtually unheard of. When an undergraduate takes a class in Scripture, it will most probably be a survey course.... Consider that many secular universities don't even have a full-time position in biblical studies. Biblical scholarship is underwritten by theological seminaries—be they independent or affixed to universities.[60]

Berlinerblau's observations depict a profound institutional reality. Can and should the field be changed under such circumstances? Who would be in favor,

---

58. Terri Kim, 'Transnational academic mobility in a global knowledge economy', in *Geographies of Knowledge*, p. 326.
59. Champagne, 'Teaching in the Corporate University', p. 5.
60. Jacques Berlinerblau, 'What's Wrong with the Society of Biblical Literature?' *Chronicle of Higher Education* 53.12 (11/10/2006), pp. B13-B15.

and why? Whose hermeneutic would become required and whose would be silenced? And most importantly, how does the academic location of biblical studies limit curricular transformation?

Yet perhaps surprisingly, the biblical curriculum is precarious also at mainline Christian theological schools despite the general acknowledgment, often repeated in a somber tone, that the academic study of the Bible is essential for future clergy and religious leaders. The situation may be different for Jewish seminaries, but the mainline Christian seminary curriculum does not include many innovative courses in biblical studies, and if it does, these courses do not usually constitute the core curriculum. Instead historical criticism rules and the curriculum covers the basics: introductory courses to the Old and New Testaments and courses on the 'Prophets', the 'Wisdom Books', the 'Gospels', 'Jesus' and 'Paul'. In contrast, courses on feminist/womanist, postcolonial, and newer hermeneutical and methodological topics are among the electives if at all.

In short, biblical studies courses are not usually a market priority at liberal arts colleges, and perhaps they should not be. Whenever universities or colleges expand into 'new markets', they develop degrees in 'new industries with new needs for expertise'. Such degrees are then found 'in industries like cybersecurity, health informatics and project management, matching programs with … industries and labor needs'.[61] The point is that the quest for marketable degrees does not include Bible courses, and hence the curricular status quo does not attract many learners beyond a perhaps-required introductory course.

Corporate Interests, Institutional Power Dynamics, and Occupying Academic Bible Teaching: Concluding Observations

When Friedrich Schleiermacher outlined the theological curriculum in 1811, he was at the pinnacle of academic power at the University of Berlin in Germany. European nations were formed into their current shapes and the industrialized-capitalist era began. Much was in flux and Schleiermacher became the visionary and builder of 'the quintessential German university',[62] the Humboldt Universität, influencing the curricular infrastructure of universities worldwide for almost two centuries. As a theologian, Schleiermacher succeeded '[o]ver the course of the nineteenth century…in assimilating theology to the realities of the modern state in order to ensure the continued survival of their discipline'.[63] He had the institutional and political power to envision, build, and implement a curriculum that fit the political and economic interests of his era. Today, these interests have changed considerably which have significantly sidelined the humanities in general and biblical studies in particular.

---

61. Tamar Lewin, 'Joining Trend, College Grows beyond Name', *New York Times* (December 28, 2011), pp. A1, A12.
62. Legaspi, *The Death of Scripture*, p. 29.
63. Legaspi, *The Death of Scripture*, p. 29.

In fact, institutions of higher education are undergoing such profound institutional changes that all academic disciplines, faculty, students, and the very vision about the purpose of a college degree have become uncertain.[64] Do scholars, theologians, and professors of religious studies and the humanities engage in substantive and pragmatic debate that articulate the purpose of the academic study of the Bible and of other research areas not conforming to neoliberal market trends? In this regard, the provocative position of biblical scholar Hector Avalos on the end of biblical studies is not even broad enough. Avalos blames biblical scholars for the field's predicament but fails to address the corporate interests and institutional power dynamics that shape so considerably all educational settings.[65]

Another anthology, entitled *Academic Repression: Reflections from the Academic-Industrial Complex*, addresses these larger societal-educational dynamics.[66] The various authors illumine the conditions within the neoliberal economic and corporate infrastructures of higher education, making connections to a wide range of socio-political, economic, and cultural developments. Although none of them addresses the state of religious, theological, or biblical studies, the editors show unambiguously that 'higher education [is] a place of hierarchical domination, bureaucratic control, hostility to radical research and teaching, and anathema to free thinking'.[67] They recognize that universities and colleges depend on corporate interests and seek conformity to and compliance with the corporate status quo. The volume thus illustrates the silencing effects of the corporate educational infrastructure on faculty, students, and even administrators.

Certainly, the decline of academic freedom is not a problem created by corporate-driven college campuses alone. Limitations to academic freedom have prevailed in religiously affiliated institutions of higher education for a long time although they have usually operated under cover. Jacques Berlinerblau referred to this problem when he exclaimed:

> As for academic freedom, something needs to be done—urgently. The obvious move is to call for a 'blue-ribbon panel' of SBL members to investigate disputes regarding alleged infringements of scholarly freedom.

---

64. See, e.g. the various online lists of wealthy entrepreneurs who did not complete their college education but were nevertheless successful: Lauren Drell, 'We Don't Need No Education: Meet the Millionaire Dropouts', (February 9, 2011), smallbusiness.aol.com/2011/02/09/we-dont-need-no-education-meet-the-millionaire-dropouts; Tina Barseghian, 'How Valuable is a College Degree?' (May 27, 2011), mindshift.kqed.org/2011/05/how-valuable-is-a-college-degree.

65. Hector Avalos, *The End of Biblical Studies* (Amherst, NY: Prometheus Books, 2007). For another critique of the field as inherently religious and neglectful of secular approaches to the Bible, see, e.g. Jacques Berlinerblau, '"Poor Bird, Not Knowing Which Way to Fly": Biblical Scholarship's Marginality, Secular Humanism, and the Laudable Occident', *Biblical Interpretation* 10. 3 (2002), pp. 267-304.

66. Anthony J. Nocella II, Steven Best and Peter McLaren (eds.), *Academic Repression: Reflections from the Academic-Industrial Complex* (Baltimore, AK Press, 2010).

67. Nocella, *Academic Repression*, p. 13.

Then again, how would any given seminary feel about having its internal affairs judged by scholars who themselves are members of seminaries affiliated with rival denominations? ... Here I have no answer. I only know that the problem exists, and the SBL is the only entity that can even begin to address it.[68]

Berlinerblau, a pragmatic thinker, made important suggestions to resolve limitations to academic freedom in the scholarly study of the Bible, certainly not prevalent only in seminar settings. For instance, he advised that we collect data on Bible scholars and that the Society of Biblical Literature (SBL) as the premier academic society of biblical studies in North America commit to gathering it. The data would provide insight into the institutional conditions of teaching Bible as an academic discipline and provide a better understanding why there is such a reticence to curricular transformation. Berlinerblau offered a whole array of questions to inquire about the field's teaching and research contexts:

> What percentage of members practice in theological institutions? What percentage work in a university not affiliated with any denomination? Of the latter, how many did their graduate work in seminaries? What is the denominational breakdown of the society? Is the persistent rumor that the SBL is dominated—if not overrun—by conservative Christians true? Does this explain the oft-heard accusation that the society takes an overly reverent, uncritical attitude toward the Bible and religion in general? And does this explain why the society has done so little to explore Scripture's aforementioned comeback in American politics?[69]

It would be interesting to have answers to these questions because they would certainly help in getting a clear picture about the inner-disciplinary power dynamics that define the field today. However, the questions are also limiting because they do not deal with the external forces. Yet, as I discussed above, they are remarkably widespread, pervasive, and influential in today's academic world. The neoliberal economic system, the increasing move toward fashioning universities and colleges like corporations, and the lack of marketability prove too strong to institute systemic curricular changes in the field. Hence, most of us teach in money-driven educational contexts in which biblical studies lack the economic cache of powerful markets, individual attempts notwithstanding. Again, this situation is not limited to biblical studies but affects many disciplines in the arts and sciences. Yet surely the curricular state in biblical studies reflects the conditions of higher education in a world in which money, greed, and speedy results rule.[70] It is high time then to occupy not only academic Bible teaching but institutions of higher education as a whole.

---

68. Berlinerblau, 'What's Wrong with the Society of Biblical Literature?', B13.
69. Berlinerblau, 'What's Wrong with the Society of Biblical Literature?', B13.
70. Wade Rowland, *Greed Inc.: Why Corporations Rule Our World and How We Let It Happen* (Toronto: Thomas Allen Publishers, 2005).

Challenges in Teaching Biblical Literature as a General Education Requirement

Stan Harstine
Friends University

Phillip Wiseley
Edison State College

As a faculty member in biblical literature at a private college that self-identifies as Christian, I have found that courses in religion have a somewhat 'sacred' position in the General Education curriculum. My question as a scholar involved in these courses every semester was whether they were valuable to the students and how such 'value' could be measured. I enlisted my colleague Phillip Wiseley from Sociology and we developed a tool to evaluate how students value biblical literature courses as well as how they value the general education curriculum as a whole. What follows is a narrative presentation of the method, analysis and conclusions of that cooperative study.

1. Survey Description

This report is based on a survey conducted at a small private liberal arts college in the Midwest during the spring and fall of 2006. Students surveyed were enrolled in religion and philosophy courses required as part of the college's general education curriculum. The courses selected for sampling were biblical literature courses: Old Testament Survey, New Testament Survey, Perspectives: Psalms or Perspectives: Romans. These are the only biblical literature courses offered in the general education curriculum.

Friends University is situated in an urban setting in south-central Kansas. The enrollment by semester in the College of Business, Arts, Sciences and Education in 2006 was 993 during spring term and 999 during fall term. The female: male ratio was approximately 5:4, while the survey sample was weighted slightly higher toward female participants.

The entire survey tool is presented in the appendix at the end of this chapter. The survey asks twelve questions regarding demographics, prior knowledge of content, expectations about learning, and student learning experience. There are forty responses in all. Most pertinent to this paper were questions 5-12 pertaining to student expectations in comparison with other courses in the General Education curriculum.

2. Survey Analysis

The main purpose of this study was to investigate the relationship between students' expectations about biblical literature courses (Question 7) and their experiences (Question 9). We also looked at students' experience in biblical literature courses in comparison to other courses in the general education curriculum (Questions 10 and 12).

As we discuss the results we will be using various sorts of descriptive information. The letter 'n' refers to the sample size and represents how many people were either sampled or responded to a particular question. Our overall sample had an 'n' of 119, meaning that a total of 119 students completed our survey. However some questions were not answered by everyone, or might not have applied to everyone; in those cases, particular questions might have fewer people answering them than the total size of our sample.

One of the key types of questions in our research involved asking students to respond to several questions by selecting a response from a 5-point scale. While the scales varied slightly based on what was being asked, the general interpretation of the responses is straightforward: low values mean less and high values mean more. For instance, questions 5, 8, 11, and 12 asked students for responses that ranged from 'none' or 'unimportant' (valued 1 on the 5-point scale) to 'very' or 'very important' (valued 5 on the 5-point scale). Questions 9 and 10 asked students to respond to the 5-point scale by comparing their experience with their prior expectations about learning or with other courses. While both sets of these questions ask for different responses the interpretation is somewhat simplified because of the symmetry of the response options. In other words, the value of 3 is the center point on all of the 5-point scale questions, regardless of how the question is worded: higher values mean more, lower values mean less.

3. Results of Survey

The first results relate to the relationship between student expectations and experiences as measured in questions 7 and 9. Question 7 asked for two responses: a) What were your expectations about the **course material**? and b) What were your expectations about **learning**? Question 9 measured responses to the question, 'how did your **experience in this course compare to what you expected as related to**…' in the following eight areas: a) Amount of reading, b) Difficulty of readings, c) Difficulty of assignments, d) Difficulty of exams, e) Useful to me personally, f) Preparing me for working with others, g) Preparing me for my future career, and h) Exposure to new information.

In general, students' experience in the areas measured exceeded their expectations with the largest mean, 3.964, appearing in question 9h. The second highest finding was in response to question 9e, where the mean was 3.705.

Question	N	mean
9a	113	3.345
9b	112	3.080
9c	112	2.830
9e	112	**3.705**
9f	112	3.116
9g	112	3.009
9h	112	**3.964**

When the results are evaluated by year in college, question 9b presents a downward trend in the mean as students matured in college, from 3.364 as first year students to 2.857 as seniors. We draw three conclusions from these results:

1. Seniors and first year students have different expectations regarding reading amount and difficulty.
2. More experienced students find the courses more useful personally than expected.
3. As college experience increases, expectations change.

When the same categories a-h are compared to other general education courses in question 10, the biblical literature courses rate well. Questions 10h and 10e again provide the largest mean responses, 3.797 and 3.622 respectively.

Question	n	Mean
10a	119	3.437
10b	119	3.277
10c	118	2.932
10e	119	**3.622**
10f	118	3.008
10g	119	2.933
10h	118	**3.797**

Based on the data we collected we are able to draw two main conclusions:

1. The amount and difficulty of readings are slightly more than students expect in general education courses.
2. The biblical literature courses are viewed as being more useful than other general education courses.

A second area of interest for the study involved determining the importance of religion and philosophy courses as part of the general education curriculum. The general education curriculum at Friends University is divided into three main categories: Foundations, Perspectives, and Competencies. Each category is subdivided into various discipline subheadings. The department of Religion and Philosophy teaches courses in both the Foundations and Perspectives categories, where the Foundations courses are typically a survey course while Perspectives courses are more focused. Questions 11 and 12 were separated to assess the perceived importance of the categories of departmental courses taught under the subheadings: 1) Foundations of Faith and 2) Perspectives of Faith, as they relate to each other and to the wider general education curriculum.

We then chose to disaggregate the information from these questions based on demographic categories. The measures used, referred to as 'ordinal measures', describe the level of measurement for the question. The term 'ordinal' refers to the fact that responses to questions with a 5-point scale can be ordered in an ascending or descending way. For example, several of the questions asked students to pick among five different response options (responding to questions by selecting a response 1 to 5). In this analysis we wanted to compare subgroups answering the same question. In other words, instead of simply looking at how all people answered a particular question, we wanted to compare how students from different majors, year in school, and gender might answer the question(s) differently. Statistically the correct way to compare ordinal responses between different groups is to compare the mean rank. The mean rank allows for the comparison of an ordinal variable across the different groups.

Many people who do not deal regularly with statistics are not familiar with the concept of mean rank. The mean rank value expresses the average ranking for a particular grouping or category. To assist those not familiar with mean rank, we also report the mean, a concept with which more people are familiar. The mean is correctly used when dealing with interval or continuous data (age, weight, height, etc.) but not with ordinal data as we have here. As you will note, the mean and the mean rank operate in the same direction: Higher means are associated with higher mean ranks. The mean shows the average response for a particular category limited to a number between 1 and 5, while the mean rank shows the average ranking for a particular category and is not limited to a number between 1 and 5.

Analysis of responses to question 12, 'Please evaluate how important you feel each category is to the general education curriculum', by major field of study, year in college, and gender each result in mean scores above 3.25. The overall mean score for Foundations of Faith courses is 3.857 and for Perspectives of Faith courses is 3.647 with an n = 119. Our conclusions for this analysis are:

1. Fine Arts majors value religion courses the most in the general education curriculum.
2. Business and Technology majors value Religion courses the least.
3. The general courses are valued more highly than more narrowly-focused courses.
4. Since both Foundations of Faith and Perspectives of Faith courses have means above 3.5 (by year in college and gender), students perceive Religion and Philosophy courses as important.

Question 12	Foundations of Faith		Perspectives of Faith	
Major Field of Study	Mean Rank	Mean	Mean Rank	Mean
Fine Arts	61.07	4.071	69.64	4.143
Natural Science/Math	46.67	3.586	49.78	3.586
Religion/Humanities	68.83	4.333	63.46	3.958
Education	46.88	3.615	43.81	**3.385**
Social/Behavioral Sciences	47.79	3.714	48.50	**3.429**
Business/Technology	44.33	3.5000	40.08	**3.250**
Year in College	Mean Rank	Mean	Mean Rank	Mean
Freshmen	58.33	3.846	63.73	3.769
Sophomore	64.56	4.000	57.29	3.583
Junior	53.09	3.656	54.50	3.500
Senior	64.19	3.946	63.89	3.730
Gender	Mean Rank	Mean	Mean Rank	Mean
Male	58.49	3.780	55.66	3.520
Female	61.09	3.913	63.14	3.739

The third analysis involves responses to question 11 comparing the importance of biblical literature courses to other departmental courses in the general education curriculum. The mean for the general religion courses is 3.797 while the mean for the biblical literature courses is 3.899. When disaggregated by major field of study, biblical literature courses have a mean ranging from 3.571 to 4.417 (Religion and Humanities) while the general religion courses have three means at or below 3.500 and a highest mean of 4.143 (Fine Arts). When disaggregated by Religion majors and non-majors, the means also increased from the general religion courses to the biblical literature courses (4.381 and 3.670 to 4.409 and 3.784).

Question 11	Religion Courses		Bible Courses	
	Mean Rank	Mean	Mean Rank	Mean
Fine Arts	64.68	4.143	47.14	3.643
Natural Science/Math	44.60	3.448	51.91	3.759
Religion/Humanities	63.52	4.043	70.88	4.417
Education	53.65	3.769	50.12	3.769
Social/Behavioral Sciences	44.82	3.500	42.50	3.571
Business/Technology	48.17	3.500	46.50	3.583

From the analysis we are able to conclude:

1. With the exception of Fine Arts majors, biblical literature courses are perceived as equal to (Education majors) or more important than general religion courses.
2. Non-majors perceive biblical literature courses to be more important than general religion courses.

But the survey pool must be considered before drawing any larger conclusions since all the students surveyed had enrolled in biblical studies courses!

A fourth analysis involves making comparisons by gender. By focusing on questions 5, 8, 9, and 11, some significant conclusions are apparent. Female students at Friends University:

1. had more exposure to the material before the course;
2. were more desirous of diversity in thoughts and ideas;
3. were less challenged by the amount and difficulty of the reading; and
4. responded positively toward new information in comparison to their expectations.

Gender:	Male		Female	
Question	Mean Rank	Mean	Mean Rank	Mean
5	56.34	2.80	62.65	**3.058**
8	**57.74**	**3.960**	**61.64**	**4.275**
9a	60.35	3.438	54.31	3.277
9b	61.88	3.250	52.47	**2.953**
9e	54.79	3.677	57.78	3.734
9h	52.73	3.854	59.33	**4.047**
11a	57.81	3.694	60.70	3.870
11b	59.58	3.840	60.30	3.942

Finally, we sought to identify any statistical relationship regarding students' level of prior knowledge, the source of that knowledge, student expectations about learning, and the reporting of their actual experience compared to their expectations. In many fields of study, students usually come to a course with a slight understanding of the subject. An additional challenge arises at a Christian school in the area of religion. As shown below, a majority of students (over 64%) reported being at least a little familiar with the material, and over 1/3 of students were somewhat or very familiar with the material.

Question 5: Prior to taking this class, how familiar were you with this material?					
Response	Not at all	Slightly	A little	Somewhat	Very
%	13.4	21.8	27.7	28.6	8.4
(n)	(16)	(26)	(33)	(34)	(10)

Of those in our survey, 86.5% (n =103) reported at least some knowledge. When asked about the source of their prior knowledge an overwhelming majority (84.4%) reported that their knowledge came from attending church or church related activities.

Question 6: Source of prior knowledge	% (n)
Taking a different course	4.4 (4)
Attending church or church related activities	84.4 (76)
On my own or with others, but not part of any organized church activities	10 (9)
Other	1.1 (1)

Given that over 1/3 of students stated that they were either 'Somewhat' or 'Very' familiar with the content, it was interesting to note that over 40% of the students thought that the course would simply be a review of prior knowledge, while 20% of the students thought that they would be learning new ways to think about the material that they felt they already knew.

Question 7b: What the student expected to learn	% (n)
No expectations	7.3 (8)
Review of prior knowledge	41.8 (46)
Review of prior knowledge and some new material	30 (33)
Learn mostly new information	0 (0)
Learn new ways to think about the material	20.9 (23)

We then asked students to compare their actual experiences with their expectations about learning.

Question 9: 'Now that you have almost completed this course, how did your experience in this course compare to what you expected as related to...' using the following 5 point scale:					
much less than I expected	less than I expected	what I expected or no expectation	more than I expected	Much more than I expected
1	2	3	4	5

We broke this scale down by students' expectations for learning (question 7b), allowing us to compare the students' actual experience across the different categories of expectations that the students reported. Those students who thought they would learn new ways to think about the material reported that they were exposed to more new information than they had expected (4.23), while those students who did not have any expectations or simply expected the course to review their prior knowledge reported being exposed to less new information.

4. Conclusions

At the end of the study, some observations are appropriate to draw about student expectations and their experiences in biblical literature courses.

1. The primary source for student 'pre-knowledge' is church.
2. First year students especially expect a review of their prior knowledge.
3. Seniors anticipate a review with some new learning.
4. Upper-level students anticipate the use of secondary materials more than primary sources.
5. The reason students enroll in the course has a positive/negative impact on their perception of the importance of the course to the general education curriculum.
6. Positive expectations toward learning by a student correlate well with positive experiences.
7. Students' initial expectations for the class are key; instructors should adjust opening days to raise expectations.

As a concluding note, in 2008–2010 Friends University established a task force to review and revise the current general education program. Although the changes proposed were ultimately not accepted by the faculty, the results of this survey were used by the task force to communicate student perceptions and to help clarify the distinctions among students and students' expectations at varying points in their academic career.

Appendix One: 2006 Survey of Biblical Literature Students at Friends University

1. I am :   ☐ Male   ☐ Female

2. I am currently a:
   ☐ First year
   ☐ Sophomore
   ☐ Junior
   ☐ Senior

3. Please write the name of your major. If you are a double major, please write the name of both majors:

4. I am taking this class –
   ☐ as a requirement to fulfill a general education requirement.
   ☐ as a requirement for my major.
   ☐ as an elective.
   ☐ I don't know / my advisor told me to take it.
   ☐ because of the reputation of the instructor.

5. Prior to taking this class, how familiar were you with this material? (Please circle the number/answer)

Not at all	Slightly	A little	Somewhat	Very
1	2	3	4	5

6. For the most part, how did you obtain that knowledge, if any? (Please indicate the mode of learning that contributed *most* to your knowledge of this material, prior to taking this course. Please select one of the following).
    - ☐ No knowledge / Not applicable
    - ☐ From taking a different course.
    - ☐ From attending church or church related activities (sermons / classes / bible study).
    - ☐ On my own or with others, but not part of any organized church activities.
    - ☐ Other—

7. The next couple of questions are about what you expected this course to be like. So think back to the beginning of the course and answer the following questions about what you expected or thought that this course would be like:
    a. What were your expectations about the **course material**? (Select the most accurate statement.)
    - ☐ I did not have any expectations about the course material.
    - ☐ I thought readings would be limited to small portions of the material directly from the Bible and mostly read in class.
    - ☐ thought readings would be limited to small portions of the material from the Bible and mostly read outside the class.
    - ☐ I thought we would read the entire book of the Bible (in or out of class).
    - ☐ I thought we would read books or material that would explain the material in the Bible.
    - ☐ I thought most of the material would be given to us in the form of lecture.

    b. What were your expectations about **learning**? (Select the most accurate statement)
    - ☐ I did not have any expectations about learning.
    - ☐ I expected this course to be a review of my prior knowledge with the material.
    - ☐ I expected to learn some new material along with reviewing some of my prior knowledge.
    - ☐ I expected to learn mostly new information.
    - ☐ I expected to learn new ways to think about the material.

8. Do you think classes that expose people to a diversity of thinking and ideas should be required to earn a college degree? (Please circle the number/answer)

Not at all	Slightly	A little	Somewhat	Very
1	2	3	4	5

9. Now that you have almost completed this course, how did your **experience in this course compare to what you expected as related to**...

Much less than I expected	less than I expected	what I expected or no expectation	more than I expected	much more than I expected
1	2	3	4	5

a. Amount of reading:
1   2   3   4   5
b. Difficulty of readings:
1   2   3   4   5
c. Difficulty of assignments:
1   2   3   4   5
d. Difficulty of exams:
1   2   3   4   5
e. Useful to me personally:
1   2   3   4   5
f. Preparing me for working with others:
1   2   3   4   5
g. Preparing me for my future career:
1   2   3   4   5
h. Exposure to new information:
1   2   3   4   5

10. Think now about this class compared to other (non-religion) general education classes that you have had. Please rate this class **compared to other general education classes** that you have had.

Much less than most	less than most	about the same	more than most	much more than most
1	2	3	4	5

a. Amount of reading:
1   2   3   4   5
b. Difficulty of readings:
1   2   3   4   5

c. Difficulty of assignments:
1   2   3   4   5

d. Difficulty of exams:
1   2   3   4   5

e. Useful to me personally:
1   2   3   4   5

f. Preparing me for working with others:
1   2   3   4   5

g. Preparing me for my future career:
1   2   3   4   5

h. Exposure to new information:
1   2   3   4   5

11. Please evaluate how important you feel it is that the following specific types of religion courses be required as part of the general education curriculum here at Friends University.

unimportant	of little importance	moderately important	important	very important
1	2	3	4	5

a. Courses on different types of religions or religious practices (Varieties of Religious Experience, Developing a Devotional Life, Basic Christian Beliefs)
1   2   3   4   5

b. Courses on the Bible (Romans, Psalms, Old Testament Survey, New Testament Survey)
1   2   3   4   5

12. Currently, there are several different categories of general education requirements. Please evaluate how important you feel each category is to the general education curriculum:

unimportant	of little importance	moderately important	important	very important
1	2	3	4	5

a. Foundations of World Civilization (for example World Civilization 1 or 2)
1   2   3   4   5

b. Foundations of American Character (for example American Government, The American Character, US History Through 1865, US History Since 1865, African American History)
1   2   3   4   5

c. Foundations of Faith (Varieties of Religious Experience, Developing a Devotional Life, Basic Christian Beliefs, Old Testament Survey, New Testament Survey)

1   2   3   4   5

d. Faith and Learning (Faith and Learning)

1   2   3   4   5

e. World Culture (History of China, History of African, History of Latin America, Cultural Anthropology, The Middle East, Literature of India)

1   2   3   4   5

f. Literature (World Masterpieces 1 or 2)

1   2   3   4   5

g. Religion and Philosophy (Introduction to Philosophy, Introduction to Ethics, Romans, Psalms, Quaker History and Beliefs)

1   2   3   4   5

h. Social and Behavioral Science (Introduction to Psychology, Principles of Sociology, Social Problems, The Individual & Family in Society)

1   2   3   4   5

i. Natural Science (Physical Science, Biological Science)

1   2   3   4   5

j. Fine Arts (The Aesthetic Experience Through the Visual Arts, Music, Dance, or Drama)

1   2   3   4   5

k. Writing (Writing 1 and 2)

1   2   3   4   5

l. Mathematics (Math for Liberal Arts, Number Concepts for Elementary Teachers, College Algebra)

1   2   3   4   5

m. Computers (Introduction to Computers, Business Software Applications, Technology in the Classroom)

1   2   3   4   5

'NOT AS THE SCRIBES': TEACHING BIBLICAL STUDIES IN THE LIBERAL ARTS CONTEXT

Glenn S. Holland
Allegheny College

The most immediate, if not perhaps the most obvious, problem in addressing how best to teach biblical studies in the liberal arts context is the contested nature of the concept of 'liberal arts' over the last century or so. Although hundreds of North American colleges and universities claim to offer a 'liberal arts' education or a 'liberal arts' curriculum, there is no wide-spread agreement about exactly what the designation 'liberal arts' actually means. There does seem to be general agreement that 'liberal arts' represents something desirable in undergraduate education, although even that is sometimes questioned by those who assert that higher education is an increasingly expensive and ultimately useless pursuit if a person's primary goal is to secure well-paying employment.[1] But both those who question the value of the liberal arts and those who are fervent supporters cannot seem to agree about how 'liberal arts' is best defined, or even in what terms: curriculum, pedagogy, skills to be acquired, philosophical outlook, or something else?

Sometimes it appears that the most useful definition is the 'baldest operational' definition offered by former Allegheny College president Louis Bénézet in his *General Education in the Progressive College* in 1943, when he asserted that liberal education is 'that kind of education which a liberal arts college program provides'.[2] Certainly this is in many ways the most practical definition for those who teach in a liberal arts program or a liberal arts college; liberal arts is what their own institution's statements and culture say it is. But of course, as Bénézet himself demonstrated, 'that kind of education which a liberal arts college program provides' itself already encompassed a myriad of ideas and

---

1. See for example Alan Ryan's discussion, 'Is Higher Education a Fraud?', chapter 3 in his *Liberal Anxieties and Liberal Education* (New York: Hill & Wang, 1998), pp. 143-84.
2. Louis T. Bénézet, *General Education in the Progressive College* (New York: Bureau of Publications, Teachers College, Columbia University, 1943; repr. New York: Arno and The New York Times, 1971), p. 28.

practices when he wrote almost seventy years ago.³ Before addressing teaching biblical studies in the liberal arts context, then, it seems advisable to provide some idea of what is meant by liberal education or 'liberal arts' in this chapter. Admittedly, my ideas will follow Bénézet's lead to the extent that they were formed by more than twenty-five years of teaching at a traditional liberal arts college, Bénézet's own Allegheny College, in northwestern Pennsylvania.

Liberal education is the modern means of achieving an ancient goal—the ideal citizen. Although the definition of 'citizen' has changed and broadened over the centuries, the idea that a citizen should be able to make intelligent decisions both as a private person and as a participant in civic life has not. Liberal education is intended to produce a person who is not only well informed about a wide range of topics but is also able to bring to bear on those topics the habits of mind associated with critical thinking: analysis, evaluation, and prudent judgment. Since a citizen is expected to take an active and interested part in civic and social discourse, liberal education also promotes the cultivation of the communication skills encompassed in intelligent reading, clear writing, and effective speaking. Part of the intention of liberal education is to produce through its efforts the sort of person who shares the goals of liberal education and does in daily life what liberal education is meant to do: encourage the accumulation of knowledge, the use of reason, and engagement in thoughtful discussion.

Although liberal education is now rarely based on the study of a particular set of 'classic' texts, it still is concerned with exposing the student to particularly poignant or evocative expressions of human insight and aspiration, whether these are found in texts, performance, music, experimentation, theory, artifacts, film, ritual, or participation in explorations of the limits of the human mind and body. In short, liberal education has shifted attention from classic texts to all sorts of expressions and evocations of what we might call 'classic' human experiences, those that strike us as quintessentially human and revelatory of what it means to be human in the world.

I will use the term 'liberal arts', then, to refer to a non-vocational and non-confessional college curriculum that emphasizes breadth in subject matter rather than depth, and pedagogically fosters exposure to a variety of ways of accumulating and evaluating knowledge, with the intention to teach students 'to think critically and creatively, write clearly, speak persuasively, and meet challenges in a diverse, interconnected world', to quote the Allegheny College mission statement.⁴

I would say further that within the 'liberal arts context' a student has the opportunity to apply similar sets of critical standards to an array of academic disciplines. Students are taught discrete subjects by professors who are specialists in the field, but they are not taught with the expectation that they will become specialists in that subject in turn. This does not mean, as some have

---

3. Bénézet, *General Education*, pp. 4-12.
4. Allegheny College 2010–2011 Catalogue, p. 2.

argued, that 'content is irrelevant' in liberal arts courses,[5] but rather that limited specialization within a major subject takes place within a larger context of broad interests across disciplinary lines and particular intellectual and rhetorical skills.

Most often this means professors too are obliged to understand their teaching in the broader liberal arts context, as part of larger common educational effort to foster the knowledge and skills that are the explicit goal of liberal arts education. Although each has a particular area of expertise, professors are expected to be competent in subjects closely related to their area of expertise, and to be able to teach a fairly wide variety of courses. For example, someone trained specifically in the Hebrew Bible might well be expected to teach New Testament as well, and perhaps courses in the history of Judaism or Christianity, or even other religious traditions. Moreover, all courses are expected not only to foster the liberal arts objectives of critical thinking, clear writing, and effective speaking, but they are all also expected to 'connect' in some way to the rest of a student's work at the college or university. In short, all faculty in a liberal arts program are expected to be committed to the liberal arts agenda, and to advance it both individually and as a group.

The liberal arts stand in particular contrast to vocational or professional education, both of which are intended to convey the methodology and body of knowledge necessary to pursue a particular career. Generally speaking, the more an academic program is aimed at credentialing students for future endeavors, or concerned with providing them the practical knowledge for a specific career, the less it is attuned to the liberal arts ideal.

In the case of biblical studies, the liberal arts context stands in contrast to the vocational or professional context of the seminary, divinity school, or university graduate studies program. Biblical studies in the context of a seminary, divinity school, or graduate program is intended to produce professional exegetes, people who can interpret and explicate the biblical texts, whether as clergy or as scholar/educators. This means biblical studies in the professional or vocational context must be concerned not only with reading and understanding the biblical texts, but also with mastering the prevailing methods of analyzing and interpreting those texts. Biblical studies in the context of professional education necessarily addresses methodology both as an approach to be understood—as one way that scholars have reached certain conclusions about the biblical texts and their contents—and as a practice to be implemented in the student's own work of interpreting the biblical texts. So in graduate programs of various kinds devoted to study of the Bible, the student learns not only what the texts *mean*—their content—but also the current acceptable scholarly procedures employed to *determine* their meaning, and how best to use those same procedures in the professions he or she will enter. Indeed, the goal of professional education is the

---

5. Cf. R. Timothy McLay, 'The Goal of Teaching Biblical and Religious Studies in the Context of an Undergraduate Education', *SBL Forum* 4.8 (2006) www.sbl-site.org/publications/article.aspx?ArticleId=581.

proper understanding and demonstrated use of scholarly methodologies instead of a particular analysis of a specific biblical text; use of the proper method is more important than its outcome.

Further, in the professional context the meaning of the texts is most often understood to be essentially unambiguous *if* deciphered through proper use of the correct methods, although the problem of what the correct methods are is subject to an unending process of discernment. Virtually the entire professional conversation among biblical scholars, as evidenced by the journals recording that conversation, is about persuading each other to accept the conclusions a scholar has reached about the correct understanding of a biblical text through application of the proper methods. In short, the purpose of instruction in biblical studies in the seminary, divinity school or graduate program is to equip the student with the accepted scholarly apparatus for making sense out of the biblical texts, and also a rationale for arguing why the conclusions the student draws are correct and definitive—not that there's anything wrong with that.

But biblical studies within the liberal arts context should be taught in a notably different way, that is, in a way consistent with the goals of liberal arts: reading intelligently and thinking critically. This can be and should be done *without* the focus on implementing specific methodologies or the drive for definitive conclusions. While methodology is important, and conclusions may be drawn, what is important in the liberal arts context is the active exchange of ideas, the challenge of approaching a text critically, and arguing persuasively for the viability of one's point of view while leaving open the possibility of consensus.

In the liberal arts context, biblical texts are best studied as literary products of their time and culture that have something worthwhile to say to our own time and culture as well—but what that 'something' is may be communicated and understood on a number of levels. This is not to deny the biblical texts have an historical content, but their historical content is presented in a thoroughly literary context, much as the historical content is present in the work of other ancient authors, not only Herodotus, Thucydides, Tacitus, and Livy, but also Plato, Aristophanes, Cicero, and Virgil. Nor would I claim that the biblical texts are in any way 'transparent' to the modern reader or student, or immediately applicable to the modern situation. But again, this is true of the majority of literary texts that students read in the liberal arts context, and just as the literary value and art of such works is not reduced to historical reconstruction, neither should the biblical texts be similarly reduced.

Rather I am arguing that in the liberal arts context, courses and instruction should approach the biblical texts as essentially literary works to be understood within their proper historical and cultural context, as texts that speak to us not only in terms of *what* they say but also *how* they say it and the portrait they present of a time and culture that enabled people to say such things in such a way. In brief, studying in the liberal arts context, instructors should help their students to study biblical texts in much the same way they should study other historic or historical texts, with understanding and openness to the world those texts create.

We may compare the study of Shakespeare's plays as a model for how the biblical texts can be taught within a liberal arts context, i.e. without regard to the methodologies and demands of professional academic exegesis. Shakespeare's works in fact provide a parallel body of texts whose similarities to the biblical texts as cultural artifacts are helpful and illuminating, despite the obvious substantial differences between the two bodies of work. For example, like the biblical texts, Shakespeare's works enjoy a status in the West that can fairly be labeled 'canonical'. Both are 'embedded' in Western and world culture in unique and inescapable ways, as cultural touchstones and as definitive portrayals of human experience. As a result, both are the source of idiomatic turns of phrase and the most quoted bodies of work in the English language. Indeed, the Bible and the works of Shakespeare are often both quoted in similarly general terms—'The Bible says . . .', 'The Bard says . . .'—rather than in reference to specific works those names encompass (cf. Romans, As You Like It) or the specific figures (Paul, Jacques) who wrote or spoke the words being quoted ('all have sinned and fall short of the glory of God', 'All the world's a stage,/ And all the men and women merely players').[6] The cultural dominance of these two bodies of texts is such that 'knowing the Bible' or 'knowing Shakespeare' is considered by many to be essential to becoming an educated person, that is, someone equipped to make sense of our own time and culture.

Both the Bible and the works of Shakespeare are necessarily subject to a process of interpretation in order for their content to be understood at even the most basic level. We are all familiar with the many translations and paraphrases of the Bible intended to make it easy for the average person to read.[7] But recent years have also seen the appearance of Shakespeare 'translations' such as The Inessential Shakespeare series published by Kabet Press or the No Fear Shakespeare series published by SparkNotes. Both the Bible and the works of Shakespeare can be and are plumbed for meaning beyond anything their creators may reasonably be conjectured to have envisioned.[8] But despite their intrinsic difficulties, both the works of Shakespeare and the Bible are widely believed to speak not only to their own time and culture, but to all times and cultures, and to that extent to be broadly accessible to the average person.

In both cases, the cultural 'embeddedness' of the Bible and Shakespeare's works inevitably affects the way students perceive these texts, and so is something an instructor must reckon with when attempting to help students read the texts effectively. Like those who teach the works of Shakespeare, those

---

6. Romans 3.23; *As You Like It* II.vii.140-41.

7. The goal of the Contemporary English Version, for example, was 'an English text that is enjoyable and easily understood by the vast majority of English speakers, regardless of their religious or educational background', according to its preface.

8. In the case of biblical texts, one may consider the early Jesus movement's interpretation of texts from the Septuagint, cf. the Immanuel prophecy of Isaiah 7.14b. In the case of Shakespeare's works, establishing limits to innovative literary interpretations was the primary concern of Richard Levin's *New Readings vs. Old Plays: Recent Trends in the Reinterpretation of English Renaissance Drama* (Chicago: University of Chicago, 1979).

teaching biblical studies in the liberal arts context should and will take advantage of some scholarly insights, but may properly do so without devoting particular attention in class to the specific methods by which those insights were gained. Moreover, in both cases there must be the recognition that analysis of the texts can render no definitive result, no 'final' interpretation that somehow fully recovers and explains the author's intention. In the liberal arts context the model for textual analysis is provocative rather than definitive, to allow the student to engage the text critically on his or her own terms. The concern in the liberal arts is perennially more about raising questions than finding answers.

The operating assumption in liberal arts is thus that literary texts may yield not only a variety of meanings but a variety of *kinds* of meaning, none of them privileged or identified as 'original' or 'intended'. This openness to a broad range of interpretation is in part an indication of the literary worth of the text being studied, but also a reflection of the liberal arts' view of knowledge: What we know is always provisional, subject to further investigation and insight, evidence and persuasion.

To take again the example of Shakespeare, historical investigation certainly forms part of the informed reader's interpretive apparatus. Historical investigation provides at the very least information about the meaning of words and social rituals, references and cultural values, among other things. Any of these may alert the reader to certain overtones or points of emphasis within a given text, but how those factors are reckoned into a final interpretation is open to debate and personal opinion. Further, whatever meaning found in Shakespeare's plays may also be explored in a non-academic context through the performance of the plays onstage or in film, where the meaning of a scene or an entire play is revealed through spoken words, actions, and *mise en scène*. Every individual performance of one of Shakespeare's play is an interpretation which is in turn interpreted by each member of the audience in the light of his or her own experience.

Similarly, the meaning of the biblical text may be illuminated by historical and cultural insights relative to their original contexts, but the work of making sense of the text in light of that information is still left to the individual student of the texts. The biblical texts also have their form of 'performance'. Both historically and in the present day, the texts have been heard more often than read silently.[9] This is true not least in the context of worship, where biblical texts are most often read in short passages with other passages related to it thematically, and then expounded in a homily or sermon. This sort of performance too may reveal new levels of meaning to the members of its audience, each interpreted

---

9. Taking again the example of the goals of the Contemporary English Version of the Bible, the translators argue in the preface, 'Today more people *hear* the Bible read aloud than read it for themselves…If this is the case, a contemporary translation must be a text that an inexperienced reader can *read aloud* without stumbling, that someone unfamiliar with traditional biblical terminology can *hear without misunderstanding*, and that everyone can *listen to with enjoyment* because the style is lucid and lyrical' (emphasis original).

through personal experience. These are meanings that would most likely not occur to the same people reading the same texts alone silently, just as silent reading might inspire insights not available in the context of worship.

As is also the case for those who teach Shakespeare, as instructors and scholars of the biblical texts we may be confronted with the question, 'Why privilege *these* particular texts with intensive study at the expense of others? Why maintain an antiquated idea of "classic" works that for some reason every educated person should supposedly be familiar with?' This is an especially pressing question in a secular institution of higher learning, where it is not assumed that knowledge of the Bible is a necessary part of the makeup of the ideal citizen. The standard, pragmatic response, based on the 'embeddedness' of both the Bible and Shakespeare's works in Western culture, is that it is necessary to be familiar with both groups of texts to make any sense out of the collective cultural history and experience of the West. In the case of the Bible, one might also argue that familiarity with its stories, characters, and language is essential to a proper understanding of United States history as well as its current political and cultural debates.[10] The importance of understanding the roots of other people's religious culture, especially as it affects their political and social behavior, should be obvious to the liberal arts' 'ideal citizen'.

I would emphasize again that I am not here advocating teaching 'the Bible as literature' as the only appropriate approach in a liberal arts context; far from it. But understanding the Bible first as a collection of literary works (i.e. stories, either explicit or implicit) that also, like all good works of literature, reflect the culture in which they were produced as well as the creative work of an author, is the key to presenting the Bible in a way most conducive to the goals and ideals of a liberal arts education. What makes these stories remarkable is that the literary works of the Bible also claim to convey information about the history of Israel lived in relationship to its God, and, in the New Testament, information about Jesus and the early movement that arose out of his ministry and teaching. Moreover, these works also claim to reveal and illustrate God's relationship with humanity and its consequences for relationship among human beings. But these claims do not change the basic character of the biblical texts as literary works, stories that by their very nature exhibit the limitations and possibilities of literature.

In fact, of course, the biblical texts represent a chorus of ideas about God's relationship with humanity, ideas that students should understand and respect even if they do not accept them. But students of all theological persuasions and none need at least to understand that although the biblical texts were written for faith communities, they can be read and understood as other literary texts are, irrespective of their own claims. One of the ideas behind 'reading critically' in the liberal arts context is that one need not accept the ideas or perspectives of

---

10. The ubiquity of the Bible's influence over the American understanding of the world is amply demonstrated by sources collected in Claudia Setzer and David Shefferman (eds.), *The Bible and American Culture* (New York: Routledge, 2011).

a given text in order to understand it. One need not be a Marxist, for example, to read and evaluate the 1848 *Manifesto of the Communist Party* or to understand its historical context and influence. In the same way, one need not be a confessing Jew or Christian to read and evaluate the Bible or to understand its historical context and influence. In short, in the liberal arts context, learning to read and understand the biblical texts is less a matter of determining their final meaning than it is a matter of assimilating information and using critical analysis to grapple with the issues the texts present. I noted earlier that professors teaching in the undergraduate liberal arts context are obliged not only to foster critical thinking and clear communication, but also to expose students to a variety of ways of accumulating and evaluating knowledge across a spectrum of fields. We have a responsibility to demonstrate in our scholarly work and in our teaching our own engagement with intellectual issues and currents that cut across disciplinary lines. Knowledge of other fields and engagement with their ideas and methods is both useful and necessary in the sort of community of learners the liberal arts college represents. This is not a matter of mere appropriation of the methods or perspectives of one disciplinary field in the service of another, but active engagement with the methods, aims, and concerns of other disciplines and the students and scholars engaged in them. Ideally, there will be formal opportunities for working across disciplinary lines, in team-taught courses or collaboration in supervising student research. In the context of a small academic community, those who reach across disciplinary lines with mutual respect in order to work and learn together benefit greatly as colleagues, as teachers, and as scholars.

But beyond that, we as instructors need to help our students discover and appreciate connections between biblical studies and other fields including, but not limited to, allied disciplines such as history, classical studies, and philosophy. Openness to other ways of thinking and other realms of discussion is basic to how liberal arts professors teach by example. Liberal arts students are encouraged to discover connections between different fields of study and to develop familiarity if not expertise in at least two distinct fields, most often represented by a major and a minor field of study. As part of their instruction, we as professors have to show, implicitly and explicitly, that we are the sort of people we wish our students to become: people conversant with a broad range of topics across disciplinary lines, people ready and willing to engage in intelligent and informed conversation with representatives of fields of study beyond our own.

This is the other major demand the liberal arts context imposes upon us as both scholars and instructors: the demand that we model for our students the ideas and practices the liberal arts represent. If we are to do this effectively, we must exemplify in our scholarly work and in our teaching the same sort of careful reading, critical thinking, and clear writing and speaking we wish our students to emulate. This of course is an old idea, perhaps older than the liberal arts themselves: The idea that one teaches as much by the example of one's character—one's *ethos*—as by what one says in a lecture or a class discussion.

An instructor's *ethos* has great persuasive power. The student wishes not only to *learn from* but also to *be like* his or her best teachers.

In conclusion I would reiterate that I do not advocate stripping away the specifically religious content of the Bible to teach its texts only as literature. I do not believe class discussion should shy away from questions with theological or philosophical implications for fear of potentially offending some class members. My point, rather, is that such questions in the liberal arts context are best addressed in terms of informed class discussion, where the instructor serves as a resource rather than an arbitrator of truth. Questions are best addressed with a focus on specific situations or problems presented by the background materials or the biblical texts themselves. The instructor in biblical studies also has to be actively engaged in the liberal arts enterprise, carrying out the business of teaching and scholarship in a way that engages other realms of academic discourse, other methodologies, other questions, and other ways of looking at things.

This is all to say that the goal of a course in biblical studies in the liberal arts context should be consistent with the more general goals of the liberal arts themselves: to give the students an opportunity to read the biblical texts carefully, to think about them critically, and to communicate effectively through both speech and writing the conclusions they reach on the basis of thoughtful analysis.

What Do Athens and Jerusalem Have to Do with Sioux Falls?

Murray Joseph Haar
Augustana College, Sioux Falls

Anna Madsen
OMG: Center for Theological Conversation

1. Introduction

MURRAY: This paper has its genesis in the role the department chair plays at Augustana College. Augustana is a school that resides on the plains of the upper Midwest. It is affiliated with the Evangelical Lutheran Church in America (ELCA), has about 1600 full-time students and is committed to being a liberal arts institution. The majority of students are Lutheran along with a substantial Roman Catholic minority and about 10% of other Christian denominations. We do have the occasional atheist and agnostic as well. It is my job as Chair of the Religion/Philosophy/Classics department of the college to mentor faculty members just starting out in the classroom. As part of my duties as Chair, I sat in on Anna Madsen's classes. I noted that when she taught her freshmen religion course, Exploring the Christian Faith, she seemed to be preaching rather than teaching. By the way, I, a practicing Jew, also teach a section of this class. Naturally, I moved as mentor to correct her aberrant behavior. I told her, in a nice and mentor-like voice, that at a liberal arts school the goal was to teach students how to think and not to get them to believe. And I also quoted to her an old Jewish saying: 'The question is more powerful than the answer to the question'.

ANNA: I responded to the chair's tactful and forthright criticism by noting that Augustana isn't just a liberal arts college. It is a Christian liberal arts college, and moreover a Lutheran liberal arts college. Here most especially a professor should have the freedom to explore the Christian faith through a Lutheran prism. After all, many students, perhaps most, come to Augustana precisely because it is Lutheran school. It is not far-fetched to assume that they, and their parents, are expecting that the classes in the religion department are being taught from the premise of faith.

MURRAY: I asked: Is our goal in the classroom to get students to evangelically believe or to think critically?

ANNA: I answered, to think critically. But a professor can demonstrate that people of faith can think critically. I make it quite clear throughout the semester, and particularly at the beginning of the term, that this is not a glorified confirmation program, there are no felt boards to be found in the department with Noah or Jonah or a manger scene. This will be an academic reflection on the Christian tradition. Just because one teaches from the premise of faith does not preclude that one has the integrity and the savvy to think critically about it.

MURRAY: I reacted by saying that I was unclear about what Anna meant by 'think critically'. To teach students to think means to examine all systems critically, even my own. The argument was joined and this paper was born.

ANNA: When I began to teach at Augustana, I presented a paper to the community titled, 'We Cannot Live by Bread Alone: The Meaning of Religion to Secular People'. The point of the piece was to pose and perhaps answer the following question: Who are religious, and per the context, specifically Christian, people, and how do we go about teaching and retelling the news about Christ risen to those who do not define themselves by our categories?

As Murray and I continued our conversations it became clear that I was operating with a notion of gospel—of Jesus—that is deeply proleptic, deeply based on the notion of self-sacrifice in the name of God, a conviction which by definition disallows any form of coercion. My 'system' springs from my embrace of resurrection, the announcement that death in all of its forms does not win. In fact, when I teach my students the term 'gospel', I tell them that gospel does not mean the forgiveness of sins, though that is so, nor does it mean that God is love, though that may well be true: In order for news to be news, it has to be an event (this distinguishes 'event' from 'idea'). Gospel, then, is that Jesus is risen. Boundaries, then, are no more.[1]

MURRAY: While I certainly understand the importance of the resurrection as event for Anna I challenged the notion that gospel need be rooted in just one thing or event. I noted that there are many different ways to be Christian. There are many different ways that the word, gospel, is defined by Christians. And the students sitting in our liberal arts religion classes are here to learn about different ways of defining what is meant by the term 'gospel'. What about those

---

1. Walt Bouman, unpublished lecture on Creeds, Confession, and Dogma.

Christians who assert that gospel is rooted in the incarnation more than the resurrection? Or of those who believe that you are saved if you accept Jesus? And even those who assert that no one comes to God except through Jesus? Or those of us who are Jewish and beg to differ with the assertions of 'gospel' at all?

Our job in the classroom, I asserted, was to be more descriptive and not prescriptive. This brought us to another question, of course, about what is the Christian faith, and how does one go about exploring it? Is there only one Christian gospel, one Christian tradition? And is it possible for someone outside the Christian faith and tradition to guide students in exploring that tradition?

ANNA: Murray is sniffing an absolutist. This is his worry. Am I or am I not insisting that there is only one way of thinking about the Christian tradition?

Again, I am a systematic theologian. This, frankly, is more my pedagogical hermeneutic than my religious persuasion. When I teach 'Exploring the Christian Faith', then, I teach it as a system. I provide my students with a system, maintaining all the while that is *one* system among *many* systems. However, if they know one system, they will more ably discern other systems, their presuppositions, and their agendas.

That said, when one's system starts with Easter, it is clear that one's teaching comes across as kerygmatic. Still and even so, in my conversations with Murray, I try to make clear that one cannot be an absolutist, at least not in a coercive fashion, if one starts with Easter, because Easter (let alone growing up with a steady diet of Lutheran theology) announces that not only might you be wrong, you definitely are. You are thereby freed to engage in conversation and questioning, trusting that you are justified regardless of where you begin or where you end up in your theological wranglings.

MURRAY: While Anna's theology affirms humility, her kerygmatic style of teaching does not. Anna's comments also raise questions about the goals we have or ought to have when we teach at such places like Augustana. Are we for faith, against faith, indifferent or just trying to be as objective as possible? What is the relationship between the faith or lack of it that the instructor brings into the classroom and the material which he or she is trying to teach? To what extent should the instructor care what happens to the faith of his or her students? Is the instructor responsible for what students do with what is being taught? Is an investigative explorative teaching methodology in the area of religion appropriate at a religiously affiliated college? When a religion professor steps into a classroom is he or she teaching religion at Augustana or proclaiming the Christian faith? And does it matter that we are teaching what we are teaching at a Lutheran-affiliated school? Indeed, the real question may be, 'Are we teaching about the tradition or for the tradition?'[2] At Augustana, we seem to be teaching

---

2. Robert Benne, *Quality of Soul: Quality with Soul, How Six Premier Colleges and Universities Keep Faith with Their Religious Traditions* (Grand Rapids: Eerdmanns, 2001), p. 129.

within the tradition. And it seems that, at Augustana, Athens and Jerusalem are wrestling with each other all the time. There is an inherent tension between our commitment to teach within the liberal arts and the Christian traditions.

ANNA: Lutherans love learning. We are heady people, and our history demonstrates that we come by it honestly. Paul Dovre, former college president and current consultant to Lutheran liberal arts colleges, writes:

> It was intellectual inquiry fed by religious anxiety that led Luther to his breakthrough reading of Romans on the nature of salvation. It was Luther's commitment to the laity, the priesthood of all believers, that led him to champion a universal education that would give people of both sexes and all ages direct access to knowledge. It was Luther's commitment to worldly truth that led him to exclaim 'how can you not know what can be known?' It was his respect for human curiosity that led him to write the catechism with its recurrent question, 'what does this mean?' following each creedal affirmation. And it was commitment to the place of learning in church and world that led Luther and Melanchthon to spearhead a reformation of the curriculum at Wittenberg University.[3]

This observation was made in a companion document to the now-adopted statement on education by the ELCA's statement on education.[4] Its scope is broad, including the optimistic goal of formulating a 'Lutheran vision of education for our time'. 'Education', as the document understands it, pertains to the vocation of all Christians, regardless of age or number of diplomas. Of course, it focuses on the relationship of the 28 colleges and universities to the ELCA. The clear hope is that these institutions will strive to keep alive a bond with their Christian roots, maintain an overt connection with their mission and service to the world, educate students in scripture, theology, church history, and ethics, and encourage interdisciplinary conversation.

Dovre details the feasibility of these reasons to strengthen Lutheran institutions. First, he points to freedom. Because we are saved by grace, we are freed to be inquisitive. This freedom leads to the possibility of uncovering truth which can then be spoken and enacted. Second, Dovre looks to Luther's 'affirmation of the world'. Luther was not troubled by the notion that secular authors can indeed be graced with knowledge which serves to build up the community. Third is the Lutheran love of the arts, seen as a vehicle for encountering God. Fourth is the concept of community, bound up in the goal of serving one's neighbor. Fifth and last is the Lutheran appreciation for the contingency of reality, summed up in the famous phrase *simul iustus et peccator* ('simultaneously righteous and sinner'). In his nod to contingency, I believe one detects that

---

3. For this and all following references to Dovre's insights, see Paul Dovre, *The Vocation of a Lutheran Liberal Arts College Revisited,* www.elca.org/What-We-Believe/Social-Issues/Social-Statements/Education.aspx.

4. www.elca.org/What-We-Believe/Social-Issues/Social-Statements/Education.aspx.

Dovre wants to point to the necessity of humility, for he explains contingency by pointing to the fallibility of reason.

Murray, of course, wonders whether Christians can really be free to examine their tradition if they are so committed to a certain way of proclaiming the truth. We may indeed be freed by grace to be inquisitive, but how inquisitive can we really be? Is not the notion of truth an absolute? And how can a claim of truth be anything but oppressive, or at the least, offensive to those who do not see it as such? And if Christians truly believe that we are saved by grace and not works, why do we have dogmas?

MURRAY: With all due respect to Luther's and Lutheran understandings of education, I find that my own training pulls me in a different direction. As a young boy attending yeshiva in New York City, I recall my fourth grade teacher Rabbi Eisenblatt leading us in a study of the Book of Exodus. We studied from a book called a Chumash which contained the text along with a commentary from the great medieval scholar, Rashi. I recall one day, being asked by Rabbi Eisenblatt to spell out what Rashi had to say about a particular text. I was proud of myself because I had prepared this part quite well and in Yiddish no less. When I was finished, the Rabbi asked me, 'So, do you think that Rashi was right?' I, of course, answered, 'yes'. But then he asked me, 'Why so?' And he went on, 'Where does Rashi's argument not hold together?' I was in the fourth grade. What did I know? But he persisted in forcing me to engage the interpretation of Rashi. And when I was haltingly able to raise a question, the Rabbi seemed quite pleased.

In Jewish tradition, to raise a question about a text or an interpretation of that text is to enter into tradition that is 3000 years old. The legitimacy and holiness of questioning in Jewish tradition goes back to the biblical and talmudic texts. In the Jewish Bible, God raises questions and interrogates Israel, and Israel feels free to question and interrogate God. In his book, *Arguing with God: A Jewish Tradition*, Anson Laytner traces the long tradition of questioning God from the biblical text, to talmudic texts, to various midrashim, to arguing with God in Eastern European tradition, to Elie Wiesel.[5]

But where does this love of questioning come from? What were the theological assumptions at work within the Jewish tradition that encouraged the questioning of God? And what pedagogical assumptions made the questioning of the text and tradition an essential part of Judaism? Of the 150 psalms in the Jewish Bible, at least 53 are laments. The psalms of lament in the Bible demonstrate certain theological assumptions that allowed and compelled Jews 2500 years ago to question and accuse God.

1. God is the creator of Israel. Israel and God are pictured as being inextricably connected. They love each other. They are pictured as being married.

---

5. Anson Laytner, *Arguing with God: A Jewish Tradition* (Northvale, NJ: Jason Aronson, 1998).

2. God and Israel have mutual unconditional covenantal obligations toward each other.
3. The fate of God is tied to the fate of Israel and the fate of Israel is tied to the fate of God. They are each reciprocally responsible to come to each other's aid.
4. The presence of sin on the part of either party does not excuse one from being covenantally obligated to act in defense of the other.
5. When either partner does not act according to covenantal obligations, the other shall be compelled to question, accuse, and argue for fidelity.
6. When Israel was being slaughtered and God appeared to be absent, questioning the deity was considered a holy, faithful, and loyal act.
7. Questioning God was a sign of the deepest fidelity and affection.

These assumptions are echoed many times in the talmudic and midrashic literature. In one famous story, Rabbi Eliezer ben Hyrcanus, a distinguished Rabbi 2000 years ago, had taken the position that the use of an oven is permissible; the other rabbis disagreed. But the story became an examination of the very nature of the issue of human versus divine interpretation of the text of the tradition:

> On that day, Rabbi Eliezer brought all the proofs in the world, but the other masters would not accept them.
> He said to them, 'If the law is according to me, let this carob tree prove it'. And the carob tree moved a hundred cubits. Some say four hundred cubits.
> They said to him, 'We do not learn proofs from a carob tree'.
> Then he said to them, 'If the law is according to me, let this stream of water prove it'. And the stream of water turned and flowed backwards.
> They said to him, 'We do not learn proofs from a stream of water'.
> Then he said to them, 'If the law is according to me, let the walls of the house of study prove it'. And the walls of the house of study began to topple.
> They said to him, 'We do not learn proofs from toppling walls'.
> Then he said to them, 'If the law is according to me, let the heavens prove it'.
> A voice came forth from heaven and said, 'Why do you dispute with Rabbi Eliezer? The law is according to him in every case'.
> Rabbi Joshua rose to his feet and said, 'It is not in heaven.'
> What is the meaning of 'it is not in heaven?'
> Rabbi Jeremiah said, 'The Torah has already been given once and for all from Mount Sinai: That means that the correct interpretation is given by the majority of scholars. After the majority must one incline'.
> Years later, Rabbi Nassan saw Elijah the prophet in heaven and, remembering the argument between the rabbis asked Elijah, 'What did the holy one, blessed be he, do at that moment when the voice from heaven was rejected?'

Elijah said to him, 'The holy one was laughing and saying: "My children have defeated me, my children have defeated me"'.[6]

This affection expressed through the questioning of God was transferred to the texts of God. In Jewish tradition the way one shows respect, passion, and affection for a text or a tradition is to engage that text and tradition through questioning and exploration with no holds barred. Does such a tradition collide with or enhance the liberal arts taught within a Church related setting? Can and should a Jew teach Christians to think critically about their own tradition?

Is it possible to teach religion or the Bible at a liberal arts religiously-affiliated college with integrity? By integrity I mean the ability to be honest and forthright about the light and darkness of the Bible, its historicity, its literary forms, its authority or lack of it, and the fact that there are three distinct monotheisms each with having different Bibles and interpretations, each with their own validity. It is possible but difficult and the professor who would step into such a classroom needs to be clear about exactly what he or she wants to accomplish. In a liberal arts setting I do not see it as my goal to encourage or discourage faith in a particular tradition. (Anna: Nor do I.) Nor am I called to convince my students of the veracity of the biblical text. (Anna: Ditto.) I do everything I can to encourage my students to raise questions honestly and explore the soul of the Christian tradition. (Anna: Whatever that is.) I use a variety of theological, historical, and practical hermeneutical methodologies. (Anna: So do I.) I do not have the power to create or destroy faith. (Anna: I agree; neither do I.) But I do have the ability to lead students into the depth of a religious tradition. I do have the power to ask questions which will compel the student to enter the religious tradition being studied with more depth.

As a practicing Jew who belongs to that long tradition of fidelity through questioning, I must be aware that for a number of my Christian students, raising questions concerning their religious faith is considered an act of unbelief. While I try to be explicitly sensitive to these concerns, I do not and cannot allow them to rule me. And after 28 years of teaching religion, I have found that for the vast majority of students taking my class 'Exploring the Christian Faith', an honest and forthright exploration with no holds or questions barred deepens and encourages their faith rather than diminishing it.

ANNA: Many elements of the conversation between Murray and me have been productive. He challenges me constantly to be vigilant that I profess rather than preach. I challenge him not to assume that the claim that merely 'raising the questions' ensures objectivism. He forces me to reconsider what I mean by absolute, and I challenge him to consider whether the Jewish tradition doesn't have its own absolutes. Is there really any such thing as objective teaching? Perhaps naming the bias is the best that one can do to move toward objective teaching.

---

6. Talmud, Bava Metzia 59b.

Still, we have discovered that although we teach depending upon different paradigms, although we come from different traditions, we do have a common purpose. Perhaps it is largely a matter of definitions: Where he speaks about the humility necessary to think that you might be wrong, I speak about the need for grace. Where he speaks about the freedom to wonder provided through the Jewish tradition of embracing questioning, I speak about the freedom to wonder provided through the Lutheran tradition of justification.

MURRAY: So, what does Athens have to do with Jerusalem in Sioux Falls? What I hear myself and Anna saying is that there is an intentional tension between these three; that is, between religious tradition, reason, and the context in which we teach. We both live and teach within this tension and we each like and defend the way we do that. But while each of us comes from different traditions and speaks about our pedagogical methods in our own way we are both wrestling with and determined to live within that tension. The argument or the conversation may be more important that its resolution.

'GOD IS NOT IN THIS CLASSROOM':
TEACHING THE BIBLE IN A SECULAR CONTEXT

Christian M. Brady
The Pennsylvania State University

It is considered a truism today to say that how we receive and read the Bible, or any text, is conditioned by our own experience. We bring as much to the text as we may get out of it. We would like to think that as scholars we are beyond this, able to read dispassionately and objectively the objects of our academic study. More importantly, the implicit, and in a secular context often explicit, assumption is that when we teach the Bible in a secular classroom we *certainly* present nothing but the most clear-eyed and unbiased presentation of the material under consideration. The reality is that how we teach the Bible is based as much upon our experience as is how we read the Bible. This should not cause us to despair, rather it should give us some sense as to how we might fruitfully engage our students and help them in their own reading and study of the Bible.

Given such a preamble it is only appropriate that I begin with a few preliminary comments about my own situation. My entire teaching career and most of my time as a student in higher education has been spent in secular institutions.[1] I spent nine years at Tulane University before moving to the Pennsylvania State University in 2006. My field of research is rabbinic literature, specifically Targumim, and the most common question I was asked at Tulane University with a student population that is one-third Jewish was, 'What is a nice Jewish boy like you doing with a name like Christian?' The perspective that I bring to the classroom and this topic of how we should teach the Bible in a secular context is as a Christian, in name and faith, researching and teaching ancient Hebrew and Jewish literature, in a secular school, often with a rather even balance of students from Jewish and Christian backgrounds.

---

1. I was at Cornell University as an undergraduate student. I majored in both Near Eastern Studies and History and was the first minor to graduate from the then newly-formed Religious Studies Program. I received an MA in Biblical and Theological Studies from Wheaton College in Illinois, an evangelical Christian college. I then received a Graduate Diploma in Jewish Studies from the Oxford Centre for Hebrew and Jewish Studies and a DPhil from the University of Oxford in Oriental Studies.

When I originally began to reflect more on how I teach the Bible I intended to share how I sprinkled my courses on the Hebrew Bible with readings of various interpretations of the text. I regularly teach a course on Genesis, for example, wherein we begin by reading the biblical text itself and then read selections from Bonhoeffer's little work on creation.[2] When we get to Noah we read the Genesis Apocryphon and when we get to the story of Tamar we consider a feminist reading of the text[3] (and make oblique references to *The Red Tent*).[4] But I think this approach is fairly self-evident, that by showing students multiple readings of the same or similar text they will begin to see the challenges and promise of reading a text that is so ancient and yet still so relevant to so many.

It seems far more useful that rather than describing *how* I teach (and arrogantly imply therefore that others ought to teach as I do) I ought to consider the *approach* that I take to teaching the Bible. In fact, the position from which I begin sometimes annoys some of my colleagues in other departments who are committed to secularism in the secular university. That is to say, I begin by recognizing and presenting the Bible to the students as a *theological* work.

The Bible as...

It seems that the sort of strategies most often employed in teaching the Bible in a secular liberal arts context involve teaching the Bible as *something*, e.g., 'The Bible as Literature', 'The Bible as History'. Or we might provide 'readings' of the Bible, as I have just suggested, such as feminist, liberationist, modern, etc. Please note, this is not a criticism *per se*; these are legitimate and useful strategies that I regularly employ, yet each of these methods is an attempt to read the biblical text as something other than it is.

Over the last few years the explosion of blogs on the internet has given rise to a community of biblical scholars online who maintain blogs where they post regularly about issues relating to biblical studies. These sites are often referred to as 'biblioblogs' and those who maintain them as 'bibliobloggers'. How the Bible ought to be taught is often a topic of debate and on one site, Kevin Wilson's BlueCord.org, where there was a lively debate over whether or not one could read the biblical text purely as 'historical' or whether or not, as Stephen Cook asserted in the comments,

> You are engaging a text whose existence is owed to the historical community's valuing of it as Word/Witness to the transcendent. There is an inherent 'theological' dimension to this text's preservation until this very day and its existence in your hands.[5]

---

2. Dietrich Bonhoeffer, *Creation and Fall: A Theological Interpretation of Genesis 1-3* (New York: Macmillan, 1959).
3. Phyllis Trible, *Texts of Terror* (Philadelphia: Fortress, 1984), pp. 37-63.
4. Anita Diamant, *The Red Tent* (New York: St. Martin's, 2005).
5. Kevin Wilson, 'Pre-Scriptural Levels', *BlueCord.org* (October 2006) web.archive.org/web/20081118175948.

In other words, by the very act of engaging with these texts that are both theological in content and theological in their preservation, we are dealing with theology.

I have become convinced that a very productive method of teaching the Bible, particularly where we are concerned with actually conveying some of the content of the text to our students, is to teach the Bible as what it is, a theological text. The vast majority of biblical texts are, after all, fundamentally *theological* texts and as Cook pointed out, Jews and Christians have viewed even the process of transmission as a theological matter. The challenge for us as teachers is that we are teaching in a fundamentally secular context. So how do we teach these theological texts *without teaching or doing theology*? Today I will offer a modest outline of a method for reading these theological texts.[6]

This brings me back to my title, 'God is not in this classroom.' This is the statement with which I begin my first lecture of most courses dealing with the Bible and I quickly follow it with the observation that it is not an assertion of fact since I cannot prove it and most religious traditions would argue otherwise. God may be in the classroom and God may not. God may be in the text and God may not. What is certain is that *the authors* (and most likely their audiences) believed that God was active and interactive and many of them, if not all, believed that God was indeed in the giving and receiving of the text. 'The word of the Lord came to me.' The next question is what do we, the faculty and the students, believe about the texts?

Internal Inventory

We must first recognize that it is very difficult to isolate one's own theological convictions (even and especially when we believe we do not have any) from those of the texts we are reading. It is difficult, but I do not think it is impossible. In an effort to deal with this I encourage students, without calling upon them to share out loud, to reflect on what effect their own background and religious convictions *or lack thereof* have on their reading of the texts. And I will then come back to that point throughout the course since often we are unaware of this influence upon our thought. This 'internal inventory' is imperative, in my opinion. For example, I never ask my students to decide whether or not they believe the miracles in the Bible occurred, but I do ask them to consider whether they believe that miracles *could* (or *could not*) occur and then consider how that conviction will influence their reading of the text.

At this point we also discuss briefly the history of textual reception, manuscript traditions, and translations. The task here is to make the students suffi-

---

6. This approach differs from that of Norman Gottwald, in that I do not assume his theoretical reconstructions of the textual traditions, but rather read the text as it has been received. This is, in my opinion, to be preferred in an introductory-level course. I believe the complex and contradictory reconstructions and textual criticism is best left to upper-level courses, although I always offer a brief introduction to these issues and present the method of source criticism in full.

ciently aware of the complexities involved in textual criticism without causing them to despair of ever knowing what the text says in its simplest form.

Historical-Theological Approach

Once a 'base text' (as fictive as that may be) has been established we engage in a simple reading of the text. This means trying to determine the basic meanings of the words we are reading and what they mean when placed together to form sentences and complete units. At this point we can begin to talk about content and ask, 'What is the text saying?' and the related question, 'What does it mean?' Whatever later application one might have, this last question must be asked first and foremost in reference to the original author and audience. The challenge here is, of course, that we are radically removed from the author by thousands of years, miles, and cultures. But we must do our best.

I try not to present an extended lecture on the beliefs and practices of ancient Israel because any such reconstruction is bound to be a synthesis of disparate sources and mar the very object of our study. Instead I begin with the text in front of us and build out from there. As a result, for example, very quickly we begin to discuss monotheism and the transcendence of God in reading Genesis 1 but only one chapter later we are discussing the immanence of the LORD God and the introduction of sin into the world. Both accounts provide very different 'theologies' while also providing opportunities to discuss source criticism, literary criticism, and developing worldviews. We even touch on the modern debates of creation, evolution, and intelligent design.

This is in many ways an 'historical' approach. The quotes around 'historical' are present because I do not refer to teaching the Bible as history, rather teaching the historical beliefs and theological convictions of the authors and the communities that preserved these texts, in so far as we are able to discover them. In our secular context, where we are not bound by a creed or code, this provides us with the reassuring protection of being able to say 'they believed', thus distancing ourselves from whatever we say following that clause and absolves us from making any judgment about the validity of that belief. We are merely observers. It also serves, I hope, both to challenge and to disarm those students who might have more traditional or orthodox views of these passages.

This is, I think, the first and necessary step in engaging both our students and the texts. If we truly want our students to understand what they are reading, they need to have some sense of its importance, if not for themselves, than at least for the people who wrote and preserved them. In describing what they believed we will invariably (or we ought to) consider why they held these convictions and this often leads to very relevant and contemporary concerns. For example, the Deuteronomic assertions that God punishes his people for their sins may be foreign and unacceptable to many of us, but once we understand that these convictions developed, at least in part, as a means of explaining the suffering of seemingly innocent people in this world, we may begin to understand that view better even if we do not espouse it ourselves.

The theological concerns of the biblical authors are not so different from our own, even if we do not identify them as theological, and of course the Bible deals with many issues that may well not be defined as purely 'theological', but are pertinent nonetheless. The psalms, for example, are full of emotion and pathos to which we all can relate, not least of all college-age students. Any number of wisdom psalms and the Book of Proverbs itself, while couched within 'god language', are espousing a way of life that most of us would still value, even if we do not call on the Lord. Thus considering the similarity between the way of life put forward within Proverbs and the modern understanding of living a 'good life' will allow an entry point into discussion of the concept of 'the fear of the LORD' found in the Book of Proverbs.

The Problem of Miracles

Perhaps the most difficult passages of all for us to teach are not, however, the assertions of God's might and law or the horrible tales of murder and rape, but accounts of the miraculous. I try to walk a fine line between appearing to espouse the plagues, the manna, and the miraculous births as 'the gospel truth' and rejecting them as fantasies and so much nonsense. I find neither extreme to be pedagogically useful. This *via media* does not, however, mean that I look for or teach naturalistic explanations for what the Bible clearly depicts as miraculous. That is certainly one possible interpretation that is included in our discussion, but I do not redefine 'miracle' in such a way that it no longer means that which is clearly the primary definition of the word.

The New Oxford American English Dictionary defines miracle as 'an event that appears to be contrary to the laws of nature and is regarded as an act of God'. The biblical authors, whether their work is represented in Tanakh or New Testament, clearly know that these things they are reporting do not usually happen. That is the whole point of a miracle! The very fact that such accounts are in the text speaks volumes about the fundamental beliefs of the authors.

Still, some scholars feel they are doing justice to the text and modern sensibilities to 'rationalize' the miracles, such as those who explain the plagues of Exodus as natural phenomena or the feeding of the thousands as acts of shame and charity. Others attribute genuine malice to the author, asserting he invented the accounts of the miracle to justify a particular action, teaching, or tradition (usually, of course, something that the modern scholar rejects). In rationalizing away the historicity of the miracles such scholars are removing an essential element of the text and context.

When I teach such passages I again start from the historical-theological perspective and point out to my students that the authors did indeed know that such events did not occur in the natural order of things and yet (at least we can be certain in many cases) the authors believed that they had occurred and they believed that they occurred through the intervention of God. The origins of these stories are lost to us and it is impossible to reconstruct what may or may not have happened (although we do discuss the various possibilities). So the next step is to ask how these stories functioned in the narrative and the life of the community. It is clear that many others at the time and since believed that these miracles occurred, 'perhaps including some of you in this room', I always point out, and that is significant. Here we can assess the literary, social, theological, and historical impact of these particular narratives, because at some point we can and should get past the question of whether or not something actually happened and acknowledge the effect of people *believing* that it occurred.

A prime example of this is the account of the ten plagues. The order, nature, and character of the plagues are themselves a commentary on YHWH's victory over Egypt and its gods. I find it important to point out that this does *not* presuppose that the Israelites did not believe in the Egyptian deities, but that they believed their god was *stronger*, even on their home turf, than those gods. The power of Exodus' story of liberation continues to infuse Judaism to this day. It also serves Christianity as one of the primary metaphors for interpreting the purpose of Jesus' death/resurrection and Christian baptism. The import of the story is thus not reliant upon the 'historicity' of the events, yet neither am I compelled to dispel a student's conviction of their veracity.

Conclusion

The biblical texts are fundamentally theological and we ignore that to the detriment of our student's education. The various historical, literary, and social critical methods that most of us were trained in and come to rely on are still valuable. This approach to the texts should, in fact, lead to their use. (I should note that Gottwald has outlined and demonstrated a similar approach of integrating all of these various concerns, including theological, in his Introduction.[7] I find, however, that his organization of the textbook and insistence upon certain hypothetical reconstructions makes it far too cumbersome for use in an introductory undergraduate class.) Once we have mined the text for as original a meaning as we can discover, we can then bring these other resources to bear as we trace the textual and hermeneutical history of the text. It is important to take the time, even if only briefly, to present other readings of the text. The student will then have an historical perspective to judge the development and adaptation of the text to meet later needs, themselves often theological.

My approach is somewhat like that of W.C. Smith, not in that I feel need to begin with a history of the formation of canon, how the Bible became *scripture*, but in that I present the Bible and attempt to have my students glimpse it, to use Smith's words, 'not merely as a set of ancient documents or even as a

---

7. Norman K. Gottwald, *The Hebrew Bible: A Brief Socio-Literary Introduction* (Minneapolis: Fortress, 2009).

first- and second-century product but as a third-century and twelfth-century and nineteenth-century and contemporary agent'.[8]

In many ways I am sure that I have not said anything new, or at least not new to those of us who teach the Bible in an academic setting. Yet at the same time I believe there is a reticence for those of us teaching in a secular context to address the theology of these texts, perhaps for fear that we will be perceived as *doing theology*. I think such a fear is misplaced; after all, can one teach Plato without dealing with philosophy? In our effort to show parallels with other ancient Near Eastern texts, provide feminist readings that cut across the text and liberate the text from its patriarchal moorings, I think we often miss and therefore fail to convey to our students, the fundamental power that these words had for their original audiences. Once we have caught a glimpse of that original vision we can then more profitably see how others have read them throughout history. After all, God may not be in the classroom, but he may be in the text.

---

8. Wilfred Cantwell Smith, 'The Study of Religion and the Study of the Bible', *Journal of the American Academy of Religion* 39. 2 (1971), pp. 131-40 (134).

Engaging Diverse Students in a Required Biblical Studies Course

Margaret Parks Cowan
Maryville College

As one of their general education requirements, students at Maryville College choose either Biblical Studies 130: Hebrew Bible World and Culture or Biblical Studies 140: New Testament World and Culture. These courses are designed as first-year core courses, not introductions to the religion major. Teaching biblical literature as a liberal arts core course taken primarily by first-year students poses a number of challenges. One of the most daunting is engaging students who enter college with wide-ranging levels of academic preparedness. Because the goals of the course require students to learn to read analytically, examine the assumptions they bring to the text, consider alternative readings of texts, and relate texts to their ancient context, differences in intellectual development and critical thinking skills are of particular concern. The course must challenge those who are better prepared for these tasks, so they will remain engaged, while supporting those who are not, so they can successfully improve their skills. Strategies for addressing these challenges discussed in this chapter are based on a review of literature related to intellectual development, critical thinking, developmental education, and active learning, and focus particularly on meeting the needs of first-year students.

Designing teaching strategies appropriate to the intellectual development of first-year students has been one of the primary goals of faculty teaching biblical studies at Maryville College. Several different models that describe the stages of intellectual development have been constructed, but there is much overlap among them. In general the models agree that many students begin their college careers viewing knowledge in black and white terms as factual information or correct answers and looking to professors and/or textbooks as authorities that can provide 'the truth'.[1] Thus, an appropriate goal of first-year courses is to move these students to a position where they recognize that definitive answers

---

1. Bette LaSere Erickson, Calvin B. Peters, and Diane Weltner Strommer, *Teaching First-Year College Students* (San Francisco: Jossey-Bass, 2006), pp. 21-33; Bette LaSere Erikson and Diane Weltner Strommer, 'Inside the First-Year Classroom' in *Challenging and Supporting the First-Year*

are not always available and that they must negotiate ambiguity or multiple interpretations.

A typical first response to such a realization is that all 'opinions' or answers are equally valid. At this stage, students think everyone has a right to his/her opinion and, therefore, every interpretation must be respected. Some first-year students come to college already having confronted conflicting ideas and reached this second level of development where knowledge is viewed as subjective so that one must choose among a multiplicity of answers.[2] At this point in their college careers, the ideal result is that students will move beyond black and white thinking, in which there is one 'correct' reading, or early multiplicity, in which all answers are equally valid, to a point where they can begin to see that some answers, i.e. readings of the text, are more cogent than others. Thus the overarching goal of the Hebrew Bible course can be defined as empowering students to find their *own, well-informed*, critical readings of text, i.e. not to mimic scholars, textbooks, parents, preachers, etc. This goal also does not mean asking, 'What is the text saying to me?' which allows for an infinite number of subjective readings and assumes no distance between the world of the text and the student's own world, but requires students to construct readings that are justifiable based on what the text itself says and what we know about the context that produced it culturally and historically.

In addition to considering the intellectual development of students, a pedagogical method should incorporate several other principles gleaned from studies of teaching and learning, the characteristics of first-year students, critical thinking, and student expectations to help meet the challenges posed by the Hebrew Bible course. These principles include:

- Balancing process and content, so that students have time to develop critical thinking skills, not simply memorize information[3]
- Encouraging self-efficacy by providing early mastery experiences; teaching note-taking, study, and test-taking strategies; providing opportunities for practice; and providing early, timely, and frequent feedback[4]

Student (ed. M. Lee Upcraft, John N. Gardner, Betsy O. Barefoot and Associates; San Francisco: Jossey-Bass, 2005), pp. 246-47.

2. Erikson and Strommer, 'Inside', p. 246.

3. Erikson and Strommer, 'Inside', pp. 249-55; Arthur Chickering and Linda Reisser, *Education and Identity* (San Francisco: Jossey-Bass, 2nd edn, 1993), pp. 344-46; Jackson Kytle, *To Want to Learn: Insights and Provocations for Engaged Learning* (New York: Palgrave Macmillan, 2004), pp. 143-46; Richard Penaskovic, *Critical Thinking and the Academic Study of Religion* (Atlanta: Scholars, 1997), pp. 21-25.

4. Albert Bandura, 'Self-efficacy' in *Encyclopedia of Human Behavior* (ed. Vilanayur S. Ramachaudran; New York: Academic, 1994), 4:71-81, reprinted in *Encyclopedia of Mental Health* (ed. Howard Friedman; San Diego: Academic, 1998), 3:421-32; Chickering and Reisser, *Education and Identity*, pp. 375-77; Kytle, *To Want to Learn*, pp. 151-55; Erickson, Peters, and Strommer, *Teaching First-Year College Students*, pp. 57, 95-96.

- Using a variety of pedagogical strategies that support diverse styles of learning and involve active, engaged learning[5]
- Helping students make connections to existing knowledge, to their own experience and to other courses[6]
- Balancing levels of challenge and support, which includes providing adequate structure while setting high expectations[7]
- Focusing on complex problems, big questions, and using Socratic questioning as a pedagogical tool[8]
- Explaining or asking students to explain why they are doing what they are doing in order to encourage them to think about and evaluate their own thinking and learning, i.e. to develop meta-cognitive skills[9]
- Establishing the class as a learning community in which the students view the instructor as a coach, mentor, facilitator—not the authoritative source of information—and in which students value learning from their peers in group activities[10]
- Avoiding strong cognitive dissonance early in the semester before students have had a chance to develop self-efficacy, recognize some of the problems and questions inherent in biblical studies, think about their own thinking, and trust the community of learning[11]
- Using writing to develop thinking[12]
- Ensuring that all communications, whether course content or instructions about assignments, between the instructor and students are clear[13]

---

5. Erickson, Peters, and Strommer, *Teaching First-Year College Students*, pp. 61-62; Erickson and Strommer, 'Inside', pp. 245-47; Chickering and Reisser, *Education and Identity*, pp. 377-78.

6. Erikson and Strommer, 'Inside', p. 248; Chickering and Reisser, *Education and Identity*, pp. 362-63; Erickson, Peters, and Strommer, *Teaching First-Year College Students*, p. 52.

7. Erikson and Strommer, 'Inside', p. 255; Chickering and Reisser, *Education and Identity*, p. 377; M. Lee Upcraft, John N. Gardner, and Betsy O. Barefoot, introduction to *Challenging and Supporting the First-Year Student* (ed. M. Lee Upcraft, John N. Gardner, Betsy O. Barefoot, *et al.*; San Francisco: Jossey-Bass, 2005), pp. 10-11; Penaskovic, *Critical Thinking*, pp. 61-65.

8. Richard Paul, *Critical Thinking: How to Prepare Students for a Rapidly Changing World* (Santa Rosa, CA: Foundation for Critical Thinking, 1995), pp. 295-97, 336-37; Erickson, Peters, and Strommer, *Teaching First-Year College Students*, pp. 140-41, 148-51.

9. Erikson and Strommer, 'Inside', p. 255; Kytle, *To Want to Learn*, pp. 155-56; Angela Provitera McGlynn, *Teaching Today's College Students: Widening the Circle of Success* (Madison, WI: Atwood, 2007), pp. 114-15.

10. Chickering and Reisser, *Education and Identity*, p. 374; Ernest T. Pascarella and Patrick T. Terenzini, *How College Affects Students* (San Francisco: Jossey-Bass, 1991), p. 146; Penaskovic, *Critical Thinking*, p. 140; McGlynn, *Teaching Today's College Students*, pp. 72-73.

11. Barbara E. Walvoord, *Teaching and Learning in College Introductory Religion Courses* (Malden, MA: Blackwell, 2008), pp. 8-9, 50, 96; Penaskovic, *Critical Thinking*, pp. 61-65.

12. John C. Bean, *Engaging Ideas* (San Francisco: Jossey-Bass, 1996); Erickson and Strommer, 'Inside', pp. 251-52; Erickson, Peters, and Strommer, *Teaching First-Year College Students*, pp. 106-108, 167-68; Kytle, *To Want to Learn*, pp. 154-55.

13. Pascarella and Terenzini, *How College Affects Students*, p. 96; Walvoord, *Teaching and Learning*, pp. 8, 81, 84, 94.

One of the first decisions instructors make about a course is whether to use a textbook and, if so, which one. The Hebrew Bible course described in this chapter focuses assignments on reading biblical texts and does not use a textbook. While a textbook can be a useful source of background information to support students' reading of the biblical text, it can also serve as the primary focus of their study time. If students are in the early stages of intellectual development and think of learning primarily in terms of memorizing information, they treat a textbook as something containing data to be memorized.[14] Such an approach does not encourage genuine engagement with the biblical texts. Asking students to write answers to questions about the biblical text as they read focuses their attention and pushes them toward understanding, not simply committing facts to memory. They are more likely to respond based on their own examination of the Bible if they do not have a textbook to turn to for 'correct' answers.

A second reason not to use a textbook is that most books present the material in canonical order, which reinforces students' assumption that the Bible should be read as an accurate chronological account of events. While it is not possible to read the Hebrew Bible in exact chronological order and maintain any coherence in the narrative, it can be valuable to begin with the Exodus and use the history of Israel/Judah to structure the course rather than begin with Genesis. This approach enables one to avoid confronting such challenging matters as the relationship to other ancient Near Eastern texts and source theories such as the Documentary Hypothesis at the very beginning of the course, before students have begun to acquire the learning strategies and thinking skills they need to negotiate these issues.

Another disadvantage of using a textbook for an introductory Hebrew Bible course for first-year students is the comprehensive coverage textbooks provide. One of the challenges of teaching any course is determining how much content is appropriate. That challenge is particularly acute for a core course for first-year students. Striking a balance between teaching enough content to enable biblical literacy and to supply students with substantive material to think about and providing the support and practice that they need to learn how to understand and think critically requires sacrificing some coverage. Using a textbook tends to encourage coverage of content at the expense of developing thinking skills.[15]

Thus, one strategy used in the course has been to focus most reading assignments on biblical texts. The selection of texts for students to read is closely tied to goals of the course. Selected texts include those that are central to Israelite/Judahite identity and theology and that illuminate the major figures, themes, and stories that are necessary for religious and cultural literacy; texts that clearly illustrate the importance of connecting texts to their historical and cultural context; texts that illustrate the development of ideas over time; texts that illustrate contrasting or differing views or perspectives within the biblical com-

---

14. Erikson, Peters and Strommer, *Teaching First-Year College Students*, p. 64.
15. Erikson and Strommer, 'Inside', pp. 248-49.

munity; and texts that have been interpreted in different ways by later religious communities.

To guide students in their reading and encourage them to consider issues to be discussed in class, the syllabus includes one or two questions for them to answer in writing, a three-level reading guide to complete, or a matrix to fill in. These tools force them to process the readings and attempt to make some sense out of them. Once or twice a week, students turn in the written assignments so that they know they are accountable and can receive frequent feedback about how well they are doing with processing the material. One example of this kind of exercise is a chart on the flood narrative in Genesis. In the left-hand column is a series of questions regarding details of the narrative. In the middle and right-hand columns are verses from the Yahwist and Priestly versions of the story. By answering the questions based on two different sets of verses, students discover for themselves the different threads of narrative that have led scholars to posit two sources. This material becomes part of the discussion of source theory and the Pentateuch, an issue we deal with fairly late in the semester.

To provide the necessary background information to enable students to read in light of the historical and cultural context in which the Bible was written, the instructor has prepared several short essays for them. These essays provide basic information about the history of ancient Israel/Judah during the Hebrew Bible period, the geography of the Levant, the structure of the household in ancient Israel, and writing in the ancient world. Short in-class PowerPoint presentations with lots of pictures replace essays on such topics as ethnicity, royal ideology, purity, and the temple. To encourage careful reading of the essays, students are asked to come to class prepared to identify what they think are the ten most important points. In small groups in class, they compare their lists, and then the class as a whole establishes a set of major points that will be the basis for a short quiz.

The use of short quizzes that focus on content rather than more difficult thinking skills is designed to give students early mastery experiences. Typically, it is those students who make little or no effort and have not attended class on the days when their peers developed learning guides who have low scores on the quizzes. In addition, comments on the short homework assignments are designed to reinforce careful readings, meaningful connections, and other positive evidence that students are learning. Being successful on these exercises encourages self-efficacy, the sense that they can master the subject matter.

Another strategy for encouraging self-efficacy is having students define their own goals. In her book *Teaching and Learning in College Introductory Religion Courses,* Barbara Walvoord argues that students often have very different goals and expectations for religion courses than those held by their professors and encourages empowering students to define their own course goals.[16] Toward the end of the first day of the Hebrew Bible class, before students have seen the syl-

---

16. Walvoord, *Teaching and Learning,* pp. 20-22.

labus, they are asked write down their goals for the course. Before the next class session, these are compiled into a short list. During the class, students compare course goals that are on the syllabus with the ones they defined in order to see where the two overlap and where they diverge. While stated differently, typically most of what they hope to accomplish fits into the overarching course goal of empowering students to construct their *own, well-informed*, critical readings of biblical texts. Seeing the connections between their own goals and those of the instructor gives students a greater sense of ownership and commitment to the course.

Another way to encourage self-efficacy among less well-prepared students, particularly those with backgrounds in a Christian tradition, is to value what they know and gradually build up to concepts and issues that are more difficult intellectually and more challenging to some religious belief systems. Students from traditions that have emphasized the truth or authority of scripture and have provided clear, unambiguous interpretations for their members face an added struggle in moving beyond the black and white stage of development, particularly in relation to biblical studies. For a number of years, the course began with a discussion of genre and immediately pushed students to make distinctions between the types of claims made by myth and history. A psychology colleague suggested that such an approach had the potential to produce such strong cognitive dissonance for some students that they would feel compelled either to give up their religious beliefs or to reject the academic study of the Bible entirely.[17] An alternative strategy is to begin with the story of Ruth. The story is a relatively short, straightforward narrative, students seldom have strong commitments to particular readings of the story, and it is set in the period of the judges, i.e. early in ancient Israelite history. As an assignment for the second class, students read the story, write a brief summary of what they think is its purpose, meaning or significance and identify two or three questions about things they do not know that might help them read the story more effectively.

As an in-class preview of the assignment, students get in small groups and 'read' a poster of 'Rosie the Riveter'. They figure out what they already know that they can use to talk about the purpose of the poster, its message, its audience, and its historical setting. Then, they try to come up with two or three questions that they would like answered to enable them to understand the poster better. Using 'Rosie' serves three purposes: first, students get to practice the homework assignment in a group before they have to do it on their own; second, they discover that they already possess some skills that they can use in reading biblical texts; and third, because the poster has been adapted by various groups at later times to convey quite different messages, it serves as a good illustration of reinterpretations of biblical motifs and stories. It provides a useful entrée into discussing how stories are adapted to meet the needs of different contexts when

---

17. Karen Beale, personal communication, March 3, 2009.

looking at the ancestral narratives, different accounts of events at Sinai, and differences between the Deuteronomistic History and Chronicles.

Most students feel fairly comfortable reading and summarizing the story of Ruth and can identify things they do not know. This gives them a very early experience of mastery. In small groups, they discuss their summaries and identify two or three questions they want to address in class. Many of the questions they raise are about history, geography, marriage and the family, etc., the kinds of things they will read about in the short essays. A discussion of the conclusion of the story makes it clear that the book of Ruth could not have been written in its current form until after the reign of David, who is mentioned at the end of the story, and so introduces the idea that biblical texts were often written long after the period of time they describe. The experience of mastery students have while reading Ruth provides a 'safe' starting point for beginning to ask questions of the text that can lead to a more critical reading.

When it is time for the first essay test, students know that they will be asked to write about the story of Ruth as one of the questions. The point is to relieve some of the anxiety that comes with the first major college test and to encourage further a sense of self-efficacy. They have already taken short-answer quizzes on the content of essays on history and geography and have, as a class, developed a list of important points from the essay on the Israelite household. The test question asks them to use material from those background essays to shed light on the story of Ruth. Thus they have to perform a more difficult intellectual task than simple recall, but are doing it with material that is, or should be, very familiar to them.

After the first test, each student whose grade is lower than 'C' is asked to make an appointment to meet individually with the instructor. The conversation begins with the instructor asking the student to explain what he/she did to prepare for each class and to prepare for the test. The most common response is that for class preparation they read the assignment, maybe more than once, and for test preparation they read over their notes, maybe several times. These two strategies are ones that Erikson and Strommer in their study of first-year students cite as common, but non-productive, study activities. Usually students are open to suggestions of things that they might consider doing, including those that Erickson and Strommer cite as productive, but less common, such as taking notes on or writing summaries of reading assignments, quizzing themselves for comprehension, or summarizing notes from past assignments or class sessions.[18]

In order to teach some basic study skills that underprepared students lack, instruction is embedded in a class session where the skill is particularly relevant. For example, after the first of the quizzes on content, students who have made high scores are asked to explain what they did to prepare. They typically identify some very good techniques for organizing information and processing it so that they were able store it in their long-term memory and recall it for

---

18. Erikson and Strommer, 'Inside', p. 243.

the quiz. The instructor may add a couple of additional ideas and then explain short-term vs. long-term memory and their significance for learning. Also early in the semester, on a day when a short lecture on the emergence of Israel in Canaan is planned, note-taking skills are introduced. After comparing accounts of the conquest in Joshua 1-10 with conflicting accounts later in Joshua and in Judges, students are asked how a historian might address the question of what happened. Usually one or more of them recognizes the possibility that other evidence might help. Before a PowerPoint presentation that explains a variety of pieces of evidence about Israel's appearance in Canaan, particularly archaeological material, students are introduced to the Cornell note-taking method and encouraged to use it. At the end of the presentation, they write a summary of their notes and identify the key or 'cue' words, two components of the Cornell method.[19] In this way they learn a specific skill and practice it in class when it is most useful.

Making connections to students' experience or helping them see some relevance without the class becoming 'what the Bible says to me' is challenging. Because Maryville College's required fall term first-year seminar begins with the topic of 'identity', it has worked well to use identity as a thematic thread for the Hebrew Bible course. Early in the semester, one can talk about the Exodus story providing one definition of the identity of the Israelites and their relationship to the God YHWH. The class can explore the role that the *bet av* plays in defining the Israelites' identity and later discuss differences in the identity of the southern kingdom of Judah, with its David-Zion ideology, from the identity of its estranged sibling Israel to the north. As students reflect on things that have influenced their own sense of identity in their seminar, they can connect their experience with the reality that different forces impacted the identities of the ancient peoples who produced the Bible.

Another strategy that has helped students connect to discussions of ancient Israel has been drawing analogies to American history, with which most of them have some familiarity. Students can understand that, just as Tennesseans view Paul Revere and the Pilgrims as part of 'their' history and identity, even though Tennessee was not part of the original colonies or earliest United States, so Israelite tribes that did not escape from slavery could consider the Exodus story as descriptive of their identity. To connect directly to issues that are current, when the class discusses the Sinai covenant and Ten Commandments, students are asked what they have learned that they think people should know about these laws before lobbying to post the commandments in public places in this country. The stories in Joshua raise the issue of genocide, which poses the question whether such killing is ever justifiable and allows students to relate the conversation to current realities such as Darfur. When students read about the household or *bet av* in ancient Israel, they are asked to define what they

---

19. Walter Pauk, *How to Study in College* (Boston: Houghton Mifflin, 7th edn, 2000), pp. 236-40.

consider to be central traditional family values. Then they compare their list to the characteristics of families in ancient Israel. When they read the prophets and discuss the concept of economic and social justice rooted in inherited land that is supposed to be inalienable, they are asked to think about what that might look like in the modern world. Job provides an obvious opportunity to discuss questions of human suffering, theodicy, etc. Learning theory confirms that making connections like these is one way for students to experience the course as relevant and embed new material in long-term memory.[20]

As some of these examples illustrate, meaningful connections students make often highlight the enormous differences between the world of the Hebrew Bible and their own world. One example that jumps out frequently is the way students from northeastern Tennessee think about the wilderness. They write essays in which they describe the Israelites wandering in the forest for forty years. If one grows up within thirty miles of the Great Smoky Mountains National Park and has lots of experience with wilderness as temperate rain forest, it is natural to think of wilderness as densely wooded terrain. To address this tendency, the class uses an online web exercise, developed as part of a project funded by the Appalachian College Association, titled *Text and Context*.[21] The exercise provides students with an interactive lesson in geography and climate in the Levant. An added advantage of this tool is that it provides students who are computer savvy or who learn best through images and hands-on activities an exercise that plays to their strengths.

Not only does highlighting the common misperception of wilderness set up readings and images about geography, but it also serves as the beginning of conversations about assumptions that students bring to their reading of biblical texts. Learning to identify assumptions is one of the key critical thinking skills that students need to develop. Another tool that addresses the issue of assumptions is a three-level reading guide. When they read the Immanuel prophecy in Isaiah 7, students bring a lot of assumptions to the text. This is one of the points in the course where the pace slows down and the class spends two days on one short text. For the first session, students read the text in Isaiah and complete a three-level guide by indicating which of several statements they consider to be justified by the text and identifying specific verses that support their conclusions. Some of the statements are evaluated based on a close reading of the text itself (level 1), some on inferences that can reasonably be drawn from the text (level 2), and some on making connections with other materials students have read or discussed in class (level 3). At the beginning of the class session, students divide into small groups and discuss their answers. In particular, they are to talk about the questions where they differed in their responses and explain

---

20. Chickering and Reisser, *Education and Identity*, pp. 362-63; Erickson, Peters, and Strommer, *Teaching First-Year College Students*, p. 52.

21. Peggy Cowan, 'Wilderness', in *Text and Context* (ed. David B. Howell, Peggy Cowan, Chris Heard, Brian K. Pennington, and Vicki Phillips; Appalachian College Association), www.ferrum.edu/dhowell/txt_cntxt/.

why they gave the answer they did. When the class comes back together to share what they have learned, generally the students have been able to correct each other in their groups. Students whose academic skills are weaker learn a great deal from the modeling of their peers who have been more successful in completing the exercise by distinguishing what the text actually says from the assumptions they brought to the text.

For the second class on the Immanuel text, students complete another web exercise, also created as part of the ACA project. This website provides a discussion of the dominance of Assyria during the eighth and ninth centuries BCE, an overview of the Syro-Ephraimite War, and a comparison of the Immanuel text in Hebrew with the Greek of the Septuagint. It also explains three different readings of the text that have been prominent in both scholarly and popular traditions.[22] After students demonstrate that they understand the historical background, they discuss the implications of the different readings and think about what it might mean for a prophecy to be 'fulfilled'. Because they have used a variety of tools to explore this text—reading, the three-level guide, small group discussion, an online interactive activity—most students, whether more or less well-prepared academically, have found some way to connect with the material.

Another tool for monitoring students' progress and helping them assess their own learning is to embed classroom assessment techniques into the class sessions periodically. Thomas Angelo and Patricia Cross have published a handbook on classroom assessment techniques that can be used to evaluate a variety of types of learning and work for students with very different learning styles. One of the simplest to administer is the one-minute essay in which students summarize important learning from the class and/or identify and explain a significant question that remains unanswered at the end of class.[23] More complicated to devise but easy to use is a 'defining features matrix', which works particularly well for comparisons. The professor creates a chart with three columns. In the first is a list of descriptors. The second and third columns are labeled with the items or concepts to be compared. Students place a plus sign or minus sign beside each descriptor in the second and third columns based on whether they think the descriptor fits the item or concept.[24] This idea can be adapted to help students compare Moses-Sinai covenant traditions with the royal ideology of the Davidic covenant traditions. Another classroom assessment technique is the one-sentence summary: Who says what to whom, when, where, how, and why?[25] This technique works well for assessing class work on a prophet. Doing classroom assessment techniques in addition to content quizzes and essay tests provides students with frequent feedback on their progress and accommodates different learning styles.

---

22. Peggy Cowan, 'Immanuel', *Text and Context*, n.p.
23. Thomas Angelo and Patricia Cross, *Classroom Assessment Techniques: A Handbook for College Teachers* (San Francisco: Jossey-Bass, 2nd edn, 1993), pp. 148-53.
24. Angelo and Cross, *Classroom Assessment*, pp. 164-67.
25. Angelo and Cross, *Classroom Assessment*, pp. 183-87.

Another strategy that seeks to take into account different learning styles is using vivid imagery when possible. Illustrations are clearly valuable in helping students envision wilderness, the various features of geography in the Levant, the traditional pillared house, the Temple and cherubim, etc., but they are also useful in talking about multiple readings of texts or the emotional impact of stories. For example, students can compare portrayals of David by Michelangelo and Donatello and think about why their renditions are so different. Similarly they can look at both Caravaggio's and Rembrandt's paintings of the *Akedah*. When confronted with different visual 'readings' of these stories, students can think about the various factors that influence how one relates to a biblical text. They begin to recognize ambiguity in the texts and in interpretations, the first step in moving beyond black and white thinking. They can also talk about what in the text might suggest a particular depiction and what seems to be the creation of the artist. This is an important step in justifying a reading by connecting it to the text itself and recognizing the tendency to read one's own views into a text.

In an attempt to provide structure without providing 'the answers' and to encourage students to work and study in groups, the course uses an online discussion board for developing study guides. In the past, a prepared study guide that listed important names, dates, terms and questions related to each class session encouraged students to write out answers and memorize them, thinking that was the best way to learn the material. To encourage more thoughtful engagement, students are assigned to groups of four or five and given the task of creating a study guide for their group. A discussion forum on the course management web site allows them to post their ideas, reply to one another, and work collaboratively to develop a study guide. It also allows the instructor to monitor who is contributing and to correct any misunderstandings that are reflected in their postings. To facilitate their getting to know one another and establish a group identity, the groups meet together during the third class session to decide on the twelve most important points they learned from the essay, 'Short History of Ancient Israel/Judah', they were assigned to read. One of the challenges in using this tool is getting all of the students to take responsibility for the study guide and not simply rely on the stronger or more diligent students to do the work.

In summary, developing a variety of strategies based on research into intellectual development, critical thinking, and active learning with a focus particularly on meeting the needs of first-year students has contributed to making Maryville College's Hebrew Bible course accessible to students who come to college less well-prepared for the rigors of our liberal arts curriculum without compromising the ultimate goals of teaching students to engage the biblical texts critically and pushing them to examine their assumptions, recognize ambiguities and uncertainties, connect text to context, and justify their readings based on evidence from the text and the ancient world. While it has meant covering less content and beginning more 'gently' than some other approaches, the process is one that is consistent with literature on effective teaching and learning.

ARTS INTEGRATION AND SERVICE-LEARNING IN INTRODUCTION TO BIBLICAL LITERATURE

Sharon Betsworth
Oklahoma City University

One of the undergraduate general education requirements for students at my church-related institution, Oklahoma City University (OCU), is to take either Introduction to Biblical Literature or Introduction to World Religions. These courses fulfill a part of the general education objectives concerned with developing a broad base of knowledge from a variety of disciplines. Until 2008, all students had to take Introduction to Biblical Literature, at which time Introduction to World Religions became an option. I wondered how this change to the general education requirements ultimately would affect the Biblical Literature classes.

The 2009 AAR-Teagle White Paper reports that sections of Introduction to World Religions are up among undergraduate institutions while sections of Introduction to Biblical Literature are down.[1] With the option to take World Religions or Biblical Literature, this trend soon became apparent at Oklahoma City University. While we once offered seven to nine sections of Introduction to Biblical Literature and four or five sections of World Religions each semester, our offerings are now more even. In the coming years, the number of sections of World Religions is likely to surpass the number of sections of Biblical Literature. There are various reasons students choose World Religions over Introduction to Biblical Literature at Oklahoma City University. One of our general education requirements is to take at least one course with a service-learning component. That is, the course has a service component directly related to the course objectives. Many of our World Religions classes contain a service-learning component. While a variety of service-learning courses are offered at OCU, World Religions also covers the 'Cross-Cultural' requirement, so students get three requirements out of the way with one course. Some students may also believe that learning about the religions of the world in today's global village is

---

1. 'The Religious Studies Major in a Post 9/11 World: New Challenges, New Opportunities', American Academy of Religion, www.aarweb.org/programs/Religion_Major_and_Liberal_Education/default.asp, p. 5. This document is also known as the AAR-Teagle White Paper.

more relevant than learning about the Bible. These realities led me to ask: Will World Religions be the death of Introduction to Biblical Literature or at least significantly reduce the number of students taking the latter?

One way to avoid the demise of Introduction to Biblical Literature is to make the class more appealing to students by providing an interdisciplinary experience. This paper examines how both arts integration and service-learning may be ways not only to improve student learning but also to pique interest in Introduction to Biblical Literature. Furthermore, integrating the arts into the class and providing service-learning opportunities makes the course more relevant to students. This then counters the most common criticism I hear regarding Introduction to Biblical Literature, that it is simply not relevant to their life.

In the fall of 2007, I was awarded a fellowship, along with seven colleagues from across the university, to spend a year learning how to integrate the arts into our curriculums.[2] We were a diverse group, representing the biology, education, and English departments from the College of Arts and Sciences, as well as the schools of theatre, business, law and religion. We spent a good deal of time reading about aesthetic education and discussing what arts integration is. We became convinced that it is more than simply tacking on art projects to a course. However, what kind and how much art is required for a course to be arts-integrated eluded us at times. A part of the fellowship was to take our year of learning and apply it to a course we would teach.[3]

I chose to teach an honors section of Introduction to Biblical Literature as an arts-integrated course. The honors classes at OCU are smaller than regular general education classes, with a maximum of 16 to 18 students rather than the usual maximum of 28 in our other general education courses in the School of Religion. Our honors program also has a rather unique focus upon service-learning courses. I knew some of the students would be resistant to the arts integration, since honors students generally seem to prefer the more academic work to creative work. On the other hand, many of the honors students at OCU are in the schools of dance, music, theatre, and visual arts so I thought they might enjoy the artistic component. I also taught the course as a service-learning course. Since then, I have integrated the arts into my Introduction to Biblical Literature courses with very positive outcomes. I am also working on a variation of my initial service-learning project for a course I will teach in the spring of 2012.

I have several learning objectives for my arts-integrated and service-learning Introduction to Biblical Literature course. At the end of the semester the students will be able to: 1) summarize the contents of the books of the Bible presented in the course; 2) describe the type of literature contained in each portion of the Bible; 3) explain the social historical context of the books; 4) discuss

---

2. The fellowship was funded by a grant from the Priddy Foundation, which supports programs in the arts and education among other areas.

3. Another part of the fellowship was to present a paper at a conference on our course. This paper is a revision of that presentation.

various academic methods used to interpret the Bible; 5) apply dramatic reading, tableau, and other artistic methods to the interpretation of selected biblical texts; and 6) teach youth how to interpret selected biblical texts through a variety of artistic methods.

I integrate art into the course in four ways. First, we begin every class session with an 'arts opening'. Students present a piece of artwork related to the theme or book of the Bible that we are studying on the day of their presentation and discuss it briefly. They also have to submit a short essay on the same. I always start with my own example: I show the music video of 'The Mesopotamians' by They Might Be Giants on the day I present an overview of the Ancient Near East. The students come up with a variety of artistic expressions for their arts opening. A student who presented on Genesis chose to read aloud James Weldon Johnson's 'Creation' for the class. Throughout the Hebrew Bible, students often select prints or paintings by well-known (and sometimes unknown) artists to show the class. When we studied the Gospel of Luke one semester, a student had us listen to Woody Guthrie's song 'Jesus Christ'. Another semester, the artwork for the Book of Acts was from an album cover by George Grie entitled 'Ascension'. After the student presents the basic information about the piece—artist, title, date—and any aspects about it which impressed him or her, I led the class through a 'deep noticing' exercise. I begin the discussion with a simple question: 'What do you notice about this piece, or what jumps out at you?' I repeat that question several times—'What else do you notice?'—in order to elicit as many responses as possible. We then discuss how the artist is interpreting the biblical text. Students comment positively on this aspect of the course on evaluations, stating that it makes the class relevant for them.

Another way I have integrated art is through an assignment the students submit the second class session. Usually, this assignment is a paper that asks the students to reflect upon what the Bible means to them and why, to describe their level of understanding of the Bible, and where they learned what they know about the Bible. The goal of the paper is to assess student knowledge of the Bible, rather than to evoke faith statements about the Bible (though that is often the result and that too is acceptable). In the honors Introduction to Biblical Literature, I instead had the students bring in a piece of artwork (not their own) depicting how they understood the Bible. Most of the presentations were quite good, such as the student who shared Michelangelo's Sistine Chapel depiction of God reaching out to Adam. She said that in the same way, the Bible is how God reaches out to humans, trying to touch them. A woman who is Jewish brought in a drawing of a family tree, because the genealogies in the Bible are the most important to her. Some of the presentations, however, were not very good. One student tried to draw an analogy between the art of pizza-making and how the Bible is a work of art. She forgot, however, to bring the 'artwork', namely the pizza. It was at that point I thought this art exercise might be a bit of a stretch for some students on the second day of class.

At the end of the semester, I usually have the students write a second version of 'My Understanding of the Bible'. For the honors course, I again had them use artwork, but this time they had to create the art. This project yielded some very fine results. Some students created collages from images they found on the Internet or in magazines. For example, one student found a series of pictures that signified the various covenants in the Hebrew Bible and New Testament. Another student made a mosaic collage of faces cut from magazines, pieced into the form of a cross on a red, yellow, and orange background (also a cut paper mosaic). One woman drew a stunning piece in charcoal symbolizing God's relationship with humanity. At the bottom of the piece, hands support an upside-down pyramid representing God as the foundation of the Bible. Inside of the pyramid are praying hands in a variety of positions, depicting humanity's connection to God through prayer. Across the top are five eyes, demonstrating the clarity of the Bible: the middle eye is open, showing that sometimes the Bible is very clear. The two eyes on either side of the middle are half open, demonstrating that the Bible is sometimes not fully clear in its meaning. The eyes on the outside are closed, revealing that parts of the Bible are not clear at all. Though the written 'My Understanding of the Bible' papers tend to provide a more concrete description of the students' progress through the semester, the art project has been meaningful for some students, and I have retained it as an option.

A third way I integrate art into my Biblical Literature course is through dramatic presentations of the text. Some students learn through their bodies, through kinesthetic learning. For this reason, I like to include some activities in which we embody the text. I have used drama in three ways. First, the students will present a tableau of a scene from a particular story. For this activity, I begin by reading the passage with the class and then asking: Who are the characters? What is each one doing in the story? How do they interact with each other? Next, I divide the passage into scenes and assign a small group to work on each scene. Each group creates a tableau or 'freeze frame' (no movement or words) of their scene. One person in each group acts as a director, who assign parts and directs the others. Then, in the order of the passage, each small group presents its tableau one at a time. The group holds their pose for a few seconds. While the group holds its pose, I ask the class what they notice about the scene. Once all the groups have presented their passage, I guide the class through a 'deep noticing' exercise: What did they notice through embodying the passage in this way? Repeating the question a few times—'What else did you notice?'—often elicits further answers.

Some variations on this theme could include having the groups add an imaginary scene before or after their biblical scene, or before or after the whole passage, and then transition into their scene. Each group could also add one line of text to the scene (not necessarily something that is in the passage), which interprets the passage further.

A second dramatic form I use is Readers' Theatre. For this activity, I prepare a script of a passage that is dialogue intensive, such as John 9. Each person receives a script and the class stands in a circle in the classroom, or another large space if it is available. I have proceeded in two ways with this activity, depending on the size of the class. I either assign each role to specific individuals, or we just read around the circle, one person reading each line. At the completion of the story, I again proceed with deep noticing: what did you notice about this passage by hearing it aloud?

The third kinesthetic activity I use is what I call 'Group Acting'. This uses the whole class to act out a passage or even a book of the Bible. I use this almost every semester with the Book of Ruth. Again, I have Ruth written out like a script, divided into parts and chapters. I divide the class into four groups and each group is assigned a chapter. I give them a bit of background about the Book of Ruth and some of the double entendre, especially in chapter three. Each group then prepares to act out their chapter for the class. The groups must use every member and can draw in persons from other groups if they need additional actors, such as for crowd scenes. The groups then perform their chapter as theatre-in-the-round (in order, of course).

Another way I have used Group Acting is with a scene from the Gospels that contains a large crowd, such as the story of the woman from the crowd whom Jesus heals from Mark 5.[4] This works best in a large open space where there is plenty of room to move around. For this story, I assign parts to various students. Then as I read the passage, they act it out. I prompt the actors to repeat their lines and to display the proper emotion called for by the text, for example at 5.38, 'When they came to the house of the leader of the synagogue, he saw a commotion, people weeping and wailing loudly'. In both cases, as with the other dramatic activities, I lead the group in a discussion about what they noticed by embodying the text in this way. Usually, the students will have keen responses. When they involve their bodies in the story, they see things they had not noticed when they quickly read the passage as a part of an assignment or heard it read aloud in class.

All of these dramatic activities have produced positive responses from the students. Course evaluations reflect the students' experiences: 'I am a very kinesthetic learner, so the dramatizations and physical pieces of art were great;' 'Arts integration was great because I am a musician and I felt really connected when we did dramatization or art works.'

Finally, I integrate art into my Introduction to Biblical Literature class through the assignments the students complete throughout the semester. The students have to turn in two assignments on the Hebrew Bible and two on the New Testament. I always give two options for each. One is usually an essay; the other is an arts option. The arts option often involves the student creating art and writing a brief reflection on the piece, or analyzing another person's work and how it interprets the biblical text. Here are a few examples of the assignments I have given:

1. *A musical review.* Read Genesis 37–46.1-7 (omitting chapter 38), then watch or listen to Andrew Lloyd Webber and Tim Rice's musical *Joseph*

---

4. An example is on YouTube by searching Oklahoma City University Methods.

and the *Amazing Technicolor Dreamcoat*. Write a paper which addresses the following: 1) briefly (only two or three paragraphs, no more than one page) summarize the musical, 2) what is the emphasis or focus of the musical? 3) How is that similar to or different from the biblical story?

2. *Respond to the story of Jonah.* Create an artistic interpretation of the story of Jonah: write a modern-day short story, a song, a poem, a script or screenplay, or prepare a visual interpretation. Submit a 500–750 word explanation and personal reflection on how your work relates to the biblical account.

3. *Visualizing Revelation.* Create a visual representation (painting, video, dance, photograph, or collage) of a passage in the book of Revelation or the whole book. Submit a 500–750 word explanation and personal reflection on how your work relates to the biblical account.

Arts integration overall has been received positively. One student said on the course evaluation: 'I loved this aspect of our class. It was intellectually and artistically stimulating. It gave me a better understanding of the material learned and my own abilities.' Another commented that creating art was 'helpful in understanding the material; created different ways of looking at things'. Other feedback from students has included an appreciation for the variety of activities in the class. In my experience, some lecture time is needed in a course such as Introduction to Biblical Literature, but that needs to be balanced with active, hands-on learning to keep the students engaged. In addition, at a university such as mine, in any given semester I may have students from not only the School of Religion or College of Arts and Sciences, but dancers, musicians, and actors, as well as nursing or business students. Using a variety of methods in the classroom, especially the arts, is welcomed and helps the students feel the class is relevant to their major and career path. It may also allow them to use a different part of the brain and express themselves in other ways than their studies usually require of them. Using the arts allowed diverse learning styles to be addressed: Linguistic, Musical, Bodily-Kinesthetic, Spatial and Spatial-Visual, Interpersonal, and Intrapersonal.[5]

The honors Introduction to Biblical Literature course in the spring of 2009 also applied this learning from the arts-integrated portions of the class to teaching the biblical material in our service-learning project. As mentioned, service-learning is a service experience that directly relates to the objectives of a course. I arranged for my class to present a program for a youth group at a church near the campus. The class was divided into four groups. Each group chose a text from a selection of passages and wrote an exegesis paper as a group. Then they had to develop a lesson on the passage that included an arts opening, a brief presentation about the passage, and a dramatic encounter with the text involv-

---

5. Howard Gardner, *Frames of Mind: The Theory of Multiple Intelligences* (New York: Basic Book, 2004).

ing all members of the youth group. The student groups were required to submit their lesson plans to me a several days before the presentation itself, so I could review their plans. After the experience, each student had to write a personal reflection paper.

We presented our programs on two Sunday evenings, two groups each evening. Each group presented their portion of the program to the youth group (a fairly small group of about 12 young people ranging from sixth-grade to seniors). From an observers' perspective, all the group's lessons went smoothly. The youth director was pleased, and the youth enjoyed it greatly. Unknown to the college students, they even drew a newcomer into the youth group and made him feel a part of the program.

My students' responses, however, were somewhat mixed. Of the fifteen evaluations, ten were positive or 'okay' with the experience. Three ranked the experience 'okay' to negative and, two were negative about experience: 'A group exegesis paper is the most ridiculous thing I have ever done!' Some students just do not like group projects. Other students were not very familiar with the biblical material they were presenting, and thus were uncomfortable with the project. To my pleasure, however, some students realized that how we structured the service-learning lesson was how our classes had been structured. I had prepared them throughout the semester for the service-learning project.

I am planning to offer the course as service-learning again in the spring of 2012. A few of the modifications the second time around will including having more class time for preparation and asking the students to include in the lesson plans who is going to do what part of the lesson. Some of the groups had only one or two students do the majority of the presentation. I will find ways for students who may not be familiar with the material to increase their comfort level and confidence. I will also work more closely with the children's minister at the site church in order to match our presentations to the educational level of the children with whom we will work. These changes will hopefully make the service-learning experience positive for all the students.

The AAR-Teagle White paper lists the Association of American Colleges and Universities' four essential learning outcomes for all American College students, including knowledge of human cultures and the physical and natural world; intellectual and practical skills; personal and social responsibility, and integrative learning.[6] An arts-integrated and service-learning approach to Introduction to Biblical Literature allows the course to address more of these objectives than a simply lecture/discussion-based class may. The arts allow students to engage in the 'big questions', with which they may be wrestling but which they may not be able to articulate verbally. The arts tap into creative thinking which is by-passed in courses based on lecture, reading, and discussion alone.

---

6. 'The Religious Studies Major in a Post 9/11 World', pp. 3-4.

Service-learning is a form of Integrative Learning. The students have to synthesize their learning for the semester and apply the 'knowledge, skills and responsibilities to new settings and complex problems'.[7] This component also allows students to put the skills acquired in the course into practice, but they must do so in an ethical and culturally sensitive manner. Such an approach to Introduction to Biblical Literature can more fully integrate the course into the Liberal Arts objectives of a college or university and make the course more relevant and appealing to the students.

---

7. 'The Religious Studies Major in a Post 9/11 World', p. 4.

Pedagogical Iconoclasm: The Role of the Upper-Level Biblical Studies Seminar in the Context of Undergraduate Religious Studies Programs

Benjamin L. White
Clemson University

Among the several courses that I took my first year of graduate school, the most curious was no doubt Religion 299: Methodology and Pedagogy in Islamic Studies, which fulfilled the 'Gateway' requirement for my program in Early Christianity at UNC-Chapel Hill. 'Gateway' courses at UNC are designed to produce more marketable graduate students, providing them with the tools necessary to teach introductory-level courses outside of their own field of expertise. I did not comprehend the genius of this curricular decision by the sages of my department until I went looking for a faculty position and began to read the kinds of job descriptions that are representative of today's ailing Humanities market, which requires that departments do increasingly more with fewer resources than in any other set of educational fields.[1] My final project for this square-peg-in-a-round-hole seminar was the construction of a usable syllabus for an undergraduate Introduction to Islam course, an eight-page document that I could wave in front of search committees to let them know I was not a one-trick pony. I have to admit, however, that after teaching in two very different educational environments (a small religiously-affiliated baccalaureate college and a large public research university) the syllabus still sits on my hard drive and has never seen the light of a college classroom. But despite its sleeping beauty, the syllabus forced me for the first time as a young educator to consider the role of the introductory religion course in the context of a liberal arts education.

---

1. The plight of the humanities and of the liberal arts has been recently highlighted by, among others, Martha Nussbaum, *Not for Profit: Why Democracy Needs the Humanities* (Princeton: Princeton University Press, 2010) and Victor E. Ferrall, Jr., *Liberal Arts at the Brink* (Cambridge: Harvard University Press, 2011).

Jonathan Z. Smith, whose writing on pedagogy I read for the first time that semester at UNC, has implored scholars of religion on numerous occasions to think deeply about the introductory course:

> For it is a fact, despite what we may sometimes claim, that the majority of us, as teachers, earn our living (and our departments get FTE'd) by means of the introductory course. This is recognized, albeit in an unfortunately grudging manner, in the widespread pejorative term, 'service course'. *As college teachers, our primary expertise is introducing.* Thinking about introducing should play the same role in our profession as meditating on first principles plays for the metaphysician.[2]

In my first two years of teaching alone I fielded both broadly conceived introductory courses (Religion 101: Introduction to Religion) as well as more specifically focused introductory-level courses in Hebrew Bible and New Testament. These kinds of courses, regardless of the institutional context, are normally populated by young people who just six to nine months prior were thinking about the prom. To their detriment, many of these students will never take another religion class during their college career. Others, hopefully, will find themselves getting hooked and reeled in by good teachers who allow the inherent value and seriousness of the subject to do its work on the souls of the next generation.[3]

Because of the truth of Smith's observation on the nature of our teaching, the literature on organizing introductory-level courses effectively is ubiquitous.[4] Much of it, however, is divorced from any consideration of the 'Program of Study', quasi-technical language used in institutional assessment circles for 'major' and/or 'curriculum'. It is language that I only recently came to know due to my time as Program Coordinator for the Religious Studies major in a

---

2. Jonathan Z. Smith, '"Narratives into Problems": The College Introductory Course and the Study of Religion', *JAAR* 56 (1988), p. 727. Emphasis original. See also 'The Introductory Course: Less is Better', in *Teaching the Introductory Course in Religious Studies: A Sourcebook* (ed. M. Juergensmeyer; Atlanta: Scholars, 1991), pp. 185-92.

3. Cf. Barbara E. Walvoord, *Teaching and Learning in College Introductory Religion Courses* (Oxford: Blackwell Publishing, 2008), pp. 82-98, for a detailed study, based on data from 533 introductory-level courses in religion, on what makes an effective teacher of religion. On the ninth anniversary of 9/11, Newsweek published an interesting piece in which it claimed that the number of students majoring in philosophy and religious studies had doubled since the 1970s: education.newsweek.com/2010/09/12/religious-studies-thrive-in-troubled-times.html. Unfortunately, the article can no longer be accessed on Newsweek's website. It can be found, however, at www.rowan.edu/colleges/las/departments/philosophy/ReligiousStudiesRevival.pdf.

4. In addition to the work of Smith, cited frequently in this essay, see also Karen I. Spear (ed.), *Rejuvenating Introductory Courses* (New Directions for Teaching and Learning 20; San Francisco: Jossey-Bass, 1984); Mark Juergensmeyer (ed.), *Teaching the Introductory Course in Religious Studies*; Russell T. McCutcheon, 'Theorizing in the Introductory Course: A Survey of Resources', *Critics Not Caretakers: Redescribing the Public Study of Religion* (Albany, NY: State University of New York Press, 2001), pp. 217-36; Bette L. Erickson, Calvin B. Peters, and Dianne W. Strommer, *Teaching First-Year College Students* (San Francisco: Jossey-Bass, rev. edn, 2006); and Walvoord, *Teaching and Learning in College Introductory Religion Courses*.

small college that had just sailed through the reaffirmation process for accreditation. For religious studies majors and minors, introductory-level courses are part of a larger program through which we move students from neophyte status to fully-fledged members of 'the club'. This is a process in which we encourage creative and critical thinking while also indoctrinating them into the institutional methods and language of our discipline. In a properly cared for departmental curriculum, much like the graduate program in which I took my PhD, each course is part of not only an interconnected web, but also a constructed hierarchy of learning that leads from information, through knowledge, to wisdom.[5] Education is a built environment.[6]

In what follows, I offer some suggestions on the rarely discussed piece near the top of this built environment: the upper-level seminar. In doing so, I will also have to make several comments on its foundation, the introductory course. My comments on the upper-level seminar will be filtered largely through my experience teaching Religion 607: Problems in Early Christian Literature and History in autumn of 2009 at UNC, for which Religion 104: Introduction to New Testament Literature was a prerequisite. In particular, I will suggest that the upper-level seminar ought to perform an act of iconoclasm: the destruction of simplistic, reified, and deceptive objects that are the necessary by-product of introductory-level courses. Any upper-level seminar worth its salt must fully engage the *prolegomena* of its subject, both deconstructing the ideological discourses that produce fixed images of the 'way things are' and providing students with the necessary methodological tools to reconstruct the subject in freedom and with a sense of empowerment.

Constructing Images, Spinning Narratives:
The Introductory-Level Bible Course in the Context
of the Program of Study in Religion

For those who have read Smith's work on pedagogy, some of what I have just claimed about the shortcomings of introductory-level courses might sound familiar. Smith has written quite a bit about the 'necessary lie' that all such courses perpetuate on unknowing students:

---

5. On the distinction between information, knowledge and wisdom, see the use of T.S. Eliot in Tim Buckley, 'Teaching the Facts, Inculcating Knowledge, or Instilling Wisdom? Rationale for a Textbook in BS101', *Teaching Theology and Religion* 12 (2009), pp. 352-3.

6. On the history of university curriculum in the United States, see Frederick Rudolph, *Curriculum: A History of the American Undergraduate Course of Study Since 1636* (San Francisco: Jossey-Bass, 1977). For more technical studies, see also John D. McNeil, *Curriculum: A Comprehensive Introduction* (Boston: Little Brown, 1977) and Arthur Levine, *Handbook on Undergraduate Curriculum* (San Francisco: Jossey-Bass, 1978). On curriculum mapping and the development of course goals within the larger context of program and institutional goals, see Robert M. Diamond, *Designing & Assessing Courses & Curricula: A Practical Guide* (San Francisco: Jossey-Bass, rev. edn, 1998), pp. 49-58, 79-105.

> We lie, it seems to me, in a number of ways. We sometimes cheerfully call the lie words like 'generalization' or 'simplification', but that's not really what we're doing. We're really lying, and lying in a relatively deep fashion, when we consistently disguise, in our introductory courses, what is problematic about our work... Moreover, we conceal from our students the fields-specific, time-bound judgments that make objects exemplary. We display them as if they are self-evidently significant and allow the students to feel guilty when they do not feel this self-evidence. We rarely do what some German critics have called a reception history of the object in front of us, examining why or how the object became in some way exemplary of humankind in a particular discipline.[7]

Smith's solution to this ethical quandary is full disclosure, along with a narrowing of focus in introductory courses to a single text, or maybe two, that can be unpacked, analyzed and treated with a large degree of nuance. Course content is of 'secondary import' to the primary focus of such a course: '*introducing the student to college-level work*'.[8] As part of the general education curriculum, introductory-level courses should be structured to help students communicate, argue, and reason better. Since no course can ever completely cover the waterfront of issues for a particular subject, 'The notion of a survey, of "coverage," becomes ludicrous.'[9] In a rather all-or-nothing moment, Smith then concludes: '*there is nothing that must be taught*, there is nothing that cannot be left out'.[10]

I came across the lengthy quotation above in one of Smith's online pieces during the same semester that I taught Religion 607, so I passed it along to my students, all of whom had previously taken Introduction to New Testament Literature. I wanted their thoughts. Was Smith right about the problem? Did it exist, in their minds, and had he landed on the right solution? Something about it bothered me, but I could not put my finger on what it was until one of my seniors, Pete Miller, posted the following reply on Blackboard. It is beautifully and frankly stated:

> I don't particularly like the Smith article. On the undergraduate level, I've been pretty satisfied with the intro classes at UNC. Smith is right that they avoid getting into the intricacies a lot of the time, but then again that's a question of the purpose of the class. Is Reli 103 [Introduction to the Hebrew Bible] meant to turn all the students into mini-professors who write articles challenging the Documentary Hypothesis? Or is it meant to be a broad survey that elevates students' understanding from the intellectual bankruptcy of the 'Moses wrote everything' view to the general consensus of the academic sphere? I would argue the latter. Of course, if a student sees Bart [Ehrman] casually placing the infamous word 'prob-

---

7. J.Z. Smith, 'The Necessary Lie: Duplicity in the Disciplines', teaching.uchicago.edu/tutorial/jz_smith.shtml.
8. 'Narratives into Problems', p. 727. Emphasis original.
9. 'Narratives into Problems', p. 728.
10. 'Narratives into Problems', p. 728.

lematic' next to the Documentary Hypothesis and wants to take it further, then he or she can. *I think that's the purpose of an upper-level class like this one.* I sense a sort of bitterness in Smith's article, and to me it undermines his argument. It's silly to suggest that a professor is 'lying' when he or she fails to spend three classes slogging through one minor point that scholarship has spent years debating. It is simply more efficient to convey the general academic consensus to the class and move on. The research is there for anyone who wants to spend more time on it. I don't like Smith's counter-proposal either. It seems like the way he would revise, say, Reli 103, would be to spend a whole semester on a case study discussing the validity of the Documentary Hypothesis vis a vis [sic] one book of the Hebrew Bible. That way, each student would have no illusions that Bart [Ehrman] or Bennie [Reynolds] know anything at all, and would then be sufficiently skeptical. There would be no academic dishonesty, and everything would be just great. Now mind you, the students would be ignorant about the other 38 books of the Hebrew Bible, but at least they wouldn't falsely attribute any certainty to a complex topic. I think anyone can see how that sucks. *The purpose of an intro level class, in my view, is to give students the basic knowledge they need to operate at the higher levels of the discipline, at which the intricacies ARE disputed and discussed.* And Ben, I know it's a major pet peeve of yours that such an oversimplified view of Paul is taught in Reli 104 [Introduction to New Testament Literature], but what's the alternative? There's just no time to slog through all the Pauline issues when you also have to cover the gospels and the "historical Jesus." Maybe the graduates of Reli 104 leave with an oversimplified view of Paul, but it's probably a damn sight better than that of 99% of Americans. And there's always this class for any student who wants to get into the meaty issues.[11]

Pete's response is so beautiful because he has answered Smith on two levels, addressing how such a course can serve to dispel basic ignorance of the Bible for the general audience, while also providing the foundation for a 'Program of Study' in biblical literature.

Recent studies like those from the Pew Forum on Religion & Public Life show that despite the religiosity of Americans, very few know much about religion, let alone the Bible. In fact, those who know the most are among the least religious (agnostics and atheists), while the devout of the Bible Belt score at the bottom of the scale of basic religious knowledge.[12] But ignorance of the basics is not limited to the study of religion. Incoming college students are, in general, increasingly unprepared for college-level work.[13] This is not because they don't

---

11. Accessed from the course Blackboard site on 11/18/2010. Used here with Pete's permission. Emphasis added.

12. religion.blogs.cnn.com/2010/09/28/dont-know-much-about-religion-youre-not-alone-study-finds/?hpt=C1.

13. See Levine, *Handbook on Undergraduate Curriculum*, pp. 54-76, and Harriet W. Sheridan, 'Where Have All the Senior Faculty Gone?', in *Rejuvenating Introductory Courses*, pp. 15-17.

know how to find information in the information age, but because, ironically, they do not know anything without recourse to an electronic device (calculator, Wikipedia, etc.). They have been taught how to succeed on standardized tests and how to respect the views of others, while also channeling a watered-down and oversimplified version of postmodernism ('But that's just your opinion'). But poverty of basic knowledge means that there is little capital with which one can grow creative and critical thinking skills. For these reasons, among others, we need to refocus much of our energy again in introductory-level courses on the lower strata of knowledge acquisition: names, dates, places, formulas, etc., while at the same time introducing students to higher levels of critical and integrative thinking. Like Pete, I fear that Smith wants to throw out the proverbial baby with the bathwater. *Content* is not a four-letter word.

There are innumerable ways for faculty to indicate the complexity of our field to neophytes without sacrificing the kind of basic images and narratives that introduce a wide variety of students to the content of the Bible and that form the foundation for organizing future scholarly pursuits.[14] Of course, striking the right balance is the key, which is both an art and a science. My experience at three different institutions in the South, where the majority of students in introductory Bible classes are conservative-leaning believers, is that even a mildly historical-critical approach that *introduces* the Documentary Hypothesis, archaeology vs. text, Deutero- and Trito-Isaiah, the Synoptic Problem, the 'Historical' Jesus, and disputed and undisputed Pauline letters is enough to get the higher-level cognitive wheels spinning in the right direction. As unsatisfied as I am, for example, with the seven-letter 'consensus' in Pauline studies, the simple recognition of stark differences among the letters bearing Paul's name in the New Testament and the suggestion that some were written by Paul and others might not be, often gets first and second year students to begin thinking about the kinds of paradigms that are appropriate for the humanities. Chances are, anyway, they had never even read the Pauline epistles before the semester began! More practically, the use of Trockmorton's *Gospel Parallels* with a set of colored pencils gives students the chance to read horizontally/critically while they also read vertically/narratively/canonically.

In order to avoid the hostile accusation from students that 'that is just your wacky, liberal opinion', a healthy dose of selected readings from the Bible is necessary. Any educator is at risk of losing their students if they have decided to mystify their subject to such a degree that its basic building blocks are left unexamined. And if we allow the primary source to be the principle textbook for the class, then there are subjects that *have* to be taught, contra Smith.[15] And

---

14. See also Margaret Parks Cowan, 'Teaching an Introductory Hebrew Bible Course without a Textbook', *Teaching Theology and Religion* 12 (2009), pp. 254-5, for several suggestions on how to balance teaching content and developing critical thinking.

15. With Smith, 'Narratives into Problems', p. 734, I now prefer to assign primary texts for introductory courses and have made the 'Introduction to the New Testament' textbook an optional purchase. I have found that covering the New Testament in a semester is a daunting task and that

in this regard, the 'reception history' of the text (cf. Smith's language above) has done the hard work for us. The Gospels, Acts and Paul, like the Torah and the Prophets, stand at the front of their respective canons for a reason. These texts provide the basic narrative(s) of faith for those for whom these texts were edited, gathered, and canonized.[16] Of course, the canonical narrative can be critiqued from a number of different perspectives, but this is normally fruitfully done only *after* a traditional portrayal has been molded.[17] Iconoclasm requires an image. 'Critique' cannot stand on its own. 'Critique of', however, is possible. And by 'turning narratives into problems', as Smith uses the language of historian John Robert Seeley, we do not remove the necessity for the category of narrative. Making dominant narratives problematic is the first step in constructing alternative narratives, non-canonical frameworks for organizing the data into different meaningful wholes.

Pedagogical Iconoclasm: The Upper-Level Biblical Studies Seminar

Outside of the general educational benefits that a well-balanced introduction to Hebrew Bible or New Testament can provide, as Pete notes, introductory-level courses and upper-level seminars exist within the same departmental curriculum and ought to play distinct roles in serving the ends of the larger Program of Study. We should not feel the need to do everything at once in our introductory-level courses:

students with limited time prefer to read someone's summary of a primary text rather than the primary text itself. My students now actually read almost all of the New Testament during the course of a semester and I provide in class the interpretive framework within which I want them to read the texts. I use meta-questions to drive their reading. 'Who was Jesus of Nazareth?' and 'What is a Christian?' provide the lenses through which they read the Gospels and Paul, respectively. For a useful discussion of the use of textbooks in introductory-level Bible classes, see the essays in *Teaching Theology and Religion* 12.3 (2009).

16. Brannon M. Wheeler, author of 'What Can't Be Left Out? The Essentials of Teaching Islam as a Religion', in *Teaching Islam* (ed. B.M. Wheeler; American Academy of Religion Teaching Religious Studies; New York: Oxford University Press, 2003), pp. 3-21, and a student of Smith's at the University of Chicago, also provides a more moderate version of Smith's pedagogical theory. While Wheeler stands close to Smith when he says that the 'introduction to Islam course is not primarily a matter of teaching students a certain corpus of facts', he does provide phenomenological categories like 'The Prophet and Prophethood', 'Canon and Law', 'Ritual', and 'Society and Culture' as 'essential' topics for an Introduction to Islam course. See also A. Kevin Reinhart, 'On the "Introduction to Islam,"' in *Teaching Islam*, pp. 22-45. It would be odd, of course, to teach Islam without reference to Muhammad, the five pillars, the differing legal traditions, and some reference to the diversity of Muslim traditions in the world today. We may take Smith's statement that 'there is nothing that cannot be left out' as hyperbolic, but even a slightly milder form of this sentiment can still absolve educators from making the kinds of critical decisions about ranking first-order, second-order, and third-order material within the context of the Program of Study.

17. See Wheeler, 'What Can't Be Left Out?' p. 11, where he recommends teaching the diversity of Islam at the end of the course, not the beginning: 'Students are usually not prepared to make the conceptual jump from ignorance to a pluralistic definition of Islam, nor are students expecting this sort of discovery.'

> As we teach our courses, we tend to lose sight of the fact that each course is but one element in a learning sequence defined as a curriculum. The closer the relationships are among courses, curriculum, and planned out-of-class activities, the more effective the learning experience will be for our students.[18]

For our majors, we have several years to shepherd them through a graduated process. And we send non-majors away impoverished if by the end of the semester we have taught them how to think, but they still do not have anything to think about. Much of what Smith has suggested as a solution for the problems of the introductory level course should wait for the upper-level seminar, when students are ready to consider the full weight of the problems that exist in the acquisition of knowledge about the past, once they know how to read and write at the acceptable level, have some clue as to what a research paper looks like, and have learned to integrate knowledge from a variety of disciplines. Only then, toward the end of a total Program of Study, are students ready for the full-scale kind of iconoclasm that I hope we began hinting at during their freshman year.[19]

Scholars of teaching and learning often reiterate that learning is a developmental process that moves from lower taxonomic levels to higher. Benjamin Bloom described cognitive learning as a path leading from knowledge, through comprehension, application, analysis, and synthesis, to evaluation.[20] More recently and building on Bloom, L. Dee Fink describes significant learning as a synthesis of six kinds of learning:

- Foundational Knowledge
- Application
- Integration
- Human Dimension
- Caring
- Learning How to Lean

---

18. Diamond, *Designing and Assessing Courses and Curricula*, p. 49.
19. Smith's proposal also seems well suited for a small, first-year seminar, which is a different kind of entity than the broadly conceived, regularly offered, and heavily populated introductory-level courses that fulfill general education requirements. Again, I want to emphasize that I do not conceive of introductory-level courses as being driven by content alone; far from it. They offer our first chance to introduce students not only to the texts themselves, but also to the various ways in which they can be studied. See McCutcheon, *Critics Not Caretakers*, p. 230: 'Some would say that only in a graduate course does one have the luxury of returning to these theoretical concerns, prompting students to think back to the inadequacies of the resources they used at the start of the university education. Although this may be a useful approach, I tend to think that we can begin this kind of meta-theoretical work in the introductory class.'
20. Benjamin S. Bloom (ed.), *Taxonomy of Educational Objectives: The Classification of Educational Goals, Handbook I: Cognitive Domain* (New York: McKay, 1956).

For Fink, 'this taxonomy . . . is not hierarchical but rather relational and interactive.'[21] I agree that learning is an integrative process and that each of these components should be present at all levels of instruction. But as students make their way through the general education curriculum and move into discipline-specific upper-level courses, the precise mix of foundational knowledge/ content, critical thinking requirements, and focus on theory/methodology will necessarily shift. Within the Program of Study there should be some 'vertical organization' that intentionally tracks with the growth in higher levels of thinking that naturally occurs in college.[22]

Religion 607 in the autumn of 2009 was my first crack at an upper-level seminar. Its generic catalogue title, '*Problems* in Early Christian Literature and History', already suggests that the course was to be driven by questions and critique and not by over-simplified solutions. The specific problems that the course addressed rotated from year to year, depending on who was teaching it and what their research interests were. The subtitle for my version of the course, 'Paul and Early Pauline Traditions', was birthed from my dissertation research. I was becoming increasingly skeptical of the regnant and rigid discourse on the 'historical' Paul vs. the Paul of 'tradition', or the 'undisputed' vs. the 'disputed' Pauline letters. I was also noticing that this same sort of rhetorical enterprise, which trades in the language of having Paul 'right', was already present in the second century, maybe earlier. Religion 607 was the perfect opportunity to help walk students through the complexities and problems of knowing 'Paul', who probably seemed like quite a static individual for them after Introduction to the New Testament Literature (Reli 104), a course that each of them had taken either with me or with Bart Ehrman. Paul often comes out looking more like a fixed image than a living and breathing human being in most introductory-level courses and textbooks on the New Testament. The normal paradigm for teaching Paul introduces differences in style and substance between Acts and the Pauline letters and among the Pauline letters themselves and then simply posits pseudonymity as the best solution, always siding with the Paul of Romans and Galatians as the 'real' or 'historical' Paul. Even at institutions where the entire Pauline letter corpus is considered authentic, the Paul of Romans and Galatians is still placed front and center. This is our academy's 'necessary lie', rooted in nineteenth-century German (Protestant) New Testament scholarship and perpetually reinforced as a byproduct of also having to cover the Jewish and

---

21. L. Dee Fink, *Creating Significant Learning Experiences: An Integrated Approach to Designing College Courses* (San Francisco: Jossey-Bass, 2003), p. 32.

22. 'Vertical organization' is based on developmental models of human psychology, whereas 'horizontal organization' is focused on the integration of diverse subjects as well as in- and out-of-classroom experiences. See McNeil, *Curriculum*, pp. 161-8, for this specific language. On the mental, social, and psychological development of college students, see Ernest T. Pascarella and Patrick T. Terenzini, *How College Affects Students: Findings and Insights from Twenty Years of Research* (San Francisco: Jossey-Bass Publishers, 1991) and *How College Affects Students: Volume 2: A Third Decade of Research* (San Francisco: Jossey-Bass Publishers, 2005).

pagan backgrounds of early Christianity, the nature of the gospels, the 'historical' Jesus, Acts, and Revelation in our introductory courses (we all know that 2 Peter and Jude normally get squeezed out). At best, Pauline biography and literature get surveyed in three to four weeks, a woefully inadequate time frame to cover this material (plus the related Hebrews and James).

There were twenty-two students in the course, most of whom were religious studies majors and minors. A few just wanted to take a course on Paul, which probably had not been offered at UNC in decades. There were twelve females and eleven males, all juniors and seniors (except one). I knew most of the students from earlier semesters. The course description read as follows:

> This upper-level research and presentation-driven seminar will focus on the Apostle Paul's wide-ranging influence in the early church. As such, we will focus on Paul as a 'persona', an authoritative image constructed in individual texts. We will explore issues related to two large 'problems' in early Christian literature and history: the 'quest for the historical Paul' (e.g.—canonical letters vs. Acts, the possibility of letters written in Paul's name, the contingency of the letters) as well as the variety of interpretive traditions about him that sprung up in the late-first and early-second centuries (e.g. non-canonical stories about Paul, second-century interpretations of his letters, and the images of Paul that develop through them). All of these Pauline traditions will be explored in the context of the growth of early Christianity and its theological variety.

I had three stated course goals:

1. Attain a high-degree of proficiency in researching and writing for the field of New Testament and Early Christianity;
2. Develop an understanding of the interrelationship between the historical-critical study of Paul and his interpreters' (modern and ancient) ideologies;
3. Master the contents and background issues pertaining to each of the 'Pauline' texts and traditions we encounter this semester.

In the course of the total Program of Study, these goals were designed to build on prior curricular experiences. For instance, students had already *begun* to do some guided research on the New Testament for in-class debates on controversial interpretive issues in Religion 104. Now they were expected to make *full use* of concordances, commentaries, monographs, and articles as well as the various search engines available for their research: ATLA, WorldCat, and Dissertations and Theses. The debates in Religion 104 also forced students to *begin* to grapple with differing interpretive perspectives on issues of gender, sexuality, and authority. By *rigorously* deconstructing the dominant Protestant discourse on the 'historical' Paul, Religion 607 helped students to see the interconnectedness between scholarship, ideology, and power. I would place this goal under Fink's 'human dimension' of learning. And whereas students come out of Religion 104 with a few *bullet points* about each of the Pauline epistles, Religion 607 gives students the opportunity to *master* the contents of these texts.

To achieve these goals, I structured the course and its assignments into four evenly divided sections, trying to run it as much like a graduate seminar as possible:

1. Prolegomena to the Study of Paul and Pauline Traditions (six meetings);
2. The So-Called 'Undisputed' Letters of the 'Historical' Paul (seven meetings);
2. Acts and the So-Called 'Pseudo-Pauline' Letters (six meetings); and
4. 'Paul' in the Second-Century (six meetings)

The first section of the semester would be driven by me, while the last three-quarters would be driven by the students. The initial weeks of class were meant to lead students through a series of considerations that I believed would deconstruct much of what they had come to know about the 'historical' Paul of the seven 'undisputed' letters, providing them with the freedom and tools to begin their own work on reconstructing a Paul that made the most sense to them from the data.

The first two classes of the semester set the tone. F.C. Baur was the subject. As the substantive father of modern Pauline studies, particularly when it comes to discourses on genuine and pseudonymous Pauline literature, Baur's historical location needed to be explained. Students read bits of Horton Harris' *The Tübingen School*, as well as the opening section of Baur's own *Paul, the Apostle of Jesus Christ*.[23] They were quite amazed to hear the following kinds of romanticized, non-critical statements by Baur:

> The comparison reveals at once how far they [shorter Pauline epistles] stand below the originality, the wealth of thought, and the whole spiritual substance and value of those other Epistles [Rom, 1-2 Cor, Gal]. They are characterized by a certain meagerness of contents, by colourlessness of treatment, by absence of motive and connexion, by monotony, by repetition, by dependence, partly on each other, and partly on the Epistles of the first class ... It is clear that the point of view from which these letters are written is not that of one seeking to make good, and to develop a general principle which has still to vindicate itself, and on which the Christian consciousness and life are to be formed ... The authentic Pauline Epistles have a true organic development; they proceed from one root idea which penetrates the whole contents of the Epistle from the very beginning, and binds all the different parts of it to an inner unity, through the deeper relations in which it holds them, even though they appear at first sight to be only outwardly connected ... Hence they exhibit a genuine dialectic movement.[24]

I gave my students the requisite notes on Lutheran Germany in the nineteenth century, the influence of Hegel on Baur, and the influence of Baur's divisions of

---

23. Horton Harris, *The Tübingen School: a Historical and Theological Investigation of the School of F.C. Baur* (Leicester: Apollos, 1990 [1975]).
24. F.C. Baur, *Paul the Apostle of Jesus Christ: His Life and Works, His Epistles and Teaching* (vol. 2; Peabody, MA: Hendrickson, 2003 [1845]), pp. 106-7.

Pauline texts on subsequent New Testament scholarship in the late-nineteenth and early-twentieth centuries. From the get-go, I wanted them to understand the ideological investments of Paul's interpreters. We stand in a long theological tradition that is unquestioning of letters like Romans and Galatians. Exhibit One: The late Harold Hoehner, several years ago in the 'Pauline Epistles' Section of the Annual Society of Biblical Literature Meeting, asked playfully, 'Did Paul Write Galatians?' Hoehner marshaled together a number of arguments that are normally made to exclude the 'disputed' Paulines in an attempt to show how these same arguments, if administered fairly, would lead to the exclusion of Galatians as authentically Pauline. Hoehner's transgressive project met the ire of at least one unnamed German scholar who told him, 'Don't do that, I like Galatians.'[25] Exhibit Two: Sometimes, one often encounters such uncritical statements as are found in the opening of James Dunn's two-volume, nearly 1,000 page-commentary on Romans: 'No doubt is today entertained regarding the author of this letter (see, e.g., Cranfield, 1-2). He identifies himself with his first word, "Paul," and is clearly the one known more or less from the beginnings of Christianity simply as "the apostle Paul."'[26] This is all the space Dunn gives to the issue of authorship in Romans. Such a statement in volumes on Ephesians, 2 Thessalonians, or the Pastoral Epistles would have never seen the light of day.

After making students wise to the ideologies that drive much of New Testament scholarship, we moved to consider a variety of other problems related to the *prolegomena* of Pauline studies:

1. How large and to what degree are the differences between Acts and the Pauline Epistles?
2. Can more 'scientific' attempts to discern authorship, like measuring differences in language and style, carry the kind of rhetorical weight that some have argued?
3. How do issues related to letter-writing in antiquity, along with circumstances surrounding the collection and transmission of Paul's letters, muddy our access to the 'real' Paul?
4. Do we really have enough data about Paul's life to make statements about what could or could not have fit within the framework of his ministry?
5. How do interpretive issues related to rhetoric, contingency, and the potential development of Paul's thought affect our ability to pin down the 'real' Paul?

All this in the first three weeks of class!

After three weeks I saw students recognizing the truth of the famous dictum, 'The more you know, the more you know you don't know.' In particular,

---

25. Harold Hoehner, 'Did Paul Write Galatians?', in *History and Exegesis: New Testament Essays in Honor of E. Earle Ellis for his 80th Birthday* (ed. Sang-wan Son and S. Aaron Son; New York: T&T Clark, 2006), p. 158.

26. James D.G. Dunn, *Romans* (2 vols.; WBC; Waco: Word, 1988), 1: p. xxxix.

I was trying to get them to find the Archimedean point from which the 'real' Paul could be constructed. On the one hand, they were frustrated upon finding none. On the other hand, I began to see a newfound sense of freedom to explore Pauline texts and traditions, unchained from the categories by which they had been previously held. I hoped that they were 'learning how to learn' (cf. Fink's classifications above).

The remainder of the semester featured student presentations and research. Working from 1 Thessalonians to Paul's late second-century proto-orthodox defenders, each student picked a text that they wanted to spend the semester studying, trying to get to the heart of its portrayal of Paul. How does Paul come across in the text? What is his relationship with his audience? What is his relationship with those around him? How does he relate to Judaism? Pagan religion? Women? Tradition? The other apostles? His opponents? What seems to matter to him in the text? Why is his persona invoked? What does his authority substantiate? A particular theology? A particular philosophy? A particular practice?

The first stage of the research process required them to give a twenty-minute presentation on a focused topic related to one of these questions and then guide a twenty-minute discussion about the day's reading. Students were required to provide a basic outline of their presentation to their classmates, along with an annotated bibliography of the five most important English-language studies on their topic. Examples of actual class presentations include:

1. The supposed interpolation in 1 Thessalonians 2.13-16 as it relates to Paul's relationship with his fellow Jews;
2. Philippians 3 in light of the 'New Perspective' on Paul;
3. The audience of Ephesians; and
4. The nature of the relationship between the Pastoral Epistles and the Acts of Paul and Thecla, particularly with respect to their treatment of women.

The presentations were graded on depth of research, clarity of argument, and originality of thought. Students continued to work on their topic until the end of the semester, at which point they produced a 12-15 page paper, arguing a specific thesis about their text. I graded the papers, returned them with corrections, comments, and suggestions for further research, and then required them submit in a revised version for their final exam. I averaged the two versions of the paper to produce a final paper score.

Since this was my first time teaching an upper-level seminar, there was a lot from which I could learn. The failures of the course were several. First, and least important from a methodological/theoretical standpoint, I have decided never again to assign Elaine Pagels' *The Gnostic Paul* for a book review. I had to read twenty-two mind-numbingly dull reviews of a book that is best used as a reference and not as a front-to-back read. I should have known better and my students let me know it. Second, I had problems organizing the class. After the first three weeks, in which I had tried to obliterate neat categories, I had no better way to structure our reading of Pauline texts than to return to those same categories. We explored the seven 'undisputed' letters first, followed by the six 'disputed'. Getting around this issue without prefiguring the field of study was a more difficult task than I had anticipated. Third, the heavy focus on student-led presentations throughout most of the course led to a very slow pace. I received numerous comments in student evaluations along the line of 'Hey—I learned a ton more about my text than I would have had I not had to give a presentation, but I would have loved to have heard you talk more about each of the other texts rather than listening to my peers.'

Overall, however, the seminar seemed to meet the goals I had laid out. Here are a few representative samples from end-of-course evaluations:

> The lecturing was good, the help with the research was great. I appreciate getting feedback *and* a chance to re-do our research papers, because I learned a lot [Goal 1].
>
> I learned how to construct an argument and build a discussion around it. The more important thing though, was how to lead people step-by-step through my argument. Feedback was great. It wasn't just stuff pertaining to my material, but also to my presenting style, which will help me in the future [Goal 1].
>
> [Dr. White] teaches effectively by asking students to delve into the field head first and giving guidance. There is no hand-holding. This truly is a graduate-style class and I learned more here than any other class at UNC [Goal 3].
>
> My knowledge of the relevant text was vastly expanded. I now feel like I could hold my own on the topic with any scholar. The presentation improved my researching skills [Goal 3].

Outside of these encouraging words, one class discussion in particular during the middle of the semester had me feeling pretty good about the ultimate, iconoclastic aim of the class, which is encapsulated to a large degree in Goal 2 above. In the midst of a debate about the relationship between 1 Timothy and the 'historical' Paul, one of my students frustratingly asked: 'But where do we begin?' I took that to mean, 'Who was the historical Paul?' I was quietly pleased to hear her thinking critically about the problems of our dominant discourse. And beyond that, to see twenty-one other heads nodding up and down in agreement suggested to me that it is possible for scholarly traditions, longstanding normative discourses, to be challenged by new scholars in ways that open up texts to new possibilities of reception, reconfigured to fit into new narratives about 'the Apostle'.

Conclusion

The upper-level biblical studies seminar exists within the context of a larger Program of Study. As such, it should function as a capstone-style course in which students toward the end of their curriculum have a chance to marshal forth a wide range of interdisciplinary skills, perspectives, and knowledge in order to engage in full-scale acts of iconoclasm. The traditional and dominant images and narratives of the past that our introductory-level Bible courses construct provide the basic, albeit grossly simplified, starting points for the organization of knowledge. Because these courses serve a dual function, meeting general education requirements for many and providing the initial entrée into a particular Program of Study for some, we should think content first. 'Turning narratives into problems' is certainly a noble goal for the introductory-level course, but the Luddite in me can hardly agree with Smith that content is secondary and that '*there is nothing that must be taught*, there is nothing that cannot be left out.'[27] Rampant societal ignorance precludes such a philosophy. But I also agree with the oft-cited and never located *agraphon* from W.B. Yeats (popular on internet quote databases): 'Education is not the filling of a pail, but the lighting of a fire.' Content always runs out the bottom of a leaky pail unless the student has been stimulated to think long, hard, and creatively about a subject. Inspired students always know more and think more deeply than those just looking for a grade.

Introductory-level courses should also provide some initial hints about the chinks in the subject's armor. We cannot afford to set up completely straw men early on. The kind of immediacy that Smith envisions, however, is never achievable and its pursuit at the introductory-level comes with too large of a price. Images, like language, function as signs and can never be identical with the objects they represent.[28] They both frustrate and grant some degree of access. Because of this, images, narratives, and language itself are necessary, despite their frustrating limits. They are all we have for interpreting the remains of the past. After we turn narratives into problems and engage in acts of iconoclasm, we still have traces of the past that must be reconfigured if we hope to make sense of them. The meta-critique of disciplinary knowledge within the field of biblical studies should be seen as a progressive journey in which the final act of iconoclasm, the exposure of images as signs encoding ideology, happens at a stage of cognitive development and educational experience at which students have the necessary materials and tools to reconstruct the past with freedom and empowerment. Education is a built environment and our Programs of Study should reflect this fact.

---

27. Smith, '"Narratives into Problems,"' p. 728.
28. W.J.T. Mitchell, *Iconology: Image, Text, Ideology* (Chicago: University of Chicago Press, 1985), p. 8.

Part II

PEDAGOGICAL THEORY AND BIBLICAL STUDIES COURSES

Teaching the Material and Teaching the Students: Reflections on Introductory Courses for Non-Majors

Shane Kirkpatrick
Anderson University

Introduction

As a biblical scholar, I teach courses that involve reading and interpreting biblical texts. I encourage students to think of the three most important criteria for real estate (in other words, location, location, location) when we talk about the three most important criteria for biblical interpretation—the first is context, the second is context, and the third is context. The same is true, I would argue, with teaching. Teaching tends to defy the notion that one size fits all and instead benefits from long, hard attention to context. In other words: Who am I, as a teacher? Where am I—what is the ethos of this institution? Who are these students? Where are they coming from? Where are we all going?

From a survey of the mission statements and educational objectives articulated by colleges and universities, one can collect any number of broad phrases pointing toward lofty goals and ideals. Quite appropriately for the setting of a liberal arts college, many of these statements evoke a broad vision, beyond any one particular discipline or field of study. For example, the *Greater Expectations* project of the Association of American Colleges and Universities reflects on liberal education and its connection to the intentional student, a person it defines as empowered, informed, and responsible.[1] If I begin with some of those general descriptions of an undergraduate setting and its goals, I am led to consider how the practice of reading and interpreting biblical texts contributes to the lives of, for example, critical thinkers, creative problem-solvers, and responsible global citizens. It can be difficult, however, to begin with these large and perhaps abstract ideals, so let me start with the particular. True to my concern for context, context, context, I begin with my own context.

---

* This work was originally published in *Teaching Theology and Religion* 13.2 (April 2010): 125-36, and is reprinted here with permission of Blackwell Publishing Ltd.

1. *Greater Expectations: A New Vision for Learning as a Nation Goes to College.* Washington, DC: Association of American Colleges and Universities, 2002; see esp. chapter 3, pp. 21-28. www.greaterexpectations.org.

Context

My reflection on these issues stems from my own experience of teaching a required, non-major, one-semester, introductory Bible course for first-year students at a church-related liberal arts college in the American Midwest. I rehearse that long string of descriptors and qualifiers because nearly every one of them adds some dimension—and often, a difficulty—to my task. Each of these dynamics is something that shapes the context in which I teach. So, for example, the course is required. This has implications for the level of interest and investment that students bring to the classroom. Even if there is some degree of interest in the subject matter, the required nature of any course tends to deflate enthusiasm for the course. Further, to the extent that students focus their attention and energy on their academic majors, a non-major course tends to be treated as an imposition, something to get out of the way, and not worthy of a student's best effort.

Introductory courses, and particularly a one-semester, stand-alone course like my own, suffer from the impossible task of introducing a whole discipline, a field of study that is so rich and deep that a scholar can devote an entire academic career to a single sub-discipline within the field. In the face of that breadth and depth, are we to spend our few weeks together getting an overview of the whole, or should we go into some detail but necessarily limit our scope? The possible answers will vary with different disciplines; for me the question is: To what does an introductory Bible course introduce students? Options include the following:

- The academic study of the Bible—if so, what methods or subspecialties are chosen and which are left aside?
- The interpretation of the Bible—if so, what periods are included, which methods are practiced, whose readings are focused upon?
- Religious, theological, or spiritual readings of the Bible— if so, what religion, or what theological tradition, or what spiritual practice is featured?
- The history of the Bible—if so, is that the history of the book itself (transmission, translation, and so forth) or the history depicted in its pages; and what of the relationship of that history to a critically-reconstructed history of the ancient Near East and Greco-Roman Mediterranean?

Of course there are other possibilities, too; the options proliferate. Additionally, the notion of an 'introduction to the Bible' differs from other college introductory courses in that there is a distinct aspect of biblical scholarship known as 'introduction'[2]—a fact of which both students and sometimes even faculty

---

2. Brevard S. Childs, *Introduction to the Old Testament as Scripture* (Philadelphia: Fortress, 1979), pp. 27-39; Werner Georg Kümmel, *Introduction to the New Testament* (trans. Howard Clark Kee; Nashville: Abingdon, rev. edn, 1975), pp. 28-34.

colleagues in other disciplines are generally unaware—which features questions of authorship, dating, and other issues that students can be surprised to find as the focus of the course.

Further, introductory courses are often taken by lower-division (or underclass) students—indeed, at my own institution, mine is a first-year course—and are thus complicated by a number of issues related to the transition from secondary to higher education and require attention to the developmental issues of adolescents and young adults. In addition to being surprised about course content, some students become concerned or even distressed because of the expectations they bring to a Bible course at a church-related college. If they have had previous encounters with the Bible, it will typically have been in worship settings within a religious community—through preaching, praying, religious education classes, peer-group Bible studies, youth group devotions, and so on. The dissonance between the behavior and forms of engagement practiced in those settings and that which is asked of students in an academic setting is experienced with varying degrees of severity. All of these elements conspire to create a difficult pedagogical challenge.

My institution offers several sections of the one-semester 'Introduction to the Bible', because it is required of every undergraduate student regardless of major. Yet we do not have a common syllabus or a mandated set of assignments or activities. Each professor is given the freedom to design and structure the course as the professor sees fit, which I appreciate. However, with that freedom comes responsibility—I have to design and structure this course. Thus, with each new semester, I am plagued again with questions about how to teach the course: What is it supposed to do? How do I understand its purpose or function? What do I want for the students who take this course; for example, how can it contribute to the life of critical thinkers, creative problem-solvers, and responsible global citizens? On what do we focus? What do we leave out? How do I make decisions like that? In other words, what are the operative criteria that guide my pedagogical decision-making, and where do I get those criteria? Am I influenced by the guild—the professional society for my discipline? Am I influenced by the students—their developmental needs, their religious concerns, their previous formation (educational, religious, social, and so forth)? Am I influenced by the material (that is, by the subject matter), or by institutional demands, or by the religious sensibilities of our school's constituency? Again, the options proliferate.[3]

In making these difficult pedagogical decisions, my own tendency is to focus less on the content and the discipline and more on the developmental and general educational needs of the students.[4] Two factors in particular in my

---

3. Jonathan Z. Smith, 'Teaching the Bible in the Context of General Education', *Teaching Theology and Religion* 1.2 (June, 1998), pp. 73-78.

4. Smith says that, 'the ways in which the Bible may be taught within the context of general education will vary, appropriately, according to the ways in which the *educational* enterprise is understood'. Smith, 'Teaching the Bible', p. 77, emphasis added.

own context make this an appropriate decision. First, my course is taken by first-year students—often in their very first semester—who are frequently also first-generation college students (that is, the first in their families ever to attend college). The first-year students I meet in my course tend not to be well-prepared for independent or critical thought, so this required introductory Bible course becomes a wonderful occasion not only for teaching the material but for using the material to teach the students, to help them become aware of themselves as learners, as agents in their own education. In addition to that, the fact that my course is for non-majors removes from me the burden (if you will) of ushering these students into the discipline of biblical studies and allows me to focus instead on what might be called 'transferable skills'—close reading, genre identification, historical awareness, argument analysis, peer critique, and self-reflection. I can use my discipline and the primary and secondary materials of the course as occasions for the development of capacities that will contribute to the broader concerns of liberal arts education—to the life of a critical thinker, a creative problem-solver, and a responsible global citizen.[5]

The way I think of my course is not unlike the approach taken by Willard Reed, a colleague of mine who teaches in philosophy. Rather than teaching an 'introduction to philosophy' course, he offers a course for non-majors entitled 'Practicing Philosophy'. As I have talked with him about how he understands the difference, he suggests that an 'introduction to philosophy' course would probably be ordered chronologically, covering the ancient Greeks and moving through significant figures and movements in the history of philosophy, considering the special contributions of different thinkers or the emphases of different eras. It would, in a sense, be a course *about* philosophy. A course entitled 'Practicing Philosophy', however, puts students in a very different posture with regard to the material and their own work. This is less a course *about* philosophy and more an experience *of* or an engagement *in* philosophy. By the end of the course, there are still major figures and significant movements within philosophy that have been the subject of some attention, but the course is assessed less in terms of what content it covered and more in terms of what effect it has had on the students and their critical capacities for practicing philosophy—and, note, not as philosophy majors but as self-reflective human beings. I make a similar move in my own course design as I think about the contribution that an introductory Bible course at a church-related college can make—a contribution not primarily to the discipline of biblical studies nor primarily to the wider Christian church (or other religious community) but primarily to the human development of the students who take the course.

My wrestling with these questions has resulted in several different versions of the course over the years I have taught it, as well as several stories of success

---

5. Andrea Leskes and Ross Miller, *Purposeful Pathways: Helping Students Achieve Key Learning Outcomes* (Washington, DC: Association of American Colleges and Universities, 2006), pp. 17-25. Leskes and Miller develop the notions of integrative learning, inquiry learning, global learning, and civic learning.

and failure on one or more of these fronts. My engagement with these questions also led me to a sabbatical project, undertaken with the support of a grant from the Wabash Center for Teaching and Learning in Theology and Religion during the 2007–2008 academic year. My thoughts here are informed by that project and by my own engagement with these issues in my particular context. The common theme that runs through my reflections is the issue of authority. In my view, critical thinkers, creative problem-solvers, and responsible global citizens are people who have a sense of their own personal agency, who can think for themselves, and who can negotiate the competing demands of authority in their lives, in part by the exercise of their own sense of authority. Let me explain what I mean by taking up, in turn, authority as a developmental issue, as an educational issue, and as a religious issue.

Authority as a Developmental Issue

I have been helped in my thinking about issues of human development by the work of Sharon Daloz Parks. She argues that developmental theories would benefit from a more differentiated structure, one that recognizes not just childhood, adolescence, and adulthood but also a distinct post-adolescent stage she terms 'young adulthood'.[6] In her book *Big Questions, Worthy Dreams: Mentoring Young Adults in Their Search for Meaning, Purpose, and Faith*, she has a rich and nuanced discussion of the distinctive issues of this emerging adulthood. She structures her presentation around not only cognition (forms of knowing) but also feelings (forms of dependence) as well as relationships (forms of community).[7]

Parks describes a developmentally-early form of knowing as 'authority-bound', by which she means a dependence for knowledge upon an authority outside the self.[8] College teachers find this demonstrated frequently as students appeal to what they have heard, or what the textbook says, or what some authority figure has told them. One does not need to press very hard on such assertions before they are recognized as being grounded in nothing more substantial than the fact that someone or something said so. In other words, this kind of 'authority-bound' repetition of someone else's conclusion does not represent knowledge in any significant or personally-relevant way.[9] Parks observes that 'the transformation that can occur (and of which higher education at its best has been a primary sponsor) is a movement from this unexamined, uncritical form of certainty to another form of knowing'.[10] That other

---

6. Sharon Daloz Parks, *Big Questions, Worthy Dreams: Mentoring Young Adults in Their Search for Meaning, Purpose, and Faith* (San Francisco: Jossey-Bass, 2000), esp. pp. 60-69.

7. Parks, *Big Questions*, pp. 53-103.

8. Parks, *Big Questions*, pp. 54-5.

9. Cf. the reflections on Plato's *Meno* in Donald L. Finkel, *Teaching with Your Mouth Shut* (Portsmouth, NH: Boynton/Cook Heinemann, 2000), pp. 34-37.

10. Parks, *Big Questions*, p. 56.

form of knowing involves critical inquiry, critical reading, critical thinking, and critical reflection.

A recent example from my own experience illustrates how this can play out in the classroom. I was encouraging the exercise of critical analysis on a position taken by our textbook author with regard to the date of the Priestly writer (one of the sources named in the standard Documentary Hypothesis as the composer of the Pentateuch). One of the students inquired about my own view on the matter. 'I'm interested to know what you think', he said. In this situation, I always wonder why: Why would a student want to know my position on any particular issue? One way to read such a request is that it seeks to establish an authority to which one can appeal (or, negatively, to which one can object; more than a few religiously-conservative students have often been warned against the hypotheses of critical biblical scholarship).

The positive developmental movement that Parks describes is the young adult work of inner-dependence and probing commitment. Rather than dependence upon an external authority (either positively or negatively), 'the developmental movement into inner-dependence occurs when one is able self-consciously to include the self within the arena of authority'.[11] 'There is greater trust in one's own experience and in one's own 'gut' or intuition. Again, this does not mean that sources of insight outside the self, or the claims of others for care, necessarily become irrelevant; it does mean, however, that the self can now take more conscious responsibility for adjudicating competing claims'.[12] Likewise, the notion of probing commitment differs from both the uncritical adoption of the position of an external authority as well as the 'unqualified relativism' of 'whatever'.[13] In probing commitment, there is instead a tentative exploration that pays attention to the 'fittingness to one's own experience of self and world'.[14] Considering authority as a developmental issue, then, I want to design educational experiences that help young adults rely less on authority-bound ways of knowing and encourage instead inner-dependence and probing commitment.

Authority as an Educational Issue

Considering authority as an educational issue, I try to emphasize the role of thinking in learning. Consider Paulo Freire's 'banking model' description of education, where students are passive recipients of deposits made by the teacher. I would argue, with Freire, that education 'consists in acts of cognition, not transferrals [sic] of information'.[15] 'Acts of cognition' is another way to say 'thinking'. When Parks writes about 'another form of knowing' (one

---

11. Parks, *Big Questions*, p. 77.
12. Parks, *Big Questions*, p. 78.
13. Parks, *Big Questions*, pp. 57-58.
14. Parks, *Big Questions*, p. 67.
15. Paulo Freire, *Pedagogy of the Oppressed* (New York: Continuum, 1970, 2000), p. 79.

that is not 'authority-bound') her voice resonates with Donald Finkel's. In a wonderful book called *Teaching With Your Mouth Shut*, Finkel points to an alternative to the appeal to authority, one that he calls 'a process of inquiry'.[16] Notice the connections between Finkel's educational concern and Parks' developmental concern. Finkel discusses a kind of genuine inquiry into the questions raised by our reading of texts (he does not limit his comments to the reading of biblical texts). Our pursuit is not for some predetermined response or settled conclusion. Instead, Finkel names a very different set of criteria for the kind of response we are pursuing. He writes of a response that is not validated by an outside authority but one that attends to the text as well as to our experience. 'If we arrive at a response that is faithful both to the text and to our own experience, then we will have learned something important from our study of [the text]. We will have deepened our grasp of the human world we inhabit. We will have taken a step in our education'.[17] Finkel's invocation of our own experience matches the developmental movement that Parks finds in the young adult work of inner-dependence and probing commitment, with its effort 'self-consciously to include the self within the arena of authority',[18] paying attention to the 'fittingness to one's own experience of self and world'.[19]

I encourage students—despite the formation many of them have received before they get to college—to think of learning not as being told something but as thinking through something. Consider again the example of the student's inquiry as to my view on the dating of the Priestly writer. As a teacher, I see this as an opportunity for thinking: 'Here is an issue we can think about together, this disputed dating of P. Others have thought about it, too, and some of them have pretty clear positions and fairly strong arguments, but this issue still confronts us—it has not been resolved or set aside.' Students, it seems to me, see it not as an issue with which they are being invited to engage but as a question for which some authority has long ago established an answer. I am looking for ways to foster and encourage a continuing conversation about the matter, while they are looking for the right answer. Notice that the function of the right answer is to close off—not open up—the conversation. If they were asking for my view so that it could contribute alongside theirs to a sustained dialogue about an unsettled issue, I would be more inclined to share my view. If they ask for my view so that it can substitute for their own thinking about the issue (instead of contribute to it), as a way to end the conversation by providing a settled resolution (rather than as a way to continue it), then I am not interested in enabling that approach. If students are inquiring about my views merely as another appeal to authority, then I will resist every time.

What I will do instead is try to make that move itself the subject of our critical thinking. I will try to make explicit what we are doing in the discussion—for

---

16. Finkel, *Teaching with Your Mouth Shut*, p. 36; see pp. 34-37.
17. Finkel, *Teaching with Your Mouth Shut*, p. 22.
18. Parks, *Big Questions*, p. 77.
19. Parks, *Big Questions*, p. 67.

example, asking what the professor thinks—and encourage reflection on that. Why is there interest in what the professor thinks; how would that contribute to our thinking? Student response to this is mixed. For some, it is simply baffling. For others, it seems positively wasteful to spend time evading the question (and thereby not teaching), getting behind in our coverage of content, and generally messing with students and their learning (one must be prepared to field some very strongly-felt complaints in this regard).[20] For still others, however, this is precisely the move that provides them an opportunity for growth and development, for insightful discovery and liberating self-reflection. They do not necessarily come to any new knowledge about the dating of the Priestly writer or any other content issue, but they come to transformative new knowledge about themselves as learners and as humans. That is a trade-off, at the cost of some content coverage, that I am willing to make every time. Especially when you consider that my course is a one-time introductory course for non-majors, that gives me all the more freedom to be concerned less with the teaching of content and more with the education of students. Indeed, this is precisely how I make sense of that old adage about not teaching the material but teaching the students.

Authority as a Religious Issue

The developmental movement away from the appeal to authority, and the way I work with it in my courses, applies in any course, not just a biblical studies course. Starting as I did with an insight about human development—the notion of an 'authority-bound' way of knowing—sets the grounds of the conversation quite broadly. On the one hand, that is not a problem. The broad educational objectives of critical thinking, creative problem-solving, and responsible global citizenship are issues that are of concern across the whole of the university, in every discipline. Additionally, many of the courses I teach—and those that were the focus of my sabbatical study project—are offered to (or required of) liberal arts students generally, not biblical or religious studies majors in particular. Specifically because these courses are required for non-majors, I as a teacher can think of their significance less with reference to the discipline or professional society to which I belong and more with reference to the educational significance of these courses in the human development of students. Engagement with biblical material thus becomes the occasion for critical reflection on ourselves as critical thinkers, creative problem-solvers, and responsible global citizens.

On the other hand, there are ways in which the fact that the subject matter of my courses is biblical material does affect my teaching, particularly at a church-related college. For example, I try to provide opportunities for students to encounter the primary material—the biblical text itself—rather than just

---

20. Cf. Parker J. Palmer, *To Know As We Are Known* (San Francisco: Harper, 1983, 1993), p. 39.

what people say about the text. Because the expectations about the Bible that students bring with them tend to have little connection to the actual contents of the text, this encounter itself will raise for many students the issue of authority and the problem of simply appealing to authority as a form of knowing. This issue can arise, for perceptive students, when they read a biblical passage that does not seem to fit what they thought they already knew about the biblical text or about the Bible in general and its claims. That lack of easy fit between the two can be the very thing that brings to consciousness for the first time the assumptions that students bring to the text. Once they see their assumptions, or become aware of them, then they can reflect on where their knowledge originated (because it clearly has not come from this particular text, at least). I find that students can name the sources of their knowledge about biblical material—usually their parents and family, as well as their church, including its leaders (pastor, youth minister) and activities (Bible study, Sunday School). I do not often find, however, that students are very aware of the implications of the fact that these various figures are their sources for information about the Bible. Students do not often recognize how strongly their ideas have been influenced by these figures until an occasion such as this wherein their own reading of the biblical text does not square with what they had always taken to be the case. Even if they had been aware of other authority figures who take different views and hold different positions, that kind of dissonance could always be dismissed by naming one authority right and the other wrong. But now, when a student is reading the primary material—the biblical text—itself, and it does not square with what they have always taken to be the case, they encounter a dissonance that is not so easy to resolve. Many have been so firmly trained to revere the authority of the Bible that they are loath to dismiss it as wrong in this case, but they have an equally strong loyalty to their parents, pastors, or others with whose views the biblical text now seems to conflict.

This leads to what is perhaps the most significant dynamic that shapes the context in which I teach biblical studies. Namely, my pedagogical and developmental concern to move away from the appeal to authority as a form of knowing runs directly counter to the accepted exercise of authority in many of the religious traditions from which my students come. It is an arrangement I describe with the declarative phrase, 'Truth is received from Authorities', and it can unfortunately work against both developmental and educational objectives. It can be detrimental to the kind of development Parks discusses because it reinforces the notion that knowledge is established by an appeal to authority. It can be detrimental to the educational notion of active learning because it puts religious people in the position of passive receivers.

Barbara Brown Taylor observes the same phenomenon when she writes in an insightful one-page column in *Christian Century* that her students' 'knowledge of what is in [the Bible] comes from their parents, their preachers and their Bible study leaders, as well as from movies such as *Left Behind*. There is no one thing that can be said about all of these interpreters, except that they all have more power than the text'.[21] The students I work with assume that the truth they have received from these various authorities (to use the terms of my descriptive phrase) was in turn derived from the biblical text, as a kind of ultimate authority, but they cannot personally vouch for that, and they certainly have no sense about how these authorities may have derived these truths from the Bible.

Teaching the Students

If Parks is right about the developmental issues, then this involves more than just texts and authorities; indeed, these issues have to do with people themselves, with 'a person's sense of self'.[22] So one of the things I am aware of working on in my course—though it is not explicitly listed as a goal or objective—is encouraging students to make decisions which are not dependent solely upon or validated by external authority. Instead, I foster a move towards what Parks calls 'inner-dependence'.[23] A prerequisite to making decisions in a self-conscious way, however, is that students need to recognize that they are, in fact, making decisions. That may sound silly; of course students are making decisions—they are living on their own for the first time, and they are deciding everything from how to spend their money, to how to dress, to what and when to eat. But I am not sure how self-reflective students are about any of these decisions, and their language often provides a revealing indication. For example, we have a twice-weekly, required, all-campus chapel/convocation session that meets at 10:00 a.m., directly after one of my class sessions. A student recently came up to me as class was beginning (at 9:00 a.m.) and told me that she was participating with a musical group in chapel. She reported that they wanted her there at 9:15, so she asked if she could leave at 9:10. Note the way in which her language did not reflect any personal responsibility or agency. She did not say, 'I decided to join this musical group', or 'I want to participate in this chapel session'. She said 'they' want her there at a certain time and she phrased a question, 'So can I leave?' Rhetorically, she is left in a position of asking permission. Whether the authority figure in question (here, the teacher) says yes or no is irrelevant to the structural fact that her decision is being made with reference to—and justified or validated or negated by—an external authority. She apparently does not even recognize it as a decision—that she is a free moral agent acting to shape her own future. The rhetorical shaping is in very passive terms, as if these events are just happening to her.

What I prefer and believe is educationally valuable in a case like this, is to play a different role from the one her question asks me to play. I would like to help her make her own decision. I can help her recognize and think through

---

21. Barbara Brown Taylor, 'Caution: Bible Class in Session', *Christian Century* (Nov 6-19, 2002), p. 39.
22. Parks, *Big Questions*, p. 74.
23. Parks, *Big Questions*, pp. 77-80.

the consequences of her decision by asking her questions (which also serves to model a set of questions she can ask of herself when faced with decisions like this). What will happen if you are late to the musical warm-up, or if you do not show up at all? What will happen if you leave class early, or miss it entirely? By asking questions, rather than telling her what to do, I put her in a position to take responsibility for her own decisions, or more modestly, to become aware that she does make her own decisions and acts as a free moral agent in shaping the events of her life.

Another example demonstrates what a developmental challenge this is, however, particularly if students come from educational environments that have reinforced a passive dependence upon external authorities. My attendance policy ties absences to the roll call—if students miss the roll they are counted absent, even if they show up later in the class session. One day a student came into class as I was calling the final names on the roster. She realized that she had missed her name and would therefore be counted absent for that day, even though she was now present in the room. She collected her things and began walking toward the door. I got her attention and tried to be strictly descriptive about the situation. I pointed out that she was making a decision. I confirmed that she would not receive attendance credit for the day, but I considered the possibility that her learning—and our learning in the class—might still benefit from her participation in the class session, and I reiterated that this was her decision. As I returned to the lectern, she did not leave but returned to her seat. As the class session ended and people were departing, she came to me and said, 'Thanks for making me stay'. Notice again the language. Even when something positive happens (in this case, she stayed in class, helping to contribute to a good learning experience), students can have trouble recognizing or claiming their own role in the event. I tried to impress upon her that she decided to stay, and I celebrated with her that she had found it to be a good decision, but I resisted her effort to reflect on the event as something that had been imposed on her by an authority. Instead, it was an experience in which she could become aware of herself as an active learner, as a participant in critical thinking, creative problem-solving, and responsible global citizenship.

These are issues that can occur in any college course, but these issues are particularly significant for a course on the Bible. They are important because, positively, I want students to recognize their own decision-making role in the work of biblical interpretation.[24] 'A new ideal of scholarly integrity and responsibility that replaces claims of unbiased objectivity with a conscientious effort to acknowledge and claim one's social location, to make one's personal as well as intellectual presuppositions conscious and explicit, and to keep one's work

---

24. See Dale B. Martin, *Pedagogy of the Bible: An Analysis and Proposal* (Louisville, KY: Westminster John Knox, 2008), pp. 29-45.

in constant dialogue with the disadvantaged is gaining ground in the academy'.[25] Indeed, not only in biblical studies but across the university, scholars are aware of and increasingly sensitive to the significant role played by readers and researchers in the construction of meaning. If students are to be self-aware and critically reflective about their interpretive decisions, they need also (perhaps first?) to be self-aware and critically reflective about themselves as active decision makers in their lives and constructors of meaning in their world. These issues are also important because, negatively, religious discourse about the Bible often mystifies our human decision-making role. Uncritical appeals to self-evident truth received from authorities can encourage the kind of passivity that proves to be educationally and developmentally detrimental.

Another way to think of this is that I, as the teacher, never want to do for students something they should be doing for themselves. Consider the issue of plagiarism. Plagiarism is an example of not doing for yourself something you can and should do for yourself. In this case, what you should be doing for yourself is thinking—thinking through issues, making observations, weighing evidence, considering implications. Plagiarism makes sense only if what really matters is the answer rather than one's own engagement with the material, one's effort to think through these issues, to synthesize, evaluate, decide, apply, and so on, for oneself. If you are a runner, you do not get faster by watching someone else run, but only by running yourself, because it is by running that you improve, not by recording times in a log book. At one level, plagiarism is the mistake of supposing that you can substitute what someone else has done for what you should be doing yourself. If I, as a teacher, do not want to encourage that with regard to plagiarism, why would I encourage it anywhere else? Therefore, when student questions put me in a position of doing for them what they should be doing for themselves, my response is an effort to deconstruct that assumed structure, to reframe and engage in a very different scenario. I pose questions of my own, hopefully drawing attention to this as the student's decision and offering a set of issues to consider. I want to help a student think through a decision—just as I want to help students think through interpretive issues in biblical studies—but I want to resist making that decision for the student.

Here again, the responses I see from students include befuddlement, frustration, confusion, anger, and resistance in addition to positive experiences, which may be delayed (sometimes for years, according to notes and letters I have received from former students). The pedagogical question for me then becomes: How can I work to manage the amount of dissonance and 'disequilibrium'[26] so that it is educationally and developmentally positive and helpful rather than detrimental? Where is that point—and it is probably different for each student—where the challenge students face is no longer formative

---

25. Sandra M. Schneiders, *The Revelatory Text: Interpreting the New Testament as Sacred Scripture* (Collegeville, MN: Liturgical, 2nd edn, 1999), p. 121.

26. Finkel's term; see *Teaching with Your Mouth Shut*, pp. 53-54.

but becomes deformative, where it no longer helps open up students' experience of learning and discovery but instead results in their closing down and disengaging?

Conclusion

I have discovered, developed, and picked up from colleagues and others along the way, a number of particular things that shape my practice in the classroom, but I have not detailed those here. Instead, I have focused on the larger conceptual framework within which any of those particular teaching practices makes sense. I have named the pedagogical criteria I use to make decisions about how and why and what I teach in a required introductory Bible course for non-majors. The notion of authority has helped structure my reflections when I consider it as a developmental issue, an educational issue, and—especially in my particular context—a religious issue.

Let me share a scenario that illustrates my vision for how I would like the introductory Bible course I teach to be able to help people in the rest of their lives—and it envisions these particular people in a religious setting. Philip Gulley and James Mulholland caused no small stir with their publication of a book advocating the theological concept of universal salvation.[27] They followed it with another volume, exploring the depth and breadth of God's grace.[28] Quite apart from theological issues, I want to draw attention to what I believe to be a fairly common scenario they describe (with a composite singular voice) in the opening of their second book. The author writes of being fired from his pastorate in a church. Later, he is hired by another church, despite his avowal of the same beliefs for which he was fired from the first church. Gulley and Mulholland go on to draw their own conclusion from this sequence of events, but the moment that captures my attention is the conversation during which the pastor is fired from the first church. He is summoned to a meeting with the church elders.

> 'This is an awkward matter', the head elder said, 'but I'm afraid we're going to have to let you go.'
> I asked if I had done something wrong.
> 'There have been concerns raised that you don't believe in Satan and hell', he said.
> 'That's right', I said. Then, eager to display my theological prowess, I asked if they wanted to know why.
> They declined my offer to enlighten them.[29]

---

27. Philip Gulley and James Mulholland, *If Grace Is True: Why God Will Save Every Person* (New York: HarperCollins, 2003).

28. Gulley and Mulholland, *If God Is Love: Rediscovering Grace in an Ungracious World* (San Francisco: Harper San Francisco, 2004).

29. Gulley and Mulholland, *If God Is Love*, pp. 3-4.

That is the point at which I am concerned as an educator. Regardless of where I stand on the theological issue, I am a staunch supporter of reasoned argument and self-reflective understanding of our own views and positions. Not only do I want potential future pastors to work in my course on the ability to articulate their own understanding of their position, so that in a moment like that envisioned in this scenario they will be able to offer reasons why they think and act the way they do, but I want potential future church elders and board members not only to be able to articulate their own views but also to be interested in and able to engage with arguments made by others. Why was this not an opportunity for a potentially fruitful dialogue between a pastor and his concerned parishioners? Rather than opening up a conversation, the circumstances appear to have become an occasion for the exercise of power and the tying of truth to authority, without engaged, critical reflection. To make a more positive and constructive alternative possible is the difference I want an introductory Bible course to make in a student's life.

SERVICE-LEARNING IN THE UNDERGRADUATE BIBLICAL STUDIES CLASSROOM[1]

Janet S. Everhart
Simpson College

Many liberal arts colleges now offer service-learning as an option or requirement in some courses; a 2008 study revealed that 44% of first year students and 53% of senior students in private US institutions of higher education had participated in service-learning. Research sponsored by the Association of American Colleges and Universities (AAC&U) suggests that service-learning is a 'high-impact educational practice' with 'positive educational results for students'.[2] Service-learning helps prepare students for the workforce, increases the likelihood they will remain in college, and encourages them to 'give back' to the community. A longitudinal study involving over 22,000 undergraduates during the 1990s revealed significant positive results in eleven areas, including academic performance, commitment to post-graduate service, leadership, values (commitment to activism and to promoting racial understanding), and choice of a service career.[3] In light of growing evidence that service-learning can be mutually beneficial for students, communities, and workforce productivity, those who teach biblical studies in undergraduate liberal arts institutions may find multiple motivations to implement this pedagogy. While educators on a wide variety of campuses recognize service-learning as a valuable pedagogy, research on service-learning in biblical studies classes is limited. This paper briefly explores the possibilities and challenges of incorporating service-learning into undergraduate biblical studies courses and suggests directions for future research as we implement and assess service-learning in our discipline.

---

1. I presented a version of this paper at the 2006 Society of Biblical Literature meeting. I am indebted to colleagues for useful questions and feedback. Bobby Nalean, Leadership Coordinator at Simpson College, offered valuable comments on a draft.

2. *The LEAP Vision for Learning: Outcomes, Practices, Impact, and Employers' Views.* (Washington, DC: American Association of Colleges and Universities, 2011), p. 15.

3. Alexander W. Astin, *et al., How Service Learning Affects Students* (Los Angeles: Higher Education Research Institute, 2000), p. ii. For a brief summary of two decades of studies on the impact of service-learning on college students, see Scott Seider, 'Deepening College Students' Engagement with Religion and Theology Through Community Service Learning', *Teaching Theology and Religion* 14.3 (July 2011), pp. 205-25 (207-208).

What Is Service-Learning?

The working definition of service-learning developed by Campus Compact (an organization of more than 1100 college and university presidents) guides the reflections in this paper: 'Service-learning is an educational methodology which combines community service with explicit academic learning objectives, preparation for community work, and deliberate reflection.'[4] Most educators agree that service-learning is **not** synonymous with community service, and that students should not receive credit for service performed. Rather, in the service-learning context, clients, volunteers, and paid staff at the service site become teachers; the student is not simply performing a needed function as a volunteer but is actively learning from multiple participants at the site. Service-learning may involve multiple goals, such as enhancing the student's grasp of disciplinary content, contributing to the well-being of a community, strengthening the relationship between community and campus, and encouraging students to develop a life-long practice of civic engagement. To be effective, the service-learning must involve service that is genuinely beneficial to the community agency and/or clients being served, and must also enhance student learning vis-à-vis the goals of the particular course.

Faculty Motivations for Service-Learning in the Biblical Studies Setting

To date only limited data is available on service-learning in a religious studies context, let alone the more specific biblical studies environment.[5] In 2002, Fred Glennon reported on a survey of professors of religion from thirty-one institutions (67% church-related, 10% 'other private', and 23% public). To assess how faculty working with service-learning employed the pedagogy, he sought

---

4. Gelman *et al.*, 'Assessing Service-Learning and Community Engagement', Campus Compact, 2001, V. For other similar definitions, see, for instance, the chapter on service-learning in Jayne E. Brownell and Lynn E. Swaner, *Five High-Impact Practices: Research on Learning Outcomes, Completion, and Quality.* (LEAP; Washington, DC: Association of American Colleges of Universities, 2010), pp. 23-29. See also the Council for the Advancement of Standards in Higher Education (CAS) Professional Standards for Higher Education: 'Service-learning is a form of experiential education in which students engage in activities that address human and community needs together with structured opportunities intentionally designed to promote student learning and development', in L. Dean (ed.), *CAS professional standards for higher education* (Washington, DC: Council for the Advancement of Standards in Higher Education, 7th edn). For more information on Campus Compact and the organization's considerable resources for service-learning, see www.compact.org. For discussion of the distinction between 'critical service-learning' that includes a social justice component, and 'traditional service-learning' with a charity focus, see Tania D. Mitchell, 'Traditional vs. Critical Service-Learning: Engaging the Literature to Differentiate Two Models', *Michigan Journal of Community Service Learning* (Spring 2008), pp. 50-65.

5. A recent study of service-learning at Ignatius University is an important addition to the small body of empirical data available on service-learning in a religious studies context; see Scott Seider, 'Deepening College Students' Engagement'. See also *Religious Studies News* 'Spotlight on Teaching' (November 2011), with articles on service-learning related to Religion and Ecology.

to answer these questions: 'Is service-learning an appropriate pedagogical tool for those interested in the science of religion who seek to bracket out questions of values and norms in the interest of knowledge for knowledge's sake?.... Or is service-learning best employed by those who see religion as a phenomenon that has the potential to change lives?'[6] Glennon's limited survey of thirty faculty members showed that professors who use service-learning in religious studies courses have educational goals **and** that most also have normative goals, wanting to promote change in student values or perspectives on social issues, encourage citizenship, and effect social change.[7] In Glennon's survey, the desire of faculty members to promote change was remarkably consistent across institution types, suggesting that the majority of professors who integrate service-learning into an academic course are interested in the connection between education and behavioral transformation.[8] In the liberal arts setting, biblical studies faculty members can think about the connection between service-learning and the stated goals of the institution, and may find a strong institutional warrant for experimenting with this pedagogy.

Many faculty members have raised good questions about the value of service-learning and how to assess its impact. When I presented an earlier version of this paper at the Society of Biblical Literature (SBL) meeting in 2006, one listener raised a concern that others have pondered: since students often lack critical thinking and other basic academic skills, does adding service-learning detract from other important goals of the course? Michael Homan raised a similar question in his 2009 article in the SBL Forum: 'Critics often observe that while they clearly see evidence of the "service component", the "learning" is all too frequently absent.'[9] Homan reports that after Saturday outings with biblical studies students to work on Habitat for Humanity homes, he realized that the interaction with the students was beneficial, but 'this experience did not increase their ability to think critically about the Bible.'[10] A creative solution was to have each student develop an individual service-learning project that linked both to the biblical studies course and the student's major. Homan reports after 534 projects over five years, he is convinced that 'students are able to articulate the challenges biblical authors had in trying to improve their own worlds and how

---

6. Fred Glennon, 'Service-Learning and the Dilemma of Religious Studies: Descriptive or Normative?' in *From Cloister to Commons: Concepts and Models for Service-Learning in Religious Studies.* (Washington, DC: American Association for Higher Education Series on Service-Learning, 2002), pp. 9-24, here 16. See also Joseph A. Favazza and Fred Glennon, 'Service Learning and Religious Studies: Propaganda or Pedagogy', *Bulletin* 29.4 (2000), pp. 105-107.

7. Glennon, 'Service-Learning', p. 18

8. 83% of respondents from public institutions reported normative goals, compared to 85% from church-related institutions and 100% from other private institutions.

9. Michael Homan, 'Service Learning, Biblical Studies, and Resurrecting Flooded Bones in New Orleans', (Society of Biblical Literature Forum, 2009), www.sbl-site.org/publications/article/aspx?articleId=822.

10. Homan, 'Service- Learning'.

this course pertains to their major.'[11] Questions about the efficacy of service-learning in achieving course goals are important, and are related to conversations about the goals of liberal learning in general. As many liberal arts colleges revise our curricula to meet the needs of students in a global environment, and quite frankly as we develop curricula that allow us to compete for students in a climate of growing demand to link college coursework to marketable skills, we may discover that service-learning courses provide a link between biblical studies course content and 'the real world'.[12] Fortunately, a growing body of resources can help faculty members develop and assess appropriate service-learning courses.[13] Hopefully the next decade will see increased data collection and analysis from service-learning courses linked to biblical studies.

Some Examples from Simpson College: Possibilities and Questions

During the past seven years, I've offered a service-learning option in twelve introductory Bible classes (both Intro to Hebrew Bible and Intro to New Testament) and in two sections of 'Feminist Interpretation of the Bible'. I have never required service-learning, though as our college inaugurates a new Engaged Citizenship Curriculum (starting with the incoming class of Fall 2011), I may experiment with a service-learning requirement in one introductory Bible course each year.[14] In the introductory classes, service-learning replaces one of five short papers and the final exam, with the percentage of the grade assigned to service-learning split about 30-70 between a service-learning journal and the service-learning paper. Students log 10-12 hours at a designated service site, keep a journal using specific journal guidelines, and write a 4-6 page paper on a text chosen in consultation

---

11. Homan, 'Service-Learning'.

12. For a provocative discussion of unexpected conclusions she came to when incorporating service-learning into a course on 'Religion in America', see Carol Harris-Shapiro, 'Service Learning and Religious Studies: An Awkward Fit?' *Bulletin/CSSR* 31.2 (2002), pp. 35-39.

13. One useful tool appears in Thomas McGowan, 'Assessment-Based Approaches to Service-Learning Course Design', in *From Cloister to Commons*, pp. 88-96. Other articles in the same volume offer syllabi and practical suggestions for designing an effective service-learning course in religious studies. The article by Bradley Dudley, '"The History and Religion of Ancient Israel"': An Introductory Course to the Hebrew Bible' focuses specifically on a biblical studies course; see pp. 169-82. See also Alicia Batten, 'Studying the Historical Jesus through Service', *Teaching Theology and Religion* 8.2 (2005), pp. 107-13.

14. I do teach a May Term interdisciplinary service-learning course that involves a week of campus preparation (reading, discussion, and team building) followed by a week of service in inner-city Denver and five days of mountain reflection experience in the Rockies. This three week course, 'Call of Service', was developed with the help of funds from Simpson's Lilly-funded PTEV (Programs for the Theological Exploration of Vocation) grant, and has become a popular and self-supporting catalog course. Experiences with the Call of Service course prompted me to develop a service-learning option in my introductory biblical studies courses. The Call of Service course seems to satisfy what Carol Harris-Shapiro identifies as students' desire for a 'combination of useful information and values and analysis in a productive synergy that could rightly be called knowledge, truth, or wisdom'. See Harris-Shapiro, 'Service Learning and Religious Studies', p. 38.

with me. The journal prompts are designed to help students prepare to write their final paper. Students receive no credit for the service itself; I emphasize that the service constitutes an additional 'text' for the course.[15] Students must tell me by the fourth week of the semester whether they plan to pursue the service-learning option. They can opt back into the last paper and the final, and so far almost half of the students who state their intention to pursue service-learning don't complete it due to transportation issues and time constraints.

After the first few semesters of allowing students great latitude in selecting a service site, I now require students in the introductory courses to serve at one of two designated sites in Des Moines, about 15 miles from our campus. The chosen sites are ones that welcome many Simpson students as volunteers, and sites where I have on-going relationships with the executive directors. Transportation is available from Simpson to one of the service sites three times each week. The site directors sometimes guest lecture in my classes, and routinely conduct a reflection meeting with the students on campus toward the end of the semester. The chance for students to interact with the directors and other staff members has been a great benefit both to the site staff, as they gain a better understanding of the needs of student volunteers, and to the students, who learn a great deal from talking with adults who are passionately committed to social justice and who read the Bible both carefully and critically. In the Feminist Interpretation of the Bible class, the service sites have varied from agencies that advocate for battered women to a refugee resettlement project focused on the needs of Iraqi girls and women. I require the students in this class to work with an agency that addresses the needs of women.

Assessment of student-learning has included pre- and post-service surveys, focus group conversations with students after the service is complete, conversations with the agency site directors after the reflection meetings, and assessment that the students provide in their papers and journals as well as occasionally in course evaluations. Without exception, every one of my students who has completed the service-learning option reports that the experience offered them a significant new lens for reading and interpreting biblical texts. One student in the Introductory Hebrew Bible course wrote in her paper that she hoped this option would always be available; she said that the experience of working with children at Shalom Zone Ministries in Des Moines and then writing her paper on Hagar as a single mother opened her eyes to new connections between biblical texts and various communities.[16] She also wondered why, in the Bible studies offered at Shalom Zone, the story of Sarah was told but never the story of Hagar. She

---

15. The idea of the service site as a text or a lens has been used by numerous colleges. See, for instance, Alicia Batten, 'Studying the Historical Jesus through Service', *Teaching Theology and Religion* 8.2 (2005), pp. 107-13 (111). See also Scott Seider, 'Deepening College Student Engagement', p. 200.

16. Student quotes from reflection groups, journals, or papers are used with their permission. Shalom Zone Ministries was a United Methodist-based after-school program in one of the poorest neighborhoods in Des Moines.

suspected that the young women of Shalom Zone would relate more readily to Hagar. Students in the Feminist Interpretation of the Bible class commented that they appreciated the chance to give back to the community; one student wrote that she would not have imagined the situation of the people she worked with in the same way without the class structure and content. Another student reported in our reflection meeting, 'I got to look through three different lenses', as she reflected on class conversations, our secondary texts, and conversations with the clients at her service site. Another said, 'This is the first class I've taken that has allowed me to go into the community to see what I can find. The connection between class and service meant that I got more out of the class and more out of my service.'

In several cases, because the service involved interacting with older adults in a retirement community, students actually read and discussed biblical texts with the people they were working with. One student wrote,

> Today I met LaJeune...she was born in China to two missionary parents; they had to flee China when civil war broke out...We talked about Ruth and that as she went with Naomi she became the foreigner. She left all that was comfortable to stay with Naomi. Why did she feel this was necessary? Did she not want to go back to her family or was she truly making a sacrifice to stay with and care for Naomi?

A later entry from the same student reported,

> I met Bryce today. We dove right in and talked about the text. He has an interesting view of Naomi and Ruth and believes that both were bold, conniving, and somewhat bawdy. It's interesting because as a female when I read the story I can see that but usually I see Naomi doing what had to be done...

And finally, 'Mary gave me many different things to consider and a lot of the way she looks at the text comes from her experiences as a single mom. She never remarried and she has loved her life.' This student recognized the deep loneliness of one widow she was visiting, and invited that woman to join her for Sunday brunch at the college. Aware that the woman's funds were quite limited, Jessica paid for lunch and drove her new friend to and from her retirement home. She remarked in her final journal entry that spending time with older women had really helped fill a void she felt being far away from her grandmother.

A student who wrote her final paper on Hagar (Genesis 16 and 21) offered this reflection:

> Ruby and I looked at Hagar's story and we got some interesting ideas from reading it together. Ruby said she was surprised she had never identified with Hagar before, because they were both sent from the comfort of a house to fend for themselves. I was surprised to hear that she found comfort in this story, because I always saw Hagar's story as somewhat negative toward women. However, Ruby said that she felt solace seeing another woman go through similar issues...I never paid attention to the end of the story of Hagar, but Ruby picked right up on it. She liked how

> Hagar was able to go on with her life and survive on her own with her son, because she feels that this is what she did.

This student suggested to Ruby that Ruby's own protection and care of her daughter was similar to Hagar's care for Ishmael. Reading and interpreting biblical texts in conversation with another adult helps students recognize how one's own social location and experiences influence how the text is received. Further, in the case of the two students quoted above, the experience of joint reading gave the student an opportunity to both receive and give useful feedback in the context of reading a biblical story in light of contemporary experience. Both students experienced the satisfaction of affirming an older adult while learning to consider new reading strategies for the text. Clearly, service experiences can help students learn firsthand the significance of social location for reading. This realization, in and of itself, is an important learning goal in my introductory classes.

Links with the Discipline: Three Possibilities

The discipline of biblical studies, particularly in the liberal arts setting, lends itself to exploring some concepts that may provide a particularly good fit with a service-learning setting. Below I cite only three of many possibilities.

A. 'The Other'

Working with the concept of 'the other', a major theme in the Bible (particularly the Hebrew Bible) can be especially fruitful in a service-learning course. As Pippin, Patterson and Bounds discuss in their article 'On En/Countering the Other', service-learning as a pedagogy brings issues of 'the other' to the forefront. For one thing, service-learning itself is side-lined in some institutions where colleagues resist the pedagogy, often because it rejects the faculty-centered model still prevalent in some higher education settings.[17] Additionally, in many service settings, students experience their own 'otherness' for the first time, particularly if they find themselves in a minority group compared to the clients who are their teachers at the service site. Since many biblical texts present the concept of 'otherness' in relation to people or practices in contrast to 'Israel', students can experience firsthand the complications of establishing one's identity in relation to difference. Reflecting on this experience through conversation, journals, and course papers can help students identify how biblical texts both construe and challenge identity based on difference.

B. Identity Formation

In an introductory Hebrew Bible course, Bradley Dudley identified a specific learning objective well-suited to a service-learning course: critical thinking with regard to the formation of Israel's society and its response to issues of social

---

17. Elizabeth Bounds, Barbara Patterson, Tina Pippin, 'En/Countering the Other', in *From Cloister to Commons*, pp. 55-68.

oppression.[18] Since the Hebrew Bible frequently addresses issues of hunger, poverty, foreignness, etc., exposing students to these realities in our own communities while they are working their way through biblical material provides a link between contemporary life and the text. Rather than asking the simplistic (and flawed) question, 'What does the Bible say about (immigration, poverty, etc.)', faculty helping students reflect on service-learning can encourage the broader questions: 'How do the writers/compilers of the Bible conceptualize community/national identity and how might those conceptions help us think about these issues today?'

C. Environmental Justice

Another timely and potentially fruitful avenue to explore in a biblical studies service-learning course involves environmental justice. Recent work in the area of biblical hermeneutics and the environment ranges from the Earth Bible project whose participants highlight the subjectivity of the Earth to those who uphold the more traditional focus on human agency but with an eye toward human responsibility vis-à-vis the non-human creation.[19] Since many liberal arts colleges are involved in 'green initiatives', LEED-certified building projects, recycling, local food production, and generally caring for the environment, opportunities for student participation in environmental projects abound.[20] Thinking about a biblical mandate for environmental care, or even exploring the biblical tension concerning the relationship between human and non-human aspects of the created order, could connect well with a service-learning project.

Campus and Community-Partner Benefits

Beyond the specific goals of a given biblical studies course, service-learning experiences offer potential benefits for an entire campus and community. Relationships between students, faculty and staff, and community partners can be enhanced and strengthened through a service-learning experience. Agency staff

---

18. Bradley Dudley, '"The History of Ancient Israel": An Introductory Course to the Hebrew Bible', in *From Cloister to Commons*, pp. 169-82.

19. For bibliographic material on biblical hermeneutics and the environment see, for instance, David G. Horrell, *et al., Greening Paul: Reading the Apostle Paul in a Time of Ecological Crisis* (Waco, Texas: Baylor University Press, 2010); Sallie McFague, *A New Climate for Theology: God, the World, and Global Warming* (Minneapolis: Fortress, 2008); Norman Habel, and Peter Rudinger (eds.), *Exploring Ecological Hermeneutics* (Atlanta: Society of Biblical Literature, 2008); there is a rapidly growing body of literature to support coursework on the environment and the Bible.

20. For a description of environmental efforts at one liberal arts college, in the context of religious studies, see James B. Martin-Schramm, *Climate Justice: Ethics, Energy, and Public Policy* (Minneapolis: Fortress, 2010). The last chapter of the book, 'Climate Justice Applied: Greenhouse Gas Reduction Strategies at Luther College', details efforts at Luther to fulfill its participation in the American College and University Presidents' Climate Commitment; Luther has pledged to reduce its carbon footprint by 50%.

members, volunteers, and clients may come to campus for specific activities or events, establishing a kind of two-way street between the agency and the campus. Recently after a reflection meeting with service-learning students on campus, an agency staff member contacted me to explore the possibility of bringing elementary children from her agency to Simpson for the purpose of implementing a service project. I put the staff member in touch with our grounds supervisor so the two of them could work out a time for children to come and help with a planting project. The staff member wanted the children to 'give back' to Simpson since Simpson students regularly volunteer at the agency; another benefit of the project is that elementary-aged children will have the experience of being on a college campus. Hopefully Simpson students will interact with the children during their time on campus to further strengthen the on-going relationship between the communities.

Inviting agency staff to participate in the classroom (as guest lecturers, on a panel, etc.) can be useful in helping students connect their service with their classroom work. Two of the agency directors of sites where my biblical studies students regularly serve are ordained ministers who are passionate about social justice and connecting the biblical text to their daily work. Their presence in the classroom helps students connect what they are reading in the biblical text with the lives of community members. Likewise, when faculty members work alongside students at a service site we may begin to think in new ways about our own futures and about how our coursework might prepare and shape our contributions to the larger world.

The pedagogy of service-learning can mesh very well with the discipline of biblical studies, since the text and its interpretations should require students to grapple with big life questions. Charles Strain argues that religious studies faculty members could be leaders in our institutions as we implement a pedagogy that helps to strengthen and perhaps transform our institutional missions.[21] At the very least, we can claim a place at the table with a pedagogy that holds promise for our discipline, our communities, and our world. A rapidly growing body of literature, practical tools, and research now exists to assist in theorizing about and implementing service-learning. We need both to draw from and add to this corpus.

Challenges of Implementing Service-Learning

While service-learning offers many benefits, professors, students, and community partners must cope with challenges. Some campuses have a service-learning center to help with logistics such as transportation, identifying appropriate sites, and providing reflection tools.[22] If a faculty member must manage

---

21. Charles R. Strain, 'Creating the Engaged University: Service-Learning, Religious Studies, and Institutional Mission', in *From Cloister to Commons*, pp. 25-39.

22. One of the downsides of a 'center' for service-learning involves reinforcing the sense that service-learning is a special pedagogy not integrated into the life of the campus. See Tina Pippin,

all of the logistics related to a service-learning course, the time involved can feel prohibitive. Potential roadblocks can become useful learning experiences, however. For instance, one student experienced frustration early in her attempts to embark on her service-learning due to major staff changes at an agency. In the end, a phone call and follow-up letter from me to the new activities director paved the way for the project to continue. The student and I talked about her frustration, the process itself, and how her need to persist was part of the course learning. While complications like these can result in additional learning for persistent students, they also require extra time of both students and professors. On-going relationships with service sites not only reduce the time involved in implementing an effective service-learning course, but also provides greater benefit to the agencies involved.

Questions for Future Exploration

In 2006 at the SBL meeting, I expressed the hope that an edited volume on service-learning might emerge from the then-new section on Teaching the Bible in the Undergraduate Liberal Arts Context. The volume in which this article appears, while not focused on service-learning, is a valuable and needed resource for those who teach biblical studies in the liberal arts setting. I hope that those of us engaged in service-learning will find additional ways to share resources and to effectively assess service-learning pedagogy as we proceed. More reflection on the ethics of teaching that self-consciously seeks to form a particular kind of citizen would be useful as well. Without imposing particular dogmatic perspectives on our students, is it still reasonable to hope that service-learning in our discipline will result in increased commitment to service in our communities and the world? Limited research to date suggests that service-learning can help students engage 'the forms of ultimate transformation that we study without asking them to engage in an explicitly religious practice'.[23] Finally, in e-mail correspondence while I was editing this paper for the current volume, colleague Robert Duke, who directs service-learning at Azusa Pacific University, suggested that it would be helpful to reflect on how service-learning in biblical studies takes different shapes at different types of institutions.[24] Hopefully during the next few years, biblical scholars working with service-learning will investigate some of these areas to broaden our understanding of the pedagogy and to improve learning outcomes for our students.

Barbara Patterson, and Elizabeth Bounds' discussion of 'otherness' related to service-learning in 'On En/Countering the Other', *Cloister to Commons*, pp. 55-68.

23. Charles Strain, 'Creating the Engaged University', p. 34.

24. E-mail correspondence with Robert Duke, June 16, 2011. While time constraints did not allow me to investigate this question here, hopefully those of us engaged in service-learning will be able to explore this issue in the future. A number of recent papers at the SBL national meetings have explored service-learning.

The Bible and World Construction:
The Reality of Multiple Voices in Biblical Religion

J. Bradley Chance
William Jewell College

Carol Barker has spoken of the need for education to offer students 'the capacity to manage change and shape their own futures and that of human society consistent with enduring and shared values'.[1] Such a statement assumes an open future and openness, I believe, assumes choices. But these are to be choices rooted in 'enduring and shared values'. Among the enduring and shared values of our society, even if not universally shared, are pluralism and diversity. While many religious traditions embrace these values, many do not. Religions regularly assert a monopolistic claim on values, and such claims, rooted as they are in divine sanctions and commandments, can be resistant to values that differ from those of the religion in question. Certain expressions of religion minimize or disparage choices by insisting that one's only legitimate 'choice' is to do the will of God and, for many Christians—the dominant religious tradition in both our larger cultural context and the specific institutional context where I teach—God's will is clearly expressed in the Bible. 'The Bible says' is, for many, synonymous with 'God says' and one must simply yield to what God says. To choose to do otherwise is to choose to do the wrong thing.

My teaching context is William Jewell College, a liberal arts college that had, for most of its history, a formal relationship with the Missouri Baptist Convention, which shares a relationship with the Southern Baptist Convention. William Jewell is no longer a Missouri Baptist college in any formal sense. With this change, Jewell is becoming deliberately and intentionally a more diverse community. The President of the College speaks often about embracing 'the other', those who are different from us. The valuing of diversity permeates our programs of service-learning and leadership. It permeates our core curriculum. Changes of policy reflect this emerging priority: Jewell no longer discriminates in employment on the basis either of religion or sexual orientation, two forms of discrimination that the law allowed Jewell to practice as a church-affiliated

---

1. Carol Barker, 'Liberal Arts Education for a Global Society' (White paper for the Carnegie Corporation of New York; New York, 2000), pp. 1-14 (7).

institution and which Jewell did in fact practice, at least officially, until recently. Given a certain inertia and trajectory, we still attract a vast majority of students who have been reared within a Christian tradition, and many of those come from an Evangelical tradition.

The College's core curriculum, the context in which I teach the course discussed in this paper, strives to introduce students to diverse perspectives and world views. Courses in the core curriculum, where appropriate, are to contribute to expanding students' exposure to varying perspectives. One of the courses that I offer within the core curriculum is Religion and Meaning. It is an interdisciplinary course which employs the theory of the sociology of knowledge as presented in Peter Berger's *The Sacred Canopy*[2] to expose students to a social-constructivist understanding of reality.[3] I use the Bible to illustrate such constructivist views of reality, attempting to show students how biblical writers 'constructed' a symbolic, social world to give order and coherence to the discrete experiences of pre- and post-Exilic Israelite and Jewish life.

1. *The Course: Religion and Meaning*

A. *An Overview*

We devote sufficient time to Berger's notion that religion strives, in so far as possible, to hide the humanly constructed character of the legitimations religion provides for the culture and society.[4] One way I try to illustrate this is through our study of the Law of Moses. Students are given a basic overview of critical understandings of the emergence of Israelite law, namely that it evolved over centuries to address the changing needs of Israelite society. To illustrate this, we explore some similar laws in the Covenant (Exod. 20.22–23.33) and Deuteronomic (Deuteronomy 12-26) Codes, such as laws dealing with slavery (e.g., Exod. 21.2-11; Deut. 15.12-18) or sacrificial altars (e.g. Exod. 20.22-26; Deut. 12.2-19). For example, we note that the laws guiding the emancipation of

---

2. Peter Berger, *The Sacred Canopy: Elements of a Sociological Theory of Religion* (New York: Anchor/Doubleday, 1967).

3. Peter Berger today laments that he unwittingly contributed to 'social-constructivist' views of reality; see Peter Berger and Anton Zijderveld, *In Praise of Doubt: How to Have Convictions Without Becoming a Fanatic* (New York: HarperOne, 2009). 'Berger and Luckmann have repeatedly announced, "We are not constructivists"…Perhaps the word "construction" in the Berger/Luckmann volume [*The Social Construction of Reality: A Treatise in the Sociology of Knowledge* (New York: Anchor, 1967)] was unfortunate, as it suggests a creation *ex nihilo*—as if one said, "There is nothing here but our constructions"…What they proposed was that all reality is subject to socially derived *interpretations*' (p. 66, emphases original). Perhaps so, though one should note that it was Berger, not those who supposedly misread him, who spoke in his book *The Sacred Canopy* of social constructions 'stamped out of the ground *ex nihilo*'. See n. 4 below.

4. E.g. 'Let the institutional order be so interpreted as to hide, as much as possible, its *constructed* character. Let that which has been stamped out of the ground *ex nihilo* appear as the manifestation of something that has been existent from the beginning of time, or at least from the beginning of this group…In sum: Set up religious legitimations' (Berger, *Sacred Canopy*, p. 33; emphasis original).

male and female slaves assume different treatment of female slaves in Exodus, while Deuteronomy explicitly does not differentiate. We then note and reflect on the obvious fact that the laws are presented in a manner so as to 'hide' their humanly constructed character. The Covenant Code is given to Moses by God, and Moses, his credibility having now been established, delivers the Deuteronomic Code. We also give attention to some features of the Holiness Code, which begins many chapters with the specific declaration that God spoke to Moses (and, sometimes, Aaron), instructing him or them what to say to the people (e.g. Lev. 11.1-2; 12.1-2; 13.1, etc.).

I understand that most students are persons of faith. That, combined with the fact that the College has not abandoned its commitment to an overall Christian mission, leads me to say that my goal is not simply to tear down what Berger would call alienated views of reality,[5] that is views of reality that essentially deny the contribution of human constructive activity to the ordering features of our cultures and societies. I do not delight in leaving students feeling naked and without any plausibility structure on which to stand. I do, however, want them to understand that this plausibility structure on which they are standing is, itself, constructed by human beings. My ultimate goal is to encourage students to take seriously the human contribution to the construction of reality, including religious realities; I do this to empower them, not to leave them feeling orphaned.

I ask the students to think about a church, synagogue, mosque, or whatever place they have worshiped, attended a wedding, etc. I ask them to think of what they have experienced there in sight or sound and then, slowly, in their minds to erase from these experiences anything that has *human fingerprints* on it: the architecture, the altar, candles, tapestries, the books, the prayers, the sermons, the songs, the stained glass, etc. Remove everything that has any human imprint and what we have left is absolutely nothing. God, if God be real, is always mediated through the experiences and externalizations of human beings, even if, should you be so mystically inclined, that human being is you. God's will and purpose is always mediated through human voices and hence as human beings we need to take responsibility for what we say and do on behalf of God.

Here I will focus on two of the assignments that contribute to this overall learning experience (see Appendix). Students are to read the biblical materials, think about the questions and be prepared to discuss them, and respond on-line to a prompt, which is given at the end of the assignment on Isaiah and Jonah.

By the time we come to these assignments, students have read chapters 1 and 2 of *The Sacred Canopy* and are familiar with Berger's overall theory of social construction and world maintenance. They are familiar with the concept of plausibility structure, social constructs that help to render as credible a given

---

5. See esp. chap. 4 of *Sacred Canopy,* 'Religion and Alienation', pp. 81-101. I will discuss this idea in more detail below.

nomos to which participants within the social world are to conform. Based on our work leading up to this lesson, students are also familiar with the Exile and the Deuteronomistic interpretation of this national tragedy: It was the result of the failure to be obedient to God, best exemplified by the failure to remain separate from other nations, which resulted in Judah imitating the ways of other nations in worship.

B. Specific Assignments and Tasks

Note in Assignment 2.8 (Appendix, *Reinforcing the Boundaries*) that I have students review certain portions of Deuteronomy. I also have them compare features of Deuteronomic theology with what they find in Ezra-Nehemiah. Ezra's prayer in Nehemiah 9 employs the Deuteronomistic pattern of rebellion, repentance, and restoration to interpret the history of Israel. Deuteronomic exhortations to be separate from the other nations are carried out in the restoration reforms implemented by the leaders in the story of Ezra-Nehemiah. Note item 2 under Assignment 2.8, where I ask students to identify specific texts that offer information about how the Judahites related to non-Judahites. A large majority of students can see the connection between specific features of the reforms implemented in the narrative of Ezra-Nehemiah and Deuteronomic materials that they had already read and were to review for this assignment.

Question 4 under Assignment 2.8 is the culminating goal of the preceding study questions. The hope is that students will recognize that the narrative depicts the leaders as attempting to construct a world that implements the Deuteronomic ideal of separation from other nations in order, in part, to avoid the repetition of the national tragedy of the Exile. A certain vision of Judahite culture and society is espoused, legitimated by appeals to the Mosaic Law and sanctioned leaders such as Zerubbabel, Ezra, and Nehemiah. It is not difficult to discern that the narrator of Ezra-Nehemiah is sympathetic with these particular reforms. From the perspective of the narrator, who is always reliable, especially since for many students the narrator is inspired by and speaks for God, it is good that post-Exilic Judahite society is separating itself, literally walling itself off from the outside world (cf. Neh.12.27-43).

Assignment 2.9 (Appendix, *Challenging Established Boundaries*) asks students to explore other biblical texts. The goal is to help them to see that within the Bible (Jonah and portions of Third Isaiah) one finds alternative visions of post-Exilic Judahite religion and society and their relationship with other nations. They are assigned brief, critical introductions to the material to make them aware of the broad historical context of the texts. The secondary reading makes clear that the texts emerged, broadly, from the same historical period as the story told in Ezra-Nehemiah (i.e. the post-Exilic Persian period). I am aware that material in Third Isaiah predates the reforms of Ezra and Nehemiah and certainly predates the composition of the narrative of Ezra-Nehemiah. In addition, dating Jonah is quite difficult (the Persian period is about as close as we can get). But it is not my goal to present material in a strict chronological order;

my goal is to present biblical materials that could be construed as espousing an ideology of other nations that challenges the defensive strategy espoused by the narrative of Ezra-Nehemiah. The prompts that guide student reading of Jonah and selections from Third Isaiah try to be open-ended enough not to compel a certain reading of the material; note, for example, questions 3 and 6 of Assignment 2.9. A large majority of students always sees that the materials from Isaiah and Jonah take a different stance toward non-Jewish people. This is apparent both from the on-line posts and class discussion.

If we take a look at the prompt to which all students must respond and post on the class web site prior to class, we can see that students are required to write specifically about the content of both Ezra-Nehemiah and Jonah and Isaiah (see *Prompt* at the end of Assignment 2.9). Furthermore, by asking which perspective they believe is 'right'—that of Ezra-Nehemiah or Isaiah and Jonah—they are encouraged to make a choice, although they are not compelled to do so and some students, in fact, affirm both perspectives. Their rationales are also interesting to explore and to this I now turn.

C. Exploring Student Responses

In this section, we will look at a sampling of student responses to these exercises.[6] We look first at four responses that affirm, in some way, the perspectives of *both* Ezra-Nehemiah and Isaiah and Jonah. Judy tries to offer an ethical rationale for the defensive strategy of Ezra-Nehemiah: perhaps these foreigners were *evil* people, not just foreigners. Note that she is careful to observe that Isaiah affirms the acceptance only of *faithful* non-Jews at the temple—and she is right about that. Her conclusion is quite comprehensive: 'Both scriptures talk about the same God, the same laws, and the same grace and forgiveness'. I think she is trying to say that, for both sets of writings, the issue is not really about 'foreigners', but about who is faithful and who is not. Ezra-Nehemiah requires separation from people because they are 'evil', not really because they are foreigners. And Isaiah accepts foreign people who are faithful. Hence in the end they both are affirming the same thing. She showed clear evidence of close and creative reading.

Helen, Holly, and James all suggest that the specific historical setting explains the stance of Ezra-Nehemiah. The texts represent a period of 'nation building' when a more defensive strategy would be necessary. Helen, one of the brightest students in the class, goes on to argue that Isaiah and Jonah would represent a period when the nation was secure, thereby allowing for a more inclusive strategy. While Helen's hypothesis of the particular social setting of Isaiah and Jonah would likely not pass critical muster, it clearly expresses awareness that biblical perspectives are rooted in specific historical and social contexts. She knows biblical ideas are not 'timeless' and detached from specific settings. Below are the comments of these three students:

---

6. The quotations below are excerpts from selected student responses to the assignments. To protect privacy, all students' names have been changed.

HELEN: I think that both plausibility structures are acceptable *when considered in the proper frame of reference*. Ezra and Nehemiah were forming the nation of Israel again. ... However, by the time of Jonah and Isaiah, the nation of Israel was functioning and strong once more, so foreigners could be associated with and even converted to Judaism. ... Ezra and Nehemiah were restarting the nation of Israel; Jonah and Isaiah were in an established Israel.

HOLLY: I think the plausibility structure that Ezra and Nehemiah were creating was necessary for the Jewish people [to] reestablish their identity as a nation set apart from others, through a history with God. It was a base for their world, but not a model that was to be used in all situations.

JAMES: E-N believed in the ways of old, non-Jewish people were a bad influence and must be separated from the Jews. I-J were all about spreading the word to non-Jewish people and welcoming them into the religion. Both were right for the time of the stories; if E-N had kept the foreigners mixed with the Jews during the rebuilding time after the Exile, it would have been a harder fight against multiple foreign cultures.

All students who took a side agreed with Isaiah and Jonah, which they perceived as more inclusive. Andy left the impression he was surprised to find varying perspectives expressed in the Bible. However once he acknowledged these different perspectives, he sided with Isaiah and Jonah.

ANDY: When I first read the texts of Jonah and Isaiah, I thought that the two texts seemed to affirm the views of the books of Ezra and Nehemiah. However, at the end of Jonah, it seems that the text rejects the views more than it affirms them…In my opinion, I think that the views expressed in Jonah and Isaiah are the right ones. I think that this is right because these views, that God accepts those who follow him, fit the *nomos* that I live in today.

The rationale given by most students for favoring Isaiah and Jonah was a perception that they offered a more inclusive understanding of God.

SALLY: 'I could not imagine that God would favor a specific group of people even when others are willing to love and accept Him'.

DREW: 'I believe that I serve a God whose powers and steadfast love is unlimited. There are no boundaries on who God loves, and where God loves'.

KIM: '…if it is true that God is full of "abundant love," then why wouldn't he bless all those who are loyal to him[?]'.

LISA: '…my limited knowledge of God leads me to believe that we do have a merciful and forgiving God'.

DAVID: 'I find it hard to believe that God would create a world with people in it whom he would not love and protect'.

TIM: 'Their message of God's universal love could have strengthened society by broadening the influence of Jewish ideas. More importantly, tolerance of foreigners was more consistent with God's broader message of loving your neighbor'.

There are two responses that affirmed the positions of Isaiah and Jonah, but offered distinctive rationales. Robert offered a very pragmatic reason:

> Jonah and Isaiah's view is one that benefits a society more in the long run. Their view would increase the influence and overall power of the Israelite nation. Since the Israelites believe so strongly that they are blessed by God and are truly the ultimate race, then why wouldn't they want to expand their influence and power? The obvious answer to this question would be that they would like to broaden their empire and influence as much as possible. The Israelites would still have the power to shed any foreigners that refused to accept the Jewish faith as their own.

Kathy's response was the most explicitly Christian and anachronistic:

> I think that Isaiah and Jonah have the right perspective. They were prophesying the new covenant through Jesus Christ. The New Testament is a record of this new creation the LORD was talking about in Isaiah. Due to the sacrifice of Jesus, anyone, Jew or Gentile, is able to be blessed by God. In Romans, Paul explains why the Gentiles can receive salvation too. Paul says, 'Inasmuch then as I am an apostle to the Gentiles, I glorify my ministry in order to make my own people (the Jews) jealous, and thus save some of them' (Romans 11.13-14).

Thus far, we can draw these conclusions from this exercise: First, students were able to perceive different perspectives within the Bible on a similar issue, in this case how Jews during the Persian period perceived their relationship with non-Jewish people. Second, some students attempted to understand different perspectives as rooted explicitly in different social or historical contexts. Third, most students, when urged to do so, chose what they perceived to be the more inclusive understanding of how God relates to people, simply because it conforms to their own understanding of God.

While my analysis of student responses for this particular paper has been limited to students who took the course in a particular semester, my memory of the responses of past student groups is similar. Students may occasionally try to reconcile the perspectives of Ezra-Nehemiah and Isaiah and Jonah, but far more students perceive differing perspectives and embrace the one they perceive as more inclusive.

D. Intended Learning Outcomes

What do I want students to achieve by the homework and what happens in class? What I have discussed so far is focused on what students do prior to coming to class. What do I do with the class period that is devoted to our discussion of this material? I prepare a summary sheet of student responses, with names omitted, distribute it, and have the students break into small groups to discuss the various responses. After small and large group discussion of the handout, we spend considerable time going over the biblical material, working our way through some of the specific homework questions. One comparative exercise we conduct in class that builds on the homework preparation compares Isaiah 56.3-8, which speaks of foreigners and eunuchs worshipping in the Temple, with Nehemiah 13.1-3, which speaks of the post-Exilic Judahite community separating from non-Jewish people in compliance with the Law of Moses. The passage in question from the Law of Moses is Deuteronomy 23.1-8, which explicitly forbids from the assembly castrated males, those born of an illicit union, and certain non-Jewish people (Ammonites and Moabites).

We look carefully at this text and observe that Nehemiah is stricter with respect to the Mosaic instruction in its exclusion of non-Jewish people; Moses forbids only Ammonites and Moabites from entry into the assembly, but Nehemiah 13 demands separation from all non-Jewish people. On the other hand, Isaiah explicitly includes within Temple worship eunuchs and foreigners, two groups explicitly forbidden inclusion in the community by Deuteronomy. It is explicit that Nehemiah 13 is based on Deuteronomy 23, as Nehemiah 13 alludes specifically to this text. Isaiah's allusion is more subtle, more of an inter-textual echo. Yet the echo is clear enough to allow students to see that within the Bible we have two perspectives concerning non-Jewish people, the more inclusive perspective of Isaiah (the one with which most students are sympathetic) and the more exclusive perspective of Nehemiah. They also see that the Isaianic perspective cuts against the grain not only of Nehemiah but also the Mosaic Law itself.

The Bible, I want students to see, invites us to listen in on its own debates and internal conversations about important issues. The Bible itself offers diverse perspectives on important issues and, by presenting us with its own diversity, urges us not only to embrace the reality of diverse perspectives but also, to whatever degree we think it important to 'listen to the Bible', to join our voices to the conversation and make choices.[7] In 'choosing' between Ezra-Nehemiah and Isaiah and Jonah, we are imitating the Bible itself, as reflected in the choice about how to respond to the Mosaic Law on the matter of foreigners and eunuchs. Appeal to the Bible does not eliminate choice (the Bible says it; I believe it; that settles it); rather appeal to the Bible requires choice, since the Bible itself *offers* choices. The Bible offers choices because the Bible is a collection of *humanly constructed* responses to and interpretations of the varied experiences of real people, trying to make sense of life. To whatever degree the Bible is authoritative or 'canonical', a term that students have learned by this stage of the course, 'choice' and 'diversity of perspectives' are also 'canonized'.

Later in the term we explore Berger's concept of alienation and dealienation. These two lessons contribute to preparing students for our later study of the idea

---

7. This approach, of course, is that constructed and employed by Walter Brueggemann in his *Theology of the Old Testament: Testimony, Dispute, Advocacy* (Minneapolis: Fortress, 1997).

of alienation, Berger's understanding of 'false consciousness', wherein a person, to varying degrees, rejects the *socially constructed character of reality*, most especially sacred, religious reality. Most students enter class, I've discovered, with an alienated view of the Bible, even if they do not have an explicitly 'high view' of the Bible as scripture. They simply have not given much thought to its origins and so have some general notion that 'God gave us the Bible'. Whatever their ideas about its origin may be, most students do not take seriously the Bible's humanly constructed character. Students who do not share this view of the Bible as a divine gift tend to see it in a very dealienated way (though they don't know this jargon yet), by which I mean they see it as purely a human book that, as such, is of no real value: It's just some ancient men's view of things. I hope to encourage both kinds of students to value the Bible and its contribution to our culture.

I encourage the more devout students to embrace a view of the Bible that does not distance them from it so much, since they see it as a book written 'back then' by people who really were not humans like us, not people wrestling as we do with making sense of life. The people who wrote the Bible, like us, had honest disagreements about what was right and what God expected of them. I encourage the more secular students, who don't see much value in the Bible because it's just the opinions of human beings, to recognize the humanly constructed character of *all* social dimensions of reality. 'Everything is humanly constructed' is a regular mantra of mine. 'Some constructions are better than others', I tell them. 'Figuring out which ones are better is the hard part'. By this I mean that it is intellectually lazy to dismiss something just because it is a 'human construction'. Should we adopt that stance with absolute consistency, we would have to dismiss all points of view.

2. Conclusion

Courses are supposed to have goals, with each lesson contributing to each unit, and all of these 'going somewhere'. A unit on the studies of Jesus follows the one described above. In preparation, we do a careful comparison of Matthew 15.1-20 and Mark 7.1-23, exploring the writers' different presentations regarding the matter of clean and unclean food. The purpose of this lesson is to help students to see that even Jesus, the one to whom most of Jewell students look as the final authority on matters of God and faith, comes to us through the interpretive lens of the gospel writers and, in the case of the texts in question, very *different* interpretive lenses.[8] We simply cannot escape human interpretations and the distinctiveness of various human interpretations.

This paves the way for our reading of *The Meaning of Jesus: Two Visions*, by Marcus Borg and N.T. Wright.[9] The purpose of this reading is not so much

---

8. I offered a more thorough presentation of this exercise before the Synoptic Gospels Section of the Society of Biblical Literature, November, 2008.

9. Marcus J. Borg and N.T. Wright, *The Meaning of Jesus: Two Visions* (New York: HarperCollins, 2007).

to offer the students a cram course on the Jesus debates, though they do learn some things about this, but to continue to press upon them *the unavoidability of debate* and *the necessity of 'constructing'* an understanding of Jesus. Reading Borg and Wright through a Bergerian lens, we see that both are credible 'constructions' of Jesus as a historical figure, constructions based on literary remains that are, themselves, *also constructions* of Jesus.

One of the expressed learning goals of Sacred and Secular courses in our college's core curriculum is 'to enable students to experience the impact that cultural diversity has on various expressions of Christianity'. I'll confess that I'm not sure how much 'impact' students 'experience' in my course. But I think that most do come to understand that Christianity is bigger than any one person's experience of it. Christianity is a 'diverse' religion. In reality, they knew this, though for many, such diverse perspectives fall too easily into 'right' and 'wrong' expressions of Christianity. What I want students to understand is that diversity within the Christian tradition and other religious traditions is not threatening. It is not the case that among the diverse options one is right and the rest, by definition, must be wrong. I want students to understand that diversity, even within a particular religious tradition, is part of the *biblical* tradition. It is not a simple matter of believing that the Bible offers *the* clear and monolithic expression of 'the true faith' and all one has to do is figure out what this is. The Bible itself offers diverse expressions of and responses to discrete experiences of life. Diversity is to be valued, not merely tolerated. Diversity is to be valued not only because the Bible encourages us to tolerate others who are different from us; diversity is also to be valued because the Bible itself gives expression to diverse perspectives on important issues. The Bible canonizes and authorizes diversity.

Appendix
Selected Assignments

Assignment 2.8: Reinforcing the Boundaries
From the Bible: Ezra 1; 3.1-4.5; 5.1-6.18; 9-10; Nehemiah 9; 13
In preparation for class, complete the following exercises and come prepared to discuss what you discovered.

1. Review our study of biblical history and refresh yourself on the basic history and historical setting of Ezra-Nehemiah. What historical event of national and even tragic significance has just come to an end? Review Deuteronomy 4.25-31, 39-40. Given this text, how would the people of Judah likely have made sense of their national tragedy? Compare this short text from Deuteronomy with Ezra's prayer of Nehemiah 9. Does Ezra essentially embrace the 'formula for national success' espoused in Deuteronomy? Be prepared to justify your response.
2. List at least three stories from your reading of Ezra-Nehemiah, providing the scriptural references, which offer a word on how the returning Judahites related to non-Judahites.

3. After you have finished the preceding exercise review Deuteronomy 7.1-6. Do you agree or disagree with the statement that Ezra and Nehemiah are attempting to firm up the boundaries that Deuteronomy attempts to establish between Israelites and non-Israelites? Why or why not?
4. Employing Berger's idea of 'plausibility structure', interpret the sociological significance of the efforts of Ezra and Nehemiah in leading the restoration of the Judahites after the exile.

Assignment 2.9: Challenging Established Boundaries
Jonah (whole book); Isaiah 56; 65-66
Read the encyclopedia articles on Jonah and Isaiah.

In preparation for class, complete the following exercises and come prepared to discuss what you discovered. Then, prior to the posted deadline, post a written response to the prompt below to the class web site.

1. Historical background and information about sources and editing is part of critical study, recall. Based on your assigned reading, what is the suggested historical background of the composition of this story about Jonah?
2. What attitude does Jonah (the character in the story) have toward non-Israelites? What attitude does God have? Can you discern the attitude of the narrator (the voice of the one telling the story that you are reading)?
3. Would the leaders of the Jews as depicted in Ezra and Nehemiah like the message of Jonah? Why or why not?
4. Given what you know about the likely historical context of the authorship of Jonah, would you consider this protest literature? Why or why not?
5. Sources and editing are part of critical study. Be prepared to summarize the history of the composition of the Book of Isaiah, as stated by the encyclopedia article.
6. What view of 'foreigners' (non-Jews) and the Temple does Isaiah 56 present? Would the leaders of the returning Jews as depicted in Ezra-Nehemiah agree or disagree with the view of non-Jews depicted in Isaiah 56? Why or why not?
7. How might texts such as Jonah and Third Isaiah have created anomy, as Berger has defined the term, in post-Exilic Jewish society?

Prompt: Respond to the following thesis statement (affirming, rejecting, or modifying): Texts such as Isaiah and Jonah could have undermined and compromised very seriously the plausibility structure that Ezra and Nehemiah were attempting to construct after the Exile. In the context of responding to this prompt, incorporate discussion about what Ezra and Nehemiah would have said was *the right thing to do* with respect to non-Jewish people. What would Isaiah and Jonah have said is *the right thing to do* with regard to non-Jewish people? Who do you think is right? *How do you know?*

COLLABORATIVE LEARNING AND THE PEDAGOGY OF THE BIBLE IN THE LIBERAL ARTS CONTEXT

Alison Schofield
University of Denver

The traditional college classroom, with its focus on individualism and competition, is increasingly a relic of the past. More than ever educators today recognize the value of active learning and student interdependence, and some researchers have shown that pedagogical techniques such as collaborative learning (C-L) engage students in meaningful, lasting learning.[1] Bible educators have not been unaware of recent trends in the college classroom; nevertheless, in spite of some potential pitfalls that may arise, more conversation could be had about C-L as a vehicle to facilitate teaching the Bible in the liberal arts context. Indeed, the theoretical underpinnings of and the active 'meaning-making' involved in C-L in many ways imitates the practice of biblical criticism itself.

Before exploring this claim further, I should place my own teaching experience in context. I have taught classes about the Bible and related literature in a religious studies context at the University of Denver (DU), a liberal arts school of just over 5,000 undergraduates (and 6,000 graduate students). During the past few years, DU has received substantial outside funding to improve the quality of the undergraduate experience. Part of this subtle shift of curricula has included additional support for instructors who develop courses with experiential and engaged learning 'for the public good'. Under the guidance of DU's Center for Teaching and Learning, I incorporated C-L components in courses, such as Introduction to the Hebrew Bible, the Bible as Literature, and the Dead Sea Scrolls. The first two general education courses included approximately 25-30 non-majors, while the latter course included undergraduates alongside both MA and PhD students; my graduate students, in general,

---

1. See the excellent synopsis of research in Elizabeth F. Barkley, *Student Engagement Techniques: A Handbook for College Faculty* (Higher and Adult Education Series; San Francisco: Jossey-Bass, 2009); and Elizabeth F. Barkley, K. Patricia Cross, and Claire Howell Major, *Collaborative Learning Techniques: A Handbook for College Faculty* (San Francisco: Jossey-Bass, 2005).

reported widely different experiences with C-L than those described by my undergraduates.[2]

The Bible in the Liberal Arts Context

Teaching the Bible in the liberal arts context brings with it its own pedagogical challenges, as one must reconcile the aims of biblical criticism with the goals of the liberal arts classroom. Although there exists no unanimously accepted definition of 'liberal arts' or 'liberal education', despite the frequent attempts of curriculum committees to find one, generally liberal arts curricula center on educating the whole person and address three general goals: 1) to expose the student to the depth and complexity of human thought, 2) to introduce the student to the process of how humans formulate beliefs, and 3) to encourage them to think critically about how humans substantiate those beliefs.[3] As part of these goals, the liberal arts experience focuses on clarifying values, self-awareness, self-direction, empathy, tolerance, and inclusion.[4] Bible instruction within the liberal context inevitably engages these questions, and in particular those of values, self-awareness, tolerance and inclusion. Regardless of one's religious beliefs about the Bible, it is nonetheless value-laden and frequently surfaces in the sphere of public discourse. As such, it constitutes fertile ground for developing students' critical thinking skills and engagement with ongoing public and private debates. But what methods are best to bridge the gap between teaching content knowledge of the Bible and fostering development of the 'whole person'?

This query is paralleled by a second, related issue debated among liberal arts institutions: What role should the instructor play in the educational process? This question is particularly poignant in the biblical studies classroom. To what extent is the instructor the authority in biblical interpretation and to what degree do students 'shape' meaning, as they engage the text from a reader-response approach? Bible educators are increasingly forced to grapple with this question, as university administrators and instructors of all sorts are rethinking the role of the instructor as the sole exemplar and source of knowledge and moving away from the traditional liberal arts model of the seminar. Current methods of active- and problem-based learning are expanding the lecture-based classroom

---

2. The response from my graduate students, particularly my PhD students, was predominantly negative, as they resisted most strongly the shift from the traditional classroom and lecture setting. They generally preferred working on their own, and, as one student put, 'being solely responsible for [his] own grade'. They also cited the difficulties of working together outside of class, given their family and other work obligations.

3. See also, Kenneth A. Bruffee, *Collaborative Learning: Higher Education, Interdependence, and the Authority of Knowledge* (Baltimore: The Johns Hopkins University Press, 1993), pp. 151-52.

4. See, for instance, A. Warmoth, '"Educating the Whole Student": Ten Essays on Learner-Centered Education', Sonoma State University, 2009, www.sonoma.edu/Senate/documents/Educating%20the%20Whole%20Student%20MS.doc.

and therefore the position of the instructor as the sole authority of knowledge. But how, and to what degree, does the Bible instructor embrace this pedagogical shift, if at all?

Wherever one falls on the pedagogical spectrum, C-L activities provide an arena to work through the ongoing tension between teacher-centered and student-centered learning, for the techniques of C-L teaching can be flexibly tailored to engage students and to instill the modes of critical thinking encouraged in a liberal education, while still retaining some traditional instructor roles.

What Is Collaborative Learning?

Collaborative learning is not just 'group work'. Collaborative (or 'cooperative') learning could best be thought of as intentionally designed group activities in which students actively work together to engage in meaningful learning and to achieve shared learning goals.

Collaborative learning techniques are just one example of a pedagogical strategy in which the instructor takes a less authoritative approach to regulating student learning. The core issue discussed by many is the degree to which the instructor should relinquish authority in the classroom, if at all, a debate which is reflected even in the nuances of the terminology 'collaborative' versus 'cooperative' learning. Although these labels are sometimes used interchangeably to identify group learning, 'cooperative' generally refers to more structured classroom learning, where there is still some maintenance of traditional understandings of classroom knowledge and authority.[5] In this regard, Johnson, Johnson and Smith maintain that instructors should shape assignments, guide the students during the working process, keep them on track, and evaluate the effectiveness of the group.[6] On the other hand, 'collaborative' often refers to the other end of the spectrum of 'constructed knowledge' with its origins in social constructivism. At the extreme end of this spectrum, some use 'collaborative' to mean that students and faculty should work together to create knowledge and that the students should not depend on the teacher as the authority or even, in many cases, as the monitor.[7] Under this definition, Bruffee would prefer to shift the responsibility away from the instructor, setting students 'clearly and unequivocally on their own to govern themselves and pursue the task in any way they see fit'.[8]

---

5. Barbara J. Millis and Philip G. Cottell, Jr., *Cooperative Learning for Higher Education Faculty* (Phoenix: Oryx, 1998). See also J.L. Flannery, 'Teacher as Co-conspirator: Knowledge and Authority in Collaborative Learning', in *Collaborative Learning: Underlying Processes and Effective Techniques* (ed. Kris Bosworth and Sharon J. Hamilton; San Francisco: Jossey-Bass, 1994), as cited in Barkley, Cross, and Major, *Collaborative Learning Techniques*, p. 5.

6. David W. Johnson, Roger T. Johnson, and Karl A. Smith, *Active Learning: Cooperation in the College Classroom* (Edina, MN: Interaction, 1998).

7. Bruffee, *Collaborative Learning*, p. 3.

8. Kenneth A. Bruffee, 'Sharing Our Toys: Cooperative Learning versus Collaborative Learning', *Change* 27 (1995), p. 17.

The differences between these terms have more to say about types of epistemology than anything else. Previous modes of pedagogy rested primarily on a cognitive understanding of knowledge, the substance of which could be transferred from the head of the instructor to the student. But cooperative—or to a greater extent, collaborative learning, by its strictest definition—assumes that knowledge is closer to that agreed upon by members of a community of 'knowledgeable peers'.[9] This epistemological perspective of knowledge as created by a community underlies collaborative ventures like Wikipedia, for example, and supports the idea, as Thomas Kuhn states, that knowledge is 'intrinsically the common property of a group or else nothing at all'.[10] Although the activities I incorporate in my Bible classroom fall somewhere between 'cooperative' and 'collaborative', per the definitions given above, I have chosen to use the terminology of 'collaborative' learning because of its emphasis on knowledge communities, such as those religious communities involved in biblical interpretation over time. I prefer that students actively participate in meaning-making within their own learning community, even though I do not completely agree with Bruffee. Rather, I believe that this creation of knowledge and knowledge communities should be modeled and regulated to some degree by the instructor.

The Case for Collaborative Learning

The craft of interdependence is not new. Whether the undergraduate student aims to go to graduate school after graduation or into the workforce, collaboration, consultation and teamwork are increasingly the norm rather than the exception. Why should their education be any different?[11] As Bruffee perhaps too boldly claims, colleges and universities do not traditionally cultivate interdependence skills because the traditional curriculum 'has little use for collaboration, does not teach it, distrusts it, and often penalizes it'.[12] Yet at the same time, in the last decade or more studies on the state of American higher education have complained that many undergraduates tend to be 'authority-dependent, passive, irresponsible, overly competitive, and suspicious of their peers', while similar complaints have been made of those in professional training.[13]

While Bruffee oversimplifies the case, C-L addresses many of these central complaints, and further, directly contributes to five of the seven good practices in undergraduate education found in the older but much-cited work by Chickering and Gamson: developing reciprocity and cooperation among students, encouraging active learning, giving prompt feedback, communicating

---

9. Bruffee, *Collaborative Learning*, p. 3.
10. Thomas S. Kuhn, *The Structure of Scientific Revolutions* (2nd edn; Chicago: University of Chicago Press, 1970), p. 210, as cited in Bruffee, *Collaborative Learning*, p. 3.
11. For similar remarks, consult Bruffee, *Collaborative Learning*, p. 1.
12. Bruffee, *Collaborative Learning*, p. 2.
13. Bruffee, *Collaborative Learning*, p. 8.

high expectations, and respecting diverse talents and ways of learning.[14] The latter three are addressed primarily through the immediacy and diversity of peer-influence and interaction in C-L activities and draw upon two of the most powerful forces underlying these best practices—cooperation and responsibility—also noted by Chickering and Gamson. In general, C-L is designed to help students learn collective responsibility, a skill that holds value both in and out of the academic setting.

Researchers increasingly affirm the role of peer influence on shaping a student's education. As early as the 1960s, Theodore Newcomb recognized that the single most powerful influence in an undergraduate's education is that coming from peer-groups, and more recent studies find that a teacher holds less direct influence on the student than fellow learners do when it comes to student development.[15] This may well be related to the effect peer interaction has in encouraging students to learn in dialogue with each other, where they 'embed' data into their own conceptual framework. Burgeoning research on cognition and brain development affirm that persons develop their own long-term memory through creating new neural pathways and storing information in context.[16] C-L and other experiential learning exercises are just one way that learners must actively create new connections in their own brains in order to process information and produce learning for themselves.[17]

Further, C-L can re-acculturate students to know what it means to be members of knowledge communities, just like those in the past, which, guided by certain hierarchical restraints, already engaged the biblical text. Given our brief, ten-week quarter system, I aim only to introduce the beginning student to the *process* and the long *history of biblical interpretation*, first by engaging them in the act of interpretation, so that they can practice as interpreters, but

14. Arthur W. Chickering and Zelda F. Gamson, 'Seven Principles for Good Practice in Undergraduate Education', *AAHE Bulletin* (1987); see also more recently, Arthur W. Chickering and S.C. Ehrmann, 'Implementing the Seven Principles: Technology as a Lever', *AAHE Bulletin* 49 (1996); Arthur W. Chickering and Zelda F. Gamson (eds.), *Applying the Seven Principles for Good Practice in Undergraduate Education* (San Francisco: Jossey-Bass, 1991); 'Development and Adaptations of the Seven Principles for Good Practice in Undergraduate Education', *New Directions for Teaching and Learning* 80 (1999). The only principles left out here are emphasizing time on task and encouraging interaction between students and faculty.

15. Theodore Mead Newcomb and Everett K. Wilson, *College Peer Groups: Problems and Prospects for Research* (Aldine, IL: Chicago, 1966), p. 6; William G. Perry, *Forms of Intellectual and Ethical Development in the College Years: A Scheme* (New York: Holt, 1968), p. 213. These references are also discussed in Bruffee, *Collaborative Learning*, p. 6. Already in the late 1960s, Newcomb spoke of mobilizing this overwhelming peer group influence on student values and attitudes around intellectual concerns (Newcomb and Wilson, *College Peer Groups*, pp. vi-vii); see more recently, Alexander W. Astin, *What Matters in College?* (San Francisco: Jossey-Bass, 1993); and Barkley, Cross, and Major, *Collaborative Learning Techniques*, pp. 14-22.

16. Christof Koch and Joel L. Davis (eds.), *Large-Scale Neuronal Theories of the Brain* (Boston: Massachusetts Institute of Technology Press, 1995).

17. See, for instance, K. Patricia Cross, *Learning is About Making Connections* (Mission Viejo, CA: League for Innovation in the Community College, 1999) and also the bibliography listed in Barkley, Cross, and Major, *Collaborative Learning Techniques*, especially pp. 10-20.

secondly, by reminding them that they are stepping into a continuing, dynamic conversation. Can beginning students really be 'turned loose' to create meaning from the Bible? Given the value-laden nature of the text, as well as its long reception-history, introductory students still need a fair amount of guidance, or reigning in, as they internalize different ways of doing biblical criticism. In my own classroom, I have kept one foot in the door of historical criticism, without having completely rushed headlong into the door of purely literary, reader-response readings of the text.

The Practicalities of Group Formation

Buzz groups. Collaborative learning groups can be loosely organized, such as in 'buzz groups', for which I gather up to six students for informal, extemporaneous discussion. For example, when introducing students to the *need* for interpretation, I begin by showing the class a quote from Socrates about the ambiguities of the written word: 'the book cannot protect or defend itself'. After some brief, individual exploratory writing on what this may mean, I gather the students in spontaneous buzz groups to discuss how this quote may apply today. Next, I offer the groups a further prompt: can the US constitution 'defend itself', to use the language of Socrates? As these groups brainstorm, they generally realize that it must be interpreted by those of sanctioned (judicial) authority, and I lead them into a general class discussion of how this may be true for the Bible, a written text, with an ongoing need for interpretation; for written texts do not speak for themselves. Just like an e-mail, text, or a tweet, written communication leaves many gaps for the reader to fill, and I use these parallels to help the student see the relevance and the immediacy of the interpretive task.

Effective learning groups. When teaching the Bible, I also establish more structured C-L learning groups, or 'effective learning groups', for the duration of the quarter, so that students can experience a longer-term knowledge community. For the best results, effective learning groups should range from two to five, possibly even six members. Size may be dictated by a number of factors and preferences, including course content and the physical arrangement of the classroom.[18] In general, I have found that groups of three have been the most efficient size for longer-term student groups, maximizing an individual's involvement in the group and best facilitating group relationships and logistics. These groups function alongside more spontaneous buzz groups, and because the buzz groups do not necessarily correspond to their C-L, or effective learn-

---

18. John C. Bean argues cogently for five as the most effective size for both formal and informal classroom groups, based on the ways these groups tend to sub-divide. According to him, six works well, but begins to dilute the experience, groups of four tend to divide in pairs, and groups of three often split into a pair and an outsider. Yet he does admit that groups of three tend to work best when they work together on a long-term basis (John C. Bean, *Engaging Ideas: The Professor's Guide to Integrating Writing, Critical Thinking, and Active Learning in the Classroom* [San Francisco: Jossey-Bass, 1996], p. 160).

ing groups, these help to mix up the student's experience when brainstorming or generating discussion for a short period of time.

Within each effective learning group, I assign a number of group roles. I allow students to assign individuals specific roles according to their own strengths. However, I do rotate roles randomly during the middle of the quarter once students are more comfortable in the classroom environment, as this challenges them to foster new skills. Sample group roles include: (1) a *group facilitator* who keeps the group on task, moderates discussions, and makes sure that all members have the opportunity to learn and contribute equally; (2) a *scribe* who takes notes of the group's discussion and writes up any written conclusions or assignments; (3) an *assessor* who takes on the responsibility of notating the group's effectiveness as a whole, as well as the participation of individual members; and (4) a *timekeeper* who monitors the time spent on task for each activity. He or she can also fill in the role of wildcard member.

The number and type of roles can vary by the course and size of groups; other possible roles for larger groups include: (5) the *checker* who makes sure that all group members grasp the concepts and understand their conclusions; (6) a *research-runner* who obtains any necessary materials and acts as a liaison between groups and the instructor; (7) a *summarizer* who restates the groups' conclusions and relates it to any prior theories, concepts, and knowledge; and finally (8) a *wildcard* member who is able to assume the role of any missing member.[19]

C-L Activities for the Bible Classroom

Anyone who has taught the Bible, particularly to non-majors, knows the challenges of trying to teach undergraduates both the content of the Bible *and* the workings of biblical criticism in all of its variety within the confines of a quarter or semester course. I structure the goals, and therefore the C-L activities, of my Bible courses with only a few modest goals in mind. First, I have increasingly had to let go of trying to cover the entire canon exhaustively (or exhaustingly) and have limited the content of the Bible covered, carefully selecting certain books and pericopes in order to spend more time engaging those passages more closely. When doing this, I have found that students have a richer experience overall and that by learning together, they better process the material we do

---

19. These group roles are similar to or are combinations of some of the roles proposed by David W. Johnson, Roger T. Johnson, and Karl A. Smith, *Cooperative Learning: Increasing College Faculty Instructional Productivity* (Washington, DC: The George Washington University, School of Education and Human Development, 1991); Millis and Cottell, *Cooperative Learning for Higher Education Faculty*; Karl A. Smith, 'Cooperative Learning: Making "Group Work" Work', in *Using Active Learning in College Classes: A Range of Options for Faculty* (ed. Tracey E. Sutherland and Charles C. Bonwell; New Directions in Teaching and Learning 67; San Francisco: Jossey-Bass, 1996); as noted also in W.C.F.E. Research, *Collaborative Learning: Small Group Learning Page* (National Institute for Science Education, 1997), www.wcer.wisc.edu/archive/cl1/CL/default.asp.

cover, in addition to remembering better the themes and characters we encounter in class. Second, by working in the same group for the quarter, students indeed learn what it means to be a part of a 'knowledge community' in all of its interworkings. Thirdly, working together necessarily requires more individual student participation, allowing students to process their learning through speech and creating their own cognitive patterns and meaningful knowledge. Even reading the Bible aloud to each other each day can help them understand the performative nature of the text and to remember the material through the use of more senses than those employed by simply reading silently alone.

Three Examples of Interpretive Exercises

Think-pair-share.[20] In my effective learning groups, I plan a number of short, low-risk, informal activities, such as 'think-pair-share' exercises, which are particularly useful when introducing new information or getting the students to brainstorm. They also help to break up lectures with a brief change in activity. For this activity, the instructor generally poses a challenging or open-ended question and allows the students one to two minutes to think about possible responses (or an alternate version allows them to engage in brief, exploratory writing). Aside from providing the student an active forum through which to process information, it also encourages individual participation and oral skills as they talk with one another, comparing and contrasting their ideas, and helps them rehearse their responses before they are asked to share with the entire class. In addition to serving as great warm up exercises at the beginning of class, think-pair-share activities help students to 'prime the pump' of their ideas and thoughts about particular passages or characters before they are exposed to established interpretations.

An example of one such introductory exercise I give in class in the think-pair-share format is *Reading Inkblots*, some of which is borrowed from Mark Roncace.[21] I ask each member to take two minutes and write down silently all of the images he or she can see in an inkblot projected for the class on Powerpoint. Then, for the next five minutes, each student takes a turn explaining and trying to convince the other group members of the various images he or she sees in the inkblot. One can even turn this into a game, for which each student tries to see how many different images he or she can both see and persuade others to see. The class winner would be the member in the class with the most

---

20. See the description of this type of activity in the section on 'Think-Pair-Share' in Barkley, Cross, and Major, *Collaborative Learning Techniques*, pp. 104-7. Compare as well F.T. Lyman, 'Think-Pair-Share, Thinktrix, Thinklinks, and Weird Facts: An Interactive System for Cooperative Learning', in *Enhancing Thinking through Cooperative Learning* (ed. Neil Davidson and Toni Worsham; New York: Teachers College Press, 1992).

21. Roncace describes a similar type of exercise using the Mattel game 'Thinkblot'. See www.thinkblot.com and Mark Roncace and Patrick Gray (eds.), *Teaching the Bible: Practical Strategies for Classroom Instruction* (Atlanta: Society of Biblical Literature, 2005), pp. 13-14.

points for images that they can convince a majority of group members to agree are there.

Together as a class we list all of the images on the board and discuss what factors may have influenced what student saw, factors such as the parts on which the student focused, the angle taken, and the different backgrounds, genders, ages, nationality, and social locations of the students. These observations clue the students into the different forces acting upon us and shaping how we read the text. With this specific example, divorced from any otherwise value-charged text, students view with some critical distance how an individual's social location influences and produces variegated interpretations of a text.

Finally, I show a close-up image of the printed words on a page of the Bible and ask, 'What about these inkblots?' Here students generally pause to make the connection. This activity helps students to look at the Bible 'wordblots' in a new light and to begin to recognize that there is no inherent meaning in the text, but that meaning is generated as they engage the shapes on the page under the influence of their own social and religious locations. Further, I ask the students to think of what it took to persuade others to see what they saw, if they could convince them. This part of the exercise introduces the students to how interpretive communities over time have come to agree on only certain established interpretations to the biblical text and to the reality that not just any individual's interpretation of the text may be considered equally valid.

Guided peer questioning. Sometimes students feel so confused or unfamiliar with the Bible that they do not even know the questions to ask of the text. 'Guided peer questioning' activities provide students with higher-order, open-ended questions to help them generate focused discussion about the Bible. With the instructor providing only generic prompts, they are encouraged to question each other and to synthesize, compare and contrast, and extrapolate from other texts; these questions allow the instructor to direct students in their questioning of the text in the service of the larger goals and outcomes of the course.

For example, in my course on the Bible as literature, one of my larger goals is for the student to recognize social location and how we are predisposed to see different emphases in the text. I lead the class in an exercise called *Reading Sodom and Gomorrah: An Interpretive Exercise*.[22] As homework the night before, students will read Genesis 18-19. In their effective learning groups, they will re-read out loud and revisit this narrative multiple times, but each time they ask questions of the text limited to only one theme at a time, such as power, sexuality, women, honor and hospitality. For each theme, I give each group a sheet of paper with open-ended prompts about that particular topic and allow them work together to generate answers. The group scribe then writes down and turns in their collective responses. Sample questions include: *Explain why_____? What conclusions can I draw about ____? What is the main idea of_____?*

---

22. Here I follow Danna Nolan Fewell and David Miller Gunn, *Gender, Power, and Promise: The Subject of the Bible's First Story* (Nashville: Abingdon, 1992), pp. 56-67.

How does _____ *relate to what I have heard before? What is another way to look at* _____*? What if* _____*?* Ultimately I ask them to think about what perspectives or new questions arise when they shift their respective lenses through which they view the same story. A variation on this exercise would be to ask students to develop their own questions about a biblical story or character or theme, after having provided them with sample analysis questions, such as those above.

Analytic teams.[23] Frequently, I break down an interpretive task and assign its component parts to different members of the effective learning group, which functions in this case as an 'analytic team'. For example, I integrate an exercise titled *Analytic Teams: Feminist Interpretations of Eve*, in which the students get to practice 'becoming' various interpreters in order to allow them to model sound biblical-critical methods. Here I use Alice Bellis' chapter on Eve, from *Helpmates, Harlots and Heroes*, where she nicely summarizes the positions and evidence from various scholars, such as Phillis Trible, Mike Bal, David Freedman, and Carol Meyers.[24]

Rarely can beginning students less familiar with the content of the Bible completely internalize the methods and conclusions of a feminist critic of this text. So I familiarize them with feminist criticism by breaking down their tasks, first assigning each member of the group to a different feminist interpreter encountered in the previous night's reading. After some time for reflection and gathering thoughts, each member assumes the identity of their respective interpreter and offers to the group a three to four minute persuasive argument for that particular reading, using the evidence given by their specific interpreter. Similar to the 'Copycat' activity in the game Cranium®, the member speaks in the first person and takes on the voice of one scholar. If you make this activity a game, the other members of the group can try to guess which interpreter they have become, based on their knowledge gained from the article. Then, the rest of the group has about two minutes to critique and debate this interpretation directly with the presenter, who maintains the identity of the original interpreter and must defend their position. This latter move often proves to be the most difficult part for the presenter, but challenges the student to 'try on' a new role and perspective on the text with some guiding parameters. As a wrap-up, the students write short, individual essays as homework, in which they synthesize their own reading of the text, based on those interpretations they found to be most persuasive. This essay also provides the instructor something concrete for assessing the activity.

---

23. Barkley, Cross, and Major describe the characteristics of this type of C-L task, which they term CoLT 17, and they list it among other effective versions of this activity, *Collaborative Learning Techniques*, p. 63.

24. See 'The Story of Eve' in Alice Ogden Bellis, *Helpmates, Harlots, and Heroes: Women's Stories in the Hebrew Bible* (Louisville, KY: Westminster/John Knox, 1994).

Challenges and Strategies

Studies have confirmed that students who learn in small groups retain more information, earn higher grades, develop better communication and teamwork skills, and are less likely to drop out of school than those taught traditionally[25]; nevertheless, challenges remain. Most studies that tout the benefits of C-L gather data on operative and effective groups. But what about those groups that are ineffective, or, at worst, entirely dysfunctional? A few general approaches can help to address the challenges posed by these groups and to safeguard C-L activities in the Bible classroom.[26] The most effective intervention I have found for negative behavior is simply that I get to know students on a personal level and honor their own experiences, difficulties, and suggestions as part of a 'co-laborer' in the learning process. This builds better relationships with the students and opens the door to discuss extreme problems with individual students in private if necessary.

Some students may resist working in groups, manifested by anger, complaining or even hostility to the instructor or other group members. An instructor can address this roadblock by trying to find the reason for such resistance, such as if certain students may have previously had bad experiences with group work. In the process of asking the students about any on-going problems, one should be sure to question *them* as to what they think is the best solution. Oftentimes, involving them in the solution can negate some of their negative reactions and discourage them from feeling they are being antagonized by the instructor.

A common complaint is that not all students participate equally. Some students may dominate the conversation or monopolize group projects, while others may say very little. Further, one or more members of a group may contribute little to the activity or come unprepared, if they attend class at all. In the former instance, an instructor can organize activities such as think-pair-share, particularly with a written component, or can build silent reflection time into the discussion to allow shyer students to gather their thoughts and to encourage domineering students to be quiet. Otherwise, 'round robin' kinds of exercises, in which everyone is forced to brainstorm and contribute something to the conversation, can help equalize participation.[27] Additional ways one can get students more invested in the success of the entire team is to have each group establish group ground rules (in conversation with general classroom rules established by the instructor) and have them incorporate their own rules into a

---

25. B. Oakley *et al.* also cite numerous other studies confirming these differences in educational outcomes, 'Turning Student Groups into Effective Teams', *Journal of Student Centered Learning* 2 (2004), p. 9.

26. Here I sometimes follow Johnson, Johnson, and Smith, *Cooperative Learning*, and Barkley, Cross, and Major, *Collaborative Learning Techniques*, especially pp. 69-82.

27. This type of exercise is effective in that it encourages the flow of ideas without interruption. It generally involves each student brainstorming a response one at a time, with one word or statement, to a question. It does not permit students to explain, analyze, elaborate on or question the responses and is particularly effective in ensuring equal participation among group members. See also Barkley, Cross, and Major, *Collaborative Learning Techniques*, pp. 108-11.

'learning contract', which each member signs at the beginning of the quarter.[28] This activity alone taps into peer pressure and reinforces student responsibilities and potential penalties for any breach of contract.

Off-task behavior can also disrupt the group learning process. Although the social relationships developed in the effective learning groups are a beneficial and desired outcome, they can also result in excessive or distractive behavior, such as chatting, distractive joking around, or drifting from the task at hand. As much as is possible, the instructor should try to break up best friends, worst enemies and romantic couples. Another effective way to keep students on task is to set a hard-to-reach time limit for each activity, which will pressure students to focus. Breaking up a larger or longer project into constituent parts and asking students to report to you at each stage can also encourage students to stay on track. Finally, as a last resort, sometimes by just physically moving closer to students, an instructor can navigate students away from disruptive behavior.

Otherwise, an instructor can respond to dysfunctional groups by varying the group's size and the roles of individual members; only as a last resort should the instructor reorganize the group(s) entirely. When left alone, less extreme problems or behaviors have a tendency to work themselves out and, in the process, allow the students to mature alongside their colleagues. In B. Tuckman's classic article, 'Development Sequence in Small Groups', he notes that student groups go through five stages in which some conflict and the testing of boundaries and relationships are normal.[29] Ideally, overcoming these challenges among themselves can prove to be important for the group's growth and a key stage in the development of the whole student, per most liberal education goals, if the educator can resist intervening in non-serious conflicts.

General Suggestions

A few final suggestions may prove helpful for those who wish to incorporate C-L techniques in the Bible classroom.[30]

1. *Keep in mind that C-L exercises, in general, require more time to cover the same amount of material than one might otherwise in a lecture.* Nev-

---

28. An excellent example of such a group learning contract can be found in Barkley, Cross, and Major, *Collaborative Learning Techniques*, p. 37. It is useful for students to see a sample form before they write up their own, given the likelihood that students will not know how to draw up such a contract on their own.

29. B. Tuckman, 'Developmental Sequence in Small Groups', *Psychological Bulletin* 63 (1965). Tuckman identifies these five stages: 1) *forming*, in which students get to know one another and shape their mutual expectations; 2) *storming*, in which the students test their relationships and struggle with each members' level of commitment; 3) *norming*, when the group clarifies their norms and roles; 4) *performing*, the period during which the work takes place; 5) *adjourning*, the wrap-up of the group project. Barkley, Cross, and Major include further discussion of this developmental process in *Collaborative Learning Techniques*, pp. 72-74.

30. Some of these follow guidelines already offered by Peter Hawkes, as republished in Bruffee, *Collaborative Learning*, pp. 41-43.

ertheless, students are more likely to retain more of what they learn by being asked to *use* their expanding knowledge; further, they are likely to be motivated to use better study habits because they may see their learning as more purposeful and interesting. In the long run, students often come to class better prepared and more invested in the content when they are motivated by and answerable to their peers.[31]

2. *When analyzing a particular Bible passage in class, limit the reading to a manageable size and instruct one person to read it aloud to the group.* Reading to each other can aid the student in hearing their own voice aloud in the classroom.

3. *List and format the instructions of every worksheet with the same general instructions.* Keeping similar types of cues and instructions in the same format across exercises can save the group time to collectively figure out what is being asked of them.

4. *Make the questions asked of the biblical text short and simple.* One need not prompt every possible angle within a question, as even the most concise of questions can generate profound and complex conversation.[32]

5. *Nevertheless, ask open-ended questions that have more than one answer.* This will ensure that the recorders' reports do not become repetitive and will generate more debate. For instance, rather than asking questions of the biblical text such as, 'What does it say?', ask instead, 'What does it assume?', etc.[33]

6. *Shape your questions to discourage over-generalizations and to encourage students to back up their assessments with specific examples.* For example, rather than simply asking, 'What is the meaning of this passage?' instead tailor your question to query, 'Which words or verses underlie your specific interpretation of this passage?', etc.

7. Finally, *make sure that individual activities clearly tie in with the overarching goals and designated outcomes of the course.* If students are made aware of how a particular activity concords with the larger course goals, they may avoid unnecessary feelings of engaging in wasteful 'busy-work'.

Concluding Reflections

As many studies have indicated, students frequently engage in more meaningful learning by working in collaborative groups rather than in classrooms that are highly competitive, individualized and hierarchical. And this type of active group learning can be equally as effective in the teaching of the Bible and of the workings of biblical criticism as it is for other liberal arts courses. Collabora-

---

31. Compare Bean, *Engaging Ideas*, p. 9.
32. Bruffee, *Collaborative Learning*, p. 42.
33. Bruffee, *Collaborative Learning*, p. 43.

tive learning evokes a new epistemology, one that understands knowledge to be something that is created among a community of readers, including the instructor, thereby imitating the long reception history of the Bible itself. Nevertheless, one could argue that in teaching the Bible through C-L activities the instructor should retain a certain amount of authority in the classroom and some monitoring of classroom learning. For although Bible students benefit from generating their own meaning-making when interacting with the text, they are positioning themselves in an ongoing conversation, one in which they should participate as responsible readers.

From Biblical Literature to Ultimate Questions: Shifting Contexts and Goals for Introducing the Bible

Bryan D. Bibb
Furman University

I recently experienced the most difficult semester I have had in twelve years of teaching, indeed even more difficult than when I began at Furman University as an optimistic and naive instructor. Several years ago, Furman began the process of completely replacing its calendar and curriculum, and I was fortunate enough to be on sabbatical during the first year that these changes went into effect. It was a temporary reprieve, however, so eventually I found myself back in the classroom, teaching a brand-new introductory Bible course in an unfamiliar curriculum with a radically different semester schedule.

These curricular changes were the latest in a series of profound transitions at Furman, which has gone from being a South Carolina Baptist college to an aspiring national university with an ecumenical and increasingly secular religious perspective. Furman disaffiliated from the Baptists in 1991, and has generally followed the pattern set by other formerly Baptist schools such as Wake Forest.[1]

The fact is that Furman as a university was functionally independent before the break, and the religion department had not been in doctrinal accord with the South Carolina Baptists for decades. Thus, Furman's disaffiliation basically assured the protection of academic freedom in the future, as well as freedom to expand our curricular offerings and to diversify the faculty without needing Convention approval. The religion department began offering world religions courses in the 1970s, and the department has continued to expand beyond biblical studies and theology to include scholars in comparative religion, religion and culture, and anthropology.

This paper is a reflection upon Furman's changing religious and curricular context, and describes how our new introductory Bible class addresses this

---

1. See James Tunstead Burtchaell, *The Dying of the Light: The Disengagement of Colleges and Universities from their Christian Churches* (Grand Rapids: Eerdmans, 1998), chapter 4, 'The Baptists'.

new environment. In past years, I taught a standard Biblical Literature survey, but the new course is more amorphous and flexible, open to diverse approaches to content and method. This new course, titled 'The Bible and Ultimate Meaning', enables the professor to engage students where they are while providing an introduction to the Bible as literature, as artifact, and as living scriptural tradition.

Biblical Literature

For many years, nearly all students at Furman took a course titled Religion 11: 'Introduction to Biblical Literature'. It satisfied the University's 'Religion' requirement, and was taught by most members of the department, even those not in biblical studies. The course description read as follows:

> The study of the Bible to heighten appreciation for its literary origins and forms, historical settings, moral wisdom and religious insight, and enduring contributions to Western culture.

Because there was not enough time to cover everything in the Bible, the professor had to choose which topics would be covered, but the emphasis was on literature survey and critical methods. In the first week of class there was an emphasis on authorship and editing of the Torah, followed by a detailed look at the differences and contradictions between the two creation stories. I spent class time discussing historical issues related to the ancestral traditions and Moses, to the models of the Israelite emergence in Canaan, and to Judean archaeology. The course continued in that vein, moving through the Deuteronomistic History and the Prophets with a brief stop in Qoheleth on the way to the historical Jesus, Paul the Jew, and the Revelation of John as an apocalyptic denunciation of ancient Rome. My sense is that most biblical scholars have taken and indeed taught this course in one form or another.

Given Furman's Baptist identity, most of our students were broadly familiar with the Bible and had some level of personal engagement with the scriptures. For that reason, it was vitally important to expose them to the most important topics in critical biblical studies, those high-impact controversies that get conservatives the most agitated. The course was a pure example of the standard liberal protestant introduction to the Bible in the late 20th century: a course designed to disabuse students of certain assumptions, deconstruct traditional views, and hopefully rebuild a stronger, more nuanced interpretive structure. Professors could (or at least did) assume that students were conversant in the tradition and that they considered the Bible to be important (culturally, religiously, and personally) and interesting.

Now, however, the religious context has changed. Before professors in universities like Furman can teach that kind of critical introduction, even to students from religious backgrounds, we have to tell them what the traditional interpretations *are* before we can disabuse them of those interpretations. The harder task these days is to engage students with the Bible, to convince them of its importance and compelling nature, and to demonstrate why it is important in our modern context to be a well-informed and critical reader of the Bible. Like many professors at formerly religious schools like Furman, I have had to alter my assumptions about what knowledge and perspectives students bring to the class. On one hand, I find in my classes more religious diversity, but a generally lower level of literacy and interest in the Bible. Teaching 'Biblical Literature' must necessarily look different in this changing religious context. I have dealt with another layer of complexity, however, presented by the changing institutional context created by a new core curriculum, in which the 'Bible' requirement was replaced with something much more diffuse.

Ultimate Questions

When Furman began to revise its curriculum in 2004, the faculty was asked to consider anew why we teach the classes we do and what we hope students will gain from them. The majority of introductory courses had been designed for two purposes: to service the university's distribution requirements in certain subjects, and to provide a disciplinary orientation for future majors. In the new curriculum, there is no single required course. Instead of stipulating that students take an 'Introduction to Biblical Literature', the new system encouraged us to think about introductory courses in a broader way.

The religion department, situated on the liberal wing of Baptist life, had originally designed its previous introductory course to make students aware of their uncritical assumptions about the Bible and to help them derive a more nuanced and critical appreciation of the scriptural tradition. Now things had changed; there was no longer a guaranteed audience of freshmen, nor a religiously homogeneous student body. There was neither a departmental consensus on what it means to 'introduce' the study of religion, nor a clear idea of what first-level Bible courses we should offer, or how might they compare (or compete) with other courses in the department and in the university.

The curriculum review committee, with input from the departments of religion and philosophy and others, concluded that students should take one course in a category titled 'Ultimate Questions'. Presently the majority of these courses are in the religion and philosophy departments, but there are offerings as well in English, political science, and the natural sciences. The category was defined in the curriculum proposal document 'Invigorating Intellectual Life', approved by the faculty in 2005.

It begins:

> Central to the experience of liberal education is the opportunity to reflect in a rigorous way on questions about the meaning and purpose of human life—about what is ultimately real and good. In accordance with Furman's mission to 'engage ethical issues and explore spiritual concerns', courses in this category invite students to engage metaphysical, religious and ethical questions in a direct and explicit way by examining ways in which individuals and societies have articulated what constitutes a good

and meaningful life—as that is reflected in various past or present cultural/ individual understandings of our obligation to others; our relation to the transcendent; and how these find expression in a rich variety of written, oral, and performative texts. While this kind of reflection can be sparked by many experiences both inside and outside of the classroom, this Core category is intended to enable students to engage such concerns in a thematic way.[2]

There are a few important code words in this description. The idea of the 'good life' ties into a classic philosophical theme. This theme is 'reflected in various past or present cultural/individual understandings'. This somewhat broad statement embraces both historical and systematic approaches, whether from a social, political, or religious perspective. The distinction between 'individual' and 'cultural' contexts reflects the increasing impact of sociology and anthropology in the field of religious and biblical studies. In the last few years the religion department has added two full-fledged anthropologists to its faculty, and one person in African-American religious traditions who works in the vein of cultural studies and philosophical ethics. The study of scriptural texts and theology is thus only one part of our identity, alongside a variety of other methodological approaches.

One phrase has caused some difficulty for the Curriculum Review Committee charged with approving courses for Ultimate Questions credit: 'our relation to the transcendent'. As the religion department debated various phrases and terms to include in the description, it became clear that we did not have ourselves a consensus about what the former Bible requirement was supposed to accomplish. In this disagreement, we compromised about certain things, including this references to the 'transcendent'. This word is supposed to communicate that the Ultimate Questions category should not be 'only' philosophy or ethics, but that courses should also address religion, i.e., God, or the transcendent, or whatever language one would like to use for 'the ultimate'.

The problem remains, of course, of how to articulate what is meant by 'transcendent' and 'ultimate', but there is room for those words to mean whatever is appropriate to the discipline in question. A course on ancient Israelite religion and course on Buddhism would address the notion of the 'transcendent' quite differently. However, how can a committee comprising faculty from across the university accurately judge whether a course outside of their fields adequately addresses 'our relation to the transcendent?' This language began as a compromise, and continues to function as a site of discussion and difference. Despite the lack of consensus, it is better to have these issues on the table, so to speak, rather than shaping the discussion in an inchoate way, as they did for many years prior to the curricular revision. The university has also committed to a thorough assessment strategy as part of its regular accreditation renewal, so these conversations will no doubt continue to evolve.

---

2. The report is available at www.furman.edu/itf/crcfinal.pdf. This quote is on p. 17.

The Bible and Ultimate Meaning

On the subject of specific classes, the Curricular Review Committee report spells out more fully what one might call the framer's intent of the Ultimate Questions category. It says this:

> Two things are thus necessary for a course to qualify for the category of Ultimate Questions. First, the written texts, the oral traditions, and/or practices studied must be interpreted as being concerned with 'ultimate questions' according to the description above. Second, the questions must be *engaged*, not merely *objectively studied or briefly mentioned*. In the pedagogy of an Ultimate Questions course, the point is to help students not only analytically examine but also empathetically respond to the questions an author, text, or situation raises.[3]

In reflecting on the new curriculum, it occurred to me that this was not a good description of how I had been teaching my 'Introduction to Biblical Literature' course. My starting point in that course had been the awareness students bring and their own personal engagement with the Bible to the course, and that my job was to help them figure out why they believe what they do, and perhaps help them refine or reconstruct their views in light of new information about the Bible's history and content. But what if students do not bring a high level of prior engagement with the biblical text, or more accurately, what if they represent a diverse array of interests and engagements, from ignorance to benevolent apathy to well-developed fundamentalism? What kind of Bible course would help those students 'engage' the 'Ultimate Questions' related to the 'Transcendent' in the Bible?

The Curriculum Review Committee document provides an example course that might be found outside of the Religion and Philosophy departments, a hypothetical course on Thoreau's Walden. It says,

> For example, a professor of English might teach an English course on *Walden* that would count as an Ultimate Questions course. While Thoreau clearly raises the kinds of questions described in this category, this by itself would not be sufficient. At some point in an Ultimate Questions course on *Walden*, the following questions must directly and explicitly arise: 'Is Thoreau right when he says that "behaving well" can be understood as a kind of demonic possession? Is he right to be critical of "acts of charity" undertaken at long distance? Would he oppose giving money for tsunami relief, for example? Why or why not? What are the arguments for his position, and are they good ones?' The educational point is not just to identify Thoreau's questions or teachings; the point is to engage those questions as a world view to be empathetically understood, reasonably considered, and critically evaluated.[4]

---

3. 'Invigorating Intellectual Life', p. 17.
4. 'Invigorating Intellectual Life', p. 18.

This course description led to me reconsider how I had been teaching the Bible. The Ultimate Questions category required me to consider not just what ancient Israelites believed about God at different points of their history, but also how contemporary readers might respond to and evaluate those claims. Should the course ask, 'Were the prophets right when they described physical idol images as mute and powerless blocks of wood?' Should it ask, 'What did Jesus mean when he said that he is the way, the truth, and the life, and would he oppose ecumenical efforts to create understanding among the world's religions? Why or why not?' Should it ask, 'The Israelite law suggests that the proper punishment for many crimes is execution. Do we have empathy for their understanding of punishment and death, and how do we feel about the modern death penalty?'

Those sound like interesting class discussions, but they are quite different from the historical and literary approach that I had learned and used for a decade. On those occasions when the class considered contemporary (rather than historical) theological questions, it was usually related to the modern church context. For example, 1 Timothy 2.11-15 says that women are not allowed to speak in church; however, this Pastoral letter was probably not written by Paul and many Christian churches would never think to enforce such a rule. For other churches, however, this passage is foundational to their ecclesiology. Even in the old class, I would consider how modern Christians might interpret the Bible in ways that bound them or freed them from patriarchal arguments. That question did not fit strictly within the biblical literature survey focus, but it was important because most students were Christian and were personally engaged in that debate. Perhaps ironically, the current Ultimate Questions requirement actively encourages such conversation, but students as a whole are not as interested in having it.

After discussion with other interested members of the department, we proposed a new introductory course titled 'The Bible and Ultimate Meaning', and its course description is as follows:

> A study of selected biblical texts with a focus on ultimate questions raised and addressed by those texts. Typically, biblical texts are studied in pairs or triads, emphasizing diverse perspectives, and in relation to other literature, ancient and modern.

This description is purposefully quite vague, but the goal is to move away from the traditional literature survey, organized historically and canonically, to a more thematic and philosophical/ethical/theological approach. There is also a course called 'The Bible in the Public Square', which focuses more on contemporary political issues, while this course is more theological or philosophical.

In this new course, designed for different students in a changing university and a revised curriculum, the professor is no longer required to 'get through' all of the material as before. There is less focus on traditional survey methodology and less concern for historical and redaction-critical issues. What does the course emphasize instead? Theological and ethical convictions and claims, as embedded in texts and within their historical context, and how contemporary religious and political discourses draw upon those texts in rhetorical and confessional ways.

In the new course, the professor has freedom to group thematically related passages across the canon, with some small attention to their historical relationship, but with a central focus on how various biblical notions compare or differ internally and with later interpretation. There is a clear incentive, a requirement even, to connect biblical texts and theology to contemporary ethical, religious, theological or political issues, whether in readings, class discussions, or written assignments.

What do students gain? Hopefully, more of them will be engaged personally and intellectually with the course content. The hope is that more students will decide that they like doing this kind of comparison and engagement, and that they would like nothing better than to declare a religion major. And most of all, students will leave the course with more confidence in addressing the biblical tradition (text and interpretation) and with more awareness of its importance and delightfulness in their lives and world.

What do students forfeit? The class does not expose them to much of the scholarly apparatus or vocabulary. They do not encounter as much of the Bible as they would in a fast-paced survey course, measured in pure volume. Theoretically, they may leave the course with a lower level of biblical and scholarly literacy than they would have in the old course. They might not be able to name the last 5 kings of Judah or to articulate the pros and cons of the gradual infiltration hypothesis. My argument at the time, which has been affirmed in my first two years in teaching the class, is that what students gain is much more significant in the long term than what students give up in this new approach.

I should also stress that the department sees this course as a university 'service' course for non-majors. A student who later declares a religion major could count this course among their credits, but the purpose of the course is not to introduce students to the academic study of the Bible. Rather, the purpose is to help them understand the Bible better, and to know better why they should study it regardless of their own religious tradition. Further, there is always the possibility that if they come away from the course being excited about biblical studies, they will sign up for an upper-level course where they will engage more of the scholarly framework of theories and arguments.

Course Structure and Topics

Let me conclude by discussing how I have arranged the course, and indicating how I address the biblical creation story as an example, freely admitting that this is a work in progress. One of the best things about this course from a professor's point of view is the freedom and encouragement to rearrange topics and assignments on a regular basis. There is no danger of me finding myself teaching this course from the proverbial yellowed notes.

I have structured the course with four 'triads' of biblical ideas, beginning with two weeks of introductory discussion of the Bible's historical and literary development. The four triads are:

1. God/Creation/Covenant, which establishes the importance of God as creator who established the world and engaged with it as partner in covenant-making. I offer more reflection about this first unit below.
2. Community/Justice/Messiah, which addresses this creator God's vision for the human community and its natural environment, culminating in the Christian tradition with Jesus, but fully expressed as well in the Hebrew prophetic tradition.
3. Worship/Wisdom/Joy, which considers the topics that Gerhard von Rad once referred to as 'Israel's Answer' to the salvation history unveiled by God.[5] In discussions of wisdom and joy, I make sure to cover their close parallels, skepticism and lament.
4. Faith/Hope/Love, based on Paul's famous triad in 1 Corinthians 13. In the faith section, I consider how Christians came to articulate their belief in Jesus in the New Testament as well as in the first four centuries of Christian history. The hope section covers the development from prophetic to apocalyptic eschatology, and the love section is usually right at the end of the course, and students always enjoy reading Song of Songs and discussing romantic relationships in light of the biblical tradition.

Below is a table of the topics with passages discussed each week. In a three-classes-per-week format, I tend to have two days devoted to particular topics, and spend the third in discussion of a book chapter from Peter Gomes' *The Good Book: Reading the Bible with Mind and Heart*.[6] A few passages show up more than once, which is intended to help them see the interconnected nature of these topics within the larger biblical worldview. In those cases, by repeating a passage that we have already discussed, I can establish a touchstone for introducing the new topic. These are the passages assigned for students to read, and I do not cover them all equally. I will sometimes focus most of my time on one passage, and will almost always bring other smaller texts into the discussion for comparison or context.

---

5. See Gerhard von Rad, *Old Testament Theology*, Volume 1 (San Francisco: Harper San Francisco, 1962), pp. 355-459.

6. Peter Gomes, *The Good Book: Reading the Bible with Mind and Heart* (San Francisco: Harper San Francisco, 1996). Chapters include topics such as 'The Bible and Race', 'The Bible and Homosexuality', 'The Bible and Suffering'.

Topic	Passages
Israel's Sacred History	Genesis 1–2, 12; Deuteronomy 4–6; 1 Samuel 17, 2 Kings 17, 24; Matthew 1–3; Luke 23–24; Acts 1–2; Revelation 1, 21–22
Literature in the Bible	Genesis 1–3; 2 Samuel 11; Psalm 1; Proverbs 1; Amos 5; Mark
God	Exodus 3, 6; Psalm 18, 29, 47, 82, 139; John 1
	Isaiah 6, 40, 44; Ezekiel 1, 8–10; Habakkuk 3; Ephesians 1
Creation	Genesis 1–5; Psalm 74, 104
	Genesis 6–11; Ecclesiastes 1–2; Isaiah 24; Romans 1–5
Covenant	Genesis 12, 15; Exodus 20, 34; Deuteronomy 28–30; Joshua 24; 2 Samuel 7; Psalm 89 and 132
	Jeremiah 7, 30–31; Romans 9–11; Galatians
Community	Ezra; Isaiah 56–66
	Matthew 5–10, Acts 1–2, 1 Corinthians
Justice	Exodus 20–23; Amos; Isaiah 1–5, 58
	Matthew 25; Romans
Messiah	Isaiah 7–11, 52–53; Psalm 22; Daniel 7–8
	John
Worship	Leviticus 1–10; 2 Samuel 6; 2 Kings 22–23; Isaiah 58
	Psalm 15, 122–125; Acts 2; 1 Timothy
Wisdom	Proverbs 1–9; Ecclesiastes
	Job 1–2, 9–10, 38–42
Joy	Psalm 38, 40, 98, 100, 102
	Lamentations 1–5; Philippians
Faith	Deuteronomy 1–8; John 1–6, 17–21
	[second day on early Church Christology]

Topic	Passages
Hope	Deuteronomy 30; Isaiah 2.1–4; Isaiah 61; Jeremiah 30.18–31.14; Ezekiel 37; Daniel 7–12
	Mark 13; 2 Thessalonians 1–2; Revelation
Love	Song of Songs; Ruth; 1 Corinthians 13; 1 John
	[second day is usually for course evaluation, once students are in a loving mood]

Creation

In order to provide a clearer idea of how I approach this course, I will conclude by illustrating how I approach the opening chapters of Genesis during Week 3 of the course. I would like to contextualize these comments in light of Jane Webster's very helpful article 'Biblical Studies in the Context of the Emerging Religion Major', in which she articulates student learning outcomes based on the recommendations in the 2008 AAR White Paper.[7] For each goal, she provides a learning outcome and examples of classroom activities related to Genesis 1-3. For 'Intercultural and Comparative', Webster says that students should do comparative myth studies between the Bible and the Enuma Elish, with some effort to have students articulate their own understanding of the earth's origins. I have always used the mythic parallel texts, but as Webster says, now there is more emphasis on what creation is rather than the differences between P and J. I still talk about P and J in the course, but not in terms of their disputed historical contexts, but rather as alternate visions of creation to be considered and evaluated.

For 'Multi-disciplinary', Webster discusses the importance of using a variety of interpretive methods, explicitly and intentionally. I am able now to do this because I can linger over the creation narratives for as long as I want. Rather than feeling like I have rush past the text of Genesis 1-3 to leave time for scholarly theories and historical survey, I have plenty of time for literary and ideological analysis of the Adam and Eve story, and to compare Genesis 1 with creation language in Psalms, Job, Colossians, Wendell Berry, etc.

For 'Critical', Webster emphasizes discussion of ethical dilemmas, and her examples cohere nicely with the Ultimate Questions category: discussions of birth control, strip mining, and patriarchy, or the question of whether Eve was right to choose knowledge over obedience. Taking time to do this requires us to rethink not only how we structure the syllabus but also how we allot class time. Instead of lecturing, there is an incentive to provide content through alternative

---

7. Jane S. Webster, 'Biblical Studies in the Context of the Emerging Religion Major', *SBL Forum*, www.sbl-site.org/publications/article.aspx?ArticleId=816.

means (readings, podcasts, online interaction) and to save class time for face-to-face discussion.

For 'Integrative', Webster suggests considering the relationship between scriptural traditions and actual religious practices in modern and contemporary contexts. The issue of women in ministry is still a hot topic for some students, though just as many wonder what the big fuss is about. How does the interpretation of Eve influence ritual and family practices in Jewish and Christian contexts?

Finally, for 'Creative and Constructive', Webster says that we should encourage students to integrate and apply their knowledge for the purpose of solving complex problems, including intensely personal issues of life, death, love, violence, suffering, and meaning. This is the goal of the Ultimate Questions category, it seems to me, though we have not articulated it so well or clearly. And it is in this area that professors must be willing to give up the most control. We can perhaps guide or force students to learn particular facts. Through the power of persuasion, we can perhaps convince them that certain ideas or facts should be prioritized or contextualized in certain ways. But we cannot live their life. The final assessment of this learning goal can be done only by the student and over the course of his or her life. The Bible, however, may be a tremendous resource along the way, whatever journey they take.

I mentioned that in my first year I was optimistic and naive. Twelve years in, I am hopefully less naive but now even more optimistic. I am optimistic that our new curriculum provides the flexibility we need to address the needs and interest of a diverse study body; I am excited about the opportunity to explore new directions in my teaching. However, I am experienced enough to know that with new approaches some things are lost or forgotten, and that we may look back wistfully on the days when our methods and assignments were more clearly defined. It is this unknown element that made me feel like a first year instructor again, and I have already enjoyed the process of finding new and fresh ways of exploring the Bible with students. The main comfort this time, of course, is that I have tenure.

Part III

CASE STUDIES

BIBLE-TREK, NEXT GENERATION: ADAPTING A BIBLE SURVEY COURSE FOR A NEW AUDIENCE

Jonathan D. Lawrence
Canisius College

What do our students want to learn about the Bible? How do they learn? As teachers, what do we want them to learn? How can we best present the material to help them learn? Barbara Walvoord's recent study indicates that there can be a large gap between student expectations and goals for introductory religion courses and the way those courses are taught.[1] What should we do about this gap? What might it look like to reinvent an introductory course in the Bible with these concerns in mind? This paper offers reflections from my own experience as a beginning teacher as I modified my courses from traditional 'survey' introductions to the Bible to more thematic approaches.[2]

Recent discussions about the nature of students in 'Generation Y' or the so-called 'Millennials' suggest that our current students are used to instant answers, information overload, and exposure to a multiplicity of viewpoints.[3] In this context, a traditional approach comprised of readings, lectures, and exams is likely to cause frustration for both students and faculty. For instance, the students may have trouble seeing why particular material is relevant or authoritative for their instructors, while professors may wonder why their students are treating Wikipedia and the Anchor Bible Commentaries as equally reliable sources. Similarly, while religious and biblical literacy may be important skills for us to encourage our students to develop, they will not accept this goal for

---

1. Barbara E. Walvoord, *Teaching and Learning in College Introductory Religion Courses* (Malden, MA: Blackwell, 2007).

2. This paper was delivered at the 2007 Annual Meeting of the Society of Biblical Literature as well as at the 2008 Eastern Great Lakes Bible Society Conference and a regional conference at Niagara University. I would like to thank those in attendance who gave comment and feedback on my approach to teaching the course. A copy of the course syllabus, assignment instructions, and rubric are available in the Society of Biblical Literature's syllabus collection.

3. Mike Hayes, *Googling God—The Religious Landscape of People in their 20s and 30s* (New York: Paulist, 2007) p. xiii and Leslie Owen Wilson, *Teaching Millennial Students* (www4.uwsp.edu/education/facets/links_resources/Millennial%20Specifics.pdf).

themselves just because we tell them to.[4]

Many students in this generation describe themselves as 'spiritual, but not religious', or some other similar formulation.[5] As 'spiritual, but not religious', they may be interested in learning more about the Bible as an exploration of spiritual matters. Many of them will not assume that the Bible is credible, authoritative, or worthy of study in and of itself, distinguishing them from previous generations and many faculty members.[6] This creates the added challenge of getting these students to engage with the material and convincing them that it is worth their time.

Some of my students expected the class to continue the doctrinal emphasis of their previous studies while others found the very idea of a required course in Bible to be offensive, even at a prominent religiously-affiliated university. A few said that their clergy had always told them that there's only one right way to read the Bible, while others said their clergy had told them never to read the Bible, just to listen to what is said in church. Even if I managed to convince them that studying the Bible could be relevant and exciting, these attitudes illustrate the kinds of assumptions our students are bringing into our classes.

Walvoord's study highlights a disconnect between the goals and expectations among students and faculty in introductory religion courses. Where students were looking for 'multi-dimensional growth', faculty were aiming for critical thinking.[7] These goals need not become mutually exclusive, but this sharp contrast demands attention by faculty who want their students to become involved in learning. We must also consider the debate over whether the 'content of our teaching is irrelevant', as R. Timothy McLay has argued.[8] He claims that our choice of content is less important than helping our students become critical thinkers. Perhaps a more useful question is whether we are teaching the content for its own sake or as a means of helping our students become critical thinkers about an important canon of texts? If the latter, we can provide opportunities for student growth while also emphasizing content and critical thinking.

As we consider shifting attitudes among our students, it is also important to consider shifting priorities among religion departments and faculty in general. For instance, many institutions have changed the focus of their religion majors from a seminary preparation model to a more broadly religious stud-

---

4. See for instance, Stephen Prothero, *Religious Literacy: What Every American Needs to Know—and Doesn't* (San Francisco: HarperOne, 2007).

5. See Reid B. Locklin, *Spiritual But Not Religious?: An Oar Stroke Closer to the Farther Shore* (Collegeville, MN: Liturgical, 2005) for a brief illustration of these viewpoints.

6. See Christian Smith, *Souls in Transition: The Religious and Spiritual Lives of Emerging Adults* (Oxford: Oxford University Press, 2009) for a study of religious attitudes among young adults.

7. Walvoord, *Teaching and Learning in College Introductory Religion Courses*, pp. 21-38.

8. R. Timothy McLay, 'The Goal of Teaching Biblical and Religious Studies in the Context of an Undergraduate Education', *SBL Forum* 4.8 (2006).

ies approach.⁹ At the same time, faculty across disciplines are considering shifts from teacher-centered or content-centered approaches to teaching that is learner-centered.¹⁰ We may still cover much of the same material and assignments, but the focus becomes how to help our students achieve the learning goals, not just how to best present the content.

Another factor to consider is changing attitudes about course design. Barbara Walvoord has argued that awareness of goals in course design can greatly improve effectiveness in grading and assessment.¹¹ Her study of introductory courses in religion and theology confirms the importance of developing clear course goals and designing a course around them.¹² Similarly, Dee Fink has proposed a system of 'integrated course design' in which instructors start with the goals and then design assignments and lesson plans, rather than starting with the content to be covered and then designing lesson plans and assignments.¹³ Once we are clear on our goals, this kind of conscious attention to learning goals and course structure can help narrow the gap between students' and professors' expectations.

During my first four years of teaching, I taught a required 'Introduction to Theology—Biblical and Historical' course at a religiously-affiliated university. In this course I was expected to cover both Old and New Testaments and five centuries of church history, all in one semester. Students would then be allowed to choose from a list of courses with a more theological focus to fulfill their second theology requirement. My learning goals were fairly standard for biblical surveys, encompassing understanding of the history of the Bible, scholarly methodologies, biblical themes and their interpretations, historical-critical reading of biblical texts, and developing personal understandings of biblical texts.

I used Stephen L. Harris's *Understanding the Bible*¹⁴ as my primary text and built the class around weekly online discussions, a midterm and final exams, group projects on a biblical topic, and a short paper based on visits to worship services in town. During the four years that I taught this course, I gradually reduced my reliance on lectures and added more discussion opportunities, along with other small adjustments to my teaching approach. My scores on

---

9. American Academy of Religion, 'The Religion Major and Liberal Education' (2009) www.aarweb.org/programs/Religion_Major_and_Liberal_Education/default.asp.

10. See Maryellen Weimer, *Learner-Centered Teaching: Five Key Changes to Practice* (San Francisco: Jossey-Bass, 2002) for an introduction to the learner-centered approach.

11. Barbara E. Walvoord and Virginia Johnson Anderson, *Effective Grading: A Tool for Learning and Assessment* (San Francisco: Jossey-Bass, 1998), pp. 1-6.

12. Walvoord, *Teaching and Learning in College Introductory Religion Courses*, pp. 10-11, 80-81.

13. L. Dee Fink, *Creating Significant Learning Experiences: An Integrated Approach to Designing College Courses* (San Francisco: Jossey-Bass, 2003).

14. Steven L. Harris, *Understanding the Bible* (New York: McGraw-Hill, 4th edn, 2011). There are many introductory textbooks available. Most of them are well-written and some even include discussion questions, self-test quizzes, and CD-ROM or online resources. However, I found few that supported the thematic approach that I developed for my reorganized class.

student evaluations improved slightly, but students' overall comprehension and application of critical thinking did not change substantially.

While many students did very well on the tests, there were also many that missed questions with answers that had been spelled out on the review sheets. In addition, many students were simply parroting back concepts we had discussed in class rather than showing evidence of critical thought. They routinely enjoyed the worship service visits, which I had included as an important experience but not related to any specific course goal. Finally I kept finding myself exhausted from the pace at which we covered material, and frustrated by the results.

I took a different approach when I started teaching at a new institution. My goals remained largely the same as before, but now the course was focused around the process of examining selected passages, rather than following a broad survey of biblical content.[15] I selected five passages (Genesis 1-4, Exodus 7-15, Isaiah 7-11, Leviticus 11-15, and the entire book of Daniel) and set up a sequence of activities for each unit:

Introducing the text and soliciting students' questions about the text
Discussing interpretations: students are to post interpretations they find
Broader issues: context, history, modern connections
Conclusion: Revisiting students' questions; often includes a movie.

The unit papers focused on the following sections:

Introducing the text and the questions the student has chosen as focus
Context: biblical, social, and historical
Interpretations: changes in interpretation, theological, artistic and literary
Conclusion: answering the questions, analyzing the sources used

The students' group projects applied the same questions to other texts from the Hebrew Bible, thus expanding the number of biblical texts students encounter during the term. Their final papers then expand on the parts of the group project that each student focused on.

I have found several benefits to designing the course in this way. First, I have been able to track students' progress easily through their papers—the same rubric is used each time so they know what they need to improve the next time and I can monitor their improvement. Second, by incorporating their questions and responses to the text, I am meeting them where they are. Third, this structure allows me to incorporate major concepts into the discussion of the texts rather than as a stand-alone topic. While I could spend several days talking about the development of the Documentary Hypothesis, I wait until the students have asked about the differences between the creation stories in Genesis 1 and 2. I then incorporate the Documentary Hypothesis into our discussion

---

15. This course was modeled closely after one found on the AAR Syllabus Project: aarweb.org/syllabus/syllabi/h/haas/RS106_syl.htm.

and the explanation of the differences. Fourth, when I ask students to bring in interpretations they have found, I also ask them to evaluate the reliability of their sources. This involves them in the process of interpreting and analyzing their sources.

Finally, this approach allows for a diversity of opinion with its focus on how students are making their arguments. My students' beliefs range from rejection of biblical authority to literal readings of the Bible or adherence to whatever their religious tradition tells them about scripture. I have seen cases where students in other classes feel pressured to give answers that contradict their beliefs just because that is what they think the instructor wants. I have not experienced this problem with this course because the focus is on how they are supporting their arguments, not on the opinions they are presenting. Thus a student who argues for a position that contradicts my own beliefs can still receive a high grade as long as the paper cites and analyzes academic sources.

In general students have responded positively in course evaluations and in personal conversations. Many have indicated that they like the way the course allows them to consider new questions and focus on learning and analysis instead of memorizing facts. Others have indicated that the course has been interesting and fun. A few have even indicated that they have left the course wanting to read more of the Bible, something that I rarely heard in my earlier classes. The biggest challenge though has been in motivating the students. There have been some students who chose to do the bare minimum needed to pass the class and who never engaged with the material any more than necessary. I have found it easier to motivate students for this course than in previous courses, but still have not won over all students.

There are of course some drawbacks to this method. Grading these papers takes a lot more time than grading the tests for my old class, but with a clear rubric that focuses on the criteria it is manageable. The rubric focuses on critical thinking and the rhetoric of the students' arguments more than just on their grasp of details. Grading thus emphasizes and reinforces the goals of the course. Another problem is the need to limit the number of Bible stories and texts examined in the class. Even though the group projects allow me to introduce the students to other passages, I have to limit severely the amount of biblical content for the course.

I developed this approach for a Hebrew Bible course, but it can be applied to other topics and disciplines as well. I have adapted the syllabus for a New Testament introduction and an honors section of Hebrew Bible. I also used the general approach but different kinds of assignments for an introduction to world religions: instead of spending two weeks talking about each religion, I have used Gary Kessler's *Studying Religion: An Introduction Through Cases*.[16] This approach could also work in literature, history, philosophy, or any other

---

16. Gary E. Kessler, *Studying Religion: An Introduction through Cases* (New York: McGraw-Hill, 3rd edn, 2007).

discipline where an in-depth examination of a few topics could substitute for a survey of many topics.

While I was not specifically thinking about the characteristics of Millennial Generation students in designing my course, I have found that several aspects of the course address their situation. First, focusing on just a few texts forces the students to slow down and stay with the story rather than move quickly from topic to topic. Second, allowing students to use interpretations they found (often online) in discussions and papers involves them in applying critical thinking skills to their internet sources. Finally, framing papers in terms of how they make their arguments rather than emphasizing what an expert has said or what religious leaders say acknowledges their awareness of multiple voices but does not allow them to get away with saying that all interpretations are equal—they still have to support their answers.

I have found this approach to teaching biblical literature very useful and have heard from several colleagues that they have adapted this approach in their own courses with good results. It may not be useful or effective for all instructors or institutions. Two crucial factors are the amount of autonomy an instructor has to choose how to teach the course and the nature of the course or departmental goals. If your school or department wants students to learn extensive content about the Bible in a semester, this course will not work. If your department expects several people to use a common approach to teaching the same course and will not allow you to experiment with other approaches, different problems may arise. I can, however, present this as a case where focusing on implementing the course goals and not just delivering material has successfully transformed how I teach my students. More important, it has transformed my students' learning experience and their interaction with biblical materials.

Dildos and Dismemberment: Reading Difficult Biblical Texts in the Undergraduate Classroom

Janet S. Everhart
Simpson College

When undergraduates enroll in a survey course on the Hebrew Bible, they expect to read about God's creation of the world, Noah and the flood, the Exodus from Egypt, and Moses receiving instructions from God on Mt. Sinai. They usually do not expect to discover multiple creation stories, to read that Noah's first act on reaching dry land was to plant a vineyard, make wine, and get so drunk that he passed out, to learn that God hardened Pharaoh's heart multiple times before the Exodus occurred, and to discover that God changed God's mind about destroying the wandering community because Moses reminded the deity to behave responsibly. Most professors who teach biblical studies have experienced the surprise, dismay, and occasional trauma that result when students read the Bible in a college classroom for the first time. Wrestling with difficult biblical texts, like the dismemberment of the Levite's concubine (Judges 19) or the misogynist pornographic images found in Ezekiel 16 and 23, can set the stage for thinking about and discussing issues at the heart of liberal arts education.

Learning Outcomes and Liberal Education

At Simpson College where I presently teach, we are in the midst of implementing a new core liberal arts curriculum. A time-consuming and tedious process, the conversations about our Engaged Citizenship Curriculum have prompted faculty to read, think about, and discuss the value of a liberal arts education. In the best tradition of the liberal arts, what outcomes do we most want for our students? While we disagree about many details, most of us want to expose our students to the rich multiplicity of the traditions that shape our culture. We want students to wrestle with diverse perspectives and to engage in big questions of meaning and purpose. We want students not only to achieve a knowledge base, but more importantly to understand how to assess information. We want students to grapple with questions like 'How do we decide what sources are authoritative for our lives?' We want students to observe and then experience how people of good will and intention can respectfully disagree, sometimes strenuously. We want students to connect their liberal arts education to the world around them, so the community and in some cases the world beyond becomes a classroom for testing ideas through interaction with individuals and communities beyond the campus. Further, we want our students to leave college with some experience of investing themselves in the community and making a positive difference in the world.

During our discussion of curriculum at Simpson we have referred often to the recent report, 'College Learning for the New Global Century', sponsored by the Association of American Colleges and Universities, or the AAC&U.[1] The Essential Learning Outcomes proposed in this report include knowledge of human cultures and the physical and natural world; intellectual and practical skills (including inquiry and analysis, critical and creative thinking, written and oral communication, quantitative and information literacy); personal and social responsibility; and integrative learning.[2] In this paper I argue that working with 'difficult' biblical texts can help undergraduates achieve several of the learning outcomes identified in the AAC&U report, particularly those outcomes listed under 'intellectual and practical skills'. As Katheryn Pfisterer Darr realized years before the AAC&U established these learning outcomes, 'Juxtaposing compelling, yet also conflicting, texts invites students to negotiate the differences between them, to evaluate the arguments of each, and to make judgments, open to future re-evaluation though those judgments be.'[3]

Connecting the Classroom to the Big Questions

While a classroom differs in many ways from a liturgical setting, my experience preaching on difficult texts has helped me navigate the same material in the classroom.[4] Early in the semester, I tell my students that in 1984, shortly after the publication of Phyllis Trible's *Texts of Terror*, three clergy colleagues and I covenanted to address at least one of Trible's four texts in our local churches.[5] The Sunday the liturgist read 2 Samuel 13, the story of the rape of Tamar by her half-brother Amnon, the congregation was so quiet one could have heard a pin drop. These words, coming from the Bible, describe the all too familiar pattern:

---

1. *College Learning for the New Global Century* (LEAP; American Association of Colleges and Universities, Washington, DC, 2008).
2. *College Learning*, p. 3.
3. Katheryn Pfisterer Darr, 'Ezekiel's Justifications of God: Teaching Troubling Texts', *Journal for the Study of the Old Testament* 55 (1992) pp. 97-117 (p. 113).
4. My preaching experience includes seventeen years as a full-time parish pastor in United Methodist churches.
5. Phyllis Trible, *Texts of Terror: Literary-Feminist Readings of Biblical Narratives* (Minneapolis: Fortress, Overtures to Biblical Theology, 1984). Trible focuses on Hagar (Gen 16.1-16; 21.9-21); Tamar (2 Sam 13.1-22); the unnamed concubine (Judges 19.1-30); and Jephthah's daughter (Judges 11.29-40).

Amnon's powerful desire for Tamar, the forced sex, his pushing her away once the rape was complete while she begged him now to receive her. David, king of Israel, was troubled but did nothing. In the course of the sermon I extended an invitation to anyone in the congregation to talk with me about experiences of sexual assault. During the following weeks, about a dozen men and women came to tell their stories. Those who had experienced abuse were relieved—in some cases comforted—to learn that their story was in the Bible. The response from students has been very similar: stories emerge. Both men and women start to think about and talk about the abuse of power, troubling images of God, and the very imperfect characters portrayed in the Bible.[6]

The questions and connections identified by students in the course of reading biblical 'texts of terror' lead straight into the heart of liberal arts inquiry. Dealing with difficult texts encourages students to apply the tools of liberal inquiry to topics and situations that many students actually care about and find themselves vested in, or at least, intrigued by.[7] For example, young adult students often explore romantic partnerships during college and some have experienced or know of violence in sexual relationships. Stories of violence in the Bible prompt questions: Why does a Levite have a concubine? Why does God look like an angry husband? What does this mean? Why are these stories less familiar than some other biblical texts? Why have I never heard these stories even though I've attended church all my life? What is the power of metaphor, and how do images of violence in biblical texts help to reinforce oppressive relationships even among individuals and communities who do not profess a Jewish or Christian faith perspective? Raising questions of the biblical text encourages the intellectual skills of inquiry and analysis as well as critical and creative thinking.

Ezekiel 16: Metaphor Gone Awry?

A student presentation in my Feminist Interpretation of the Bible class illustrates how hearing a difficult biblical text in the classroom can help students engage in some of the learning processes cited above.[8] A senior student read Mary Shields' article, 'Multiple Exposures: Body Rhetoric and Gender Characterization in Ezekiel 16'.[9] She began her class presentation by asking each of us to take out paper and pen, and draw a line down the middle of the paper. She

---

6. For a useful article on working with difficult texts in a seminary setting, see Harold W. Attridge, 'Living with Difficult Texts at YDS', *Reflections* (Spring 2008), pp. 22-24.

7. Here one's teaching context will make a difference in student investment in the subject. At a church-related liberal arts college, many students are intrigued to struggle with unfamiliar biblical stories. For a helpful discussion of pedagogical objectives involved in dealing with difficult texts, see Linda Day, 'Teaching the Prophetic Marriage Metaphor Texts', *Teaching Theology and Religion* 2.3 (1999), pp. 173-79.

8. My thanks to Anne Alesch, now pursuing graduate theological studies.

9. Mary Shields, 'Multiple Exposures: Body Rhetoric and Gender Characterization in Ezekiel 16', *Journal of Feminist Studies* 14.1 (2008), pp. 5-18.

instructed us to note on the left hand of the sheet any images we heard that were affirming for women; on the right hand, we were to note images that seemed oppressive. She then read, out loud, the first 42 verses of Ezekiel 16. The entire chapter is structured as a metaphor depicting the city of Jerusalem as a woman whose sexual appetite knows no bounds. 'The word of the Lord was addressed to me as follows, 'ben-adam, confront Jerusalem with her filthy crimes'. The single reference to Jerusalem occurs in verse 1. The remaining 62 verses of the chapter describe, in some detail, the whoring behavior of a female character. The student read 42 of the 63 verses. A sample from the NRSV will suffice here:

> You have become infatuated with your own beauty; you have used your fame to make yourself a prostitute; You have taken your clothes to brighten your high places and there you have played the whore...in all your filthy practices and whorings you have never remembered your youth or the time when you were quite naked and struggling in your own blood. You have piled whoring on whoring. You have lain down for those big-membered neighbors, the Egyptians; you have piled whoring on whoring to provoke me, and now I have raised my hand against you. How easily you were led to behave no better than a bold-faced whore...The Lord says this: I am going to band together all the lovers who have pleasured you; I will strip you in front of them, and let them see you naked. And I mean to punish you like women who commit adultery and murder; I intend to hand you over to fury and jealousy....

Each of us made notes as the student read. The presenter's first point was already clear: each listener had made numerous entries on the right side of her page where we recorded images derogatory toward women. Most had little or nothing on the left hand side. One student said, 'I counted some version of the word "whore" 21 times.' Most of us had long forgotten that the text was supposed to be a metaphor, since the sole mention of Jerusalem occurred in the first verse. We discussed how easily a metaphor depicts reality. Through most of the long chapter, it surely seemed that God was talking about a real woman, a woman who bled and dressed and undressed herself, a woman so desperate for sex that she paid her partners, a woman whose restoration, according to the Lord, means shame (Ezek. 16.61).

The presenter asked her peers for their responses to the text. 'I had no idea this was in the Bible', some said. Other comments included, 'It seems like God is justifying abuse against women', and 'This text makes me really angry', and 'I think we should throw this out of the canon.' Our classroom conversation continued. We discussed the power of biblical texts to both oppress and liberate. We discussed the possibility of resisting texts that condone violence against a particular population. At the end of that class period, I asked the students, 'Do you think it's important to know about this text?' Without exception in our seminar of 12 students, the response was a definitive 'Yes!' When I asked why, the students explained that they felt it was important to know what is actually in the Bible. One linked this story with a long-standing tendency to blame women for men's behavior. Another wondered whether this is one of the texts contributing to the acceptance of violence against women. Encouraging students to wrestle with possible unintended consequences of the metaphor in Ezekiel does not prevent exploration of the text using the tools of historical criticism, trying to unpack how the metaphor worked in Ezekiel's context. Indeed, approaching the text from several methodological perspectives is a useful exercise and illustrates how asking different questions of the text necessarily results in different readings. As they wrestle with the discovery that the Bible includes complex and troubling stories, and consider the ethical implications of how the stories are read and interpreted, students have the chance to develop the learning outcomes specified in the AAC&U's 'intellectual and practical skills' as well as 'personal and social responsibility'.

In my introductory Hebrew Bible class, I do not shield students from some of the violent and troubling texts in the Tanakh. Reading the story of David's adultery with Bathsheba and the arranged murder of Uriah, for example, usually raises questions about why God continues to favor David. Students often protest, 'I thought God would punish someone for committing adultery.' This story often prompts good discussion about the notion of fairness, or lack thereof, on God's part. Is God free to choose? Why does God choose anyone—Abraham, Saul, David? We also talk about the perspective of the narrator and the possible settings for the stories. Why, for instance, does the Chronicler 'clean up' David's story? Why do multiple versions of stories appear in biblical texts? Many undergraduate students want to read the Bible as history. When a student asks, 'which story is correct?' we are able to discuss concepts like social location, ideological perspective, and the notion of multiple voices in the canon. Dealing with complexity and multiplicity is a significant part of a liberal arts education. Students are required to think critically in new ways, to adopt alternative perspectives, to reconsider what they may have been taught about the Bible, and to grapple with the reality that both within and outside the canon, differing perspectives and interpretations are possible.[10]

The tools required to pose and wrestle with some of the questions that emerge when reading biblical texts translate usefully into life beyond college. Most students can think of someone whose character is as complex as David's—a strong leader with compassionate qualities, yet at times self-centered and capable of odious behavior. Recognizing the complexity of human nature and learning to identify both admirable and despicable qualities within a single biblical character helps students reevaluate their own tendencies to characterize certain members of the community as 'good' or 'bad', 'insider' or 'outsider'. As we consult some of the diverse perspectives found in the Bible, such as conflicting evaluations of monarchy or the participation of 'foreigners' in the life of the

---

10. Research suggests that problem-based assignments for both papers and discussion help to engage students and promote critical thinking skills. Difficult biblical texts lend themselves to problem-based assignments! A useful resource is John C. Bean, *Engaging Ideas: The Professor's Guide to Integrating Writing, Critical Thinking, and Active Learning in the Classroom* (San Francisco: John Wiley and Sons, 2nd edn, 2011).

community, students learn that the Bible does not present a singular viewpoint. Most students know that in almost any group of people, multiple perspectives about a given situation or issue can coexist; it is not hard to illustrate diverse perspectives among peers in a classroom. Sometimes classroom conversations about biblical texts lead naturally into conversations about our own campus community or the broader community of our country and world. How to deal with diverse perspectives thoughtfully and creatively is one of the goals of a liberal arts education.

The students I work with are often surprised to discover that the 'life rules' they thought were in the Bible don't appear, at least not in the form they expect. One semester, a student in my introductory Hebrew Bible class wanted to find a clear condemnation of pre-marital sex in the Bible. When I explained that the world of the Hebrew Bible accepts multiple sexual partners for men, unless a man has robbed another man of 'his woman', and that the biblical concept of marriage is quite different from a modern Western concept, he was confused. He desperately wanted the heroes of the Tanakh to behave in ways that were morally defensible in his worldview. As he slowly grappled with the realization that his view of the Bible has been significantly and sometimes inaccurately filtered through the lens of a particular faith community, he began to ask other significant questions about life, meaning, and authority. Another student in the introductory class probably spoke for some of her classmates when she exclaimed one day, 'People who use the Bible to support their religious and political views should read it first!' When students recognize the responsibilities that come with interpreting biblical texts and grappling with the (often unintended) results of those interpretations, they have an opportunity to develop the 'personal and social responsibility' skills that are part of the AAC&U's essential learning outcomes.

Specific Reading Strategies

As teachers, I'm convinced we need to resist the temptation of the Chronicler to revise certain stories in order to create more palatable biblical characters. But like my students, I struggle with how to respond to texts of violence and degradation. One strategy is prompted by biblical portrayals of Abraham and Moses, who at critical moments in the narrative invite God to act in a manner that is befitting to God. Abraham, for instance, in Genesis 19, suggests that God should not destroy the city of Sodom if a few good righteous men are found therein. And God agrees. Moses persuades God to desist from the impulse to wipe out the entire community of Israelites after the incident of the Golden Calf in the Sinai desert (Exodus 32). In the spirit of these ancient characters, I wonder whether some of my students and I might think about inviting God to reconsider the metaphors of rape in the prophetic literature, pointing out to the deity the perhaps unintended and hopefully unwanted effects of such metaphors on the lives of real women. This creative strategy does not require the reader to assume any of these accounts is 'historical' or 'factual'. Of course, our words will not become part of the canon, but the process of developing a contemporary response, patterned on responses of canonical characters, allows students to place the biblical narrative in creative and critical dialogue with contemporary problems. This endeavor addresses the learning outcomes of personal and social responsibility.

Another useful strategy involves helping students see what Seth Goldstein calls 'fluidity in action' by tracing the use of a particular word or image throughout the Tanakh.[11] Goldstein uses the example of *toevah*, often translated 'abomination'. By examining the use of this term in the three books where it is most prominent, Deuteronomy, Proverbs, and Ezekiel, Goldstein provides a new perspective on the occurrences of *toevah* in the Holiness Code in Leviticus. Demonstrating that in the 'transmission and shifts in the meaning of *toevah*, what has often been translated as "abomination" or "abhorrent" actually refers to a socially constructed boundary.'[12] If a professor prefers to demonstrate the process of inner biblical interpretation with a less 'loaded' topic, many other terms could be explored. For example, one could trace the view of 'Moabites' and or 'Ammonites' through various parts of the Tanakh to explore how the concept of who is excluded seems to change over time. Exploring dialogue among biblical texts can help students develop the intellectual skills identified among the essential learning outcomes.

Yet another strategy focuses on the hints within violent texts that suggest disapproval from the community that constructed and/or edited the text. A teacher can use the tools of biblical criticism (e.g. redaction) to help expose the stratigraphy of a given text. As students explore various layers of a text and its transmission, they are learning important skills of analysis and critical thinking. Where does the text hint at a later community's commentary? The story of the Levite and the dismembered concubine, for example, is set in a larger context (Judges) that negatively evaluates much of the community's attempt at self-governance.[13] 'Everyone who saw it cried out, "Never has such a thing happened or been seen from the day the Israelites came out of Egypt until this day. Put your mind to this: take counsel and decide."' (Judg. 19.30) A class might consider how this conclusion invites readers to think about the story. What counsel should we take, and will we decide to resist the story as one which should be told for the sole purpose of never repeating the violence?[14] The concluding chapters of Judges recount the revenge that 'all the Israelites' (Judg.

---

11. Seth Goldstein, 'Reading *Toevah:* Biblical Scholarship and Difficult Texts', *The Reconstructionist* (Fall 2003), pp. 48-60 (p. 48).

12. Goldstein, p. 55.

13. For a recent exploration of Judges 19 that reads the text as a post-exilic 'metaphor of admonition' encouraging 'Israel' to act as a unit, see Heidi M. Szpek, 'The Levite's Concubine: The Story that Never Was', *Women in Judaism: A Multidisciplinary Journal* 5.1 (2007), pp. 1-7 (p. 7).

14. If a teacher wants to alert students to variations between the Masoretic Text and the Septuagint, s/he can alert students to the different wording found in Judg. 19.30a.

20.1) inflicted on the Benjaminites for their failure to provide hospitality to the traveling Levite and his concubine; the rape and murder of one woman results in civil war. As students consider whether and how the text justifies the leadership transition from judges to kings, they must engage the text in its complexity. What kind of literature is this? What is our responsibility as readers? What are the possible unintended consequences of a story that describes a woman whose body is cut into twelve pieces to muster troops for battle? Do the transmitters of the text condone the rape/murder and the subsequent war, or is the entire scenario an indictment of community life gone awry?

Just as a careful reading of Judges 19-21 reveals multiple voices in the ext, so the incest story in 2 Samuel 13 hints at the narrator's distress. Tamar tries to persuade Amnon, before he rapes her, 'Don't, brother! Don't force me. For such a thing is not done in Israel' (2 Sam. 13.12). In both stories, despite the protest that such things are 'not done in Israel', the reader learns that such things *do* occur. The texts both expose and question the violence. Thinking about strategies for reading and resisting texts of violence links well with the goal of learning to become responsible global citizens, since rape, torture, and violence are rampant in our world today. If we invite students to consider the difference between descriptive and prescriptive biblical texts, they may also discover strategies for responding to such texts. Incest, rape, and murder occur, but ought not to occur.

Directly confronting difficult texts in the biblical studies classroom provides much fodder for helping students achieve essential learning outcomes that many of our colleges have adopted. Further, students find themselves talking outside the classroom about the surprising stories they are reading in the biblical text. Young adult students, in particular, discover that the Bible is a more complex and more interesting library than they had imagined. The tools required to become responsible readers of the Bible are significant life tools that will help students engage the world beyond the text and beyond the classroom.

Reading Textual Violence as 'Real' Violence in the Liberal Arts Context

Amy C. Cottrill
Birmingham-Southern College

At Birmingham-Southern College, a liberal arts school in Birmingham, Alabama, I have developed a course called Violence and the Bible, an upper-level seminar course in which we explore the violent narratives, imagery, symbolism, and rhetoric of the Hebrew Bible and New Testament. That the Bible contains violent themes and stories is not a new observation.[1] In fact, one of the fundamental assumptions of this class is that violence occurs in biblical texts and that the Bible, as well as other sacred texts, has frequently authorized and legitimated acts of physical violence in the world on many occasions.[2]

---

1. See, for example, Phyllis Trible, *Texts of Terror: Literary-Feminist Readings of Biblical Narratives* (Philadelphia: Fortress, 1984); Robert Allen Warrior, 'Canaanites, Cowboys, and Indians: Deliverance, Conquest, and Liberation Theology Today', *Christianity and Crisis* 49 (1989), pp. 261-65; David R. Blumenthal, *Facing the Abusing God: A Theology of Protest* (Louisville, KY: Westminster John Knox, 1993); Susan Niditch, *War in the Hebrew Bible: A Study in the Ethics of Violence* (New York: Oxford University Press, 1993); Renita J. Weems, *Battered Love: Marriage, Sex, and Violence in the Hebrew Prophets* (Minneapolis: Fortress, 1995); Gerd Lüdemann, *The Unholy in Holy Scripture: The Dark Side of the Bible*, trans. John Bowden (Louisville, KY: Westminster John Knox, 1996); Harold Washington, 'Violence and the Construction of Gender in the Hebrew Bible: A New Historicist Approach', *Biblical Interpretation* 5.4 (October 1997), pp. 324-63; Regina Schwartz, *The Curse of Cain: The Violent Legacy of Monotheism* (Chicago: University of Chicago Press, 1997); David Penchansky, *What Rough Beast?: Images of God in the Hebrew Bible* (Louisville, KY: Westminster John Knox, 1999); John Collins, 'The Zeal of Phinehas: The Bible and the Legitimation of Violence', *JBL* 122 (2003), pp. 3-21; Jack Nelson-Pallmeyer, *Is Religion Killing Us? Violence in the Bible and the Quran* (Harrisburg: Trinity International, 2003); Terence E. Fretheim, 'God and Violence in the Old Testament', *Word & World* 24 (2004), pp. 18-28; Eryl W. Davies, 'The Morally Dubious Passages of the Hebrew Bible: An Examination of Some Proposed Solutions', *Currents in Biblical Research* 3 (2005), pp. 197-228; Joel Kaminsky, 'Violence in the Bible', *SBL Forum*, www.sbl-site.org/Article.aspx?ArticleID=159.

2. Of course, one cannot draw a straight line from violent texts to violent actions. There is no simple cause and effect formula in the relationship between textual and physical violence. Yet, as John Collins notes, 'the line between actual killing and verbal, symbolic, or imaginary violence is thin and permeable' (Collins, 'The Zeal of Phinehas', 4.) See also Mark Juergensmeyer, *Terror in the Mind of God: The Global Rise of Religious Violence* (3rd edn; Berkeley: University of Califor-

In this course, we consider how violence functions within the textual world of the Bible. Students quickly discover that violence does not function the same way in all texts. The challenge of the course involves confronting a range of assumptions about reading, language and the concept of the self, as well as violence itself. Here, I share the story of this class, the questions I pose, student difficulties with addressing those questions, and some pedagogical strategies I have developed to overcome those obstacles.

The first question addressed by the class is this: What assumptions do the biblical texts make about violence? My hope is that, at the end, students will have a more sophisticated awareness of the range of definitions of violence and of the diverse ways violence functions in the various texts we examine. In this upper-level course, students start to differentiate between kinds of violence in the text, the way the texts thematize and/or obscure violence, and the ways students experience these texts as readers. There are some instances of violence that students expect and are acquainted with from earlier exposure to the Hebrew Bible, especially the conquest narrative in Joshua. They easily recognize Samson's aggressive antics as violent. Less familiar texts, especially in the prophets, and texts they are not predisposed to associate with violence, like the Psalms, challenge their notions about what violence is and where it occurs. Further, some seemingly comic or satirical stories nonetheless include violence, like the Ehud story of Judges. In short, violence is part of texts in a wide variety of ways and calls for different types of engagement from the reader in particular narrative and poetic settings.

The second central question of the class is this: How does the text position the reader to the violence? My intention is that, by the end of the course, students will be able to recognize the ways texts position them in relation to the violence of the narrative. Because there are different kinds of textual violence in the Bible, a one-size-fits-all response to violence in the Bible would be a cloddish and heavy-handed response. Sometimes the texts invite the reader to agree with them, justify, or excuse violence and thus become complicit. Other times readers are asked to appreciate the wit or humor of a violent story, such as in the Ehud narrative of Judges 3. Sometimes they are invited to be horrified and repelled, as in the story of Judges 19, the rape and dismemberment of the Levite's concubine. Other times they are chilled, such as in Psalm 137 and its prayer to see the babies of the Babylonians dashed against the rocks. For my students, the idea of the reader's subject position—the ways they are afforded roles in texts and invited to or discouraged from particular conclusions as readers—is new and important.

And finally, the third central question is this: What happens when one *reads* violence? Answering this question is by far the most difficult and challeng-

---

nia Press, 2003); Andrew Kille, '"The Bible Made Me Do It:" Text, Interpretation, and Violence', in *The Destructive Power of Religion: Violence in Judaism, Christianity, and Islam* (ed. J. Harold Ellens; Westport: Praeger, 2004), pp. 55-73.

ing issue. The question assumes that textual violence, encountered through the practice of reading, affects and shapes the reader in significant ways. While my students become adept at exploring the literary and rhetorical dynamics of violence, they frequently resist engaging the question of the effect of encountering textual violence. For many students, reading textual violence is simply not an encounter with 'real' violence. After all, they say, no one is physically harmed by reading the Bible. They do not operate with a definition of violence that includes the act of reading a deceptively passive written text. They often regard reading as a transfer of knowledge from one location, the text, to another location, their minds, and believe their minds are disembodied, computer-like mechanisms that simply register information. Moreover, they do not regard reading as a practice in which their ethical sensibilities are informed and shaped. Perhaps as symptom of our increasingly aliterate society, my students frequently assume that nothing really happens in reading, or nothing of real consequence.

In my experience, three main assumptions lead to student resistance to understanding the practice of reading the Bible as an experience of real violence. First, some of my students have a powerful need to dismiss biblical violence as influential largely because of theological commitments to what they deeply desire to understand as the 'good' book. Students frequently recognize the violence of the Hebrew Bible, but many of them adopt a reading strategy that offers an extremely satisfying interpretive solution: The violent presentation of God and God's people in the Old Testament is corrected by the peaceful Jesus of the New Testament. To counter this assumption, it is important to address the violence of the New Testament.[3]

The second reason my students often resist the idea of biblical violence as 'real' violence is that many students are reluctant to explore the idea that media (film, video games, television, images, music, and verbal texts) shape them in unconscious ways. They are attracted, as many are, to the concept of the person as impermeable to influence that he or she does not consciously accept. Anthropologist Clifford Geertz describes this notion of the self well: 'The Western conception of the person [is] as a bounded, unique, more or less integrated motivational and cognitive universe, a dynamic center of awareness, emotion, judgment, and action organized into a distinctive whole and set contrastively both against other such wholes and against its social and natural background.'

---

3. See, for example, Michel Desjardins, *Peace, Violence and the New Testament* (Sheffield: Sheffield Academic Press, 1997); George Aichele, 'Jesus' Violence', in *Violence, Utopia and the Kingdom of God: Fantasy and Ideology in the Bible* (ed. George Aichele and Tina Pippin; New York: Routledge, 1998), pp. 72-91; Denny J. Weaver, *The Nonviolent Atonement* (Grand Rapids: Eerdmans, 2001); Shelly Matthews and Leigh Gibson, eds., *Violence and the New Testament* (New York: T & T Clark, 2005); John Sanders, ed., *Atonement and Violence: A Theological Conversation* (Nashville: Abingdon, 2006); David J. Neville, 'Toward a Teleology of Peace: Contesting Matthew's Violent Eschatology', *JSOT* 30.2 (2007): pp. 131-61.

Geertz further notes, 'however incorrigible it may seem to us, [this is] a rather peculiar idea within the context of the world's cultures.'[4] The idea of a bounded self, impervious to outside influence unless judgment deems it necessary, seems to be the dominant understanding of the self for many of my students.[5] They have a deep faith in their ability to make judgments about what to allow to affect them and what to disregard as irrelevant.[6]

This 'bounded' understanding of the self presents a difficulty in my class for several reasons. Many students enter the class with the assumption that they can rationally make decisions about the violent media they consume, how it will affect them, or, more importantly, how it will not. Their self exists outside of the media they consume and is not constituted by it. They assume that they are impenetrable to influences that they consciously and rationally decide are ethically suspect.

In order to posit biblical violence as an encounter that is affective, that forms readers in particular ways, we as a class explore together other ways of thinking about violence in media, ways that understand the self as permeable, porous, and interdependent with the surrounding world. Fortunately, there is no lack of literature that makes the connection between violent media and its effect on the violent imagination of individuals.[7] For instance, Mark Juergensmeyer draws the connection between violent texts and rituals (symbolic violence) and the construction of a culture of violence that authorizes violent acts.[8] Through such sources, the class introduces a concept of the self that is permeable to the effect of language and images of violent texts.

I am interested in how the violent texts of the Bible configure our ability to become aware of, interpret, and respond to other acts of violence. Because of the attraction of so many undergraduate students to video games, we often start there, but I have used several helpful articles that discuss the implications of

---

4. Clifford Geertz, *Local Knowledge: Further Essays in Interpretive Anthropology* (New York: Basic, 1983), p. 59.

5. George Lakoff and Mark Johnson argue that the notion of the independent, boundaried self is actually a dominant Western misunderstanding of the human mind. They argue, 'The mind is inherently embodied. Thought is mostly unconscious. Abstract concepts are largely metaphorical' (Lakoff and Johnson, *Philosophy in the Flesh: The Embodied Mind and its Challenge to Western Thought* [New York: Basic Books, 1999], p. 3).

6. See Lakoff and Johnson: 'Real human beings are not, for the most part, in conscious control of—or even consciously aware of—their reasoning' (Lakoff and Johnson, *Philosophy in the Flesh*, p. 5).

7. For instance, see Kostas A. Fanti, Eric Vanman, Christopher C. Henrich, Marios N. Avraamides, 'Desensitization to Media Violence Over a Short Period of Time', *Aggressive Behavior* 35.2 (March/April 2009), pp. 179-87; Richard B. Felson, 'Mass Media Effects on Violent Behavior', *Annual Review of Sociology* 22 (1996), pp. 103-28; Arthur Kleinman, 'The Violences of Everyday Life: The Multiple Forms and Dynamics of Social Violence', in *Violence and Subjectivity* (ed. Veena Das, Arthur Kleinman, Mamphela Ramphele and Pamela Reynolds; Berkeley: University of California Press, 2000), pp. 226-41, esp. pp. 231-33.

8. Juergensmeyer, *Terror in the Mind of God*, pp. 10, 163-64.

consumption of violent media and the effects, individual and interpersonal, of witnessing media violence.[9]

The gaming literature deserves special comment largely because it has provoked the most heated debate in my classes to date, mostly among the 'gamers'. Rachel Wagner, in her book *Godwired: Religion, Ritual, and Virtual Reality*, provides a useful conceptual vocabulary for the way video games attempt to create an alternate reality, or a magic circle, a closed and impermeable boundary in which the rules of the game are distinct from the rules of daily life.[10] The concept of a magic circle has been intriguing to my students and has also helped me to theorize the encounter with violence in the Bible. In a video game, so the argument goes, one enters a magic circle, a liminal space in which players immerse themselves in violent, war-time experience in which it is permissible to shoot Iraqis who have invaded the United States, as in the most recent version of the game *Call of Duty*, or virtually re-enact the Iraq war in *KumaWar*.[11] Within the magic circle, one can actually pull the trigger, shoot to kill, commit acts of extraordinary violence, and then simply leave the magic circle when one chooses and go on with one's life with no tangible consequences.

The concept of the magic circle has been scrutinized, of course. Game theorists Katie Salen and Eric Zimmerman question the degree to which video reality is distinct from daily life.[12] Further, Wagner argues, 'Games can and do affect us when we put down the joysticks and turn off our screens.'[13] Yet the 'magic circle' is an attractive, if problematic, theory. Those of my students who spend significant time in the worlds of video games find the magic circle to be a particularly appealing concept, possibly because it affords a means of avoiding difficult ethical questions about the effects of 'playing' with extreme physical violence and the implications of being willing, even if only for the duration of a game, to shoot an Iraqi enemy. Bringing the concept of the magic circle into the classroom launches a new way of asking questions of the Bible: Do we enter a

---

9. For instance, see Kathryn Reklis, 'Prime-Time Torture: Jack Bauer as a Hero of Our Time', *Christian Century* 125.2 (June 3, 2008), pp. 11-12; David Grossman, 'Trained to Kill: A Military Expert on the Psychology of Killing Explains How Today's Media Condition Kids to Pull the Trigger', *Christianity Today* 42.9 (August 10, 1998), pp. 30-39; Dan Mathewson, 'End Times Entertainment: The Left Behind Series, Evangelicals, and Death Pornography', *Journal of Contemporary Religion* 24.3 (October 2009), pp. 319-337.

10. Rachel Wagner, *Godwired: Religion, Ritual, and Virtual Reality* (New York: Routledge, 2011), p. 3. See also *Godwired*, pp. 162-64.

11. See Wagner's mention of *KumaWar* in *Godwired*, 162.

12. Katie Salen and Eric Zimmerman argue, the 'wider our cultural frame grows in defining games as culture, the more their artificiality begins to unravel. As culture, games are open systems. They are not isolated from their environment, but are intrinsically part of it, participating in the ebb and flow of ideas and values that make up a larger cultural setting...the magic circle is not an impermeable curtain but is instead a border that can be crossed. Cultural elements from outside the circle enter in and have an impact on the game; simultaneously, cultural meanings ripple outward from the game to interact with numerous cultural contexts' (*Rules of Play: Game Design Fundamentals* [Cambridge, MA: MIT, 2004], 572), quoted in Wagner, *Godwired*, 3-4.

13. Wagner, *Godwired*, 3.

magic circle when we read the Bible? Do violent texts have any lived, embodied effect, any implications for the way we structure our own worlds, or do we simply leave that experience behind when we close the book? Is a text 'really' violent if no actual Cannanites get killed?

The third reason my students often resist the idea of biblical violence as 'real' violence is that they tend to operate with habitual understandings of the reading process in which reading is simply the comprehension of symbols on a page rather than a consequential encounter. My experience is that students must be introduced to other understandings of reading, specifically reading as an encounter, as effective, not just in the transfer of knowledge, but also in the construction of the ethical sensibilities of the individual.

To this end, I use a reading by Wayne Booth in *The Company We Keep*.[14] Booth is a literary scholar who connects literary and ethical criticism. He offers a provocative metaphor for reading, the relational metaphor of friendship. As Booth says, 'Considered under the friendship metaphor, the implied authors of all stories, fictional or historical, elevated or vulgar, welcoming or hostile on the surface, purport to offer ... friendship.'[15] He encourages readers to view their reading material as a potential friend, though not in a sentimental or trivial way. Booth believes that friendships have tremendous shaping influence. According to Booth, we are what we read. He asks the reader to scrutinize what the text, or the friend, wants the reader to feel, experience, desire, pursue, accept, and deny. Does the text, or the friend, draw us into a complex narrative world in which violence is a feature and invite us to encounter characters and situations that may not ultimately be able to be categorized as good or bad, or does the text 'dumb-down' our emotional range and ability to engage complex moral worlds?

Two facets of this metaphor of reading as friendship are particularly helpful when reading the violent texts of the Bible. First, it helps me ask a set of suggestive questions: What kind of friend is this particular text? Who will I become through spending time with this text? That is, what kind of reading experiences is offered the reader in this text? What kind of response does the text elicit and how does it do that? Part of what is involved in answering these questions is developing sensitivity to the kinds of information the text offers, the kind of language it uses, what kinds of things are obscured or not addressed in the text.

A second area of reflection that the metaphor of reading as friendship brings into relief has to do not with the kind of friend the text is, but the kind of friend the reader is to the text. Friendship is, after all, a two-way street. Am I the kind of friend who listens attentively? That is, as a reader, do I challenge myself to really listen to the contours of the voice in the text and not force it to conform to my pre-established interpretation of what the texts says and means? Do I allow

---

14. Wayne C. Booth, *The Company We Keep: An Ethics of Fiction* (Berkeley: University of California Press, 1988).

15. Wayne Booth, *The Company We Keep*, p. 174.

it to be different from me? Am I the kind of friend who empathizes, who is emotionally open to the concerns of my friend? That is, as a reader, am I brave enough to let myself be affected by the text and engage the concerns of the text in a real way? Am I the kind of friend who is able to speak back in dialogue with my friend, to ask questions that are risky and challenging, but are ultimately about raising the level of the friendship? That is, as a reader, am I willing to maintain my own voice and respond to the text in ways that are not necessarily about affirming the text, but are about scrutinizing and criticizing the embedded assumptions and worldview of the text? I have found friendship to be a rich metaphor for students as they begin the process of interpreting biblical violence. Within this metaphor, reading is not a flat or inconsequential activity, but a place of encounter and interaction where something is at stake.

The friendship metaphor informs two assignments in the course. First, the major writing and research paper of the class is an exploration of a violent text as a friendship offering. Through their attention to the literary and rhetorical dynamics of the story, students are asked to describe the kind of friendship offered within the text. What are they made to desire in the story? How does the violence of the text function? Then, students are asked to reflect on their assessment of this friendship offering. Does the friend offer a chance to think about violence in ways that are valuable and helpful, or is this a text that obscures or hides aspects of violence in ways that are ethically problematic? Finally, as a potential friend to the text, how does the reader, the student, respond to the text? Sometimes being a good friend means offering affirmation, and other times being a good friend means challenging what is happening.

Second, in future iterations of the course, I plan to use the concept of friendship in an earlier, smaller assignment that will prepare them to write the larger paper. In a 3-5 page reflection paper, this assignment will ask them to analyze two or three of their human friendships. The stipulation will be that the friendships should be from different stages of life, and at least one of them should be a friendship that failed in some way, or simply ended. In other words, I want to use my student's obvious interest in their human friends to help them become more intentional and serious about the way they read. The questions they will answer will be largely the same as those I ask them to consider of the biblical text, creating a direct connection between the shaping effect of time spent with humans and time spent with written texts.

In conclusion, my hope is to reinforce the concept of reading, especially reading violent texts, as an activity of real consequence, one that matters in the ongoing construction of the self in a complicated world. Learning to be a better reader and interpreter, like learning to be a better friend, is intimately connected to developing one's skills of empathy, questioning, and response, all of which are deeply ethical skills that have wide-ranging implications for how one lives in relation with others.

Engaging Students Online: Using Wiki Technology to Improve Your Class Notes

Carl N. Toney
Hope International University

Introduction

The internet continues to present enormous opportunities for creating dynamic classroom experiences both for traditional students and distance learners. For instructors, the rapidly changing teaching environment poses numerous challenges and opportunities, including being aware of available tools to promote online learning. One such tool is a wiki. A wiki is a website that promotes user-generated content through editing, adding, and deleting material in order to produce collaborative documents, projects, or webpages. The most famous wiki is Wikipedia, the online encyclopedia.[1] Google also offers group collaboration on projects when using its online office suite. Wikis may be used to supplement distance learning facilitated by Blackboard, eCollege, Moodle and others, or to extend learning beyond the confines of a traditional classroom. Like other online resources that promote active learning, one key to a wiki's success or failure is both the students' and the instructor's regular engagement in the online collaboration. This paper will explore the benefits and challenges of online collaboration by presenting a case study which used Wetpaint.com as the medium for creating a collaborative set of online class notes in an undergraduate class.[2]

Welcome to Web 2.0 and Beyond

Wikis are part of what has been called 'Web 2.0', a term popularized by O'Reilly Media in 2004.[3] Web 1.0 refers to primarily read-only websites that

---

1. Well known websites will be listed by name, without including 'www.' or '.com'.
2. For examples of wiki class notes see carltoney.wetpaint.com or ns500.wetpaint.com. Of course, one challenge when writing a paper about internet tools is the ever shifting sands of websites being created, renamed, modified, and deleted. I apologize if any links listed become inactive or produce an error. Active links are usually maintained by Wikipedia's article on 'wikis' and www.wikimatrix.org provides a searchable list of wikis based on features needed.
3. 'What Is Web 2.0: Design Patterns and Business Models for the Next Generation of Software', www.oreillynet.com/pub/a/oreilly/tim/news/2005/09/30/what-is-web-20.html#mememap.

host static information usually created by the website owner. One example would be traditional news sites. However, Web 2.0 websites are dynamic and are constantly evolving by facilitating user-generate content and encouraging on-going user participation. Examples of Web 2.0 include anything from social media like Facebook and Twitter to photo-sharing like Picasa to video sharing like YouTube to knowledge sharing like Wikipedia to virtual reality sites like Second Life (where users create alter-egos). Web 2.0 sites become platforms and springboards for collaboration. Essentially, any website that encourages users to participate actively by adding or editing content is using a Web 2.0 model. Those parts of a course that rely upon the instructor, as the specialist who creates material using writing, audio, video, or PowerPoint lectures/presentations, follow a Web 1.0 approach. Those parts of a course that encourage active, ongoing contributions by students such as threaded discussions, blogs, peer-reviewed papers, and group projects are indebted to the Web 2.0 model.

One type of Web 2.0 site is a wiki, which is a website specifically designed for visitors to quickly and easily collaborate by editing, adding, and removing content. In 1995, Ward Cunningham created the first wiki, www.wikiwikiweb. com.[4] However, the most popularly known and infamous wiki is Wikipedia. Visitors to Wikipedia have the option both to read and to contribute to its ever-increasing storehouse of knowledge.[5] Wikipedia reflects some of the current values of our up-and-coming students. These students are technology orientated and savvy. They are attracted to collaboration and value a presence on the internet. They gravitate toward easily obtained information that is just a few keystrokes away. They decreasingly see their teachers as authorities and guardians of information because of the competing authorities found on the web. Less value is placed on memorizing facts; rather, value is placed on ease of obtaining information.

Rather than rejecting these technological advancements, instructors need to teach our students to handle resources critically. We need to help them distinguish good information from bad, and we need to help them contribute to the good. One tool is the wiki, which allows students to create and edit a collabora-

---

4. WikiWikiWeb was the first site to be called a wiki. Ward Cunningham started developing WikiWikiWeb in 1994, and installed it on Internet domain c2.com on March 25, 1995. It was named by Cunningham, who remembered a Honolulu International Airport counter employee telling him to take the so-called 'Wiki Wiki' Chance RT-52 shuttle bus line that runs between the airport's terminals. According to Cunningham, 'I chose wiki-wiki as an alliterative substitute for "quick" and thereby avoided naming this stuff quick-web.' Wiki Wiki is a reduplication of wiki, a Hawaiian-language word for fast. The word 'wiki' is a shorter form of wiki wiki' (www.wikiwikiweb.com).

5. With Wikipedia comes the supposed democratization of knowledge. Unfortunately, at times, ignorance can easily breed further ignorance, and a 'groupthink' paradigm is introduced where if enough people consent to a fact, then it must be true. One simple solution to concerns about 'unscholarly' websites is for instructors to create sites, which are based on research of scholarly works and undergo academic review at least in the classroom setting. Another solution is to create class assignments where instructors help students to verify and cite information on Wikipedia's pages.

tive set of notes on a class website. For each class, students can be divided into groups that are responsible for contributing to the online notes. This is different from a blog or threaded discussion because the students are working together on the same document/webpage. And wiki websites facilitate the ease of this group collaboration because each student can edit the page using their own personal computers.

These wikis offer unique benefits and opportunities to educators. First, wikis encourage student-directed pedagogy because students actively contribute to the class materials. Second, wikis promote collaborative learning by allowing students to work on common projects. Third, wikis facilitate quantifiable assessment of students' participation by tracking their contributions. Fourth, wikis use cutting-edge technology. Fifth, when using wikis, it is easier for users to fix mistakes than to make them. And sixth, wikis can be fun for students because they are using a medium with which they are very comfortable.

The Wiki Way of Wetpaint

The first step towards a collaborative set of class notes is to choose your wiki. For selecting your own wiki, you may wish to use the choice wizard at www.wikimatrix.org or to look at the wikis listed at Wikipedia. If your institution is using Google for email, then you may wish to consider using Google Docs (which allows multiple users to simultaneously edit a document online, but currently does not have as many features for tracking user contributions). For this case study, we used Wetpaint.com. In picking a wiki, several factors should be considered.

1. *Cost*: What is your budget, and what is the cost? In my opinion, free is always good, but you may want a specific website name or need to match your institution's branding or may not want advertisements. This case study used Wetpaint's free, ad-supported service.
2. *Privacy*: You must decide whether you want students' work to be public or private. If you decide to have a public space, then you must ensure students' academic privacy rights (such as using aliases). If the course is offered multiple times, then you need to decide if you want previous content to be available to future classes. Wetpaint allows students to register and pick their own usernames. Be sure that students pick names that allow the instructor/moderator to easily identify them.
3. *Ease of use*: Look for a wiki that is *easy* to edit. Specifically, you will want to avoid a wiki which requires any technical knowledge of programming codes (such as html), so look for W.Y.S.I.W.Y.G. editing (What You See Is What You Get). Google and Wetpaint are examples of sites that use a simple interface. Many wikis make editing easy by using toolbars similar to word processing programs.
4. *Users*: Make sure that you can identify users and can control who adds information to the site. While some wikis allow any person who visits the

site to edit the content, for a class project, it is best to limit contributions only to students. Also, make sure to use a site that fits the number of users in you class, and consider the ease for students to register.
5. *History*: Most importantly, be sure that you can monitor the history of changes (both when and who made the changes). This allows instructors to measure learning and to give personalized feedback. Be sure that the 'history' page allows users to revert to a previous version of the website if mistakes are made.[6] The history should also provide basic information such as the number of words added or deleted by particular students. In Wetpaint, the teacher can see the actual words added and removed on a particular page (including word count), and the teacher can monitor the specific contributions of each student by clicking on her or his name and viewing the profile.
6. *Content*: Is the site capable of adding links to other websites? What organizational features does it have? Can it make outlines using bullet points or add tables? Will students be able to take notes on their computer/tablet/smart phone, then cut and paste them in and out of word processing programs? Can the wiki import/export pdf or word documents?
7. *Accessibility*: Is the site accessible using broadband, dial-up, or cell phone networks? Is the site compatible on PCs, Macs, Android, smart phones, and/or tablets?
8. *Multiple pages*: Make sure you get a wiki that is capable of handling multiple pages and has an easy navigation bar.
9. *Optional features*: Do you want to be able to upload documents? Would you like to add pictures and video? Do you want students to have threaded discussions? Blog? You may wish to control who can view your site. You may wish to control the name of your wiki. Before you begin, take time to consider what you value as important features.

Case Study: Romans-Galatians Course

1. The Assignment
I used Wetpaint to create a collaborative set of class notes for an undergraduate class on Romans-Galatians.[7] (I have also successfully used this assignment in graduate classes.) The common set of class notes became the basis for the midterm and final examinations. Students were offered extra credit to participate in the creation of the class notes. Students were required to post their own class notes for one class session, as well as edit/improve/respond to the class notes posted by another student. Participants were given two weeks from the original day of class to complete the notes. Once notes were posted, students

---

6. One of the foundational principles of a wiki is that it should be twice as easy to fix a mistake as it is to make a mistake.
7. See carltoney.wetpaint.com.

had one week to edit and/or to respond. In addition, I also kept track of the notes and edited content. In order to keep track of contributions, each student was assigned her or his own unique user identification.

2. Evaluation and Future Implementation
Overall, I found the experiment to be successful. Through this project, students took greater ownership of the course. Students expressed a great appreciation for having a collected set of notes because it took away a degree of uncertainty when preparing for exams and meeting course learning outcomes. It also helped fill in the gaps in students' notes and helped if students missed class. I also found it easier to prepare the exams because I knew exactly what information the students should know. However, it also created a proof-reading challenge because I had to be sure that incorrect information was not being perpetuated in the class notes. I encouraged to students to check for 'final' versions of the notes prior to exams.

I discovered that allowing two weeks to post the notes was too great of a time lag. I found the quality of the notes diminished as time moved on, and it did not allow enough opportunity for others to edit or add to the notes. Many students procrastinated, so that by the time they posted the notes, the information was not fresh in their minds. This lack of freshness also created difficulty for those students who had to edit those notes. Further, the specific lecture was no longer fresh in my mind, so it was hard to remember the specific details myself. When I have used this assignment in subsequent classes, I have given less lag time, such as one to three days after the class for the notes to be posted and edited. This shorter lag time works better and encourages greater student participation throughout the week and more detailed notes. For online only classes, shorter deadlines, which involve more frequent interaction, work better.

At times, the quality of the notes could also be improved. Because I only had two students working on a day's notes, some days the notes suffered because of the poor note-taking skills of one or both the students. I had to make up these shortcomings with my own contributions. In subsequent courses, I have required more students to edit and contribute to each day's notes to help offset problematic students. I have also appointed more skilled students to act as TAs to help edit multiple sets of notes. In addition, some students have the tendency to contribute the bare minimum, so at times the notes would be a bit sparse. However, other students provide over-detailed notes, being unable to discern important material. So I have found that placing a minimum and maximum word count is helpful, such as 250-500 words for each original contributor and 50-100 words for each secondary editor. Word counts often vary depending up the length and depth of a class. As an instructor, you have to decide how much time you will spend reading these notes. It can also be helpful to teach students to highlight key words and concepts. Another option is for students to write study guide questions or self-quizzes at the end of the day's notes.

Finally, because I found that taking good quality notes collectively can be a great deal of work, I sometimes make these class notes part of the students' regularly assigned and graded work. Since writing notes constitutes a regular assignment, students can be graded on the quality of their notes. I would grade the notes a bit like a paper where inaccurate information and spelling mistakes would potentially be points against the student, while insight and assimilation is rewarded. Wetpaint has a 'comments' feature, which allows instructors to offer public praise to highlight particular successes. Email is useful for more private comments.

Benefits of Using Wiki Notes

1. For Students

There are many benefits to using wiki notes for both students and instructors. One of the greatest benefits of wiki notes for students is that note-taking becomes a corporate responsibility. Because notes are a corporate responsibility, it takes pressure off individual students to be mere transcribers of information in the classroom setting because they might 'miss something'. This can encourage active learning through discussion and reflection upon the material presented in class. For online only courses, class notes covering assigned reading, webinars, etc. can help students feel part of a learning community and bring focus to forum discussions.

Wiki notes can help students develop the skills of note-taking in class and for required reading. In my experience, many students are developing the basic skills of prioritizing information and identifying both key words and concepts. Students' notes tend to either be too full by transcribing every detail of class or too bare by cherry-picking ideas from class or merely writing down only what appears on a PowerPoint slide or whiteboard. The public forum of notes allows students to compare their notes with others. The maximalist will be edited down by the minimalist, and the minimalist will be expanded by having information contributed by the maximalist.

Further, in a typical note-taking scenario, students may only look at their notes a second time prior to taking their examinations. By requiring the contributing and editing of online notes, students will engage with class materials several times before their examinations. This can help students retain what is gained in classroom instruction. Thus, the often missed steps of synthesis and reflection can potentially occur. Synthesis occurs when students attempt to evaluate which portions of their own notes are worthy of being contributed to the collective notes. Synthesis also occurs when students attempt to fit their notes and ideas into the notes and ideas of others. Reflection also occurs in this process because the students revisit their notes after class. If the students use the comments feature of the wiki, then students can also post comments about how the material is applicable to other facets of life.

For traditional classes, online notes extend the learning experience outside the classroom. For distance learning, it creates another medium of collaboration, allowing 'lecture' style material or readings to be an opportunity for group learning. Students join a learning community each time they interact with the wiki. It fosters an environment of co-learning as students make meaningful contributions which will aid themselves and other students in their education. It can also help students take ownership of their learning because they are contributing original content to the course. And all of this is done in a medium which may be familiar and comfortable for younger students.

2. For Instructors
For instructors, wiki notes can provide measurable feedback about what is being communicated and learned by students. Using the 'history' feature, an instructor can actually see what work a student contributes to the site. This allows the instructor to quantifiably evaluate individual students. Minimum word contributions through additions and editing can provide specific measurable criteria for grading. Instructors can also pinpoint which students are taking notes well and which students need help, and instructors can help, possibly by pairing-up such students.

An instructor may learn ways to improve his or her own teaching. For example, an instructor may learn how organized or unorganized the material presented in class is. He or she may also learn if important information, such as key concepts, is being sufficiently highlighted and conveyed in class or through assigned readings. Because an instructor is a fellow editor, she or he can also make up for any insufficiencies by helping to reorganize notes, highlight key concepts, and even add and explain missed material. Thus, the instructor gets the opportunity for a second or third pass at teaching the same material to students. Instructors can even provide additional commentary to the notes using the comments features of the wiki.

Challenges of Using Wiki Notes

1. For Students
While there are many benefits to wiki notes, there can also be some challenges. As an instructor, I find myself having a love/hate relationship with technology. Using wiki notes encourages students to bring their computers, tablets, and other devices to class. With all the joys of computers also comes the distractions, whether games or the internet. I also find that students on computers can be slower to engage in dialogue than other students. However, in an ever-increasingly 'wired' world, instructors need to think creatively about how to use technology to engage students effectively both inside and outside the classroom. Wiki notes can allow students to use technology meaningfully in the classroom. Wikis can also allow students to create group projects or papers in the classroom (replacing the traditional 'go up to the blackboard and write your answers').

Wiki notes can also prey on vices of passivity and doing the bare minimum. If students are not careful in their effort to create class notes responsibly, they can become more scribes than active participants. Students can also become lax when they realize that they are not responsible for every day's class notes. This is especially true for students taking a class merely for the grade. Some students may not see the importance of attending class or reading assignments if they can access the information online. Part of the solution is to move students away from seeing the goal of the class as obtaining facts and information; instead, they need to view class as a chance to develop skills. Instructors need to be mindful of what makes classroom interaction different from other learning activities, such as reading a book, and to create class sessions that provide transformative experiences and teach skills alongside ideas.[8] This can be especially challenging for larger classes. Another solution may be to require students to write a reflection journal highlighting one or two key concepts from lectures or class reading and applying those concepts to their personal lives.

Another challenge can be to ensure the quality of the wiki notes. Unfortunately, poor note-takers can diminish the quality of the notes. However, the collective nature of the note-taking enterprise can help offset these shortcomings. Hopefully, instructors can pair good note-takers with poorer note-takers. In addition, not everything an instructor deems important will make it into the notes. As a fellow contributor, an instructor can supplement the notes in these cases. This requires a degree of finesse from the instructor because students should not become dependent upon the expertise of the instructor for the quality of the notes. At times, it is important to allow students to have control over the notes, so that they take responsibility for them. At other times, material may be too important to pass over.

There is also a format limitation. The wiki is limited in style to standard paragraphs, outlines, basic charts, or possibly even Cornell notes. This can be difficult for students who prefer flow charts, webs, or other graphic representations for their notes. It is important to develop a degree of consistency to the notes, which can be difficult for some students. Part of the solution is to encourage students of different styles to maintain their own style in the personal notes while stretching themselves in the collective notes. It can be helpful to establish the criteria for the format, so that students know what the class notes should look like. This could include giving a lecture about taking class notes and/or providing samples. Another option would be for an instructor to post a basic outline or template, in which students provide details.

It can be harder to implement evaluation of individual student's work when collective notes are used. It may be harder to evaluate individual skills of acquiring knowledge and synthesis of ideas. Additionally, it may be harder to evaluate personal reading if note-taking is the basis of evaluation. Further, students can become overly dependent upon others for producing good quality notes. Also, these notes may work best the first time a class is taught, but may encourage

---

8. See John Dewey, *How We Think* (Boston: D.C. Heath and Company, 1910), for a good discussion of the tension between ideas and skills.

plagiarism in future classes. Part of this solution is to emphasize the skill-set being taught rather than focusing on the information. In addition, the 'history' portion also helps with the evaluation of individuals. A more pragmatic solution is to use a wiki that has restricted access, so that only class members of an active class can access the information.

2. For Instructors
Instructors are faced with the challenge of the technology gap. A wiki can be one more program to master, and in a rapidly changing world, new tools will quickly outpace and replace this tool. The good news is that certain wikis are relatively easy to use, since they have interfaces similar to word processing programs. If the task still seems too daunting, another solution is to have a TA create and monitor the site.

More problematic may be that wiki notes can create more work for the instructor (as well as the students). By extending the class outside the walls of the classroom, an instructor also gets drawn outside the four walls of a building. This may involve making choices of where and how class preparation time is being spent as well as where and how grading time is spent. So a final consideration for the use of the wiki is a time-management decision.

Other Uses of a Wiki

After using the wiki for class notes, I realized that there were other possibilities for using a wiki. For example, class papers might be improved by putting them on a wiki because students can incorporate pictures, videos, and links to other websites. Students can write traditional research papers using the non-traditional platform of a wiki. Of course, caution needs to be taken on the quality of information being referenced. While some wikis do not use footnotes, students can still write research papers by documenting research using parenthetical citations. The web design can also create an 'entertainment' element for the project. Value can be gained because the student's work may be immediately published on the web. Some wikis have a comments feature, which allows the student to receive feedback from others. This technology could be especially helpful for group projects because an instructor can see *exactly* what each student contributes to the project by looking at the 'history' page. This would help overcome the problem of stellar students doing the work for slacker students.

Conclusion

Wikis are an exciting medium for doing traditional tasks of the classroom, such as taking notes in class or on required reading (and possibly writing papers and group projects), in a non-traditional fashion. Wiki notes allow collective learning to occur in either on-site or distance learning environments. Students learn team dynamics by working together for a common goal. They also learn to improve the content of their class notes and develop note-taking skills. Instructors are given a tool for tangibly evaluating students' contributions and the ability to assimilate information. Further, as a fellow editor, the instructor can take on the role of facilitator and give dynamic feedback to students. Of course, colleges and universities continue to tap into the riches and challenges of web technology like Blackboard and eCollege, but if teachers want to stay abreast of current trends and useful tools, the apt instructor will find herself or himself venturing beyond the digital boundaries of these applications. One such tool which can be useful is the wiki.

What's the Harm in Harmonization?
Using Jesus Films in the Classroom
to Examine the Crucifixion Narratives

Margaret E. Ramey
Messiah College

Shepherds together with magi huddle around an infant king.
A dying Jesus agonizingly speaks seven statements from the cross.
Multiple women, disciples, and angels are all present at an empty tomb.

The above descriptions are only some of the harmonized images that many students carry into our classrooms. These mixed messages are given to them via various avenues not only inside the church but also from popular culture outside it. Art, theatre, film, novels, children's books, and even coloring books have all been known to merge elements from the gospels.

Harmonizations tend to be the norm rather than the exception in society, perhaps in part because artists and shapers of the popular imagination are unhampered by the same guidelines that limit biblical scholars in reconstructing Jesus' life. They are free to draw upon any, and sometimes all, available resources and to shape them together uncritically in order to create a fuller and more harmonious picture.[1] While these blended depictions can sometimes serve a positive role, such as in simplifying these events for a children's Bible storybook or in providing a contemplative reflection for a Good Friday service, they can also unintentionally hinder students' ability to understand the biblical texts themselves.

One of the many challenges facing biblical studies professors is helping students disentangle these images so that they can begin to evaluate the four canonical gospels on their own terms. Using Jesus films in the classroom is an excellent way to empower students to become critics capable of deconstructing

---

1. According to Dorothy Sayers, 'The playwright, in any case, is not concerned, like the textual critic, to establish one version of a story as the older, purer, or sole authoritative version. He does not want to select and reject, but to harmonise.' Dorothy Sayers, *The Man Born To Be King* (London: Victor Gollancz, [1941–1942], 1946), p. 35.

harmonizations for themselves and of recognizing how these mixed messages may actually hinder their full appreciation of the portraits constructed by each evangelist.

Lesson preparation

One of the most effective scenes to screen in class is that of the crucifixion because it appears in all four gospels. In addition, while there is agreement between the gospels on most of the basic facts about that event (i.e., Jesus was crucified on a Friday, by the Romans, along with other convicted criminals, etc.), there are some significant details along with varying stylistic and theological perspectives that differ among these versions.

Before reaching this point in the semester, students already have had an introductory overview of the four canonical gospels. They are aware not only of the striking diversity between the Synoptics and John but also of the particular themes, special interests, and quirks of Matthew, Mark, and Luke. When we turn to examine the crucifixion narratives, students are better prepared for the discovery that even when narrating so central an event the evangelists are not uniform in their portrayals. Students also have begun to see that most of their mental pictures of what the life of Jesus was like are harmonized ones drawn from bits and pieces of each of the gospels.[2]

In order to prompt their thinking about the implications of harmonization, I assign in advance of our class meeting an essay from Walter Moberly's *From Eden to Golgotha* that examines the use and the potential abuse of the gospels by analyzing some typical evangelical harmonizations of the crucifixion.[3] I also have them read the four canonical accounts (i.e., Matt. 27.27-61; Mark 15.15b-47; Luke 23.26-56; John 19.16-42). Moberly's article focuses on the Markan and Lukan accounts and by comparing them points out some significant problems raised by blending these two distinct accounts. When students arrive in class, Moberly has prepared them to address the issues raised by harmonization.

---

2. They are also aware that some of the gaps left in the canonical narratives have been filled in with traditional and often imaginative elements that are now firmly embedded in society's collective psyche. One of the very first examples that my students read about in their introductory textbook is the mistranslation of *kataluma* as 'inn' rather than as 'guest room'. This now ingrained tradition of the inn has led to the creation of extra-biblical characters, such as the innkeeper and his wife. For further information, see Michael R. Cosby, *Interpreting Biblical Literature: An Introduction to Biblical Studies* (Grantham, PA: Stony Run, 2009), pp. 7-9.

3. R.W.L. Moberly, 'Proclaiming Christ Crucified: Some Reflections on the Use and Abuse of the Gospels', in *From Eden to Golgotha: Essays in Biblical Theology* (Atlanta: Scholars, 1992), pp. 83-104. When possible, I like to have students in my introductory courses read at least one example of an academic essay because the predominant textbook culture found in the USA higher education system often ensures that students in general education classes encounter only the biblical literature and the course textbooks.

Class discussion

I like to begin class by focusing our discussion of harmonization around three potential types of problems: literary, historical, and theological. By dividing the issues into these categories, it reinforces the idea that there are different kinds of information, or truth if you will, and that one cannot assume that any deficiencies found in one category subsequently impinge upon the others.[4] Students apply this compartmentalization to their later analysis of the cinematic crucifixion scenes, and it is my hope that by first practicing these skills with film they will be better prepared to use them when they return to read the gospels synoptically.

1. Literary

First, we focus on the literary (some might say artistic) difficulties raised by harmonization. In his article, Moberly compares the Markan portrayal of the crucifixion to Grunewald's rather agonizing crucifixion scene on the Isenheim Altarpiece and the Lukan account to Fra Angelico's much more serene portrayal. Since most students have never seen these works, the stark contrast of the comparison is lost on them until I project the images on screen. While a picture may not be worth precisely a thousand words, sometimes a visual juxtaposition of differing artistic interpretations is worth more than a verbal description, or at least it is often more easily grasped by students.

In order to reinforce the role that interpretation plays in renditions of the crucifixion, I go on to show them a wide variety of paintings from various centuries. Some of my favorite examples to compare are Tintoretto's 1565 crucifixion, which clearly embodies the *Christus Victor* interpretation of the event with the Jesus on the cross resembling a conquering Roman more than a condemned Galilean peasant, against Nikolai Nikoaliovitch Gay's 1905 *Le Calvaire*, which displays the agony of Jesus' cry of dereliction and his utter abandonment. I also enjoy placing side by side El Greco's *Crucifixion* (1596), Dali's *Christ of Saint John of the Cross* (1951), and James B. Janknegt's *Cruxifiction at Barton Creek Mall* (1985). As we examine the various images, I am always pleased with the analysis students provide and their ability to critique each portrayal's view of the significance and meaning of Jesus' death. When I ask whether we would possibly lose something if we were to try to combine all of these artistic interpretations, students are quick to respond in the affirmative.

Once students have a sense of just how differently the same event can be portrayed artistically, we turn back to the various literary portrayals, and I ask

---

4. So too Moberly states, '[S]ome might argue that any historical uncertainty would mean uncertainty about the truth and reliability of the gospels. It is hard to emphasize sufficiently, however, how important it is not to beg the question of the relationship of truth to historicity or impose anachronistic criteria of truth on the biblical text. . . . Our neat modern categories of "history" and "fiction" had not in fact been formulated in the world of the evangelists, who move freely and easily between the two' (Moberly, 'Proclaiming Christ Crucified', p. 101).

them to think again about the potential losses versus the potential gains in harmonizing the gospels. Can such a complex event be captured by one portrayal, or do we possibly need more than one to see the various angles, colors, shades, and implications of that Friday?

Of course, these are leading questions, so after hearing their opinions, I expose my own hand by using a food analogy. My culinary practices apparently have never improved since childhood, and like many children, I still hate it when different types of food run together on my plate invading one another's space and polluting each other's taste. I prefer to eat each type of food in turn partly because I love to savor the individual flavors. When the food is mixed, it becomes harder to appreciate the subtly and uniqueness of each taste, and I am afraid that I will miss out on the experience of each if I were to combine them. In a similar way, we can better taste and appreciate the different flavors of the gospels and the unique literary styles of each evangelist when we read them side by side rather than mushing them together.

2. Historical

Second, we discuss how harmonizations can often lead to a confusion of the harmonized presentation with what *actually* happened. If one assumes that all the events described in each of the gospels are historically accurate, then one might also assume that a more complete picture of the crucifixion could be constructed by including all the events in a new narrative. The new narrative is given priority over the four gospels because it is thought to contain even more historical data than any individual one could.

At this stage, I like to point out that there is a sequential order of movement from the actual, historical Jesus to the gospel presentations of Jesus to these harmonized presentations. While some may think that they are moving closer to what Jesus was actually like with these harmonizations, they have in fact moved another step away. The gospel versions are closer to the events than a harmonized portrait could be because even if one were to conclude that all of the events in the gospels were historically accurate, that does not guarantee that these pieces are arranged in the correct chronological order by any reconstruction.

One other important comparison that can be made here is between harmonizations and scholarly reconstructions of the historical Jesus. While the first in trying to include all the gospel material, often uncritically, produces a type of hyper-gospel, critical scholarship deconstructs the gospels by judging the historicity of individual sayings and events in an effort to uncover the 'historical Jesus' behind the gospels. The former reconstructed portrait, in effect, becomes something more than the gospels while the latter creates something that is generally less than the gospels, but both create a new narrative that is in essence in competition with the Gospel portraits.

A positive benefit of exposing students to a myriad of interpretations is that they can begin to recognize the difference between a person and his many presentations. Then perhaps they are less likely to mistake the representations for the referent and to lapse into bibliolatry, a reverence for the text itself as if it were God. At the very least, students begin to become more attuned to the role that interpretation inevitably plays in any type of reconstruction of history and more aware of the impossibility of one text's ability to convey the totality of a person or of an event.

3. Theological

Third, we examine the theological impact of harmonization. Harmonization attempts are often driven by a desire to present as 'historical' a picture as possible, one that is able to somehow merge together divergent pieces from each account and thus to affirm the veracity of each of them. Unfortunately, harmonizers fail to grasp that the blending of these narratives may privilege the theology of one gospel over another, thus effectively silencing the voices and authority of the others. Just as there are different literary and artistic flavors to each of the gospels, so too there are varying theological senses. To mix them together may result in the loss of one or more of the distinct flavors.

In Moberly's article, he notes how evangelicals tend to gravitate towards the subsitutionary atonement theory when explaining the significance of Jesus' death. While this particular theology may be in line with Mark's Gospel and Paul's letters, it is certainly not the viewpoint that Luke's Gospel, for instance, provides. Moberly likens Luke's portrayal to a mixture between Aulen's *Christus Victor* and Abelard's 'moral influence' models and says that presenting one harmonized view of the crucifixion in affect foists a Markan theology onto Luke and privileges the harmonization, and subsequently its preferred theology, as the normative and therefore authoritative interpretation.[5]

Here, I like to remind my students that the early church rejected Tatian's harmonization and opted for having four distinct versions instead of one and to have them think about why those ancient leaders seemed to think that each one was necessary and valuable for Christian instruction. For those students who regard the canon passed down from those early believers as an authoritative text, I ask them whether or not they personally think it is valid to privilege any harmonized version over the four authorized versions. As Moberly points out, '[I]t is all too easy to use the rhetoric of being "biblical", while in reality adopting a partial and selective reading of scripture in which the ultimate, and often unacknowledged, authority is the theological emphasis of a particular Christian tradition.'[6]

Using Jesus Films in the Classroom

Since roughly about thirty Jesus films have been produced in the last century, there are plenty of options from which to choose, although not enough time to

---

5. Moberly, 'Preaching Christ Crucified', p. 103.
6. Moberly, 'Preaching Christ Crucified', p. 105.

view them all in class. The films range from sentimentalized Hollywood epics, to merry musicals, to humorous spoofs, to graphically violent adventures, and even to animated versions. Most of the films are harmonizations of some sort, but there are a select few that purport to draw from one gospel only.[7] Sometimes I like to start off with one that is not a harmonization without telling my students and then ask them to determine from which gospel the film primarily pulls its material and theology. Pasolini's *The Gospel according to St. Matthew* is one of my favorite non-harmonized versions to use, but occasionally I do choose to begin with Saville's *The Gospel of John*.

As we watch the clips together, students try to identify elements drawn from specific gospels and to detect whether one evangelist's theological portrait is being favored above any others. While the single-source films, such as *The Jesus Film* based on Luke, are obvious in their inclinations, the harmonized versions also tend to have certain leanings as well. For example, even though the crucifixion scene in Gibson's *The Passion of the Christ* is a true harmonization drawing together most of the details described by the four evangelists, including all of the seven statements, it also has a decidedly Markan flavor to it as it emphasizes the agony, the utter abandonment, and the idea of substitutionary atonement.[8] Another film that I enjoy using is Hayes' *The Miracle Maker* because in it the animated Jesus appears like a rippling superhero as he hangs from the cross. Though theologically this film more closely resembles the *Christus Victor* image found in Luke, it too is a harmonization.

I try to give students as varied a selection as possible from the types mentioned above. Ray's *King of Kings* is a fascinating example of a harmonization precisely because while it appears to attempt to combine most of the material found in the canonical gospel accounts the director then makes bizarre choices regarding which material is left out. For example, he includes final sayings from all four gospels but then leaves out one of the seven statements.[9] We often ponder in class what motivated the director to exclude only one and why it was that particular one. Also useful for demonstrating the role of interpretation and perspective, *King of Kings* with its overly sentimentalized nature stands in stark contrast with other portrayals, such as Pasolini's *Matthew*. The latter offers a desolate picture while the former is more peaceful and, of course, infused with an extra dose of saccharine. Similarly, watching a movie that focuses more on the violence of the crucifixion, such as Gibson's *Passion* or Deasy's *Passion* put out by the BBC, also provides a stark contrast to the more peaceful death scene

---

7. The single-source films include the following: *The Gospel according to St. Matthew* (Pasolini, 1965); *Godspell* (Greene, 1973); *The Visual Bible: Matthew* (van den Bergh, 1993), all based on the Gospel of Matthew; *The Jesus Film* (Sykes and Krisch, 1979), based on the Gospel of Luke; and *The Visual Bible: The Gospel of John* (Saville, 2003), based on the Gospel of John.

8. One of the ways in which Gibson makes his substitutionary atonement theology clear is by casting himself in the role of a soldier who hammers the nails into Jesus' wrists.

9. 'I thirst' (John 19.28).

in either version of the *King of Kings* (DeMille, 1927 or Ray, 1961).[10] Because of time constraints, I rarely get to show any of the parodies, such as Jones's *Life of Brian*, musicals, such as Jewison's *Jesus Christ Superstar*, or modern-day parallel versions, such as Arcand's *Jesus of Montreal*.[11]

To be sure, the amount of advance work required to screen these films and prepare clips for class is not minor and can be quite time consuming. For the overly burdened and busy professor, I would suggest consulting Staley and Walsh's *Jesus, the Gospels, and Cinematic Imagination*.[12] This incredibly helpful resource provides overviews of 18 different Jesus films and provides plot summaries for each. Also included in each chapter dedicated to a different film are a list of memorable characters and scenes, a discussion on each film's genre and film setting, and key biblical passages portrayed. By reading these reviews first, professors can gauge which films would be most beneficial for their course objectives and so save hours of time in watching the many cinematic versions of Jesus' life. Perhaps most beneficial though are the book's scene by scene breakdowns that even list the time mark for each scene so that finding precisely what you want to view becomes even easier. Tatum's *Jesus at the Movies* and Stern's *Savior on the Silver Screen* are also good resources offering analyses of some of the more popular Jesus films, but Staley and Walsh's guide is definitely the first stop for a concise introduction and overview.

Conclusion

The use of Jesus film clips in class supports not only the liberal arts ideal of cross-disciplinary integration but also promotes critical thinking skills as it moves students gently from analyzing harmonized dramatizations of the crucifixion to the gospels themselves. Viewing cinematic crucifixion scenes together enables students to recognize more easily the role that interpretation and culture play in the retelling of this renowned event. They are able to critique the possible biases or agendas of directors and the influence of popular cultural forces on the films. Once students become comfortable with analyzing the films from this perspective, they are more likely to be able to see the gospels anew as depictions of Jesus that are also influenced by their own cultural context and

---

10. I have never actually used Gibson's film in class precisely because it is so gory and includes an unnecessary excess of graphically violent footage. If I have any reservations about the use of crucifixion scenes in the classroom, they revolve around the issue of violence. I worry a bit that the repetition of watching these executions may desensitize students, so I usually view films that do not focus as much on the violence but that still offer interesting examples of harmonization and interpretation.

11. Arcand's film would certainly be worthwhile to view in class because it is one of the few that incorporates any historical critical scholarship that challenges more traditional versions of the crucifixion.

12. Richard Walsh and Jeffrey L. Staley, *Jesus, the Gospels, and Cinematic Imagination: A Handbook to Jesus on DVD* (Louisville, KY: Westminster John Knox, 2007).

by different theological views regarding the meaning of Jesus' life, death, and resurrection.

Screening Jesus films in class can help students perceive through a visual medium the potential difficulties of mixing together the individual literary, historical, and theological flavors of each of the canonical gospels. They begin to see that while there may not be extreme harm done through harmonization there are certainly important perspectives lost through the process. To be truly 'biblical' in reading the Bible, students need to learn to read the books on their own terms and not replace their stories with a harmonized version, no matter how spectacular the special effects may be.

TEACHING WITH META-QUESTIONS

Jane S. Webster
Barton College

In seminaries and graduate schools, instructors in biblical studies have clearly defined goals, such as to teach students how to prepare sermons, to think theologically, or to conduct historical-critical research. In religiously-affiliated or confessional Bible colleges, instructors teach the Bible in order to promote understanding and faith within a religious tradition. In the undergraduate liberal arts context, however, instructors do not have such well-defined purposes. Often teaching biblical studies as part of the core education, instructors hope that their students will develop cultural literacy and the skills to conduct civil religious discourse, and to research, write, and think critically in the discipline; they will deliberately steer clear of promoting religious affiliation or commitment. But as Barbara Walvoord has argued, students take introductory courses in religion, not to learn how to think critically as their instructors had long imagined, but to make personal meaning.[1] And as each successive generation enters college, they bring with them new questions about who they are and what their place in the world might be. So as teachers of biblical literature in a non-religious context, how can we find a way to create the space for individual meaning-making—without imposing a religious agenda—and at the same time, encourage skill development?

I have often found it helpful to organize a course around a central question, one that I frequently return to in class and use on exams to encourage students to consider how the various parts of the course might contribute to one particular theme. Can we now find a common question that will satisfy the academic rigor of the college classroom to lay a foundation for further studies *and* create the space for students to make personal meaning? Can we find a perennial question that speaks to the human condition, one that will find students where they are and lead them into a fervent search for answers in the biblical text? This question would combine both the criteria of academic integrity and personal meaning-making, satisfying both the needs of the instructor and the student.

---

1. Barbara E. Fassler Walvoord, *Teaching and Learning in College Introductory Religion Courses* (Oxford: Blackwell, 2007).

In the last few years, I have been experimenting with designing biblical literature courses around what I will call a meta-question. In this essay, I will outline the pedagogical theory that underlies this method of course design, apply the theory to a course called *The Life and Teachings of Jesus*, and then identify the principles learned from this experiment. Meta-questions, if carefully selected and communicated, contribute to academic skill building and personal meaning-making.

1. Theory

In *Understanding by Design*, Grant Wiggins and Jay McTighe describe a way of designing courses 'backwards'.[2] In other words, they say, start with the things that we want students to understand by the time we finish the course—what they call 'enduring understandings'. Here are some possible understandings for a biblical studies course:

> Each religion that draws from the Bible (Judaism, Islam, and the many branches of Christianity) defends its faith, in part, by a selective, human interpretation of the key Bible passages from which the faith springs.

> It is difficult to reconcile the literalist view of the Bible with a historical understanding of the text(s) written by many men over many years.

> One need not believe in the God of the Bible to appreciate the power of image, language, and history in the text and the influence of the text on all the arts from the time it was written.

While the idea of communicating a clear 'understanding' is appealing, college students might be better served, not with a statement but with a question from which they might begin to articulate their own understandings. They are also more likely to adopt a question for themselves—and that perhaps they have already considered—if the answer does not come in a prepared package. For this reason, rather than seek an understanding upon which to base a course, I chose to begin with a meta-question.

The next task is to determine how students can show that they have arrived at understanding: what type of 'authentic tasks' and assessments will give them an opportunity to delve deeply into the topic, do research, and formulate an answer that makes sense to them. Thus, the summative assessment begins to take shape that will bring all the various aspects of a course together into a coherent and organized form, perhaps including such things as demonstrating writing or presentation skills or critical thinking. It might be something like a

---

2. Grant P. Wiggins and Jay McTighe, *Understanding by Design* (Alexandria, VA: Association for Supervision and Curriculum Development, expanded 2nd edn, 2005).

class presentation, a debate, or an essay—some kind of project. Ideally, this would be 'authentic', something done by professionals in the discipline.

In the final step, we need to identify the specific steps that students need to make in order to arrive at a successful summative performance, or to use a common metaphor, we need to provide 'scaffolding' for their learning. Do students need to learn the skills required to write an essay, give a presentation, or conduct a debate? Do they need to learn how to research? Do they need to learn how to read the Bible with understanding? And so on. Then we organize the scaffolding so that it logically builds one piece on top of another, and give formative assessments along the way to test the structure before it bears too much weight. This gives students an opportunity to practice the various skills and get feedback before their summative assessment, and it gives us valuable information to adjust the pace, complexity, process, and work environment in order to meet the students where they actually are (and not where we would hope they would be). The first formative assessment should be a pre-assessment that measures what students understand at the beginning of the course. Well-designed formative assessments will culminate in an authentic summative performance that demonstrates student understanding.

2. Application

Now we will turn to a particular example and application of this method of course design. First, the context: Barton College is a non-profit liberal arts college of about 1,100 undergraduates in eastern (read 'rural') North Carolina. Although it was founded by and retains its affiliation with the Disciples of Christ (Christian) Church, Barton College has no mandatory religion courses or chapel attendance; in fact, students can easily avoid all religion courses. The 3-member Religion and Philosophy Department thus attracts students by offering courses that fulfill the general education skill requirements of written and oral communication and critical thinking. We also attract occasional students interested in ministry or law, with about 10 majors at any one time.

Since my arrival at Barton College some 12 years ago, I have struggled with the structure of a course called 'The Life and Teachings of Jesus'. In the past, I have focused the course on the question 'Why are there four gospels?' and have asked students to write a final summative take-home essay exam based on their synthesis of the ideas we explored through class work; they would explain the relationship between the gospels, the different perspectives, agendas, and tendencies of each, relative dating, and historical context. They also became very familiar with the life and teachings of Jesus in order to do this. And while this was an interesting *academic* question, it was by no means a question the students brought into the class with them, nor a question that was part of their everyday conversations, or of ultimate concern to them. As a result, I set out to identify a question that 'transcends the discipline' and is therefore transferable to other courses, not limited to those who are only interested in ministry or religious studies; I also wanted a question that has a global and social impact. I wanted to focus the attention of students, not so much on the details of the life and teachings of Jesus, but rather on why we would want to know anything about Jesus at all. In particular, I wanted to explore the Christian idea of 'exclusive truth' with its far-reaching global impact. I decided the meta-question should be: 'What is truth and how do we know it?'

With my question articulated, I then designed the course around a final assessment that would give me some sense that the students understood not only the question, but a range of possible enduring understandings. Students would write a take-home essay exam that answered this question using the life and teachings of Jesus as examples. In order to identify clearly what these essays should look like, I used a rubric to identify the various components of the summative assessment. Students would need to be able to write clear sentences without mechanical errors, identify and evaluate evidence, develop a thesis, make transitions, and extend their thesis to the larger question about truth. If they were able to practice these skills often and get feedback, they would be well-prepared for the summative assessment. I thus assigned learning logs— one page papers that reflect on specific course content, citing primary and secondary sources as evidence and place it in the framework of the meta-question. At midterm and at the end of the semester, students would collate their various learning logs, revise, edit, and submit them for a weighted grade, the final being significantly higher than the first. These assignments were formative in nature: they gave me a chance to evaluate and address the developmental needs of the students, and they gave students a chance to improve their skills with low risk but ultimate reward.

Finally, I measured what students knew when they came into the class. Not only did it cue me into where the students were starting, but it gave me an opportunity to pitch the question as 1) multidisciplinary, 2) relevant in biblical studies, and 3) valuable for personal meaning-making. So on the first day, I asked students to write an in-class paragraph answering the question, 'What is truth?' After students had a chance to identify what they themselves thought about truth, I invited them to discuss their ideas in class. I used such prompts as 'How do you know that's true?' 'Is that more or less true?' 'What's your evidence for that?' They claimed that they knew truth because the Bible, parents, tradition, or teachers said so. In each weekly class we returned to this question and reflected on the content of the class and how it shaped our understanding of what we thought truth was. I returned these preliminary paragraphs to the students at the end of the semester so that they could remember where they had started and then could evaluate what they had learned.

3. Meta-Questions: Principles Learned

So how did it work to teach with a meta-question? What principles can I take away from this experiment?

The meta-question about truth was particularly interesting in a course on the life and teachings of Jesus. As one student pointed out at the beginning of the semester, the Gospel of John states that 'Jesus is the way the truth and the life;' that's that then. As we explored each gospel in turn—starting first with Mark, then Matthew, then Luke, an excursion to Q, then John, then the extra-canonicals, the Infancy Gospel of Thomas, the Protoevangelium of James, the Gospel of Thomas, and the Gospel of Peter—students quickly saw that some of the gospels contradicted each other, that Jesus' sayings sometimes had different meanings when set in a new context, that not all the stories and sayings of Jesus are included in the canonical gospels, and that each gospel had a different agenda. Through the differences in these gospels, students learned to be careful observers of details, to identify bias, and to raise questions about location, date, and authorship. This led us naturally into an exploration of possible theories and methods to explain the differences, giving students an appreciation for academic debates on these every same issues. Students practiced all this in their learning logs, and at the end of the semester, drew together all of their observations in their final take-home essay exam by framing them with a discussion of truth. Each student demonstrated that they could make and break an argument using evidence and appropriate methodologies. I was satisfied that students had developed their biblical literacy, methodology in the discipline, and communications skills. My questions were answered. But were the students' questions?

I used a course evaluation to see if this question worked for them. First, I asked if the students knew what the meta-question was. There was no ambiguity there. *A meta-question should be explicit.*

Second, when I asked how the question was raised throughout the course, students were able to give a range of answers, showing they understood how the same question could shape their whole approach to a topic. The question also did not have only one answer. *A meta-question should be open-ended and multi-dimensional.*

I asked if students did extra research because they were interested. Here is a sample of the responses: 'I am reading the textbook and trying to determine truth and my beliefs'. 'For the first time, I took advantage of the library. I used a lot of different books, including commentaries'. 'I read several articles about what is historical about Jesus, and found Bible dictionaries to be very helpful'. *A meta-question should provoke independent research.*

I asked students if they discussed this question outside of the classroom; here are some sample responses: 'Yes, because it is a real life question and comes up in everyday life'. 'It came up all the time'. 'I was so excited; I talked to anyone who would listen!' *A meta-question should be relevant.*

When I asked students if they had faced this question in other classes, they said this sort of thing: 'Not really because most of my other courses focus on attaining the information and not analyzing it, which I feel is sad'. One said, 'Only if we brought it up'. *A meta-question should be cross-disciplinary.*

When I asked students if the question provoked them to make personal meaning, they said: 'This class forced me to read and learn something I thought I knew. I was forced to open my mind and [it] challenged everything I've always believed. The course has forced me to look at my faith and figure out what I believe. As of now, I don't know what I believe, but I am working to rebuild that faith based on the knowledge I have gained, giving me a whole new faith'. *A meta-question should promote personal meaning-making.*

Finally, I wondered if students had been able to discover an enduring understanding for themselves about the nature of truth. Their final essay exam showed me that they had learned how to identify and evaluate evidence, to gather it thoughtfully, to construct and test a thesis, and to reflect on the meaning of truth. They learned that truth is not stable, that it can be used to oppress and to liberate, that it is constructed and so can be deconstructed, that it can and should be challenged. '[This course] helped me to question what others present as truth. I no longer accept information solely on someone else's opinion. I do research to support my research now'. 'This class led me not only to think critically, but also to ask critical questions and only accept critical answers'. *A meta-question should lead to enduring understandings.*

4. Conclusion

This experiment taught me the importance of using meta-questions to design a course in biblical literature. Because students found the question relevant and interesting, they were provoked to explore the contours of their faith and developed their understanding of the world. Students engaged the question with enthusiasm; in the process, they also learned content about the life and teachings of Jesus, methodologies of the discipline, civil religious discourse, and critical thinking, and honed their communication skills. We found a common question that met the needs of both groups. It was a win-win.

COURSE DESIGN AND THE USE OF META-QUESTIONS IN AN INTERDISCIPLINARY FIRST-YEAR SEMINAR ON THE ETHICS OF BIBLICAL INTERPRETATION

Russell C.D. Arnold
DePauw University

Introduction

Discussions in our sessions have focused attention on the complex process of designing courses in ways that provide the best opportunities for real learning to take place. Two of the pedagogical tools raised in this regard are 'backward' course design and the use of metaquestions. In Jane Webster's endeavor to design a course that would provide students the opportunity to discover their own 'enduring understandings' she turned to metaquestions, the use of an overarching question (e.g., 'What is truth?') that could tie together the learning in the course.

In contrast, I came to the intersection of course design and metaquestions because I was confronted with a difficult question that I wanted some help in answering. The question was, how do we make judgments about interpretations of the Bible as either good or bad, better or worse? Like many biblical scholars, I was trained to focus on historical critical questions alone, but have become increasingly convinced that this approach is just as culturally influenced (Euro-American male) as any other kind of reading.[1] So, if I thought the historical method was better, I decided that I had to be able to explain why. I also wanted to be able to explain why I rejected readings of the text that promoted violence, economic oppression, exclusive claims to God's favor, etc. It is easy to acknowledge that vastly different interpretations of biblical texts exist, but I wanted to know how readers could be held morally responsible for their interpretations.

I am fortunate that my job supported me in my attempt to create a first year seminar course in which students and I could wrestle with these questions together. The course came to be called 'Ethics of Biblical Interpretation: Read-

---

1. I was especially influenced by Daniel Patte, *Ethics of Biblical Interpretation: A Reevaluation* (Louisville, KY: Westminster John Knox, 1995).

ing the Bible in Contemporary Controversies'. During the time I was deciding to develop this course, I was introduced to the integrated model of course design presented by L. Dee Fink in his 2003 book, *Creating Significant Learning Experiences*.[2] Intrigued by the creative possibilities of his work, I set out to apply Fink's method to the creation of this course revolving around this basic question, 'how do we make moral decisions about interpretations?'

Taxonomy of Significant Learning

The first consequence of focusing on this metaquestion was that it forced me to focus on learning outside of knowledge acquisition and analysis. This is not a question we can answer simply by gaining a certain amount of factual knowledge. To begin to respond, the students and I would need to think and learn about who we are, how we think, how we make moral judgments, how we understand our responsibility to others, and how our interpretations might affect others. From the beginning I found common cause with Fink's taxonomy of significant learning pictured in the figure below.[3]

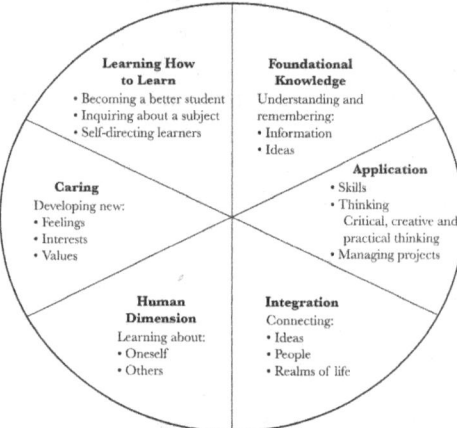

Fig. 1. Taxonomy of Significant Learning

Unlike Bloom's hierarchical taxonomy of learning, Fink sees different types of learning as a circle, interrelated and nonhierarchical. He argues that investing in one category of learning improves the engagement in the others.[4] So the more we engage in each kind of learning, the more significant the learning experience overall. For example, we learn foundational knowledge better if we integrate it with other ideas from various fields, or if we connect this learning with the human dimensions of learning about self or others. Similarly, if we are asked

---

2. L. Dee Fink, *Creating Significant Learning Experiences* (San Francisco: Jossey-Bass, 2003).
3. Figure used by permission from Fink, *Creating Significant Learning*, p. 30.
4. Fink, *Creating Significant Learning*, pp. 32-33.

to apply appropriately what we have learned to real-life situations, we will be more likely to see value in and care about what we are learning.[5]

This engagement with other kinds of learning is especially important in religious studies. Walvoord's study of pedagogy within introductory courses in religious studies indicates a significant gap between what professors typically declare as course goals and what students want when they register for a class.[6] Faculty members want critical thinking while our students typically indicate a desire for personal or spiritual development. Recognizing this 'great divide', as faculty we can press on with what we want and ignore our students' goals, or we can create opportunities to engage the human dimension and invest in active integration of the range of realms of life in the classroom. I agree with Walvoord's conclusion that we should work to 'create spaces and voices for students to integrate academic with spiritual/religious development'.[7] Not only will our students be more satisfied with their experience in our classes, but according to Fink's taxonomy, they will more effectively attain the knowledge and critical thinking that we say we want them to learn.

Integrated Course Design

This relational taxonomy of learning informs the basic structure of Fink's model for course design. Once again the model is not hierarchical, but rather focuses on the complex integration of situational factors, learning goals, feedback and assessment, and teaching and learning activities.[8]

We begin with reflection on situational factors, at the bottom, because they influence everything else. Learning goals, feedback and assessment, and teaching and learning activities form three points on a triangle, each one relating to both the others. Fink recommends, following the principles of 'backward design', that we develop goals first, rather than starting with content or topics to be covered.[9] Each course's learning goals ought to be based primarily on what I want them to be able to do or know five years from now. After developing these goals, I imagine how they can show me, and themselves, that they have done that kind of learning (assessment). Then I develop activities we can do during the course to build their competence to do what I want them to do in the end.

---

5. Fink, *Creating Significant Learning*, p. 32.
6. Barbara E. Walvoord, *Teaching and Learning in College: Introductory Religion Courses* (Malden, MA: Blackwell, 2008). See also John K. Simmons, 'Vanishing Boundaries: When Teaching about Religion Becomes *Spiritual* Guidance in the Classroom', *Teaching Theology and Religion* 9 (2006), pp. 37-43.
7. Walvoord, *Teaching and Learning*, p. 94.
8. Figure used by permission from Fink, *Creating Significant Learning*, p. 62.
9. Fink (*Creating Significant Learning*, p. 63) refers to the work of Grant Wiggins, *Educative Assessment: Designing Assessments to Inform and Improve Student Performance* (San Francisco: Jossey-Bass, 1998).

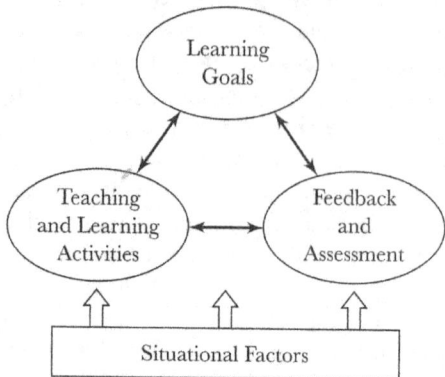

Fig. 2. Key Components of Integrated Course Design

The final step is to make sure that the three sides of this triangle are connected and integrated in such a way that 'they reflect and support each other'.[10]

Situational Factors

We turn now to discuss how this model was applied in the development of my First Year Seminar (FYS) course. I began by brainstorming the various types of situational factors relating to the setting (time, room, semester, etc.), the students (number, background, year, requirement, major, etc.), the teacher (experience, busyness, commitments, etc.), and the subject (nature of field, history of discourse, etc.). Some of these issues may not be known, but it is best to take into account as many as possible from the beginning.

Here are some of the most salient factors for my class. In a First Year Seminar, made up of 14 first year students, there were two built-in features that greatly enhanced this project. First, DePauw's FYS program is designed to be interdisciplinary; it encourages courses that make connections across departmental lines and employ a variety of modes of inquiry. All students enroll in a FYS, but each course in independently designed and the subject matter chosen by the faculty member who teaches the course. This provided me with the freedom to take on a new and controversial topic and approach it in creative ways. Second, the students in my FYS form a mentor group for their entire First Year experience. They have a student mentor who meets with them as a group and individually throughout the year, and I serve as their faculty advisor. When

---

10. Fink explains that if there is a breakdown in the link between any two of these parts, there will inevitably also be a break in one of the other links. As a result, this final element of integration is essential for achieving a satisfying, fair, and effective learning experience (*Creating Significant Learning*, pp. 64-66).

the students arrive on campus for orientation, they spend much of their time together with their mentor group. As a result, the students have a chance to form friendships with one another and to form some group cohesion before we get into the real controversies in the class. This contributes to creating a learning community that serves as a safe space for open discussion of controversial topics, even though they have very different religious, political, and personal backgrounds.

With respect to the students' religious backgrounds, in the two years I have taught this seminar I have had students representing, among other things, King-James-only fundamentalism, evangelical Protestantism, liberal Protestantism, Catholicism, African-American Christianity, and philosophical atheism, as well as international students from China and India. Most of these students chose this course as one of their top three choices, but others ranked it lower on their list. Some knew the Bible quite well, and others had never opened it before.

Some other factors relate to my own engagement with the class. The focus on contemporary uses of the Bible stands outside my area of training, which is Hebrew Bible and early Judaism. I have often worked on questions of biblical interpretation, but seldom regarding contemporary questions such as abortion, capital punishment, homosexuality, environmentalism, and evolution. Whatever investigations I had undertaken on these topics had been outside of the academic setting, in my own personal interactions with various contemporary religious communities.

The most important situational factor relating to my approach to the subject is that the metaquestion at the heart of the course remains an open question for me. I cannot say that I have settled on any sort of satisfactory explanation for how I make moral choices between interpretations of controversial biblical passages. While the openness of this situation can be frightening for me, I believe that it is also an asset. I can honestly enter into the course alongside the students, not as the expert with the right answers, but as a fellow learner who can just as easily learn from them. I certainly have strongly held positions on each of the controversies we discussed, but my own unanswered questions about the moral basis of the biblical interpretations that support those positions allows the class to keep returning to the primary question about how we make moral choices instead of getting stuck on the details of any particular 'answer'.

Learning Goals

After reflecting on the situational factors, I began developing learning goals that derived from the metaquestion and Fink's relational taxonomy. At first I wrote out a set of learning goals myself and asked the students if they had anything they wanted to add. The second time I taught the class, we spent the first few days as a class developing our learning goals together. In both cases, the list was framed as OUR learning goals, things that WE are going to learn, not what I expect them to learn. Here is one form of the list:

- Our primary goal is to provide safe, directed opportunities to develop our skills in critical thinking through discussion of the methods of reasoning used in contemporary arguments based on biblical interpretations.
- We will develop our research skills, as well as skills in the use of sources in argumentation.
- We will come to understand some different approaches to biblical interpretation, and learn to analyze the ways the Bible is used in an argument. In being exposed to others' interpretations, we will be encouraged to hear each other's perspective with empathy and generosity of spirit.
- We will be challenged to consider the ethical implications of both the methods and the interpretations that derive from them, as well as how we make such ethical judgments.
- We will learn to recognize the role of the reader's context in the process of interpretation as we place different interpretations within the religious landscape of our society.
- We will learn about ourselves, about our own contexts of interpretation, and about our ethical responsibilities as a reader and member of society.
- We will all be challenged to think critically about, and more effectively articulate in speech and in writing, our own interpretations of important biblical texts, the bases for these interpretations, and their ethical implications.
- Finally, we will take ownership of the direction of the course and of our own learning. We will be encouraged to seek out and bring to the class additional resources, issues, and perspectives that are of interest to us.

For the purposes of simplifying the integration stage of the course design process, I have grouped these goals into three main areas: research skills (choosing and using sources), critical thinking (analysis of other people's readings, application of principles to new readings), and self-understanding (understanding our own context as readers, becoming self-directing learners,[11] articulating our own views).

Feedback and Assessment

Building on these goals, I started to think about feedback and assessment. How are students going to show me they are working toward these goals? Fink talks about four aspects of feedback and assessment based on models of educative assessment: forward-looking assessment, clear criteria and standards, opportunities for self-assessment, and Frequent, Immediate, Discriminating feedback

---

11. Fink prefers this term to the more traditional 'self-directed learning' because it is more active, and it keeps the focus on the learners rather than the learning, *Creating Significant Learning*, p. 53.

delivered Lovingly (FIDeLity).¹² For this class, I focused attention on the first of these, but although I recognize the importance of the others, I continue to struggle to implement them effectively.

In most of my previous courses I have assigned a combination of exams and papers, in which I want students to show me they understood what we just did. I ask them to tell me what these terms mean, who these people are, or what this text is about. This epitomizes a backward looking approach. Forward-looking assessment asks students to take what we did and use it for something. Can you use it in a real situation? This goes beyond application of technique to a new problem in order to practice it (for example, source criticism on a new section of text). Instead, the situation should be as real-life as possible and it should require students to build on the work done in class in ways that encourage innovation and require them to use their own judgment. Ideally such assignments would also incorporate opportunities for trial, error, feedback, and revision.¹³ One of the examples I developed for the class came at the end of a section in which we discussed, and then staged a debate about, the Bible's views on the use of drugs and alcohol. I asked students to write a letter to our university's president, the town's mayor, or some other figure in authority in government or the Church, making a case for what their drug/alcohol policy should be based on the Bible (they had to assume that the recipient would care about what the Bible says). Taking what they had learned about the different texts relating to the topic, and the different ways others had interpreted those texts, they had to use their judgment to make a real argument that could conceivably have been sent to a person of influence.¹⁴

Other aspects of feedback and assessment include clear criteria and standards, reflective self-assessment and frequent, immediate, discriminating feedback delivered lovingly. A key aspect of this last principle encourages separating feedback from assessment.¹⁵ All of this feedback may not be tied to grading directly. For example, I could give students feedback to something someone said in class, or others could. If this practice is a regular part of the class, then students are always getting feedback; if the feedback is discriminating (i.e., it highlights a specific strength or weakness rather than providing a general comment like 'good') then it can be very helpful for them. Grades are given separately, based on clear criteria, and possibly with input from their own self-assessments. Fink's approach to feedback and grading seems to me the way to go, although I am still figuring out how to put it into practice in my courses.

---

12. Fink, *Creating Significant Learning*, pp. 82-100. In this section, Fink draws on the work of Wiggins, *Educative Assessment*, and Barbara E. Walvoord and Virginia J. Anderson, *Effective Grading: A Tool for Learning and Assessment* (San Francisco: Jossey-Bass, 1998).
13. Fink, *Creating Significant Learning*, pp. 86-87.
14. There are significant similarities here to work on 'problem-based learning' as described by Barbara J. Duch, Susan E. Groh and Deborah E. Allen (eds.), *The Power of Problem-Based Learning: A Practical 'How To' for Teaching Undergraduate Courses in Any Discipline* (Sterling, VA: Stylus, 2001).
15. Fink, *Creating Significant Learning*, p. 95.

Learning Activities

Once we have a sense of where we want to go, and how we will know if we are getting there, the next task is to develop a range of different kinds of learning activities to prepare us. Since the FYS program at DePauw has historically been seen as an introduction to general education competencies, I have separated these activities out as they relate to 'W', writing and 'S', speaking and listening.

I chose to employ all three types of reflective writing Fink describes: one-minute papers, journals, and learning portfolios.[16] The one-minute reflections (usually closer to five minutes) were done at the end of class each Thursday, and focused on some aspect of the learning process. I asked students to write what was the most compelling or most confusing thing that came up in that day's class. Or I asked them to write down some questions that remained unanswered for them. Or in one case, after a particularly charged and productive discussion about creationism and evolution, I asked them simply to write down whatever they were thinking about at that moment.

The journals took different forms. Sometimes I asked them, at the end of each two- to three-week section, to reflect on the intersections of ideas across the topics covered, or to write the kind of letter mentioned above, or simply to reflect on any aspect of our discussions over those weeks. The second year, I gave each student a yellow notepad on which they could write down any thoughts, ideas, questions, or drawings that came to them during the class period.[17]

The final writing project was a learning portfolio.[18] I asked students to create a portfolio that articulated how they approached reading the text, i.e., their own philosophy of interpretation. Essentially I asked them to explain how they answer the metaquestion: How they decide what is good and bad interpretation. Their philosophy statement was then supported by an appendix that included examples of texts and interpretations we had encountered throughout the semester.

On the S (oral communication) side, I focused on class discussion, presentations and debates. Early in the semester these provided practice with interpreting a single text, or analyzing and presenting someone else's interpretation of a text. The debates in the second half of the semester challenged students to articulate and defend a position on a controversial topic (e.g., abortion, homosexuality, heaven/hell, drugs and alcohol, premarital sex, etc.) using biblical interpretations in the face of counterarguments based on different interpretations.

---

16. Fink, *Creating Significant Learning*, pp. 117-18.

17. This was originally recommended to me as a way to provide an outlet of expression for a student in the class with Asperger's, but I found it to be quite helpful for all the students.

18. Fink describes a few different ways of using portfolios and their benefits, *Creating Significant Learning*, pp. 119-20.

Integration

In the final stage of the course design process, we check to make sure that all of the course material was integrated, that the goals, assessments and activities work together. The following diagram shows how the learning activities and assessments related to the key learning goals.

Integration Diagram

                                                                                      Self-Inventory
     Presentations on Topics of Interest   List of Moral Principles
Text Analysis Worksheets

                                            Weekly Reflections
    Text Interpretation Analysis   Journals
                                          Advocacy Letters

                     Debates / Town Hall Meetings

         Learning Portfolios   (Philosophy of Interpretation)

Research Skills   **Critical Thinking**   **Self-Understanding**

At the bottom are the three basic types of goals: research skills, critical thinking, and self-understanding. Above are the various learning activities and assessments used in class. Those activities on the far right, like the self-inventory, develop only an awareness of one's background and perspective. The reflection writing begins to bring in more critical thinking and analysis, so it is placed slightly more toward the middle of the chart. On the left side, activities like the text analysis worksheets (finding a secondary source and identifying its thesis) focus on basic research and analysis, while others incorporate more critical thinking. The final projects are designed to require the effective integration of all three areas. The students will only be able to complete the portfolio effectively if they have achieved some proficiency in these learning areas, and can employ what they have learned to produce something of meaning to them.

Conclusions

Having undergone this involved course design process, I came to realize that this course reflects the goals I have always had for my students, although I had never before set them out this way, or developed clear ways to assess them. As a result I had seldom known whether students were really achieving those goals. The feedback I received about the course indicated many students very clearly liked the portfolio and appreciated the opportunity to articulate their ideas in this way. The students showed that, although they may not have known exactly how to answer the metaquestion that framed the course, they had developed some tools and avenues for trying to address that kind of question. They also recognized that they could use what they'd learned from wrestling with this question to address things outside the Bible, both in their classes and in their lives. Some students were clearly empowered by the experience of leaving their first semester of college having completed a thoughtful, detailed statement that articulated their personal approach to reading the Bible.

One of the comments from the Student Opinion Forms reflects how successful this project was:

> I like how much this course challenged me. Countless times throughout the course while completing assignments I have had to stretch so far outside of my boundaries to be able to complete assignments. It challenged what I knew and taught me so much more in the process. It was not just a class and completing assignments to receive a grade, it was literally learning solely for the sake of understanding. I did not do the work solely because I wanted a good grade, I did the work because I wanted to understand the topics we discussed and further understand the Bible, controversy, etc.

I had never received something quite like this comment before. Comments like this reflect the ideal learning experience: self-directing, seeking real understanding, reflecting on the student's own sense of self as a learner, etc. The overwhelmingly positive response from my students and the enlivening and transformative power of the experience for me has convinced me that all my courses should be redesigned based on these principles. The combination of the compelling metaquestion and a process of course design that helped integrate the entire class in the service of the metaquestion, clearly resulted in experiences of significant learning, both for the students and for me.

BIBLICAL STUDIES AND METACOGNITIVE READING SKILLS

Rodney K. Duke
Appalachian State University

According to the ACT 'The Condition of College and Career Readiness' report of 2011, only one student out of four coming out of high school has the basic skill level necessary to succeed in college in the four areas of writing, math, science and reading.[1] In my experience, many incoming students have few learning skills and a mistaken notion about what constitutes learning; this is particularly noticeable in my students' lack of reading comprehension skills.[2] Moreover, when it comes to reading the Bible, a subject about which students often have preconceived notions and some vested interest, students tend to abandon what reading skills they have acquired and read the Bible 'on the flat' without nuance. This is to say that they read culturally familiar genres with much more sophistication, albeit unselfconsciously, than they read biblical texts.

This paper discusses how I have used metacognitive learning, and specifically metacognition and reading strategies, in order to improve students' reading skills and comprehension of the biblical literature. My main goals are to increase our recognition as teachers of the role of metacognitive learning in the classroom and to give some specific exercises for building metacognitive reading skills in our students. My target audience for this paper is not instructors who see their role as merely passing on factual data, but teachers who are trying to provide a skills-based education in the traditional liberal arts educational setting. Such teachers seek to motivate their students to be life-long learners and to equip them with reading skills that apply across disciplines.

One of my working assumptions is that training students in reading skills presupposes the possibility of successful communication. Such an assumption may be questionable to some readers of the currently popular theories of literary criticism. Due to the goals and constraints of this paper, I offer only this brief explanation. Once it became popular to read the biblical texts as literary

---

1. The report may be found at www.act.org/research/policymakers/cccr11/index.html. See page 2 for support for the specific statement made above.
2. See below, 'Addressing a Basic Problem through Metacognitive Learning'.

art, the methodologies of New Criticism and Formalism were applied to them. Such approaches were in part correctly based on the recognition that one cannot get into the mind of the author/artist and that one does not even need to know the author's intention in order to appreciate literary art. More recently, the vogue has been the postmodern emphasis on reader-response criticism leading to deconstruction and various proprietary readings of the biblical texts. Such methodological approaches correctly note that in one sense a text has no meaning apart from the reader and that in every act of re-reading new meaning is created. I do not dispute the value of such hermeneutical insights, but I do recognize the limits of their presuppositions when pushed to the extreme. I start with the understanding that the biblical texts are works of communication. While it is true that we cannot get into the minds of the authors and that the results of our efforts will always be flawed, there are things we can do to understand something of what the biblical texts might have communicated to their original audiences. In fact, if that were not true, there would be no point in producing this paper. None of us can get into one another's minds and yet we communicate fairly successfully through texts and other means. If we did not, there would be no social structures. My basic approach with my students, then, is to explore with them these questions: What is learning? How do we communicate successfully? How do we read? How can we apply these skills to the biblical texts?

Addressing a Basic Problem through Metacognitive Learning

Identifying the Problem and a Solution
Many of my students have not learned in the current school system how to be learners. They cannot articulate well what learning means or entails. At the beginning of my courses, particularly at the lower levels, I try to make them aware of this problem, so that they can address it. This direct approach was something that I learned recently through an online workshop by Saundra McGuire, Director of the Center for Academic Success at Louisiana State University.[3] With my students, we explore the difference between studying and learning. According to McGuire, and confirmed by my students:

- Most incoming students state that to achieve a good grade in high school they had to show up in class the day before the test in order to receive the answers.
- They believe that learning is accomplished by listening or taking notes in class.
- They say that they are studying what they have learned when they reread their notes to prepare for a test.

---

3. Saundra Y. McGuire, On-line workshop, 'Teach Students How to Learn: Metacognition is the Key': www2.nemcc.edu/IR/Spring2007_PresentationbySMcGuire.pdf.

To address this issue, I will employ a definition of 'learning' as a function of deliberative behaviour (not IQ) that results in an end goal.[4] That is, when a student can take new data, concepts, and skills, and apply them to new situations and/or teach them to another person, then learning has taken place. The class looks at Bloom's Revised Taxonomy[5] of levels of learning (e.g. remembering, understanding, applying, analyzing, evaluating, and creating) and I ask them to identify what levels of learning they operated at in high school and for what levels they believe college learning should strive. I make it clear that at the least we will be working toward a level of application. Such a clarification of our learning goals gives students an objective means for evaluating their learning prior to evaluative tests. When they can teach someone else the data, skills, and concepts, then they are well prepared. (In fact, from the first day of class on, I employ a common teaching strategy that engages one of the metacognitive protocols of assessment. I will pause after stating a concept and ask students to turn to a partner and rearticulate that concept in their words. Immediately they have a means of assessing whether or not learning has taken place.)

Moreover, I clarify for students that in this process of reflection about studying and learning we are engaged in what is often called 'metacognitive learning', also called 'self-regulated learning'. 'Metacognition', a term coined by John H. Flavell[6], is basically being aware of one's own thinking processes. 'Metacognitive learning' is thinking about how one learns, having a conscious approach to learning, and assessing accurately one's level of learning.[7]

Metacognitive Learning and Motivation
A metacognitive approach to learning treats students with respect and enables them to embrace learning. Hacker, Dunlosky and Graesser, in 'A Growing Sense of "Agency"', point out how some people in cognitive science, having moved somewhat away from treating people as empty-headed behavioural machines, still treat them only as more sophisticated processors of information. However, a metacognitive approach has a fuller perspective on people as self-aware agents who guide their own learning and are involved in constructing their sense of the world.[8] Teaching students to be guided by meta-

---

4. See further discussion below at, 'Metacognitive Learning and Motivation'.
5. See Lorin W. Anderson, David R. Krathwohl and Benjamin Samuel Bloom (eds.), *A Taxonomy for Learning, Teaching and Assessing: A Revision of Bloom's Taxonomy of Educational Objectives: Complete Edition* (New York: Longman, 2001). Chart at www.odu.edu/educ/roverbau/ Bloom/blooms_taxonomy.htm.
6. John H. Flavell, 'Metacognitive Aspects of Problem Solving', in *The Nature of Intelligence* (ed. Lauren B. Resnick; Hillsdale, NJ: Lawrence Erlbaum Associates, 1976), pp. 231-5.
7. McGuire, 'Teach Students How to Learn'.
8. Douglas J. Hacker, John Dunlosky and Arthur C. Graesser, 'A Growing Sense of "Agency"', in *Handbook of Metacognition in Education* (ed. Douglas J. Hacker, John Dunlosky and Arthur C. Graesser; New York: Routledge, 2009), pp. 1-2. For a theoretical work on intelligence and the role of metacognition, see Cesare Cornoldi, 'Metacognition, Intelligence, and Academic Performance', in *Metacognition, Strategy Use, and Instruction* (ed. Harriet Salatas Waters and Wolfgang Schneider; New York: Guilford, 2010), pp. 257-77. Cornoldi's research supports the conclusion

cognition addresses their perceptions about learning. Studies have shown that when students believe that failure is due to a lack of ability (I.Q.), they tend to feel shame, they decrease their effort, and their performance goes down. When students believe that failure is due to a lack of effort, they tend to feel guilt, increase their effort, and their performance improves.[9] Introducing metacognitive learning also addresses students' motivation. Non-self-regulated learners are characterized by extrinsic motivation (e.g. grades and praise), self-handicapping, and avoidance of failure by procrastination and by avoiding challenge. Encouraging metacognitive learning promotes intrinsic motivation, awareness of one's strengths and weaknesses, a belief in successful incremental learning, and the ability to adapt and cope with classroom stress, all traits which lead to success in school and beyond. It also shifts their motivation from performance goals, where there is fear of failure, to mastery goals which encourage persistence. Students become more likely to take on challenging tasks and practice their learning, leading to greater academic success.[10]

In my classes, I am trying to take the process of self-motivation forward another step. I discuss with my students how studies have shown that people are attaching their self-worth to their ideologies. When such people encounter new knowledge that challenges their ideology, it can feel like a personal attack, and they sometimes refuse to learn.[11] Surveys show that many people only turn to the 'news' source that promotes their ideology and ignore other sources.[12] I ask my students to think about what difference it would make if a person based one's self-worth on being a learner, on being a person who wants to grow in knowledge. For such a person, new knowledge would never be threatening. Based solely on my anecdotal experience in the classroom, I believe that this information and challenge appear to be motivating my students to become more engaged in biblical studies than in the past and with less apprehension that they and their beliefs will be threatened. I suggest the class motto:

> Learning comes with humility, at the expense of ego.
> But, the cost of ignorance is higher—one's self-respect.

---

that metacognition, a component of intellectual ability that can be promoted by education, is one of the critical components that enables one to apply the basic structures of intelligence to daily life.

9. Nancy E. Perry, Lynda Phillips and Lynda Hutchinson, 'Mentoring Student Teachers to Support Self-Regulated Learning', *The Elementary School Journal* 106.3 (2006), pp. 237-54.

10. See survey of research listed by Perry, Phillips, and Hutchinson, 'Mentoring Student Teachers', pp. 238-39.

11. Brendan Nyhan and Jason Reifler, 'When Corrections Fail: The Persistence of Political Misperceptions', *Political Behavior* 32.2 (2010), pp. 303-30.

12. Pew Research Center for the People & the Press, 'News Audiences Increasingly Politicized': www.people-press.org/2004/06/08/news-audiences-increasingly-politicized; 'Partisanship and Cable News Audiences': pewresearch.org/pubs/1395/partisanship-fox-news-and--other-cable-news-audiences; 'Press Widely Criticized, But Trusted More Than Other Information Sources': www.people-press.org/2011/09/22/press-widely-criticized-but-trusted-more-than-other-institutions.

Metacognition and Metacognitive Reading
As noted above, 'metacognition' is a term that was coined in a 1976 article by John H. Flavell, a developmental psychologist. His article called attention to the role that metacognition plays, at least theoretically, in successful learning. Primarily due to the work of Flavell, the academic community became engaged in research in metamemory and metacognition.[13] In education, one main field of research has been in the area of learning theory, primarily in the sense of memory retention for children. In fact, most research has been done with elementary school-age children, although some studies, particularly in linguistics and second-language learning have turned to adult students.[14] For instance, the Center for Academic Success at Louisiana State University offers various workshops on study and learning skills that are based on a metacognitive approach.[15] Still, metacognitive learning is a rather new field in terms of empirical evidence. As recently as 2010 one researcher notes there is still a lack of sufficient empirical evidence because not enough teachers have been trained in teaching metacognitive skills, although the number is increasing.[16]

A particular field that has developed in education is metacognitive reading. Actually, in educational psychology, 'think aloud' studies, in which one identifies and comments on what one is doing or thinking, have been applied to reading for over one hundred years.[17] This method has also been called the 'think-aloud protocol', which is basically a type of 'protocol analysis'—a phrase that was much later coined for a type of qualitative research in usability testing. Still, it is essentially a form of metacognition. Working with the interest in metacognition prompted by Flavell, studies have focused more specifically on teaching the reading process metacognitively.[18] In terms of reading, Pressley and Afflerbach created a compendium of reading strategies that people may employ for reading a variety of texts.[19] A recent study has noted how some strategies have changed for Internet-based reading.[20]

---

13. Wolfgang Schneider, 'Metacognition and Memory Development in Childhood and Adolescence', in Waters and Schneider, *Metacognition, Strategy Use, and Instruction*, pp. 54-81, particularly pp. 54-6, 72-4.

14. For some initial work on college-level implementation, see Roman Taraban, Marcel Kerr and Kimberly Rynearson, 'Analytic and Pragmatic Factors in College Students' Metacognitive Reading Strategies', *Reading Psychology* 25 (2004), pp. 67-81. They provide a helpful list of college-level analytic and pragmatic reading strategies on page 75.

15. www.cas.lsu.edu.

16. Schneider, 'Metacognition and Memory Development', p. 74.

17. Michael Pressley and Peter Afflerbach, *Verbal Protocols of Reading: The Nature of Constructively Responsive Reading* (Hillsdale, NJ: Erlbaum, 1995), p. 1.

18. For instance, see Chapters 2-5 in Hacker, Dunlosky, and Graesser, *Handbook of Metacognition in Education*.

19. Pressley and Afflerbach, *Verbal Protocols*.

20. Peter Afflerbach and Byeong-Young Cho, 'Determining and Describing Reading Strategies: Internet and Traditional Forms of Reading', in Waters and Schneider, *Metacognition, Strategy Use, and Instruction*, pp. 201-25.

As I learned more about the theories of metacognitive learning and metacognitive reading, I realized that I had been teaching in this manner for many years in my classroom. My guess is that many of my colleagues who teach biblical studies have been as well. However, learning about this approach has influenced my teaching in two ways. It has made me more deliberate about applying this approach; and, more importantly, I now explicitly explain to students what we are doing, so that they may be consciously engaged in metacognitive learning. In my case, I have not been simply giving the students strategies for reading the biblical texts; I have been attempting to teach them how to devise reading strategies. So, I want to turn at this point to some specific illustrations of what those teaching biblical studies can do.

Moving toward Metacognitive Reading Strategies

Genre Awareness

We all know that we need to help our students place the biblical texts in their historical and cultural contexts. Often though, students do not think about the literary context of genre. As I am helping the students place the texts in their historical-cultural contexts, I also try to get them to see the significance of different genres and different reading strategies. Metacognitive learning works particularly well in developing genre awareness, because college students can draw on previously acquired skills and knowledge in the area of reading and communication in general. Most often, however, my students employ such skills unconsciously, without foresight and deliberation. My main objective is to draw out their skills and prior knowledge so that they begin to process and to employ metacognitive reading systematically. For several years now I have used the following collaborative-learning exercise successfully to create an 'ah-ha moment' regarding genre awareness.

Genre-criticism exercise.[21] I inform the students that we will be developing metacognitive reading skills by drawing on their current ability to recognize different genres and to read different genres differently. The students are given a handout with the beginning lines of a few different, common types of written communication (e.g. a formal letter, a lead news article, a want ad, a technical journal article, a fairy tale). First, as a class-wide project, I read the samples aloud one-by-one and ask the students to speak out and record all of the descriptive terms that apply to each genre. They find this part quite easy and wonder what it has to do with biblical studies. I point out how skilled they had been at identifying different genres, but how they had been rather unconsciously responding correctly to specific literary features. The second procedure is to have them identify the specific literary features that generated the descriptive

---

21. This exercise in fuller form, but without reflection on metacognition, was previously published in Rodney Duke, 'Spotlight on Teaching', *Religious Studies News* 13.4 (November 1998), pp. 5-7.

terms. I work through one of the genres with them, using the terms they generated, giving them three basic categories to think about (formal features, stylistic features, and specific content) and identifying what they must have noticed to come up with their descriptors. They then work in groups, each group working on one of the genres, and practice what I have demonstrated.

The third procedure in this exercise moves on to the next point; that is, to realize that they are reading each genre differently. Again, demonstrating to the class, I pick out one of the genres and explore what I am doing when I read it. I do so by raising and answering the following (admittedly overlapping) questions:

- Who was its intended audience?
- What is/are the purpose/s of this literary type?
- Once we recognize the type, what other features or characteristics do we expect to find?
- Once we recognize the purpose of this type, what do we focus on in order that the purpose might be achieved?
- What must we do or ask as readers in order to understand this type?

The students then work in groups again with their genre, answering these questions and reflecting on how the responses differ for different genres. After the group work, I assemble the class and ask them for some brief reports in which they give one literary feature that sets their genre off from other genres and one thing that they do when reading their genre that is different than what they do when reading other genres.

The last procedure may be the most important one. The students write a brief reflective paper on the prompts: a) What new learning or point of emphasis from the exercise seems the most significant? and b) How does this exercise apply to reading the Bible? The results are exciting! Many students write about how they now recognize that, as obvious as it is, they had never thought about there being different types of literature; they had never thought about how they read different genres differently; and they had not realized that they already had some sophisticated skills that they could apply to reading the Bible. With this exercise, we identify the first step of our metacognitive reading protocol: What is my text's genre?

Communicative Functions and Evaluation
After getting students to the initial insight about reading different genres differently, I move into a series of exercises. These exercises have the goals of getting the students to recognize that different genres generally carry out different communicative functions, that communicative functions are closely related to what we call a text's 'meaning' (a text's total impact), and that, when we read different genres differently, we evaluate them for meaning differently. I expose the students to some basic theory about the poles of communication (i.e. addresser, addressee, means, and referent) and how different forms of commu-

nication emphasize those poles in various blends of functions (emotive, conative, poetic, and referential). We then do the next exercise.

Function and evaluation exercise
First I inform the students of the objective of the exercise, that at its conclusion, they should be able to explain and illustrate the relationship between a text's literary function and how its meaning is evaluated. I then raise the following set of questions for each of the numbered texts (below):

- Does this text have meaning?
- What is its main function(s)?
- Is it legitimate to ask whether or not its meaning is true or false?
- How would you assess whether or not the text carried out its intended function(s)?

   1. Water consists of 2 parts hydrogen and 1 part oxygen.
   2. Napoleon originated the custom of sewing buttons on the cuffs of dress jackets.
   3. I am the best candidate!
   4. Use this deodorant and you will become more romantically appealing.
   5. It is so hot outside, I'm burning up.
   6. I love you.
   7. Once upon a time a tortoise and a hare had a race.... (assume the rest of the story).
   8. [I also include a E.E. Cummings graphic-style poem with words one might associate with a fall scene arrayed on the page as if they were tumbling down.]

The students readily see that the main functions of 1 and 2 are referential and that we may legitimately ask whether or not the statements are true or false. However, again using a simple collaborative learning technique, I ask them to discuss in pairs: How do these texts represent two different classes of referential statements? How is what we mean by 'proof' for each of these quite different? How would they go about proving each of these? Which class of referential statement do they think they will find represented more in the Bible?

As we move onto 3 and 4, the texts shift to a more conative (persuasive) function. Some students, in their first response, will state that one can assess the texts as true or false. With the prompting of other students, and after further reflection on the communicative function, most students realize that such texts are not primarily providing facts, but seeking to change behavior, something that would have to be assessed differently for its effectiveness than primarily referential statements.

With 5 and 6 the texts move to a more emotive function. The more thoughtful students, however, will prompt discussion on whether 6 sometimes might function more conatively and manipulatively than emotively in certain situations.

A poetic, or entertaining, function blends with a conative (and to some degree, referential) function in 7. The last example, 8, initially stumps many students who will say that it has no meaning. However, when I ask them if the text, by virtue of its vocabulary and word placement on the page, had prompted them to picture anything, they tend to have another 'ah-ha moment' about different kinds of meaning and evaluation.

After some more processing of the exercise and how it might apply to the Bible, the students come to the conclusion that before we as readers assess the value and meaning of a literary text, we first need to understand the intended communicative function of that text. In essence, we have added two more steps to our metacognitive reading protocol. The first is to determine the communicative function(s) of a text. The second is to ask what one should focus on for assessing a text's meaning and value. I further illustrate this point by giving real-life examples of mis-readings of biblical texts and ask the students to identify what the mistakes are behind the mis-readings.

Reading Strategies

The ultimate goal of the class literary approach is to get students to recognize that when dealing with genres that are foreign to them, they will need to develop new reading strategies deliberatively; that is, they will need strategies for biblical narratives, parables, letters, laws, etc. just like we have strategies for lead news articles and fairy tales. We set out to follow a basic metacognitive protocol for reading:

General Steps
 1. Identify the literary genre and its function in general.
 2. Identify the general literary features of that genre and their intended impact (i.e. create a 'Reading Strategy')

Specific Steps
 3. Identify the literary features of a specific text and their specific impacts (i.e. apply the 'Reading Strategy')
 4. Evaluate in terms of intended function/impact.

In reality, we all follow these steps in everyday reading. However, in daily reading, we tend to employ these steps unselfconsciously and uncritically, particularly the first two steps.

In order to develop more consciously employed skills, I introduce the students to some basic communication theory using the 'Process of Communication Chart' below.

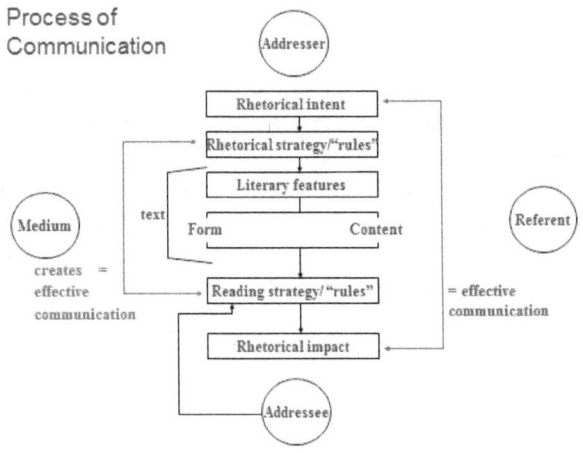

I illustrate the chart by walking through a story about how one student ends up in an awkward situation and needs to apologize to another student. The basic idea is that some such situation calls for communication. The addresser has a rhetorical intent he wants to achieve. To do so effectively, he must create a rhetorical strategy that is going to 'play by the same rules' of communication that he assumes the addressee will employ. The form of communication in this case is a text, the literary features of which can be examined abstractly in terms of their form and content. (I note that the horizontal axis of medium-form-content-referent is explored further in such fields as semiotics.) The end process is the rhetorical impact on the addressee. When the rhetorical impact at least closely approximates the rhetorical intent, then communication has been effective. However, involved in this process is the fact that the addressee will bring her reading strategy to the text, by which she derives the rhetorical impact. Both parties must be 'playing by the same rules' of communication. Therefore, it is only when the strategy by which the text is read (reading strategy) is close to the strategy by which the text was created (rhetorical strategy), will the rhetorical impact approximate the rhetorical intent. I explain that, although we can never get into the mind of the original addresser of the biblical texts, there are some things we can do to try to put ourselves in the role of the intended addressee and to develop a reading strategy.

We then spend the semester working through a few biblical genres one at a time, creating reading strategies for them. I employ a teaching method that is typically used in metacognitive learning. I first model the skills involved for the students. Then I employ group peer work in which the students practice employing those skills in a context in which they can learn from each other. Finally, the goal for tests is for the students to demonstrate that they can employ those skills by themselves.

Students, with guided exercises, first use the categories of the chart to come up with a descriptive definition of a given biblical genre (e.g. kind of addresser, nature of the addressee, typical content, rhetorical intentions). After getting a handle on the basic intention(s) of a given genre, we brainstorm the kinds of rhetorical strategies a good communicator might use to carry out those functions effectively. For example, to get students thinking about conative strategies used in wisdom literature, I will ask them to compare the strategies used in two TV illustrations. The first is a talking head that says, 'Drugs are bad. Do not use drugs'. The second is an old image, but still somehow known by most of my students, of a hot frying pan that has bacon and eggs sizzling in grease, over which one hears, 'This is your brain on drugs'.[22] With a list of strategies in mind, we then begin to identify the specific literary features in our texts that carry out such strategies. At this point we are beginning to shape a reading strategy that looks for those literary features. Again, we even try to be metacognitive about the nature of those literary features. For example, when we recognize that a text uses such figures of speech as metaphors and similes, we reflect on just how figures of comparisons work to create both cognitive and affective responses. The final result is a reading strategy. Below is a suggested metacognitive reading strategy for the literary genre of the two-line proverb.

Wisdom Literature
Reading Strategy for the Two-Line Proverb

A. *Formal Level of Analysis* (how the 'parts' function)
  1. What kind of relationship exists between the two lines? (e.g. comparison, contrast, 'building', etc.)
  2. How does that relationship work? (Consider diagramming the relationship.)
  3. What figurative language is in the 1st line? How does it work?
  4. What figurative language is in the 2nd line? How does it work?

B. *Level of Specific Content* (what the 'parts' are)
  1. What are the specific elements (words, phrases, concepts) that are being related between lines 1 and 2?
  2. What are the specific images, feeling, and thoughts which are evoked and developed through the relationship?

C. *Synthesis*
  1. What is the intended total impact of the whole proverb? (Write out the mental process of how the literary features create their individual and cumulative impacts.)

D. *Application*
  1. How does the proverb cause you to push 'backwards' and dwell on your own past experience? What kind of experience/observation/perspective do you imagine prompted this particular piece of wisdom?

---

22. The 'Fried Egg' TV spot created by the Partnership for a Drug-Free America (www.drugfree.org/) which can be viewed at www.youtube.com/watch?v=nl5gBJGnaXs.

2. How does this proverb then invite self-assessment in the present moment?
3. How does this proverb lead you to push 'forwards' toward future application? In what future kinds of settings might this piece of wisdom be applicable?

Conclusion

I have been pleased with the overall results of this metacognitive approach to reading the biblical literature. First, this approach has successfully engaged many students, although not every one of them. Initially, some students will complain that they want 'just the Bible' and not 'this literature stuff'. As the semester progresses, most students become persuaded about the significance of what they are learning. (In a recent class, in which we were conducting a close reading of Gen. 1.1–2.3, a student had an 'ah ha moment' and blurted out, 'There wouldn't be so much fighting over this text, if people would just read what it says!') Second, students have applied what they have learned outside of class. Although I certainly do not have a goal of stirring up trouble, I must admit that it is rewarding when a church-going student comes back to class and says that a pastor was missing the communicative purpose of the sermon text. Also, students who have gone on to graduate studies in biblical studies or theology have reported back to me that our approach had provided them a solid foundation for biblical interpretation. Third, occasionally students have come back to me after the semester is over and told me that these skills had helped them to be more successful in their other classes in other disciplines. Finally, I am learning that the more my incoming students have been 'trained' not to be self-learners through the current educational system, the more my primary function as a teacher has become that of challenging and training my students to become self-learners. Engaging them in the process of metacognitive learning is helping me to carry out that function successfully.

Teaching Revelation to the *Left Behind* Generation

Susan E. Hylen
Vanderbilt University

I teach Revelation in an introductory-level New Testament course in which my overall goal is for students to learn scholarly practices of NT interpretation. In the earlier parts of the course, students learn basic tools of literary analysis of texts, along with resources for understanding the historical and social context. As we discuss their interpretations of assigned texts, I have drawn their attention to the diversity in their readings. Our study of the Book of Revelation, situated at the end of the course, underscores this goal for student learning: to understand that more than one interpretation of the text is possible. The imagery of the text and the gaps it leaves regarding sequence and the logic of events give rise to many possible good interpretations.

A problem I have encountered is that many students have difficulty imagining more than one interpretation of Revelation. A majority of my students at Vanderbilt come from conservative religious traditions. When I poll the class, about half of students have read portions of the *Left Behind* series.[1] These students' understanding of Revelation is already shaped by the world they entered in reading *Left Behind*, and the power of that story line can be difficult to shake. The half of the class that has not read *Left Behind* usually has little contact with Revelation at all. Even so, their expectations of what they will find in Revelation often coincide with the *Left Behind* approach. The problem for me as a teacher is the dominance of this way of reading. As one student said in response to an alternative way of viewing the text, 'I understand what you're saying, but I have a hard time imagining it that way.' One particular reading of Revelation already shapes the student's understanding of the text.

This problem of students' imaginations being limited by the *Left Behind* approach led me to change the way I teach Revelation. The primary change has been a shift in the performance task I assign for this section of the class. I discuss that task here, followed by two specific strategies I employ in lectures.

---

1. Tim LaHaye and Jerry B. Jenkins, *Left Behind*, Wheaton, IL: Tyndale House Publishers, 1995. The best-selling book initiated a series of books and other products, including movies and a video game.

Performance Task: Generate Two Interpretations of Revelation

In an older version of this class, I evaluated student learning by asking students to analyze and evaluate the choices other interpreters have made. I prepared students to identify interpretive decisions regarding the vocabulary and syntax, relevant historical background, and the relationship of the passage to other biblical texts. This task was on the right track. For the most part, students were able to point to specific choices each interpreter made that supported his or her interpretation. My frustration was always that students never had to step outside of their own framework of interpretation. They could comfortably critique another interpreter, yet rarely brought the assumptions of their own framework into a critical perspective. My hope has never been for students to change their minds about a particular way of interpreting Revelation, but I do want them to see it as only one way of interpreting among many possible ways. And to do that requires a critical engagement with one's own prior assumptions about and experiences of the text.

My new performance task requires students to generate two possible interpretations of one text of Revelation. In the final exam I give them a short passage of Revelation and ask them to provide two different interpretations, discussing the choices represented by each. This strategy has worked much better. Having the students create interpretations rather than simply analyze them requires them to imagine more than one way of viewing the text. I explain ahead of time that each of their interpretations needs to be presented as a legitimate way of viewing the passage. Thus although they will likely prefer one or the other, they must communicate two distinct and coherent ways of interpreting this complex book.

Having set a new task for evaluation, I also had to back up through the course material to prepare students adequately to perform in this way. I developed two specific strategies for this. First, in my own lectures I created two options for interpreting Revelation. Each time we discussed a different passage or interpretive choice, we discussed more than one legitimate way of approaching the question. Second, I incorporated images of Revelation to help them to 'see' the text in different ways.

Option 1 and Option 2
In the prior manifestations of the course, I had primarily spent my time presenting the scholarly consensus: for example, that the author is an unknown 'John', not the author of the gospel or letters, or that 'apocalyptic literature' is a recognized genre, of which we have many extant examples. In preparing students to create two different interpretations, I framed these issues as open questions about which interpreters make decisions. With each topic I presented two possible options that interpreters choose. As we went, we fleshed out two different ways of interpreting Revelation, which we called simply 'Option 1' and 'Option 2'. Option 1 is the mode of interpretation represented by the *Left Behind* series. It understands Revelation as a prediction of real future events. The chronologi-

cal sequencing of these events is important, as the interpreter's job is to place the events in order and give a clear indication of what will happen. Option 2 is a message about the present. Revelation provides a vision of who God is, and who Christians are in relationship to God and the world. The seer critiques the attitudes and behavior of people in his own time, and calls them to change by realigning their understanding of the world with the vision of Revelation.

A caveat: These options are a heuristic device. They do not always correspond to actual interpretations, nor do they circumscribe all of the options interpreters face. I find that many scholarly interpretations actually lie between these two. My intention in creating the contrast is to lend clarity to a complex conversation for students who approach it at a beginner's level.

By way of expansion, I briefly describe the interpretive issues I identify for students and the different choices represented by the two options. The first interpretive choice I discuss is the identification of the author. Option 1 interpreters insist that the apostle John wrote this and other books of the NT. This choice affects the way they interpret Revelation, because it makes it possible to look for consistency across the works attributed to John. For Option 2 interpreters, either an unknown person named John wrote Revelation, or someone drew on John's already established authority as an apostle to reinforce the authority of the work. Revelation should then be read on its own terms, or perhaps as reinterpreting imagery and concepts from the other Johannine works.

The second issue is the question of what it means to have a 'revelation'. For Option 1 interpreters John's revelation is a direct experience of God, a view into heaven and into the future. John sees what will really unfold at some point in time. For Option 2 interpreters, an *apokalypsis* (ἀποκάλυψις, Rev. 1.1), or 'revelation' was a relatively common experience in the ancient world. Paul speaks of a revelation as an element of Christian worship (1 Cor. 14.6, 26), and has revelations himself (Gal. 1.12; 2.2). Additionally, immersion in the genre of literature we think of as 'apocalyptic' makes the language of Revelation seem more familiar. Like other apocalypses of its time, John's 'revelation' is a way of communicating a transcendent message about the current state of affairs.[2]

A third question for interpreters is defining 'prophecy', a term Revelation uses to describe itself (1.3; 22.7). In Option 1, a prophecy predicts future events. The prophet hears the word of God regarding the future and communicates this to God's people. Option 2 understands the prophet's message as a critique of his own time. The future elements of Revelation are a reminder to the hearer that God remains consistent through time and will act to fulfill God's promises. These elements do not provide information about the future but communicate something about the character of God or the world, or about who humans are

---

2. See the definition by John J. Collins, 'Towards the Morphology of a Genre: Introduction', *Semeia* 14 (1979), pp. 1-20 (p. 9): '"Apocalypse" is a genre of revelatory literature with a narrative framework, in which a revelation is mediated by an otherworldly being to a human recipient, disclosing a transcendent reality which is both temporal, insofar as it envisages eschatological salvation, and spatial insofar as it involves another, supernatural world.'

in relationship to God. Therefore, the prophetic message is a critique of the injustices and idolatries of the status quo. Both of these options regarding the function of prophecy were available in the ancient world. Thus the interpreter is left to assess the use of the word 'prophecy' in relation to the content of the rest of the book.

A fourth question for interpreters is the relationship of the Hebrew Bible to Revelation. Much of the language of Revelation echoes at least one and often multiple HB texts. From the perspective of Option 1, this reiteration validates the truth of Revelation. John sees the same thing that prophets before him have seen: the four living creatures (Rev. 4.6b-8; cf. Ezek. 1.5-12), the sun darkening (Rev. 6.12; Joel 2.31), the sky rolling up like a scroll (Rev. 6.14; Isa. 34.4). Like the prophets, the author of Revelation predicts these future events, and so it is not surprising that they see the same things. Within Option 2, however, an interpreter may notice that the imagery of Revelation both does and does not match up with the ancient prophets. The four living creatures have the same four faces that Ezekiel sees, but in Revelation each creature has one face, not all four. And these creatures sing the song of the cherubim of Isaiah 6.3. Revelation does not simply see the same thing but uses familiar imagery to communicate something new. This causes the Option 2 interpreter to ask about the literary function of the HB in Revelation. The use of prophetic imagery may indeed add authority to the vision. It also adds content. When John sees a beast with heads and horns, the imagery draws on Daniel's vision, including the political nature of that beast (cf. Dan. 7). Furthermore, the layers of HB imagery add a sense of culmination to John's vision. The expected signs of the end time from Joel, Isaiah, Ezekiel, and Daniel become visible together. John sees what all of the prophets have predicted coming to pass within the scope of his vision.

Fifth, interpreters make decisions about how to understand time. As I have mentioned, Option 1 interpreters understand the entire book as a vision of the future. Option 2 places more weight on the verb tenses in Revelation, relatively few of which occur in the future tense. The author sees a vision of the way things are, and the verb tenses reflect this. For example, in the description of the rider on the white horse of Revelation 19, John writes, 'Its rider is called Faithful and True, and in righteousness he judges and makes war' (19.11). From the perspective of Option 2, the rider on the white horse is not simply a future event, but an aspect of the identity of Christ that is unchanging. He is already Faithful and True. He judges and makes war. John mentions future aspects of Christ as well (e.g. 'he will rule them with a rod of iron' [19.15]), and these aspects relate to the promises of the last day. But the point for Option 2 is that the events of the end time are consistent with who God already is, and that people should act in the present with that understanding of God in mind.

A sixth problem is the sequencing of events. Option 1 interpreters understand the events of Revelation as sequential. Events are largely narrated in order of future appearance, and the occasional time markers (e.g. 42 months, 11.2; 13.5) are clues to aid the interpreter in establishing a clear chronology. In Option 2, the sequencing in the text is a part of the narrative. For example, the words 'then

I saw', which often introduce a new scene in the vision (e.g. 19.11, 17; 20.1, 4, 11; 21.1), are part of the narrative framework of Revelation. They indicate the order of John's vision, not the sequence of future events. When the images of Revelation are not viewed sequentially, they may be seen as distinct metaphors for understanding the complex theological concept of the end time.[3] John sees the end as the eschatological final battle, but also as the binding of Satan, and as the new Jerusalem, with the river of the water of life running through it. Just as humans draw on many metaphors to understand complex concepts like death or time, so also John uses many images, each of which captures something important about the end time. Instead of predicting future events, these images help the reader to understand different aspects of the day of the Lord.

A seventh issue is how the interpreter understands the imagery of Revelation. Option 1 is not a literal interpretation, a point that I underscore again and again for students. Some aspects of the text are taken literally, yet many are metaphorical. In the *Left Behind* series, for example, the locusts of Rev. 9.1–11 are read literally. Actual locusts come out of the ground to torture people. However, the beast of Revelation 13 is a symbol of a future person, the anti-Christ. Thus both Options 1 and 2 are metaphorical on some level. However, each option operates with a different understanding of what a metaphor is. Within Option 1, metaphors are referential. Images have a one-to-one correspondence with concrete people or events of the future. The beast is a metaphor, but it represents an actual future person. The metaphors of Option 2 are conceptual in nature.[4] The beast represents economic and political forces in this world that appear to be powerful from a human perspective yet are actually subordinate to the power of God.

Leaving Options 1 and 2 unnamed is one way that I try to engage the student's imagination in the process of understanding. In one of the final lectures, I invite students to suggest names for Option 1 and Option 2, or to encapsulate what each interpretation involves in a few words. I give them time to write something down, to push them each toward synthetic learning, before asking for answers orally. In a recent class, one student described Option 1 as depicting a future reality, and Option 2 as giving the reader a concept of God. Another student said Option 1 looks for sequential facts, while Option 2 finds eternal truths. A third student offered his own metaphors: Option 1 is a crystal ball, and Option 2 is a dream. When asked to elaborate, he responded that Option 1 understands the text as an enactment of the future, like one might see in a crystal ball. Option 2 sees the text as a dream, something that requires interpretation and is often

---

3. See Susan E. Hylen, 'Metaphor Matters: Violence and Ethics in Revelation', *CBQ* 73 (2011), pp. 777-96.
4. Although I do not communicate much of the theoretical background to students, my own thinking here engages the work of conceptual metaphor theorists. See e.g. George Lakoff and Mark Johnson, *Metaphors We Live By* (Chicago: University of Chicago Press), 1980; Mark Johnson, *The Body in the Mind* (Chicago: University of Chicago Press), 1987.

250 *Teaching the Bible in the Liberal Arts Classroom*

understood metaphorically. To my mind, each of these answers shows significant comprehension of the course material.

Using Imagery to Shape the Imagination
A second strategy that I employ as an aid to student imagination is the use of art to depict differences in interpretation.[5] I use art to present different interpretations of the opening of the first four seals in Revelation 6. In a prior class period I presented an interpretation of Revelation 6 that aligns with Option 2, and a convenient one-page handout from *Left Behind*, which serves as our example of Option 1.[6] In the next class, I begin with the Bamberg Apocalypse, an early 11th century work by an unknown artist, commissioned for the Cathedral of Bamberg. The first of four very similar images depicting the four horses and their riders is found in Figure 1.[7] I ask students to have the text of Revelation open in front of them, and to identify aspects of the text that they see in the image. They invariably notice elements the riders carry: the bow, the sword, the scales. They also notice what is not in these images: the first rider has no crown, the fourth horse is not green. They invariably say that the horses' heads look too small and that the riders do not appear powerful or frightening.

Figure 1: The Bamberg Apocalypse, 'The First Horseman'.

---

5. I am indebted to Lynn R. Huber of Elon University for many of the ideas I have for using art in the undergraduate classroom.

6. LaHaye and Jenkins, *Left Behind*, pp. 311-12.

7. The other three images are similar to the first. Unknown artist, 'The First Horseman', Wikimedia Commons, accessed 18 August 2011, commons.wikimedia.org/wiki/File:BambergApocalypseFolio014rFirstHorseman.JPG?uselang=de

Figure 2: Albrecht Dürer, 'The Four Horsemen of the Apocalypse'

When I turn to Albrecht Dürer's 'Four Horsemen of the Apocalypse' (Fig. 2)[8], there are often audible sighs or exclamations in the room. This is more like it! This is what we imagine these verses to look like. I again ask the students to identify what they see depicted from the text: the bow, the sword, the scales. 'Death' looks dead, as does his horse. Then I ask them what is found in the text that is missing in the image. They say, for example, that there is no color, and that all four images appear in the same frame.

Finally, and most importantly, I ask them to identify what is found in the image that is not in the text. Because we have already agreed that this interpretation corresponds more closely with what we imagine about the text, this is a way of pushing the students to notice the interpretive choices we are making, as well as those that Dürer has made. The contrast with the Bamberg images prepares students to be able to notice things about this interpretation that would otherwise remain hidden from view. Someone will usually notice that the horsemen appear to be on earth rather than in heaven. They also notice that the horses are moving, apparently at great speed, and that people are already dying as a result. None of these facets are mentioned in Revelation 6, but they are common assumptions that readers bring to the text, assumptions that say a good deal about how interpreters understand the overall function or purpose of Revelation.

The last thing I do is to go back to the Bamberg sequence and ask the students to reconsider these images. They do not conform to our expectations, but they capture certain aspects of Revelation 6 better than Albrecht Dürer. I pose the question, 'Which aspects?' and make them come up with answers. There is a long silence. Then, drawing on our discussion of the Dürer image and our prior discussion of the text, at least one student will say that these images capture a sense of calm that is present in Revelation. Either that student or I will remind the class of the narration of the climactic opening of the seventh seal, when 'there was silence in heaven for about half an hour' (8.1). John often returns to a vision of worship in the heavenly throne room, and his vision of the horsemen emerges within that space. Perhaps this artist's view of the horsemen communicates that quality of heaven. Another student will point out that Revelation 6 does not actually depict death and destruction in progress. The second horseman is 'permitted to take peace from the earth, so that people would slaughter one another' (6.4). He is given a great sword, but John does not narrate that he kills anyone. The fourth rider is 'given authority over a fourth of the earth, to kill' (6.8), yet again John does not narrate this killing. The Bamberg images are true to the text of Revelation in that they also do not depict death and destruction in progress.

The contrasting images offer the class a way to uncover some of our own presuppositions, and to see the validity behind a different set of interpretive

---

8. Albrecht Dürer, 'Four Horsemen of the Apocalypse', commons.wikimedia.org/wiki/File:Durer_Revelation_Four_Riders.jpg

choices. I do have to push students to take this last step, to locate what makes the Bamberg images a good possible interpretation of Revelation 6. But I find that if I prepare them for the task, they are capable of it. It has the potential to help students integrate what they have been learning and to reach a new level of understanding.

To my mind, teaching the Bible is always an exercise of imagination. We ask students to suspend for a moment their prior knowledge and experiences of a text and to see it in a new way. Revelation is not really different from other texts, it is only more vivid. There is a pattern here that I recognize from other parts of my teaching. Naming the dominant mode of interpretation, historicizing and explaining it, does as much to counteract its dominance as anything I offer as an alternative. I find teaching Revelation in this way somewhat counter-intuitive. My first inclination is not to lend an air of legitimacy to the *Left Behind* approach. Yet this is what I have ended up doing. I validate this perspective as one possible set of interpretive judgments. However, doing so involves the recognition that these *are* interpretive judgments and not the necessary or inevitable reading of the text. This paves the way for students to imagine other possibilities.

BIBLIOGRAPHY

AAR Syllabus Project: http://aarweb.org/syllabus/syllabi/h/haas/RS106_syl.htm.
'AAR Undergraduate Departments Survey Methodology', Focus on the Undergraduate Study of Religion, *Religious Studies News* (May 2008) p. 13.
'AAR Undergraduate Departments Survey Shows Increases in Religious Studies', Focus on the Undergraduate Study of Religion, *Religious Studies News* (May 2008), pp. 11-12.
Adam, A.K.M., *What Is Postmodern Biblical Criticism?* (Minneapolis: Fortress, 1981).
— (ed.), *Postmodern Interpretation of the Bible: A Reader* (St. Louis: Chalice, 2001).
— *Faithful Interpretation* (Minneapolis: Fortress, 2006).
Adam, A.K.M., D.B. Martin, *et al.*, 'Should we be teaching the historical-critical method?' *Teaching Theology and Religion* 12.2 (2009), pp. 162–187.
Adams, David E., 'The Teaching of Religion in the Liberal Arts College', *Journal of the National Association of Biblical Instructors* 2.2 (1934), pp. 56–60.
Afflerbach, Peter and Byeong-Young Cho, 'Determining and Describing Reading Strategies: Internet and Traditional Forms of Reading', in Waters and Schneider (eds.), *Metacognition, Strategy Use, and Instruction*, pp. 201-25.
American Academy of Religion, 'The Religion Major and Liberal Education' (2009) www.aarweb.org/programs/Religion_Major_and_Liberal_Education/default.asp.
Anderson, Lorin W., Krathwohl, David R. and Bloom, Benjamin Samuel, *A Taxonomy for Learning, Teaching and Assessing: A Revision of Bloom's Taxonomy of Educational Objectives: Complete Edition* (New York: Longman, 2001).
Angelo, Thomas and Patricia Cross, *Classroom Assessment Techniques: A Handbook for College Teachers* (San Francisco: Jossey-Bass, 2nd edn, 1993).
Aichele, George, 'Jesus' Violence', in Aichele and Pippin (eds.) *Violence, Utopia and the Kingdom of God: Fantasy and Ideology in the Bible*, pp. 72-91.
Aichele, George and Tina Pippin (eds.), *Violence, Utopia and the Kingdom of God: Fantasy and Ideology in the Bible* (New York: Routledge, 1998).
Association of American Colleges and Universities, *The Challenge of Connecting Learning: Project on Liberal Learning, Study-in-Depth, and the Arts and Sciences Major* (Liberal Learning and the Arts and Sciences Major 1; Washington, DC: Association of American Colleges and Universities, 1990).
— *Greater Expectations: A New Vision for Learning as a Nation Goes to College* (Washington, DC: Association of American Colleges and Universities, 2002), www.greaterexpectations.org.
Astin, Alexander W., *What Matters in College?* (San Francisco: Jossey-Bass, 1993).
Astin Alexander W., *et al., How Service Learning Affects Students* (Los Angeles: Higher Education Research Institute 2000).
Attridge, Harold W., 'Living with Difficult Texts at YDS', *Reflections* (2008), pp. 22-24.

Avalos, Hector, *The End of Biblical Studies* (Amherst, NY: Prometheus Books, 2007).
— *The End of Biblical Studies* (Amherst, NY: Prometheus Books, 2007).
— 'Wither Biblical Studies?' *Bulletin of the Council of Societies for the Study of Religion* 38.1 (2009), pp. 13–15.
— 'The Ideology of the Society of Biblical Literature and the Demise of an Academic Profession' *SBL Forum* www.sbl-site.org/Article.aspx?ArticleId=520.
Avioz, Michael, Ronald M. Hinson, Paul D. Brassey, K.L. Noll, James E. Bowley, 'In Response to the Fox Article', *SBL Forum* www.sbl-site.org/Article.aspx?ArticleId=502.
Bader, Mary 'Strategies for Moving Students from Faith-based to Academic Biblical Studies', *SBL Forum* www.sbl-site.org/Article.aspx?ArticleId=467.
Baker, Carol M., *Liberal Arts Education for a Global Society* (2000), carnegie.org/fileadmin/Media/Publications/PDF/libarts.pdf.
Bandura, Albert, 'Self-efficacy', in V.S. Ramachaudran (ed.), *Encyclopedia of Human Behavior*. IV, pp. 71-81.
Banya, Kingsly, 'Globalization, Social Justice, and Education in Africa: Neoliberalism, Knowledge Capitalism in Sub-Saharan Africa', in Joseph I. Zajda (ed.), *Globalization, Education, and Social Justice*, pp. 15-31.
Barker, Carol, 'Liberal Arts Education for a Global Society' (White paper for the Carnegie Corporation of New York; New York, 2000), pp. 1-14.
Barkley, Elizabeth F., K. Patricia Cross, and Claire Howell Major, *Collaborative Learning Techniques: A Handbook for College Faculty* (San Francisco: Jossey-Bass, 2005).
Barr, David L. and Nicholas Piediscalzi (eds.), *The Bible in American Education: From Source Book to Textbook* (Philadelphia: Fortress, 1982).
Barseghian, Tina, 'How Valuable is a College Degree?' mindshift.kqed.org/2011/05/how-valuable-is-a-college-degree.
Batten, Alicia, 'Studying the Historical Jesus through Service', *Teaching Theology and Religion* 8.2 (2005), pp. 107-13.
Baur, F.C., *Paul the Apostle of Jesus Christ: His Life and Works, His Epistles and Teaching* (Peabody, MA: Hendrickson, 2003 [1845]).
Bean, John C., *Engaging Ideas: The Professor's Guide to Integrating Writing, Critical Thinking, and Active Learning in the Classroom* (San Francisco: John Wiley and Sons, 2nd edn, 2011).
Bellis, Alice Ogden, *Helpmates, Harlots, and Heroes: Women's Stories in the Hebrew Bible* (Louisville, KY: Westminster/John Knox, 1994).
Bénézet, Louis T., *General Education in the Progressive College* (New York: Bureau of Publications, Teachers College, Columbia University, 1943; repr. New York: Arno & The New York Times, 1971).
Bénilde, Marie, 'The End of Newspapers?' *New York Times* (March 16, 2010), www.nytimes.com/2010/03/17/opinion/17iht-edbenilde.html?pagewanted=all.
Benne, Robert, *Quality of Soul: Quality with Soul, How Six Premier Colleges and Universities Keep Faith with Their Religious Traditions* (Grand Rapids: Eerdmanns, 2001).
Berger, Peter, *The Sacred Canopy: Elements of a Sociological Theory of Religion* (New York: Anchor/Doubleday, 1967).
Berger, Peter and Anton Zijderveld, *In Praise of Doubt: How to Have Convictions Without Becoming a Fanatic* (New York: HarperOne, 2009).

Berlinerblau, Jacques, '"Poor Bird, Not Knowing Which Way to Fly": Biblical Scholarship's Marginality, Secular Humanism, and the Laudable Occident', *Biblical Interpretation* 10.3 (2002), pp. 267-304.
— 'What's Wrong with the Society of Biblical Literature?' *Chronicle of Higher Education* 53.12 (2006), pp. B13-B15.
— 'The Unspeakable in Biblical Scholarship', *SBL Forum* www.sbl-site.org/Article. aspx?ArticleId=503.
Bloom, Benjamin S. (ed.), *Taxonomy of Educational Objectives: The Classification of Educational Goals. Handbook I: Cognitive Domain* (New York: McKay, 1956).
Blumenthal, David R., *Facing the Abusing God: A Theology of Protest* (Louisville, KY: Westminster John Knox, 1993).
Bonhoeffer, Dietrich, *Creation and Fall: A Theological Interpretation of Genesis 1-3* (New York: Macmillan, 1959).
Booth, Wayne C., *The Company We Keep: An Ethics of Fiction* (Berkeley: University of California Press, 1988).
Borg, Marcus J. and N.T. Wright, *The Meaning of Jesus: Two Visions* (New York: HarperCollins, 2007).
Bosworth, Kris and Sharon J. Hamilton, *Collaborative Learning: Underlying Processes and Effective Techniques* (San Francisco: Jossey-Bass, 1994)
Botta, Alejandro F. and Pablo Andinach (eds.), *The Bible and the Hermeneutics of Liberation* (Atlanta, GA: Society of Biblical Literature, 2009).
Bousquet, Marc, *How the University Works: Higher Education and the Low-Wage Nation* (New York: New York University Press, 2008).
Brereton, Virginia Lieson, 'The Bible Schools and Conservative Evangelical Higher Education, 1880–1940', in Carpenter and Shipps (eds.), *Making Higher Education Christian*, pp. 110–136.
Brewington, David V., 'AAR Undergraduate Departments Survey Comparative Analysis of Wave I and II', Focus on the Undergraduate Study of Religion, *Religious Studies News* (May 2008), pp. 14-15. www.aarweb.org/programs/Department_Services/Survey_Data/RSN_UndergradSurvey_May2008.pdf.
Brownell, Jayne E. and Lynn E. Swaner, *Five High-Impact Practices: Research on Learning Outcomes, Completion, and Quality* (LEAP; Washington, DC: Association of American Colleges and Universities, 2010).
Brueggemann, Walter, *Theology of the Old Testament: Testimony, Dispute, Advocacy* (Minneapolis: Fortress, 1997).
Bruffee, Kenneth A., *Collaborative Learning: Higher Education, Interdependence, and the Authority of Knowledge* (Baltimore: Johns Hopkins University Press, 1993).
— 'Sharing Our Toys: Cooperative Learning versus Collaborative Learning', *Change* 27.1 (1995), pp. 12-18.
Buckley, Tim, 'Teaching the Facts, Inculcating Knowledge, or Instilling Wisdom? Rationale for a Textbook in BS101', *Teaching Theology and Religion* 12 (2009), pp. 352-53.
Bureau of Labor Statistics, 'Occupational Employment and Wages, May 2010: Clergy', US Dept. of Labor Website, www.bls.gov/oes/current/oes212011.htm.
Bureau of Labor Statistics, 'Economic News Release, Table 1-A, Employment Status of the Civilian Population by Sex and Age', US Dept. of Labor Website, www.bls.gov/news.release/empsit.t01.htm.
Burtchaell, James Tunstead, *The Dying of the Light: The Disengagement of Colleges and Universities from their Christian Churches* (Grand Rapids: Eerdmans, 1998).

Cady, Linell, 'What Does the Census Data Say about the Study of Religion? A Public Sector Perspective', *Religious Studies News* 17.2 (March 2002), pp. 7, 21.

Cantwell Smith, Wilfred, 'The Study of Religion and the Study of the Bible', *Journal of the American Academy of Religion* 39.2 (1971), pp. 131-40.

Carpenter, Joel A. and Kenneth W. Shipps (eds.), *Making Higher Education Christian: The History and Mission of Evangelical Colleges in America* (Grand Rapids: Eerdmans, 1987).

Chambers, M.M., 'The University as a Corporation', *The Journal of Higher Education* 2.1 (January 1931), p. 24.

Champagne, John, 'Teaching in the Corporate University: Assessment as a Labor Issue', *AAUP Journal of Academic Freedom* 2 (2011), p. 4. www.academicfreedom journal.org/VolumeTwo/Champagne.pdf

Chickering, Arthur W., and S.C. Ehrmann, 'Implementing the Seven Principles: Technology as a Lever', *AAHE Bulletin* 49.2 (1996), pp. 3-6.

Chickering, Arthur W., and Zelda F. Gamson, 'Development and Adaptations of the Seven Principles for Good Practice in Undergraduate Education', *New Directions for Teaching and Learning* 80 (1999), pp. 75-81.

— 'Seven Principles for Good Practice in Undergraduate Education', *AAHE Bulletin* (1987), pp. 3-7.

Chickering, Arthur W., and Zelda F. Gamson (eds.), *Applying the Seven Principles for Good Practice in Undergraduate Education* (San Francisco: Jossey-Bass, 1991).

Chickering, Arthur W., and Linda Reisser, *Education and Identity* (San Francisco: Jossey-Bass, 2nd edn, 1993).

Childs, Brevard S., *Introduction to the Old Testament as Scripture* (Philadelphia: Fortress, 1979).

Cohen, Patricia, 'In Tough Times, the Humanities Must Justify Their Worth', *New York Times* (February 25, 2009), p. C1.

College Learning for the New Global Century (LEAP; American Association of Colleges and Universities, Washington, DC, 2008).

Collins, John J., 'The Zeal of Phinehas: The Bible and the Legitimation of Violence', *Journal of Biblical Literature* 122 (2003), pp. 3-21.

—'Towards the Morphology of a Genre: Introduction', *Semeia* 14 (1979), pp. 1-20.

Cornoldi, Cesare, 'Metacognition, Intelligence, and Academic Performance', in *Metacognition, Strategy Use, and Instruction*, in Waters and Schneider (eds.), (New York: Guilford, 2010), pp. 257-77.

Cosby, Michael R., *Interpreting Biblical Literature: An Introduction to Biblical Studies* (Grantham, PA: Stony Run, 2009).

Cowan, Margaret Parks, 'Teaching an Introductory Hebrew Bible Course without a Textbook', *Teaching Theology and Religion* 12 (2009), pp. 254-55.

— 'Wilderness', 'Immanuel', in *Text and Context* (ed. David B. Howell, Peggy Cowan, Chris Heard, Brian K. Pennington, and Vicki Phillips; Appalachian College Association), www.ferrum.edu/dhowell/txt_cntxt.

Cross, K. Patricia, *Learning Is about Making Connections* (Mission Viejo, CA: League for Innovation in the Community College, 1999).

Dahl, George, 'The Scientific Approach to the Bible', *Journal of the National Association of Biblical Instructors* 1.2 (1933), pp. 1–4.

Darr, Katheryn Pfisterer, 'Ezekiel's Justifications of God: Teaching Troubling Texts', *Journal for the Study of the Old Testament* 55 (1992), pp. 97-117.

Das, Veena, Arthur Kleinman, Mamphela Ramphele and Pamela Reynolds (eds.), *Violence and Subjectivity* (Berkeley: University of California Press, 2000).

Davidson, Clara Willoughby, 'Re-thinking Our Aims as Biblical Instructors', *Journal of the National Association of Biblical Instructors* 2.2 (1934), pp. 49–55.

Davidson, Neil and Toni Worsham (eds.), *Enhancing Thinking through Cooperative Learning* (New York: Teachers College Press, 1992).

Davies, Eryl W., 'The Morally Dubious Passages of the Hebrew Bible: An Examination of Some Proposed Solutions', *Currents in Biblical Research* 3 (2005), pp. 197-228.

Day, Linda, 'Teaching the Prophetic Marriage Metaphor', *Teaching Theology and Religion* 2.3 (1999), pp. 173-79.

Dept. of Labor Website, www.bls.gov/oes/current/oes212011.htm.

Deresiewicz, William, 'Faulty Towers: The Crisis in Higher Education', *The Nation* (May 4, 2011), www.thenation.com.

Desjardins, Michel, *Peace, Violence and the New Testament* (Sheffield: Sheffield Academic Press, 1997).

Devine, Richard, Joseph A. Favazza and Michael F. McLain (eds.), *From Cloister to Commons: Concepts and Models for Service-Learning in Religious Studies* (AAHE Series on Service-Learning; American Association for Higher Education, 2002).

Dewey, John, *How We Think* (Boston: D.C. Heath and Company, 1910).

Diamant, Anita, *The Red Tent* (New York: St. Martin's, 2005).

Diamond, Robert M., *Designing and Assessing Courses and Curricula: A Practical Guide* (San Francisco: Jossey-Bass, rev. edn, 1998 [1989]).

Dierckxsens, Wim, *et al.* (eds.), *XXI Century: Crisis of Civilization: The End of History or the Birth of a New Society?* (DEI: San José, 2010), www.observatoriodelacrisis.org/what-encourages-us/?lang=en.

Dovre, Paul, *The Vocation of a Lutheran Liberal Arts College Revisited,* www.elca.org/What-We-Believe/Social-Issues/Social-Statements/Education.aspx.

Drell, Lauren, 'We Don't Need No Education: Meet the Millionaire Dropouts', small business.aol.com/2011/02/09/we-dont-need-no-education-meet-the-millionaire-dropouts.

Duch, Barbara J., Susan E. Groh and Deborah E. Allen (eds.), *The Power of Problem-Based Learning: A Practical 'How To' for Teaching Undergraduate Courses in Any Discipline* (Sterling, VA: Stylus, 2001).

Duke, Rodney, 'Spotlight on Teaching', *Religious Studies News* 13.4 (1998), pp. 5-7.

Dunn, James D.G., *Romans* (Word Biblical Commentary, Waco, TX: Word Books, 1988).

Ellens, J. Harold (ed.), *The Destructive Power of Religion: Violence in Judaism, Christianity, and Islam* (Westport: Praeger, 2004).

Elmore, John M., 'Institutionalized Attacks on Academic Freedom: The Impact of Mandates by State Departments of Education and National Accreditation Agencies on Academic Freedom', *AAUP Journal of Academic Freedom* (2011), www.academicfreedomjournal.org/VolumeOne/Elmore.pdf.

Engwall, Lars, 'The University: A Multinational Corporation?' (Portland Press, 2008), www.portlandpress.com/pp/books/online/univmark/084/0009/0840009.pdf.

Epstein, Debbie, *et al.* (eds.), *Geographies of Knowledge, Geometries of Power: Framing the Future of Higher Education* (World Yearbook of Education 2008; New York/London: Routledge, 2007).

Erickson, Bette L., Calvin B. Peters, and Dianne W. Strommer, *Teaching First-Year College Students* (San Francisco: Jossey-Bass, rev. edn, 2006).
Fanti, Kostas A., and Eric Vanman, Christopher C. Henrich, Marios N. Avraamides, 'Desensitization to Media Violence over a Short Period of Time', *Aggressive Behavior* 35.2 (2009), pp. 179-87.
Faiola, Anthony, 'The End of American Capitalism?' *The Washington Post* (October 10, 2008), www.washingtonpost.com/wp-dyn/content/article/2008/10/09/AR2008100903425.html.
Favazza, Joseph A. and Fred Glennon, 'Serving Learning and Religious Studies: Propaganda or Pedagogy' *Bulletin/CSSR* 29.4 (2000), pp. 105-107.
Felson, Richard B., 'Mass Media Effects on Violent Behavior', *Annual Review of Sociology* 22 (1996), pp. 103-28.
Ferguson, James, *Global Shadows: Africa in the Neoliberal World Order* (Durham, NC: Duke University Press, 2006).
Ferrall, Victor E., Jr., *Liberal Arts at the Brink* (Cambridge, MA: Harvard University Press, 2011).
Fewell, Danna Nolan, and David Miller Gunn, *Gender, Power, and Promise: The Subject of the Bible's First Story* (Nashville, TN: Abingdon, 1992).
Fink, L. Dee, *Creating Significant Learning Experiences* (San Francisco: Jossey-Bass, 2003).
Finkel, Donald L., *Teaching with Your Mouth Shut* (Portsmouth, NH: Boynton/Cook Heinemann, 2000).
Fish, Stanley, 'The Crisis of the Humanities Officially Arrives', *New York Times* (October 11, 2010), opinionator.blogs.nytimes.com/2010/10/11/the-crisis-of-the-humanities-officially-arrives.
—'Reading Confirms Physics Closure', *BBC* (November 21, 2006), news.bbc.co.uk/2/hi/uk_news/education/6159106.stm.
Fitch, Florence Mary, 'The Historical Approach to the Study of the Bible', *Journal of the National Association of Biblical Instructors* 1.2 (1933), pp. 11–14.
Flannery, J.L., 'Teacher as Co-conspirator: Knowledge and Authority in Collaborative Learning', in Bosworth and Hamilton, (eds.), *Collaborative Learning: Underlying Processes and Effective Techniques*, pp. 15-23.
Flavell, John H., 'Metacognitive Aspects of Problem Solving', in *The Nature of Intelligence* (ed. Lauren B. Resnick; Hillside, NJ: Lawrence Erlbaum, 1976), pp. 231-35.
Foderaro, Lisa W., 'Budget-Cutting Colleges Bid Some Languages Adieu', *New York Times* (December 5, 2010), p. MB1.
Fowler, Henry T. 'The Place of the Bible in the College Curriculum', *Journal of the National Association of Biblical Instructors* 1.2 (1933) pp. 25–28.
— untitled remarks from the 25th anniversary dinner of NABI, held in December, 1934, *Journal of the National Association of Biblical Instructors* 3.1 (1935), pp. 41–42.
Fox, Michael V., 'Bible Scholarship and Faith-Based Study: My View', *SBL Forum* www.sbl-site.org/Article.aspx?ArticleId=490.
Fretheim, Terence E., 'God and Violence in the Old Testament', *Word & World* 24 (2004), pp. 18-28.
— '"I Was Only a Little Angry:" Divine Violence in the Prophets', *Interpretation* 58 (2004), pp. 365-75.
Freire, Paulo, *Pedagogy of the Oppressed* (New York: Continuum, 1970, 2000).
Fukuyama, Francis, *End of History and the Last Man* (New York: Free Press, 1992).

Gardner, Howard, *Frames of Mind: The Theory of Multiple Intelligences* (New York: Basic Book, 2004).

Gaston, Paul, et al., *General Education and Liberal Learning: Principles of Effective Practice* (LEAP; Washington, DC: Association of American Colleges and Universities, 2010).

Gaztambide, Daniel J., Matthew W.I. Dunn, Shawn C. Madden, and Ron Clark, 'Responses to Bader Article' *SBL Forum* www.sbl-site.org/Article.aspx?ArticleId=473.

Gaztambide, Daniel J., 'If You Can't Take the Heat, Stay Out of the Classroom: Re-evaluating the Student-Teacher Relationship, Classroom Ambiance, and Religion', *SBL Forum* www.sbl-site.org/Article.aspx?ArticleId=437.

Geertz, Clifford, *Local Knowledge: Further Essays in Interpretive Anthropology* (New York: Basic, 1983).

Gerstenberger, Erhard, 'Liberation Hermeneutics in Old Europe, Especially Germany', in Botta and Andinach (eds.), *The Bible and the Hermeneutics of Liberation*, pp. 61-84.

Gifford, Carey J., 'AAR Surveys of Religion and Theology Programs in the U.S.: Numbers Count', *Religious Studies News* 18.4 (October 2003), p. 14.

Gilpin, W. Clark 'The Creation of a New Order: Colonial Education and the Bible', in Barr and Piediscalzi (eds.), *The Bible in American Education*, pp. 5-24.

Giroux, Henry A., 'Why Faculty Should Join Occupy Movement Protesters on College Campuses', *truthout* (December 19, 2011), www.truth-out.org/why-faculty-should-join-occupy-movement-protesters-college-campuses/1324328832.

Goldstein, Seth, 'Reading *Toevah*: Biblical Scholarship and Difficult Texts', *The Reconstructionist* (Fall 2003), pp. 48-60.

Gomes, Peter, *The Good Book: Reading the Bible with Mind and Heart* (San Francisco: Harper San Francisco, 1996).

Gottwald, Norman K., *The Hebrew Bible: A Brief Socio-Literary Introduction* (Minneapolis: Fortress, 2009).

Gray, Edward R., 'What We Have Learned from the Census of Religion and Theology Programs', *Religious Studies News* 16.2 (Fall 2001) Special Pullout Section, pp. i-iii.

Grossman, David, 'Trained to Kill: A Military Expert on the Psychology of Killing Explains How Today's Media Condition Kids to Pull the Trigger', *Christianity Today* 42.9 (August 10, 1998), pp. 30-39.

Guéhenno, Jean-Marie, *The End of the Nation-State* (Minneapolis: University of Minnesota Press, 1995).

Gulley, Philip, and James Mulholland, *If Grace Is True: Why God Will Save Every Person* (New York: HarperCollins, 2003).

— *If God Is Love: Rediscovering Grace in an Ungracious World* (San Francisco: Harper San Francisco, 2004).

Habel, Norman C. (ed.), *The Earth Bible* (Cleveland: Pilgrim, 2001–2007).

Habel, Norman C. and Peter Rudinger (eds.), *Exploring Ecological Hermeneutics* (Atlanta: Society of Biblical Literature, 2008).

Hacker, Douglas J., John Dunlosky and Arthur C. Graesser (eds.), *Handbook of Metacognition in Education* (New York: Routledge, 2009).

Hamilton, Reeve, 'Budget Woes, Calls for Efficiency Imperil Physics', *The Texas Tribune* (September 16, 2011), www.texastribune.org/texas-education/higher-education/underenrolled-physics-program-fight-survival.

Harris, Horton, *The Tübingen School: A Historical and Theological Investigation of the School of F.C. Baur* (Leicester: Apollos, 1990 [1975]).
Harris, Steven L., *Understanding the Bible* (New York: McGraw-Hill, 4th edn, 2011).
Harris-Shapiro, Carol, 'Service Learning and Religious Studies: An Awkward Fit?' *Bulletin/CSSR* 31.2 (2002), pp. 35-39.
Hartshorne, Hugh 'The Future of the Bible in the American College', *Journal of the National Association of Biblical Instructors* 1.1 (1933), pp. 9-10.
Haroutunian, Joseph, 'The Bible and Modern Education', *Journal of the National Association of Biblical Instructors* 1.1 (1933), pp. 10–15.
Hayes, Mike, *Googling God—The Religious Landscape of People in their 20s and 30s* (New York: Paulist, 2007).
Hillerbrand, Hans J., 'Going Our Way: The 2000 Survey of Departments of Religion', *Religious Studies News, AAR Edition* 19.2 (March 2004), pp. 6, 19.
Hoehner, Harold, 'Did Paul Write Galatians?' in Son and Son (eds.), *History and Exegesis*, pp. 150-69
Homan, Michael M., 'Service-Learning, Biblical Studies, and Resurrecting Flooded Bones in New Orleans', *SBL Forum* (April 2009), www.sbl-site.org/publications/article.aspx?articleId=822.
Horrell, David G., Francesca Stavrakopoulou, Cherryl Hunt and Christopher Southgate (eds.), *Ecological Hermeneutics: Biblical, Historical, and Theological Perspectives* (New York: T&T Clark International, 2010).
Horrell, David G., Cherryl Hunt and Christopher Southgate, *Greening Paul: Rereading the Apostle Paul in a Time of Ecological Crisis* (Waco, Texas: Baylor University Press, 2010).
Humphries-Brooks, Stephenson, *Cinematic Savior: Hollywood's Making of the American Christ* (London: Praeger, 2006).
Hylen, Susan E., 'Metaphor Matters: Violence and Ethics in Revelation', *CBQ* 73 (2011), pp. 777-96.
International Forum on Globalization. ifg.org/index.htm
Jaschik, Scott, 'Turning Off the Lights', *Inside Higher Ed* (March 4, 2010), www.insidehighered.com/news/2010/03/04/clark.
Johnson, David W., Roger T. Johnson, and Karl A. Smith, *Cooperative Learning: Increasing College Faculty Instructional Productivity* (ANSH-ERIC Higher Education Report No. 4; Washington, DC: The George Washington University, School of Education and Human Development, 1991).
— *Active Learning: Cooperation in the College Classroom* (Edina, MN: Interaction Book Company, 1998).
Johnson, Kayla and Gianna Cruet, 'Cost of Cutting: Philosophy Tied to Campus', *The Nevada Sagebrush* (April 25, 2011), nevadasagebrush.com/blog/2011/04/25/cost-of-cutting-philosophy-tied-to-campus.
Johnson, Mark, *The Body in the Mind* (Chicago: University of Chicago Press, 1987).
Juergensmeyer, Mark (ed.), *Teaching the Introductory Course in Religious Studies: A Sourcebook* (Atlanta: Scholars Press, 1991).
— *Terror in the Mind of God: The Global Rise of Religious Violence* (Berkeley: University of California Press, 3rd edn, 2003).
Kaminsky, Joel, 'Violence in the Bible', *SBL Forum*, sbl-site.org/Article.aspx?ArticleID=159.
Kendrick, Eliza H., 'Twenty Five Years of the National Society of Biblical Instructors', *Journal of the National Association of Biblical Instructors* 3.1 (1935), pp. 37–40.

Kessler, Gary E., *Studying Religion: An Introduction through Cases* (New York: McGraw-Hill, 3rd edn, 2007).

Kille, Andrew, '"The Bible Made Me Do It:" Text, Interpretation, and Violence', in Ellens (ed.), *The Destructive Power of Religion,* volume 1, pp. 55-73.

Kleinman, Arthur, 'The Violences of Everyday Life: The Multiple Forms and Dynamics of Social Violence' in Das *et al.* (eds.), *Violence and Subjectivity*, pp. 226-41.

Kniker, Charles R., 'New Attitudes and New Curricula: the Changing Role of the Bible in Protestant Education, 1880–1920', in Barr and Piediscalzi (eds.), *The Bible in American Education*, pp. 121-42.

Koch, Christof and Joel L. Davis (eds.), *Large-Scale Neuronal Theories of the Brain* (Boston: Massachusetts Institute of Technology Press, 1995).

Korten, David C., *When Corporations Rule the World* (West Hartford, CT: Kumarian, 2nd edn, 2001).

Kovel, Joel, *The Enemy of Nature: The End of Capitalism or the End of the World?* (New York: Zed Books, 2002).

Kuh, George D., *High Impact Educational Practices: What They Are, Who Has Access to Them, and Why They Matter* (LEAP; Washington, DC: Association of American Colleges and Universities, 2008).

Kuhn, Thomas S., *The Structure of Scientific Revolutions* (Chicago: University of Chicago Press, 2nd edn, 1970).

Kümmel, Werner Georg, *Introduction to the New Testament* (trans. Howard Clark Kee; Nashville: Abingdon, rev. edn, 1975).

Kytle, Jackson, *To Want to Learn: Insights and Provocations for Engaged Learning* (New York: Palgrave Macmillan, 2004).

Lagaspi, Michael C., *The Death of Scripture and the Rise of Biblical Studies* (Oxford: Oxford University Press, 2010).

LaHaye, Tim and Jerry B. Jenkins, *Left Behind* (Wheaton, IL: Tyndale House Publishers, 1995).

Lake, Richard, 'Proposal Would Eliminate Nevada State College, Other Schools', *Las Vegas Review Journal* (March 10, 2011), www.lvrj.com.

Lakoff, George and Mark Johnson, *Metaphors We Live By* (Chicago: University of Chicago Press, 1980).

— *Philosophy in the Flesh: The Embodied Mind and its Challenge to Western Thought* (New York: Basic Books, 1999).

Laytner, Anson, *Arguing with God: A Jewish Tradition* (Northvale, NJ: Jason Aronson, 1998).

The LEAP Vision for Learning: Outcomes, Practices, Impact, and Employers' Views (LEAP; American Association of Colleges and Universities, Washington, DC, 2011).

Leonard, Angela, 'Service Learning as a Transgressive Pedagody: A Must for Today's Generation', *Crosscurrents* (Summer 2004), pp. 61-72.

Leskes, Andrea, and Ross Miller, *Purposeful Pathways: Helping Students Achieve Key Learning Outcomes* (Washington, DC: Association of American Colleges and Universities, 2006).

Levine, Arthur, *Handbook on Undergraduate Curriculum* (San Francisco: Jossey-Bass, 1978).

Levin, Richard, *New Readings vs. Old Plays: Recent Trends in the Reinterpretation of English Renaissance Drama* (Chicago: University of Chicago, 1979).

Lewin, Tamar, 'Joining Trend, College Grows beyond Name', *New York Times* (December 28, 2011), pp. A1, A12.
Locklin, Reid B., *Spiritual But Not Religious?: An Oar Stroke Closer to the Farther Shore* (Collegeville, MN: Liturgical, 2005).
Lüdemann, Gerd, *The Unholy in Holy Scripture: The Dark Side of the Bible* (trans. John Bowden; Louisville, KY: Westminster John Knox, 1996).
Lyman, F.T., 'Think-Pair-Share, Thinktrix, Thinklinks, and Weird Facts: An Interactive System for Cooperative Learning', in *Enhancing Thinking through Cooperative Learning* (ed. Neil Davidson and Toni Worsham; New York: Teachers College Press, 1992), pp. 169-81.
Manji, Firoze and Carl O'Coill, 'The Missionary Position: NGOs and the Development of Africa', *International Affairs* 78.3 (2002), pp. 567-83.
Marchal, Joseph A., 'To What End(s)? Biblical Studies and Critical Rhetorical Engagement(s) for a 'Safer' World' *SBL Forum* www.sbl-site.org/Article.aspx?ArticleId=550.
Marquand, David, *The End of the West: The Once and Future Europe* (Princeton: Princeton University Press, 2011).
Marsden, George M., 'The Collapse of American Evangelical Academia' in *Faith and Rationality: Reason and Belief in God* (ed. Alvin Plantinga and Nicholas Wolterstorff; Notre Dame: University of Notre Dame Press, 1983), pp. 219–264.
Martin, Dale B. *Pedagogy of the Bible: An Analysis and Proposal* (Louisville, KY: Westminster John Knox, 2008).
Martin, Nathan, 'Interfaith Service Learning: A New Model for Muslim-Jewish Dialogue?' *The Reconstructionist* 72.1 (2007), pp. 26-33.
Mathewson, Dan, 'End Times Entertainment: The Left Behind Series, Evangelicals, and Death Pornography', *Journal of Contemporary Religion* 24.3 (2009), pp. 319-37.
Matthews, Shelly and Leigh Gibson (eds.), *Violence in the New Testament* (New York: T&T Clark, 2005).
Mazwi, A.E. and R.G. Sultana, *Education and the Arab 'World', Political Projects, Struggles, and Geometrics of Power* (World Yearbook of Education 2010; New York/London: Routledge, 2009).
McCarraher, Eugene, 'The End of Capitalism and the Wellsprings of Radical Hope', *The Nation* (June 27, 2011), www.thenation.com/article/161237/end-capitalism-and-wellsprings-radical-hope.
McCutcheon, Russell T., *Critics Not Caretakers: Redescribing the Public Study of Religion* (Albany, NY: State University of New York Press, 2001).
McFague, Sallie, *A New Climate for Theology: God, the World, and Global Warming* (Minneapolis: Fortress, 2008).
McGlynn, Angela Provitera, *Teaching Today's College Students: Widening the Circle of Success* (Madison, WI: Atwood, 2007).
McGuire, Saundra Y., Online workshop, 'Teach Students How to Learn: Metacognition is the Key', www2.nemcc.edu/IR/Spring2007_PresentationbySMcGuire.pdf.
McLay, R. Timothy, 'The Goal of Teaching Biblical and Religious Studies in the Context of an Undergraduate Education', *SBL Forum* 4.8 (2006), www.sbl-site.org/publications/article.aspx?ArticleId=581.
McNeil, John D., *Curriculum: A Comprehensive Introduction* (Boston: Little Brown, 1977).
Millis, Barbara J., and Philip G. Cottell, Jr., *Cooperative Learning for Higher Education Faculty* (Phoenix: Oryx, 1998).

Mitchell, Tania D., 'Traditional vs. Critical Service-Learning: Engaging the Literature to Differentiate Two Models', *Michigan Journal of Community Service Learning* (2008), pp. 50-65.

Mitchell, W.J.T., *Iconology: Image, Text, Ideology* (Chicago: University of Chicago Press, 1985).

Moberly, R.W.L., *From Eden to Golgotha: Essays in Biblical Theology* (Atlanta: Scholars, 1992).

Mokhiber, Russell and Robert Weissman, *On the Rampage: Corporate Power and the Destruction of Democracy* (Monroe, ME: Common Courage, 2005).

Mould, Elmer W.K., 'The National Association of Bible Instructors: An Historical Account', *Journal of Bible and Religion* 18.1 (1950), pp. 11–28.

Nelson-Pallmeyer, Jack, *Is Religion Killing Us? Violence in the Bible and the Quran* (Harrisburg: Trinity International, 2003).

Neville, David J., 'Toward a Teleology of Peace: Contesting Matthew's Violent Eschatology', *Journal for the Study of the New Testament* 30.2 (2007), pp. 131-61.

'New Information on the Undergraduate Study of Religion', AAR Website, www.aarweb.org/programs/Department_Services/Survey_Data/Undergraduate/default.asp.

Newcomb, Theodore Mead, and Everett K. Wilson, *College Peer Groups: Problems and Prospects for Research* (Aldine, IL: Chicago, 1966).

Niditch, Susan, *War in the Hebrew Bible: A Study in the Ethics of Violence* (New York: Oxford University Press, 1993).

Nocella, Anthony J. II, Steven Best, and Peter McLaren (eds.), *Academic Repression: Reflections from the Academic-Industrial Complex* (Baltimore: AK, 2010).

Noll, Mark A., 'The Revolution, the Enlightenment, and Christian Higher Education in the Early Republic', in Carpenter and Shipps (eds.), *Making Higher Education Christian*, pp. 56–76.

— 'The University Arrives in America, 1870–1930: Christian Traditionalism during the Academic Revolution', in Carpenter and Shipps (eds.), *Making Higher Education Christian*, pp. 98–109.

Nussbaum, Martha, *Not for Profit: Why Democracy Needs the Humanities* (Princeton: Princeton University Press, 2010).

Nyhan, Brendan and Jason Reifler, 'When Corrections Fail: The Persistence of Political Misperceptions', *Political Behavior* 32.2 (2010), pp. 303-30.

Oakley, B., *et al.*, 'Turning Student Groups into Effective Teams', *Journal of Student Centered Learning* 2.1 (2004), pp. 9-34.

Olbricht, Thomas H., 'Intellectual Ferment and Instruction in the Scriptures: The Bible in Higher Education', in Barr and Piediscalzi (eds.), *The Bible in American Education*, pp. 97-120.

Page, Matt, 'Bible Films Blog' biblefilms.blogspot.com.

Palmer, Parker J., *To Know As We Are Known* (San Francisco: Harper, 1983, 1993).

Parks, Sharon Daloz, *Big Questions, Worthy Dreams: Mentoring Young Adults in Their Search for Meaning, Purpose, and Faith* (San Francisco: Jossey-Bass, 2000).

Pascarella, Ernest T. and Patrick T. Terenzini, *How College Affects Students: Findings and Insights from Twenty Years of Research* (San Francisco: Jossey-Bass Publishers, 1991).

—*How College Affects Students: Volume 2: A Third Decade of Research* (San Francisco: Jossey-Bass Publishers, 2005).

Patte, Daniel, *Ethics of Biblical Interpretation: A Reevaluation* (Louisville, KY: Westminster John Knox, 1995).
Pauk, Walter, *How to Study in College* (Boston: Houghton Mifflin, 7th edn, 2000).
Paul, Richard, *Critical Thinking: How to Prepare Students for a Rapidly Changing World* (Santa Rosa, CA: Foundation for Critical Thinking, 1995).
Penaskovic, Richard, *Critical Thinking and the Academic Study of Religion* (Atlanta: Scholars, 1997).
Penchansky, David, *What Rough Beast?: Images of God in the Hebrew Bible* (Louisville, KY: Westminster John Knox, 1999).
Peoples, Timothy, 'Pedagogy of the Bible in the Liberal Arts Context: Paradigms and Perspectives', unpublished paper presented to the Teaching Biblical Studies in the Undergraduate Liberal Arts Context group of the Society of Biblical Literature, Annual Meeting, November 19–22, 2011.
Peritz, Ismer J., 'Editorial: The National Association of Bible Instructors and the Society of Biblical Literature and Exegesis', *Journal of the National Association of Biblical Instructors* 1.2 (1933), p. 29.
Perry, Nancy E., Lynda Phillips and Lynda Hutchinson, 'Mentoring Student Teachers to Support Self-Regulated Learning', *The Elementary School Journal* 106.3 (2006), pp. 237-54.
Perry, William G., *Forms of Intellectual and Ethical Development in the College Years: A Scheme* (New York: Holt, 1968).
Pew Research Center for the People & the Press, 'News Audiences Increasingly Politicized'. www.people-press.org/2004/06/08/news-audiences-increasingly-politicized.
Pew Research Center for the People & the Press, 'Partisanship and Cable News Audiences'. pewresearch.org/pubs/1395/partisanship-fox-news-and-other-cable-news-audiences.
Pew Forum on Religion and Public Life, 'U.S. Religious Landscape Survey', religions.pewforum.org/reports.
Pew Research Center for the People and the Press, 'Press Widely Criticized, But Trusted More Than Other Information Sources', http://www.people-press.org/2011/09/22/press-widely-criticized-but-trusted-more-than-other-institutions/.
Plantinga, Alvin and Nicholas Wolterstorff (eds.), *Faith and Rationality: Reason and Belief in God* (Notre Dame: University of Notre Dame Press, 1983).
Plater, William M., 'The Twenty-First-Century Professoriate: We Need a New Vision if We Want to Create a Positive Future for the Faculty', *Academe Online*, www.aaup.org/AAUP/pubsres/academe/2008/JA/Feat/plat.htm.
Population statistics from US Census Bureau, 'Population Estimates', www.census.gov/popest/data/national/totals/2011/index.html.
Powell, John W. 'Outcomes Assessment: Conceptual and Other Problems', *AAUP Journal of Academic Freedom* 2 (2011), p. 9, www.academicfreedomjournal.org/VolumeTwo/Powell.pdf.
Pressley, Michael and Peter Afflerbach, *Verbal Protocols of Reading: The Nature of Constructively Responsive Reading* (Hillsdale, NJ: Erlbaum, 1995).
Prothero, Stephen, *Religious Literacy: What Every American Needs to Know—and Doesn't* (San Francisco: HarperOne, 2007).
Quimby, Chester Warren 'The Word of God', *Journal of the National Association of Biblical Instructors* 1.1 (1933), pp. 1–6.

Ramachaudran, Vilanayur S. (ed.), *Encyclopedia of Human Behavior* (New York: Academic, 1994); repr. Howard Friedman (ed.), *Encyclopedia of Mental Health* (San Diego: Academic, 1998).

Readings, Bill, *The University in Ruins* (Cambridge, MA: Harvard University Press, 1996).

Reinhartz, Adele, *Jesus of Hollywood* (Oxford: Oxford University Press, 2007).

Reklis, Kathryn, 'Prime-Time Torture: Jack Bauer as a Hero of Our Time', *Christian Century* 125.2 (June 3, 2008), pp. 11-12.

Renick, Timothy, *et al.*, 'The Religious Studies Major in a Post-9/11 World: New Challenges, New Opportunities', *Religious Studies News* (October 2008), pp. 21-24.

— 'The Religion Major and Liberal Education: A White Paper', www.aarweb.org/ Programs/Religion_Major_and_Liberal_Education.

— 'The Religious Studies Major and Liberal Education', *Liberal Education* 95.2 (2009), pp. 48–55.

Report of the Twenty-Third Annual Meeting of the National Association of Biblical Instructors, 1932, *Journal of the National Association of Biblical Instructors* 1.1 (1933), pp. 23–28.

Resnick, Lauren B. (ed.), *The Nature of Intelligence* (Hillside, NJ: Lawrence Erlbaum, 1976).

Ringenberg, William C., 'The Old-Time College, 1800–1865', in Carpenter and Shipps (eds.), *Making Higher Education Christian*, pp. 77-97.

Roncace, Mark and Patrick Gray (eds.), *Teaching the Bible: Practical Strategies for Classroom Instruction* (Resources for Biblical Study; Atlanta: Society of Biblical Literature, 2005).

Rosengarten, Richard A., 'The AAR Graduate Survey at First Blush: Some Initial Thoughts on Institutional Definition and Doctoral Areas of Concentration', *Religious Studies News* 19.2 (March, 2004), pp. 7, 18.

Rosenthal, Laurel, 'Some California University Degrees Disappear amid Budget Cuts', *The Sacramento Bee* (July 9, 2011), www.sacbee.com.

Rowland, Wade, *Greed Inc.: Why Corporations Rule Our World and How We Let It Happen* (Toronto: Thomas Allen, 2005).

Rudolph, Frederick, *Curriculum: A History of the American Undergraduate Course of Study Since 1636* (San Francisco: Jossey-Bass, 1977).

Ryan, Alan, *Liberal Anxieties and Liberal Education* (New York: Hill and Wang, 1998).

Salen, Katie and Eric Zimmerman, *Rules of Play: Game Design Fundamentals* (Cambridge, MA: MIT Press, 2003).

Sanders, John (ed.), *Atonement and Violence: A Theological Conversation* (Nashville: Abingdon, 2006).

Saunders, Ernest W., *Searching the Scriptures: A History of the Society of Biblical Literature 1880–1980* (Biblical Scholarship in North America 8; Chico, CA: Scholars Press, 1983).

Sayers, Dorothy, *The Man Born To Be King* (London: Victor Gollancz, 1943).

'SBL Educational Resources', www.sbl-site.org/educational/thebibleinpublicschools.aspx.

Schneider, Carol Geary, 'Practicing Liberal Education: Formative Themes in the Reinvention of Liberal Learning', *Liberal Education* 90.2 (2004), pp. 6–11.

Schneider, Wolfgang, 'Metacognition and Memory Development in Childhood and Adolescence', in *Metacognition, Strategy Use, and Instruction* (ed. Harriet Salatas Waters and Wolfgang Schneider; New York: Guilford, 2010), pp. 54-81.

Schneiders, Sandra M., *The Revelatory Text: Interpreting the New Testament as Sacred Scripture* (Collegeville, MN: Liturgical, 2nd edn, 1999).

Scholz, Susanne (ed.), *Biblical Studies Alternatively: An Introductory Reader* (Upper Saddle River, NJ: Prentice Hall, 2003).

Schüssler Fiorenza, Elisabeth, *Democratizing Biblical Studies: Toward an Emancipatory Educational Space* (Louisville, KY: Westminster John Knox, 2009).

Schüssler Fiorenza, Elisabeth and Kent Harold Richards (eds.), *Transforming Biblical Education: Ethos and Discipline* (Atlanta, GA: Society of Biblical Literature, 2010).

Schwartz, Regina M., *The Curse of Cain: The Violent Legacy of Monotheism* (Chicago: University of Chicago Press, 1997).

Segovia, Fernando F., *Toward a New Heaven and a New Earth* (Maryknoll, NY: Orbis Books, 2003).

Seider, Scott, 'Deepening College Students' Engagement with Religion and Theology through Community Service Learning', *Teaching Theology and Religion* 14.3 (July 2011), pp. 205-25.

Setzer, Claudia and David Shefferman (eds.), *The Bible and American Culture* (New York: Routledge, 2011).

Shea, Christopher. 'The End of Tenure?' *New York Times* (September 3, 2010), www.nytimes.com.

Shields, Mary, 'Multiple Exposures: Body Rhetoric and Gender Characterization in Ezekiel 16', *Journal of Feminist Studies in Religion* 14 (1998), pp. 5-18.

—'An Abusive God? Identity and Power/Gender and Violence in Ezekiel 23', in *Postmodern Interpretation of the Bible: A Reader* (ed. A.K.M. Adam; St. Louis: Chalice, 2001), pp. 129-51.

Simmons, John K., 'Vanishing Boundaries: When Teaching about Religion Becomes Spiritual Guidance in the Classroom', *Teaching Theology and Religion* 9 (2006), pp. 37-43.

Smith, Christian, *Souls in Transition: The Religious and Spiritual Lives of Emerging Adults* (Oxford: Oxford University Press, 2009).

Smith, Drew, '"Between Athens and Jerusalem": Reading Liberal Books at Church-Based Universities', *SBL Forum* www.sbl-site.org/Article.aspx?ArticleId=389.

Smith, James Howard and Rosalind I.J. Hackett, *Displacing the State: Religion and Conflict in Neoliberal Africa* (Notre Dame, IN: Notre Dame Press, 2011).

Smith, Jonathan Z., '"Narratives into Problems": The College Introductory Course and the Study of Religion', *Journal of the American Academy of Religion* 56 (1988), pp. 727-39.

— 'Teaching the Bible in the Context of General Education', *Teaching Theology and Religion* 1.2 (June 1998), pp. 73-78.

— 'The Necessary Lie: Duplicity in the Disciplines'. teaching.uchicago.edu/tutorial/jz_smith.shtml.

— 'What Does the Census Data Say about the Study of Religion? A Private Sector Perspective', *Religious Studies News* 17.2 (March 2002), pp. 7, 23.

— 'Bible and Religion', *Bulletin of the Council of Societies for the Study of Religion* 29.4 (2000), pp. 87-93. Reprinted in *Relating Religion: Essays in the Study of Religion* (Chicago: University of Chicago Press, 2004), pp. 197-214.

Smith, Karl A., 'Cooperative Learning: Making "Group Work" Work', in Sutherland and Bonwell (eds.), *Using Active Learning in College Classes: A Range of Options for Faculty,* pp. 71-82.

Smith, Wilfred Cantwell, 'The Study of Religion and the Study of the Bible', *Journal of the American Academy of Religion* 39.2 (1971), pp. 131-40.

Soederberg, Susanne, *Corporate Power and Ownership in Contemporary Capitalism: The Politics of Resistance and Domination* (London/New York: Routledge, 2010).

Solvang, Elna K 'Teaching Difference: College Students and the Bible', *SBL Forum* www.sbl-site.org/Article.aspx?ArticleId=224C.

Sommerville, C. John, *Religious Ideas for Secular Universities* (Grand Rapids: Eerdmans, 2009).

Son, Sang-Won and S. Aaron Son (eds.), *History and Exegesis: New Testament Essays in Honor of Dr. E. Earle Ellis on his Eightieth Birthday* (New York: T&T Clark, 2006).

Spear, Karen I. (ed.), *Rejuvenating Introductory Courses* (New Directions for Teaching and Learning 20; San Francisco: Jossey-Bass, 1984).

Staley, Jeffrey L., 'The Crucifixion of Jesus in Films and in the Gospels', *Teaching the Bible: An e-newsletter for public school teachers by Society of Biblical Literature* (www.sbl-site.org/assets/media/TBv2_i6.htm).

Staley, Jeffrey L. and Richard Walsh, *Jesus, the Gospels, and Cinematic Imagination: A Handbook to Jesus on DVD* (London: Westminster John Knox, 2007).

Stern, Richard C., Clayton N. Jefford, and Guerric Debona, *Savior on the Silver Screen* (New York: Paulist, 1999).

'Survey of Graduate Programs in Religion and Theology', AAR Website, www.aarweb.org/programs/Department_Services/Survey_Data/Graduate/default.asp.

Sutherland, Tracey E., and Charles C. Bonwell, (eds.), *Using Active Learning in College Classes: A Range of Options for Faculty* (New Directions in Teaching and Learning 67; San Francisco: Jossey-Bass, 1996).

Suzrez-Villa, Luis, *Globalization and Technocapitalism: The Political Economy of Corporate Power and Technological Domination* (Burlington, VT: Ashgate, 2011).

Szpek, Heidi M., 'The Levite's Concubine: The Story that Never Was', *Women in Judaism: A Multidisciplinary Journal* 5.1 (2007), pp. 1-7.

Taraban, Roman, Marcel Kerr and Kimberly Rynearson, 'Analytic and Pragmatic Factors in College Students' Metacognitive Reading Strategies', *Reading Psychology* 25 (2004), pp. 67-81.

Tatum, W. Barnes, *Jesus at the Movies: A Guide to the First Hundred Years* (Santa Rosa, CA: Polebridge, rev. and expanded edn., 2004).

Taylor, Barbara Brown, 'Caution: Bible Class in Session', *Christian Century* (Nov 6-19, 2002), p. 39.

Trible, Phyllis, *Texts of Terror: Literary-Feminist Readings of Biblical Narratives* (Minneapolis, MN: Fortress, 1984).

Tuckman, B., 'Developmental Sequence in Small Groups', *Psychological Bulletin* 63 (1965), pp. 384-89.

Upcraft, M. Lee, John N. Gardner, and Betsy O. Barefoot, *et al.* (eds.), *Challenging and Supporting the First-Year Student* (San Francisco: Jossey-Bass, 2005).

US Census Bureau, 'Population Estimates: National Intercensal Estimates (2000–2010)', www.census.gov/popest/data/intercensal/national/nat2010.html.

von Rad, Gerhard, *Old Testament Theology*, Volume 1 (San Francisco: Harper San Francisco, 1962).

Wagner, Rachel, *Godwired: Religion, Ritual, and Virtual Reality* (New York: Routledge, 2011).

Walker-Jones, Arthur, 'New Life in the Biblical Studies Classroom', *SBL Forum* www.sbl-site.org/Article.aspx?ArticleId=423.

Walsh, Richard, *Reading the Gospels in the Dark: Portrayals of Jesus in Film* (Harrisburg, PA: Trinity Press International, 2003).

Walvoord, Barbara E., *Teaching and Learning in College Introductory Religion Courses* (Oxford: Blackwell Publishing, 2008).

Walvoord, Barbara E. and Virginia Johnson Anderson, *Effective Grading: A Tool for Learning and Assessment* (San Francisco: Jossey-Bass, 1998).

Warmoth, A., '"Educating the Whole Student": Ten Essays on Learner-Centered Education'. Sonoma State University, 2009, www.sonoma.edu/Senate/documents/Educating%20the%20Whole%20Student%20MS.doc.

Warrior, Robert Allen, 'Canaanites, Cowboys, and Indians: Deliverance, Conquest, and Liberation Theology Today', *Christianity and Crisis* 49 (1989), pp. 261-65.

Washington, Harold, 'Violence and the Construction of Gender in the Hebrew Bible: A New Historicist Approach', *Biblical Interpretation* 5.4 (October 1997), pp. 324-63.

Waters, Harriet Salatas and Wolfgang Schneider (eds.), *Metacognition, Strategy Use, and Instruction* (New York: Guilford, 2010).

W.C.E.R. Research, *Collaborative Learning: Small Group Learning Page* (National Institute for Science Education, 1997), www.wcer.wisc.edu/archive/cl1/CL/default.asp.

Weaver, Denny J. *The Nonviolent Atonement* (Grand Rapids: Eerdmans, 2001).

Weber, Max, *The Protestant Ethic and the Spirit of Capitalism* (trans. Talcott Parsons; Mineola, NY: Dover, 2003).

Webster, Jane S. 'Biblical Studies in the Context of the Emerging Religion Major', *SBL Forum*, www.sbl-site.org/publications/article.aspx?ArticleId=816

Webster, Jane S., James J. Buckley, Tim Jensen, and Stacey M. Floyd-Thomas, 'Responses to the AAR-Teagle White Paper: "The Religious Studies Major in a Post-9/11 World"', *Teaching Theology and Religion* 14.1 (2011), pp. 34–71.

Weems, R.J., *Battered Love: Marriage, Sex, and Violence in the Hebrew Prophets* (Minneapolis: Fortress, 1995).

Weimer, Maryellen, *Learner-Centered Teaching: Five Key Changes to Practice* (San Francisco: Jossey-Bass, 2002).

West, Gerald O. and Musa W. Dube (eds.), *The Bible in Africa: Transactions, Trajectories and Trends* (Leiden/Boston/Köln: Brill, 2000).

'What Is Web 2.0: Design Patterns and Business Models for the Next Generation of Software', www.oreillynet.com/pub/a/oreilly/tim/news/2005/09/30/what-is-web-20.html#mememap.

Wheeler, Brannon M. (ed.), *Teaching Islam* (American Academy of Religion Teaching Religious Studies; New York: Oxford University Press, 2003).

Wiggins, Grant, *Educative Assessment: Designing Assessments to Inform and Improve Student Performance* (San Francisco: Jossey-Bass, 1998).

Wiggins, Grant P. and Jay McTighe, *Understanding by Design* (Alexandria, VA: Association for Supervision and Curriculum Development, expanded 2nd edn, 2005).

Wilson, Kevin, 'Pre-Scriptural Levels', *BlueCord.org* (October 2006), web.archive.org/web/20081118175948.

Wilson, Leslie Owen, *Teaching Millennial Students*, www4.uwsp.edu/education/facets/links_resources/Millennial%20Specifics.pdf.

Wolf, Naomi, *The End of America: Letter of Warning to a Young Patriot* (White River Junction, VT: Chelsea Green Publishing, 2007).

World Alliance of Reformed Churches, 'Neoliberalism contradicts Christian faith, Argentine forum says' (May 2003), www.warc.ch/pc/confess/00.html.

World Council of Churches, 'African Women's Statement on Poverty, Wealth and Ecology' (November 5-6, 2007, Dar Es Salaam, Tanzania), www.oikoumene.org/en/resources/documents/wcc-programmes/public-witness-addressing-power-affirming-peace/poverty-wealth-and-ecology/neoliberal-paradigm/african-womens-statement-on-poverty-wealth-and-ecology.html.

Zajda, Joseph I. (ed.), *Globalization, Education, and Social Justice* (Series Globalization, Comparative Education and Policy Research, vol. 10; Dordrecht, Netherlands/New York, NY: Springer, 2010).

Websites

www.wikiwikiweb.com
www.compact.org
carltoney.wetpaint.com
ns500.wetpaint.com.
www.wikimatrix.org

Art

Unknown artist, 'The First Horseman', commons.wikimedia.org/wiki/File:Bamberg Apocalypse Folio014rFirstHorseman.JPG?uselang=de.

Dürer, Albrecht, 'Four Horsemen of the Apocalypse', commons.wikimedia.org/wiki/File:Durer_Revelation_Four_Riders.jpg.

Index of Subjects

AAHE Bulletin 155
AAR Surveys of Religion and Theology Programs 13
AAR-Teagle group 1-2
AAUP Journal of Academic Freedom 30, 36
Abraham 5, 188-89
academic disciplines 3, 7, 9, 15, 32-33, 42-43, 57
academic freedom 30, 36, 42-43, 165
affiliations, religious 25, 217
Africa 34-35, 255, 259, 263, 269
agency 27, 125, 134, 138-39, 235
American Academy of Religion 12, 14-15, 17-18, 79, 91
American Association for Higher Education Series on Service-Learning 132
American Education 19-20
ancient world 84, 90, 247-48
Apocalypse 247, 251-52
Appalachian College Association 88
artists 90, 93, 209, 252
arts 4, 43-44, 48, 59, 68, 92-97, 104, 209, 218, 234, 250
arts integration 7, 91-92, 95-96
artwork 93-94
assessment 7, 30, 36, 134, 163, 180, 198, 218, 225, 228-29, 231, 235
   summative 218-20
assignments, problem-based 188
Association of American Colleges and Universities 20, 27, 97, 116, 119, 130, 185
authority, external 121, 125-26

beliefs 2-4, 21, 55, 76, 128, 152, 172, 182, 221, 236
   religious 3, 85, 152
Bible requirement 167-68

biblical interpretation ix, 9, 14, 25, 42, 116, 126, 134, 136, 152, 154-55, 189, 192, 223, 227-28, 244
biblical studies curriculum vii, 7, 28-32, 36, 40
blogs 74, 200-202
buzz groups 156

capitalism 32-34
Christian history 2, 13, 172
church-related college 1, 8, 118-19, 123
class materials 9, 201, 204
class notes ix, 9, 199, 202-208
class presentations 111, 186, 219
class work 89, 219
classroom
   traditional 152, 199
   undergraduate viii, 8, 184, 250
classroom assessment techniques 89
classroom conversations 4, 187, 189
collaboration 63, 154, 200, 204
collaborative learning viii, 8, 151-55, 157, 162-63, 201
collaborative learning techniques 151, 153, 155, 158, 160-62, 240
content, coverage of 83, 123
cooperative learning 153, 157-58, 161
Cooperative Learning for Higher Education Faculty 153, 157
core curriculum 41, 140-41
corporations 31, 36-37, 39, 43
crucifixion 210-15
cultural contexts 3, 29, 59, 83-84, 140, 168, 196, 215, 238
curricular transformation 28, 31, 34, 41, 43

Daniel 173-74, 181, 248
David 86, 90, 145, 186, 188

Deuteronomy 141-43, 147, 149-50, 173-74, 190
development, intellectual 22, 80-81, 83, 90
developmental issues 118, 120-21, 125, 128
difficult texts 185-86, 190-91
diversity xiii, 49, 53, 105, 140, 147, 149, 155, 182, 210, 245
Documentary Hypothesis 83, 102-104, 181
Dürer, Albrecht 251-52

Earth Bible 137
economic system 32-33, 35, 43
educational objectives 3, 106, 116, 123-24, 235
engaged learning 81-82, 151
epistles, Pauline 104, 108-10
ethics of biblical interpretation ix, 9, 223
evangelists 9, 210-12, 214
exams 45, 53-54, 178, 203, 217, 229
exercises 84, 88-89, 120-21, 124, 129, 144, 146, 148-50, 158-63, 233, 238-41, 253
Exodus 77-78, 83, 142, 173, 181, 184, 189
experience, religious 4, 54-55
Ezekiel 173-74, 184, 186-88, 190, 248, 267
Ezra 143, 145, 149-50, 173
Ezra-Nehemiah 143-44, 146-47, 149-50

feedback 96, 112, 130, 178, 207, 219-20, 225, 228-29, 231
Feminist Interpretation 133-35, 160, 186
films 57, 61, 194, 209, 211, 214-15
First Year Seminar (FYS) 223, 226

Galatians 107, 110, 173
games 158, 160, 196, 205
gender 47-49, 108, 159, 192
general education classes 53
general education courses 46, 92, 151
general education curriculum 7, 44-48, 51, 54, 102, 107
general education requirements vii, xiv, 7, 44, 51, 54, 80, 91, 106, 113

Genesis 74, 83-84, 93, 95, 135, 159, 173-74, 181, 189
genres 85, 238-39, 241, 247
geography 26, 84, 86, 88, 90
global citizens, responsible 116, 118-20, 123, 191
globalization 29, 34, 37
goals 8, 58-62, 64-68, 80-81, 83-85, 108-109, 112, 131-33, 142-44, 152, 178-83, 225, 228, 231, 244-45
  educational 106, 132
good practice 154-55
gospels, canonical 209-10, 216, 221
grading 180, 182, 205, 229
group learning 153, 156
  effective 156-60, 162
group projects 97, 162, 180-82, 200, 205, 207
groups, mentor 226-27

Hagar 5, 134-36, 185
harmonizations ix, 9, 209-16
heaven 70, 247, 252
higher learning 1-2, 62
historical approach 22-23, 76
historical context 63, 143, 146, 171, 219
historical-critical paradigm 5-6
historical criticism 23, 32, 156, 188
Historical Jesus 103-104, 108, 133-34, 166, 212
historical Paul 107-109, 112
historicity 71, 77-78, 211-12
human development 119-20, 123, 157, 261
humanities xiv, 31, 33-34, 36-38, 40-42, 48, 62, 94, 99, 104

iconoclasm 101, 105-106, 112-13
identity 81-82, 87-88, 136, 145, 160, 168, 248
ideology 16, 108, 110, 113, 144, 194, 236
insiders 14, 16, 26, 188
institutional contexts 23, 100, 140
interpretations, artistic 96, 211
introductory Bible classes 104, 133
introductory Bible courses 6-7, 13, 16, 91-92, 95-98, 101, 113, 117, 119, 128-29, 133
  required 8, 119, 128, 166-67, 169

Index of Subjects

introductory courses 5, 41, 100-102, 104-106, 108, 113, 116-18, 133-34, 136, 167, 180, 189, 210, 217, 225
Introductory Hebrew Bible 83, 104, 134, 136
introductory religion courses 178-79, 225
Isaiah 88, 142, 144-47, 150, 173-74, 181, 248
Israel 62, 69-70, 87, 136, 143, 145, 173, 186, 190-91
Israelites 78, 83, 87, 146, 150, 189-90

Jewish Tradition 69, 71, 262
Jews 26, 65, 71, 75, 145-46, 150, 166
Joel 248
John 94, 166, 173-74, 210, 214, 221, 246-49, 252
Jonah 66, 96, 142-47, 150
Journal of Bible and Religion 18
journals 34, 133-34, 136, 230
Judges 78, 87, 168, 184-85, 190-91, 193
judgments 76, 185, 194-95, 223, 229
justice, social 34, 88, 134, 138

King of Kings (film) 214-15
kings 171, 173, 186, 191, 209, 214-15
knowledge, prior 44, 49-52, 238, 253
knowledge communities 154-55, 158

language 9-10, 62, 100-101, 105, 107, 110, 113, 125-26, 156, 168, 193, 195, 197, 218, 243
laws 70, 77, 87, 92, 140-42, 144, 147, 219, 241
LEAP 131, 185
learning
    active 80, 90, 124, 151, 153-54, 156, 188, 199, 204
    college 185, 235
    integrative 97-98, 119, 185
learning activities 206, 225, 230-31
learning community 82, 154, 204-205, 227
learning experience 106, 128, 142, 183, 204, 224
learning goals 36, 175, 180, 191, 225, 227, 235

learning outcomes 8, 37, 97, 131, 139, 174, 185, 188-91, 203
learning portfolios 230
learning processes 161, 186, 230
learning styles 82, 89-90, 96
liberal arts vii, 1, 3, 6-7, 11, 55-59, 61-64, 68, 71, 99, 152, 184, 215
liberal arts colleges, church-related 117, 186
liberal arts education xiii, 14, 18, 26, 29, 56, 58, 62, 99, 119, 140, 184-85, 188-89
liberal education, goals of 7, 22, 57
Liberal Learning 20, 27, 133
literary features 238-39, 241-3
literary works 59, 62
Luke 93, 173, 210, 213-14, 221

Mark 19-20, 95, 148, 173-74, 210, 221
Matthew vii, 148, 173, 210, 214, 221
memory, long-term 86-88, 155
meta-questions ix, 9, 217-21, 220-24, 225, 227, 229, 230-32
metacognition 9, 233-38
metacognitive learning 9, 233-38, 242, 244
metaphors 186-89, 197-98, 243, 249
methodologies 4, 9, 58-60, 64, 99, 221-22, 234
Miracle Maker, The (film) 214
Moses 141-42, 147, 166, 184, 189

narratives 100, 102, 104-105, 113, 213
narrator 143, 150, 188
National Association of Biblical Instructors (NABI) 17-23, 25
nations 1-2, 27, 33, 38, 116, 143-45
Nehemiah 143, 145, 147, 149-50
Neoliberalism 31-36, 42-43
New Directions for Teaching and Learning 100, 155, 157
New Testament xiii, 13, 15, 41, 62, 77, 95, 104-105, 107-108, 117, 127, 146, 172, 194
New Testament scholarship 107, 110
New Testament survey 44, 54-55
non-majors 8, 48-49, 106, 116, 119, 123, 128, 151, 157, 171
notes 86-87, 127, 157, 162, 187, 195, 201-206, 213, 234

outsiders 26, 156, 188

Paul 41, 60, 82, 103-105, 107-11, 146, 166, 170, 172, 247
Pauline texts 108, 110-11
pedagogy viii, xiii, 5, 8-9, 17, 23, 56, 99-101, 121, 126, 130-32, 136, 138-39, 151
performance 57, 61, 236
personal meaning 4, 217, 221
plagiarism 127, 207
presentations 87, 92-93, 96-97, 111-12, 120, 148, 212, 219, 230
problem-based learning 152, 229
problems xiii, 9, 18, 30, 42-43, 56, 59, 100-102, 106-108, 110-13, 123-24, 182-83, 234, 245
programs 12, 21, 92, 96-97, 99, 101, 105, 107, 112, 133-34, 140, 207
prophecy 89, 247-48
Proverbs 77, 173, 190, 243-44
Psalms 44, 54-55, 69, 77, 173-74, 193

rabbis 69-70
rape 77, 185-86, 189, 191, 193
reading biblical texts 83, 85, 188
reading skills 9, 233
reading strategies 9, 189, 194, 233, 237-38, 241-43
religion, study of 2, 6, 12-17, 40, 103, 167
religion and philosophy departments 167, 169
religion departments 13-14, 27, 47, 66, 165, 167-68, 179
religion major xiv, 48, 179
religion requirement 13, 166
religious backgrounds 166, 227
religious context 8, 166
religious discourse, civil 217, 222
religious practices 14, 54, 139, 175
religious studies departments 3, 25, 40
religious studies major 1-5, 15, 91, 97-98, 101, 108, 123
Religious Studies News 1, 12-13, 15-16, 131, 238
religious studies programs 23, 99
religious traditions 3-4, 34, 58, 67, 71-72, 124, 140, 149, 171, 182, 217
    particular 15, 149

research, historical-critical 18, 217
research skills 228, 231
responsibility, social 4, 27, 32, 97, 185, 188-90
resurrection 66-67, 216
Revelation 9, 96, 108, 166, 173-74, 245-50, 252-53
rituals 4-5, 57, 105, 195-96
Romans 44, 54-55, 60, 68, 107, 110, 146, 173, 210
Ruth 85-86, 95, 135, 174

Samuel 173, 185, 191
scriptures, sacred 14, 25-26, 127
secular context vii, 7-8, 73, 75-76, 79
secular universities 39-40, 74, 268
self-efficacy 81-82, 84-86
seminaries xiii, 1-2, 6, 12, 15, 43, 58-59, 217
seminary model 2-4, 13-14, 19, 26
service-learning viii, xiv, 7, 91-92, 96-98, 130-34, 136-40
Shakespeare 1, 60-62
situational factors 225-27
social locations 32, 126, 136, 159, 188
Society of Biblical Literature (SBL) ii, xiii, 5, 12, 14, 16, 18, 25-26, 28, 34, 43, 132, 178
Society of Biblical Literature and Exegesis 18
standards 21, 131, 228-29
strategies xiv, 9, 74, 80, 83-87, 90, 161, 189-91, 237, 241-43, 245-46
    defensive 144
    rhetorical 242-43
structure, plausibility 142, 145, 150
student expectations 45, 49, 51, 81, 178
student response 123, 144, 146
study, classical 10, 63
survey of undergraduate programs 12
syllabi 5-6, 84-85, 99, 133, 174, 178, 182
synthesis 76, 106, 204, 206, 219, 243

Tanakh 77, 188-90
Teaching and Learning in College Introductory Religion Courses 4, 82, 84, 100, 178-80, 217
Teaching First-Year College Students 80-83, 88, 100

Teaching Theology and Religion 15, 101, 104-105, 116, 118, 130, 133-34, 186, 225
texts
  eastern 79, 83
  literary 59, 61-62, 241
  primary 104-105, 180
  resisting 187, 191
  touchstone vii, 12-13
  violent 190, 192, 195, 197-98
textual violence 193-94
Third Isaiah 143-44, 150
tools 26, 44, 84, 88-90, 99, 109, 113, 138, 180, 186, 188, 190-91, 199-200, 207-208, 229
traditions ii, 3-4, 25-26, 67-72, 77, 85, 107-108, 111, 166, 184, 220

ultimate questions 165, 167-70
undergraduate education 17, 20, 38, 56, 58, 154-55, 179

universities, religiously-affiliated 179-80
using wiki notes 204-205

values 3, 14, 29, 32-33, 35, 39, 44-45, 56, 77, 132-33, 140, 148, 151-52, 200, 241
video games 194-96, 245
violence viii, 5, 9, 175, 186, 188-98, 214-15, 249
  in the Bible 192, 262
violent media 195-96

websites 89, 144, 150, 199-200, 202, 207
Wetpaint 201-202, 204
wiki notes 204-207
Wikipedia 33, 104, 154, 178, 199-201
wikis 199-202, 204-208
wisdom 101, 133, 172-73, 243-44
women 5, 60, 111, 134-35, 159, 170, 175, 186-88, 190
world religions 91-92, 165, 182

INDEX OF AUTHORS

Adam, A.K.M. 6, 23-24, 27
Adams, D.E. 23
Afflerback, P. 237
Allen, D.E. 229
Anderson, L.W. 235
Anderson, V.J. 229
Angelo, T. 89
Aichele, G. 194
Andinach, P. 34
Astin, A.W. 130, 155
Attridge, H. 186
Avalos, H. 16, 25, 33, 42
Avioz, M. 16
Avraamides, M.N. 195

Bader, M. 16
Baker, C.M. 29
Bandura, A. 81
Banya, K. 34
Barefoot, B.O. 81-82
Barker, C. 140
Barkley, E.F. 151, 153, 155, 158, 160-62
Barr, D.L. 19
Barseghian, T. 42
Baur, F.C. 109
Bean, J.C. 82, 156, 163, 188
Bellis, A.O. 160
Bénézet, L.T. 56-57
Bénilde, M. 33
Benne, R. 67
Berger, P. 8, 141-42, 147-50
Berlinerblau, J. 16, 26, 40, 42-43
Best, S. 42
Bloom, B.S. 106, 235, 254
Blumenthal, D.R. 192
Bonhoeffer, D. 74
Bonwell, C.C. 157
Booth, W.C. 197
Borg, M.J. 148-49

Bosworth, K. 163
Botta, A.F. 34
Bousquet, M. 30, 39
Bowley, J.E. 16
Brassey, P.D. 16
Brereton, V.L. 22
Brewington, D.V. 12, 15-16
Brownell, J.E. 131
Brueggemann, W. 147
Bruffee, K.A. 152-55, 162-63
Buckley, J.J. 15
Buckley, T. 15, 105
Burtchaell, J.T. 165

Cady, L. 12-13
Cantwell Smith, W. 79
Carpenter, J.A. 19
Chambers, M.M. 36
Champagne, J. 30, 34, 40
Chickering, A.W. 81-82, 88, 154-55
Childs, B.S. 117
Clark, R. 16
Cohen, P. 38
Collins, J.J. 192, 247
Cornoldi, C. 235
Cottell, P.G. Jr. 153, 157
Cross, K.P. 89, 151, 153, 155, 158, 160-62
Cruet, G. 39

Dahl, G. 20, 22
Darr, K.P. 185
Das, V. 195
Davidson, C.W. 22-23
Davidson, N. 158
Davies, E.W. 192
Davis, J.L. 155
Day, L. 186
Debona, G. 215

Deresiewicz, W. 38
Desjardins, M. 194
Dewey, J. 74
Diamant, A. 74
Diamond, R.M. 101, 106
Dierckxsens, W. 35-36
Dovre, P. 68-69
Drell, L. 42
Dube, M.W. 35
Duch, B.J. 229
Duke, R. 9, 139, 233, 238
Dunlosky, J. 235, 237
Dunn, J.D.G. 110
Dunn, M.W.I. 16

Ellens, J.H. 193
Elmore, J.M. 36
Engwall, L. 39
Epstein, D. 31
Erickson, B.L. 80-82, 86, 88, 100
Ehrmann, S.C. 155

Fanti, K.A. 195
Faiola, A. 33
Favazza, J.A. 132
Felson, R.B. 195
Ferguson, J. 35
Ferrall, V.E., Jr. 99
Fewell, D.N. 159
Fink, L.D. 106-108, 111, 180, 224-30
Finkel, D.L. 120, 122, 127
Fish, S. 39
Fitch, F.M. 22-23
Flannery, J.L. 153
Flavell, J.H. 235, 237
Floyd-Thomas, S.M. 15
Foderaro, L.W. 39
Fowler, H.T. 19-21
Fox, M.V. 16
Fretheim, T.E. 192
Freire, P. 121
Fukuyama, F. 33

Gamson, Z.F. 154-55
Gardner, J.N. 81-82, 96
Gaztambide, D.J. 16
Geertz, C. 194-95
Gerstenberger, E. 34
Gibson, L. 194

Gifford, C.J. 13
Gilpin, W.C. 19
Giroux, H.A. 31-32
Glennon, F. 132
Goldstein, S. 190
Gomes, P. 172
Gottwald, N.K. 75, 78
Graesser, A.C. 235, 237
Gray, E.R. 12-13
Gray, P. 158
Groh, S.E. 229
Grossman, D. 196
Guéhenno, J.-M. 33
Gulley, P. 128
Gunn, D.M. 159

Habel, N.C. 137
Hacker, D.J. 235, 237
Hackett, R.I.J. 35
Hamilton, R. 39
Hamilton, S.J. 163
Harris, H. 109
Harris, S.L. 180
Harris-Shapiro, C. 133
Hartshorne, H. 19
Haroutunian, J. 22-23
Hayes, M. 178
Henrich, C.C. 195
Hillerbrand, H.J. 13, 24
Hoehner, H. 110
Homan, M.M. 132-33
Horrell, D.G. 137
Hunt, C. 137
Hutchinson, L. 236
Hylen, S.E. 9, 249

Jaschik, S. 39
Jefford, C.N. 215
Jenkins, J.B. 245, 250
Jensen, T. 15
Johnson, D.W. 153, 157, 161
Johnson, K. 39
Johnson, M. 149, 195, 249
Johnson, R.T. 153, 157, 161
Juergensmeyer, M. 100, 192, 195

Kaminsky, J. 192
Kendrick, E.H. 21
Kerr, M. 237

Kessler, G.E. 182
Kille, A. 193
Kleinman, A. 195
Kniker, C.R. 20
Koch, C. 155
Korten, D.C. 36-37
Kovel, J. 33
Kuhn, T.S. 154
Kümmel, W.G. 117
Kytle, J. 81-82

Lagaspi, M.C. 32-33
LaHaye, T. 245, 250
Lake, R. 34
Lakoff, G. 195, 249
Laytner, A. 69
Leskes, A. 119
Levine, A. 101, 103
Levin, R. 60
Lewin, T. 41
Locklin, R.B. 179
Lüdemann, G. 192
Lyman, F.T. 158

Madden, S.C. 16
Major, C.H. 151, 153, 155, 158, 160-62
Manji, F. 34-35
Marchal, J.A. 17
Marquand, D. 33
Martin, D.B. 23-24, 27, 126
Mathewson, D. 196
Matthews, S. 194
Mazwi, A.E. 31
McCarraher, E. 33
McCutcheon, R.T. 100, 106
McFague, S. 137
McGlynn, A.P. 82
McGuire, S.Y. 234-35
McLaren, P. 42
McLay, R.T. 17, 58, 179
McNeil, J.D. 101, 107
McTighe, J. 218
Miller, R. 119
Millis, B.J. 153, 157
Mitchell, T.D. 131
Mitchell, W.J.T. 113
Moberly, R.W.L. 210-11, 213
Mokhiber, R. 37
Mould, E.W.K. 18, 20-21

Mulholland, J. 128

Nelson-Pallmeyer, J. 192
Neville, D.J. 194
Newcomb, T.M. 155
Niditch, S. 192
Nocella, A.J. II 42
Noll, K.L. 16
Noll, M. 16, 19, 20
Nussbaum, M. 99
Nyhan, B. 236

Oakley, B. 161
O'Coill, C. 34-35
Olbricht, T.H. 20

Palmer, P.J. 123
Parks, S.D. 120-22, 124-25
Pascarella, E.T. 82, 107
Patte, D. 223
Pauk, W. 87
Paul, R. 82
Penaskovic, R. 81-82
Penchansky, D. 192
Peoples, T. 5-6
Peritz, I.J. 18-19
Perry, N.E. 236
Perry, W.G. 155
Peters, C.B. 80-82, 86, 88, 100
Phillips, L. 236
Pippin, T. 136, 138, 194
Plantinga, A. 21
Plater, W.M. 30
Powell, J.W. 30
Pressley, M. 237
Prothero, S. 179

Quimby, C.W. 19, 21

Ramachandran, V.S. 81
Ramphele, M. 195
Readings, B. 37-38
Reifler, J. 236
Reisser, L. 81-82, 88
Reklis, K. 196
Renick, T. 1-5, 15
Resnick, L.B. 235
Reynolds, P. 195
Richards, K.H. 28

Ringenberg, W.C. 20
Roncace, M. 158
Rosengarten, R.A. 13
Rosenthal, L. 34
Rowland, W. 43
Rudinger, P. 137
Rudolph, F. 101
Ryan, A. 56
Rynearson, K. 237

Salen, K. 196
Sanders, J. 194
Saunders, E.W. 18
Sayers, D. 209
Schneider, C.G. 27
Schneider, W. 235, 237
Schneiders, S.M. 127
Scholz, S. 7, 28-29, 30
Schüssler Fiorenza, E. 28-29
Schwartz, R.M. 192
Segovia, F.F. 29
Seider, S. 130-31, 134
Setzer, C. 62
Shakespeare, W. 1, 60-61
Shea, C. 38
Shefferman, D. 62
Shields, M. 186
Shipps, K.W. 19
Simmons, J.K. 225
Smith, A. 31
Smith, C. 179
Smith, D. 16
Smith, J.H. 35
Smith, J.Z. 13-14, 17-8, 20, 26, 100-106, 113, 118
Smith, K.A. 153, 157, 161
Smith, W.C. 78-79
Soederberg, S. 37
Sommerville, C.J. 39
Son, S.A. 110
Son, S.-W. 110
Southgate, C. 137
Spear, K.I. 100
Staley, J.L. 215
Stern, R.C. 215
Strommer, D.W. 80-82, 86, 88, 100

Sultana, R.G. 31
Sutherland, T.E. 157
Suzrez-Villa, L. 37
Swaner, L.E. 131
Szpek, H.M. 190

Taraban, R. 237
Tatum, W.B. 215
Taylor, B.B. 124-25
Terenzini, P.T. 82, 107
Trible, P. 160, 185, 192
Tuckman, B. 162

Upcraft, M.L. 81-82

Vanman, E. 195

Wagner, R. 196
Walker-Jones, A. 16
Walsh, R. 215
Walvoord, B.E. 4, 82, 84, 100, 178-80, 217, 225, 229
Warmoth, A. 152
Warrior, R.A. 192
Washington, H. 192
Waters, H.S. 235, 237
Weaver, D.J. 194
Weber, M. 32
Webster, J. 15, 17, 174-75
Weems, R.J. 192
Weimer, M. 180
Weissman, R. 37
West, G.O. 35
Wheeler, B.M. 105
Wiggins, G. 218, 225, 229
Wilson, E.K. 155
Wilson, K. 74
Wilson, L.O. 178
Wolf, N. 33
Wolterstorff, N. 21
Worsham, T. 158
Wright, N.T. 148-49

Zajda, J.I. 34
Zijderveld, A. 141
Zimmerman, E. 196

www.ingramcontent.com/pod-product-compliance
Lightning Source LLC
Chambersburg PA
CBHW051049230426
43666CB00012B/2628